To FRIEDA —
WITH THANKS
FOR SHARING
IDEAS AND IDEAS
WITH ME.

BEST WISHES,

Jim

ONE NATION
UNDER GOODS

One Nation
UNDER GOODS
Malls and the Seductions of American Shopping

JAMES J. FARRELL

Smithsonian Books • Washington and London

Copy Editor: Karin Kaufman

Production Editor: Ruth G. Thomson

Designer: Brian Barth

Library of Congress Cataloging-in-Publication Data

Farrell, James J., 1949–

    One nation under goods : malls and the seductions of American shopping / James J. Farrell.

        p.   cm.

    Includes bibliographical references and index.

    ISBN 1-58834-152-6 (alk. paper)

    1. Shopping malls—United States—History.

2. Shopping centers—United States—History.

3. Popular culture—United States—History. I. Title.

    HF5430.3.F37   2003

    381'.1—dc21   2003041447

British Library Cataloging-in-Publication Data available

Manufactured in the United States of America

10 09 08 07 06 05 04 03   5 4 3 2 1

∞ The paper used in this publication meets the minimum requirements of the American National Standard for Information Sciences—Permanence of Paper for Printed Library Materials ANSI Z39.48-1984.

To my students, who are also my best teachers

What would become of us, if we walked only in a garden or a mall?
—Henry David Thoreau, "Walking"

An age that has lost its consciousness of the things that shape its life will know
neither where it stands, nor, even less, at what it aims.
—Siegfried Giedion, *Mechanization Takes Command*

There's a place for fun in your life.
—Mall of America

We cannot begin to know ourselves until we can see the real reasons why we do
the things we do, and we cannot be ourselves until our actions
correspond to our intentions, and our intentions are
appropriate to our own situation.
—Thomas Merton

The primary task is to design environments where it will be possible for
[people] to lead the lives of free and responsible citizens,
where they can give expression to the social or
political side of their nature.
—J. B. Jackson, *Landscape*

Contents

Acknowledgments

There are many debts incurred in America's malls. There have also been debts incurred in writing this book *about* malls. The absent-minded professor will surely forget some of them, but because scholarship is always a community endeavor, it pays to acknowledge our debts.

I am indebted to America's libraries, especially to the librarians of St. Olaf College. A church-related liberal arts institution doesn't regularly shelve such books as *The Shopping Center Development Handbook* or *Design for Effective Selling Space*, but my colleagues in the Interlibrary Loan office have been persistent in finding such volumes for me. And librarians all across the country have been generous with their time and collections.

One Nation under Goods also owes a lot to people who work in malls of America for sharing insights and materials with me. Malls themselves are a visual spectacle, and this book's visual dimension is due in large part to people who generously granted permission to reprint photographs and cartoons. Even when people couldn't grant permission for precisely the images I wanted, they went out of their way to help me find materials that would work just as well.

I owe this work to my friends and colleagues at St. Olaf College who have created an intellectual community that makes an eccentric professor like me feel right at home. More specifically, I owe a debt of gratitude to the Faculty Development Committee at St. Olaf, who—at just the right time—gave me time (the scarcest of academic resources) for research and writing. I also owe thanks to the college for a timely sabbatical to complete the project.

I'm also thankful to the people of St. Joan of Arc, a radical Catholic community in Minneapolis that continually raises my consciousness and engages my conscience. The services at St. Joan are inspiring—in every sense of the word. St. Joan of Arc challenges members to think continually about the moral ecology of everyday life and to do something about it—changing the world, in small ways and large, with our own wild and precious lives.

I am indebted to several generations of St. Olaf students, who have been inquisitive and imaginative in thinking about the social construction of shopping in classes on American consumer culture and Minnesota's Mall of America. I owe a lot to Kendra Smith and Kahla Foster, who shared ideas with me for most of their senior year, and I'm especially indebted to Laura Henderson and Elise Braaten, whose thoughtfulness, expressed as cogitation *and* care, never ceases to amaze me.

Many of these reflections have been influenced by Dr. America, the curator of the magnificent (but wholly imaginary) American Studies Museum. Since April Fool's Day of 1996, Dr. America has made his home on public radio station WCAL in Northfield, Minnesota. Both the good doctor and I are indebted to program director and grand poohbah Marty Pelikan for his invitation to think about the invisible complexity of American culture and for his careful editing of individual essays. Marty has a way with words—and with ideas—that makes it a pleasure to put ideas into words every week.

Finally, I owe a debt of gratitude to my family. I am indebted to both of my sons, John and Paul, who read my chapters in addition to assignments from their other professors, and who taught their old man about today's youth culture. And as always, this book belongs to Barb, who has shared my life and work for more than thirty years.

Introduction

Shopping for American Culture

Malls are an American cultural phenomenon. The United States now has more shopping centers than high schools, and in the last forty years, shopping center space has increased by a factor of twelve. By 2000, there were more than forty-five thousand shopping malls with 5.47 billion square feet of gross leasable space in the United States. Currently, America's shopping centers (most of which are strip malls) generate more than a trillion dollars in annual sales. Not counting sales of cars and gasoline, that's slightly more than half of the nation's retail activity. The International Council of Shopping Centers (ICSC) reported that in 2000, America's shopping centers served 196 million Americans a month and employed more than 10.6 million workers, about 8 percent of the nonfarm workforce in the country. We go to malls 3.2 times a month and spend an average of $71.04 each time (a one-third increase in spending from 1995 to 2000). Shopping centers also support our state and city govern-

Table 1

Shopping Centers in the United States

	1970	1980	1990	2000
Number of shopping centers	11,000	22,100	36,500	45,000
Total leasable sales area				
(billions of square feet)	1.49	2.96	4.39	5.57
Retail sales in shopping centers				
(billions of dollars)	82.0	305.4	681.4	1,136.0
Employment in shopping centers				
(millions of people)	2.49	5.28	8.60	10.69

Source: Data from ICSC, *Scope.* (*Scope* is a publication of the International Council of Shopping Centers, Inc., New York, N.Y.; reprinted by permission.)

ments, generating $46.6 billion in sales taxes, almost half of all state tax revenue (see table 1).[1]

Shopping is such a common part of America's pursuit of happiness that we usually take shopping centers for granted. But although malls are usually places of consumer forgetfulness, they can inspire a sense of thoughtfulness. It's no particular problem if we come back from the mall empty-handed, but it should be a deep disappointment if we come back empty-headed.[2]

But why should we think about malls?

Quite simply, because Americans go to malls. We may not like the malling of America, but if we want to understand Americans, we have to look for them where they are, not where we think they ought to be. We need to follow Americans to the mall and see what they're doing because shopping centers can reveal cultural patterns that we don't usually see. In some ways, culture is what happens when we are not paying attention. When we are fully conscious of our choices, they are likely to express our individual values and preferences, but when we're going about our daily business with little thought about what we're doing, we act according to the habits of our hearts, and those habits are shaped as much by culture as by character.[3]

Malls are a great place for the pleasures of shopping, but they're an even better place for the pleasures of thinking, in part because they help us think about the cultural contours of shopping. Shopping is, etymologically, the process of going to shops to purchase goods and services. According to Webster, a shop is a small retail store; the word comes from a root that denoted the booths or stalls of the marketplace. The verb *to shop* appeared in the late eighteenth century; by the late twentieth century, shopping had become a way of life. Measured in constant dollars, the average American of today consumes twice as many goods and services as the average American of 1950 and ten times as much as a counterpart from 1928. On average, we each consume more than one hundred pounds of materials a day. Shopping, it seems, might be more American than apple pie.[4]

Sometimes shopping is a utilitarian act. We need a shirt or a suitcase, and we go to the mall to get it. Sometimes, though, shopping is intrinsically pleasurable, and we go to the mall to just do it. Shopping itself can be therapeutic, even fun, whether or not anything ends up in the shopping bag. So an exploration of malls can help us think about what we have in mind—as well as what we don't have in mind—when we are shopping.[5]

When we get home from the mall, we tell the family, "I was shopping." It sounds simple. Yet shopping is a complex act, or, more precisely, a complex interaction. It's not just a matter of choosing items and paying for them; it's an act of desire that is shaped individually and culturally, an interaction with shops and with a complex infrastructure of production and distribution. It's an act of conscience in which our own values interact with commercial and cultural values. Shopping requires a biological being to enter an architectural space outfitted with commercial art and designed to sell artifacts manufactured and distributed in a market economy. Shopping centers are built of solid materials, but the spaces are also socially constructed and regulated by political entities. Our malls reflect and affect personal perceptions, social norms, religious beliefs, ethical values, cultural geography, domestic architecture, foreign policy, and social psychology. And the artifacts within shopping centers are equally complex, synthesizing material form and symbolic meaning. Shopping is no simple task.

Malls are a good place to think about retailing and retail culture, an important subset of American commercial culture. Because we are consumers, we think we know how consumption works, but we don't usually pay attention to how consumption is *produced*. In malls of America, consumption is not just happenstance. It's carefully planned and programmed. To be informed consumers, therefore, we need information

The mall as American success story—in this case,
Roosevelt Field (Courtesy of Simon Property Group)

not just about the products we buy but also about the spaces—architectural and social—where we buy them.

Malls are America's public architecture, a primary form of public space, the town halls of the twentieth and twenty-first centuries. Sociologist Mark Gottdiener contends that the mall "has become the most successful form of environmental design in contemporary settlement space." The late nineteenth century was known for its train stations and department stores. In the early twentieth century it was skyscrapers and subways. Mid-twentieth-century Americans created suburban forms, including subdivisions, malls, and office parks. The late twentieth century was an era of malls and airports, and the airports increasingly looked like malls.[6]

Malls are also art galleries, carefully crafted collections of commercial art. To the connoisseur, they offer an unending display of artful design, including product design, package design, retail design, visual merchandising, sculpture, and architecture. The artists we find in museums often challenge our conceptions of ourselves and unsettle our sense of society. The artists who exhibit their skills in the museums we call malls, on the other hand, tend to reinforce our sense of ourselves, producing a commercial art that makes malls more popular than museums in American culture. But even people who have taken courses in art appreciation don't always take time to appreciate the creativity of commercial art.

Malls are also outstanding museums of contemporary American material culture. In them, we find a huge collection of the artifacts that help us make sense of our world. And as in most museums, reading these artifacts can help us read the culture.

Indeed, as cultural institutions, malls perform what Paul Lauter calls "cultural work," a term that describes "the ways in which a book or other kind of 'text'—a movie, a Supreme Court decision, an advertisement, an anthology, an international treaty, a material object—helps construct the frameworks, fashion the metaphors, create the very language by which people comprehend their experience and think about their world." In short, malls help teach us the common sense of our culture. If we look closely at malls, we will soon be looking inside our own heads. So it is partly the purpose of this book to explain this social construction of common sense—the way we teach each other, both explicitly and implicitly, the common sense of our culture.[7]

Understanding a single act of shopping means understanding the culture in which it occurs. When we go to the mall looking for jeans, we find ourselves embedded in a cultural fabric that fits us like a pair of jeans. Shopping centers are constructed of steel and concrete, bricks and mortar, but they are also made of culture. Indeed, culture is about the only thing they *can* be made of. Retailers routinely use our cultural values to stimulate sales. Shopping centers reinforce these values even as they distract us from other American values—justice, equality, democracy, and spirituality—that might also animate our lives (see table 2).[8]

As this suggests, malls are a manifestation of popular philosophy. They're a place where we answer important questions: What does it mean to be human? What are people for? What is the meaning of things? Why do we work? What do we work for? And what, in fact, are we shopping for? Like colleges and churches, malls provide answers to these critical questions. Like colleges, malls are places where we make

Table 2

Summary of American Core Values

Value	General Features	Relevance to Consumer Behavior
Achievement and success	Hard work is good; success flows from hard work.	Acts as a justification for acquisition of goods ("You deserve it.")
Activity	Keeping busy is healthy and natural	Stimulates interest in products that are time-savers and enhance leisure time
Efficiency and practicality	Admiration of things that solve problems (e.g., save time and effort)	Stimulates purchase of products that function well and save time.
Progress	People can improve themselves; tomorrow should be better than today	Stimulates desire for new products that fulfill unsatisfied needs; ready acceptance of products that claim to be "new" or "improved"
Material comfort	"The good life"	Fosters acceptance of convenience and luxury products that make life more comfortable and enjoyable
Individualism	Being oneself (e.g., self-reliance, self-interest, self-esteem)	Stimulates acceptance of customized or unique products that enable a person to "express his or her own personality"
Freedom	Freedom of choice	Fosters interest in wide product lines and differentiated products
External conformity	Uniformity of observable behavior; desire for acceptance	Stimulates interest in products that are used or owned by others in the same social group
Humanitarianism	Caring for others,	Stimulates patronage

	particularly the underdog	of firms that compete with market leaders
Youthfulness	A state of mind that stresses being "young at heart" and having a youthful appearance	Stimulates acceptance of products that provide the illusion of maintaining or fostering youthfulness
Fitness and health	Caring about one's body, including the desire to be physically fit and healthy	Stimulates acceptance of food products, activities, and equipment perceived to maintain or increase physical fitness

Source: Consumer Behavior, 5th ed. by Schiffman/Kanuck. © Reprinted by permission of Pearson Education, Inc., Upper Saddle River, N.J.

statements about the good, the true, and the beautiful. Like churches, they are places where we decide what is ultimately valuable and how we will value it. And malls are places where we act out, and institutionalize, our values.[9]

As the local outlet of the new world order, malls can teach us a great deal about the central institutions of our American lives. Malls are the intersection of manufacturing and merchandising, nature and culture, home and away, love and money. At the mall, we can see the market at work, and we can contemplate what it means to live in a society shaped by the powerful institutions of commercial capitalism. American individualism often makes it hard for Americans to understand institutions and the prescriptions and patterns that structure our lives. We forget that when we walk into a mall, we walk into a market full of *cultural* questions and controversies. Anthropologists Mary Douglas and Baron Isherwood contend that "consumption is the very arena in which culture is fought over and licked into shape." Malls, therefore, are one place where we make significant decisions both as individuals and as a society.[10]

Yet if we want to understand malls, we must examine them within a broader framework. The mall makes sense in the flow of our whole lives, as we compare and contrast it to what we experience every day. The mall, for example, tells us immediately that it's not home and it's not work. It's an architecture of pleasure, not of comfort or efficiency. Shopping is what academics would call an "intertextual experience," an activity that only makes sense if we know how to read many different cultural "texts": ads, stores, mannequins, clothes, logos, race, class, gender, and sexuality. And the mall's complexities are multiplied by its customers.

There are many malls in America, and each mall is many things to many people. Architecturally, a mall is singular, but sociologically, psychologically, and culturally, it's plural. Each store is a variety store, not just because it sells a variety of products but because it evokes different responses from a variety of people. Each of us brings our own cognitive map to the mall, so it's a different place to a mother and her child, to a mall worker and a mall walker. It's different if we're different in any way—and we all are. Malls mean different things to women and men, to blacks and whites, to gay people and their heterosexual friends, to teenagers and senior citizens. The mall looks and feels different to poor people than it does to the affluent. Although the mall may try to be all things to all people, it succeeds mainly by being different things to different people. It's possible to speak truthfully about an American consumer culture, but if we look closely, we'll see that we are a consumption society with many different and interconnected consumer cultures.[11]

Even though I understand these differences, I often use a language of "we" in this book. I am a tall white guy, middle-aged and middle class, married with children. I use "we" not because all Americans experience shopping centers in the same way, but because we have many experiences in common. I use "we" because I don't want to pretend that I'm not involved in American consumer culture, and I don't want to act like an "objective" outsider observing shoppers as a different species. One of the important questions this book poses is, How much are you a part of "we"? Only you will know the final answer to that question. In the meantime, though, let's assume that, in many important ways, we are "we, the people."

One Nation under Goods is about shopping centers, but it's also a story about us—you and me and the millions of other Americans who routinely visit those centers. We often go to malls to buy things we don't have—a pair of pants, a toaster, a new lamp, a book, or a CD. Yet we also go to buy more important things—an identity, a secure sense of self, a set of social relationships, a deeper sense of community, an expression of who we are and who we would like to be. We go to shopping centers with the unfulfilled needs of our American lives, so the mall's attractions are one way of studying the deficiencies of American life. We can use the things we carry *at* the mall to help us understand the things we carry *to* the mall. We can use the mall to make sense of our everyday life.

Telling stories: St. Mark's Square in Las Vegas (Photo by the author; published with permission of the Grand Canal Shoppes, Las Vegas, Nevada)

This book is the story of the stories we tell at the mall. Whatever else they may be, shopping centers are places where we tell stories about ourselves—about who we are and what we value. In the plot to separate us from our money, malls are also plotted. They tell stories—about business, about shoppers, about work and leisure, about good and evil, about American culture(s). Stores, and not just bookstores, are full of stories. Victoria's Secret is a romance novel about sex, seduction, and desire, about bodies and beauty, about femininity and masculinity. Sportsmart is the sports page of the mall, telling stories about striving and success. Abercrombie & Fitch combines adventure stories with coming-of-age stories. The Gap started by telling stories about the generation gap, but now their stories are about "cool" characters and their "casual" lives. The stories of progress at Radio Shack are often futuristic fantasies, and Hot Topic tells stories about individualism and conformity, dissent and deviance. The

Rainforest Café spins adventure yarns and nature stories. The department stores tell stories about abundance and choice. All of the retailers tell stories about "the good life" and about America. All of the *things* in the mall also have a story. Each artifact is a story of nature becoming culture, of raw material (com)modified to make it meaningful to Americans. At the mall, it's always story time, and, at least according to the publicity, there's almost always a happy ending.

This book is the story of all those stories. It's a storybook.

It's also my story. It's a story by me, of course, but it's also a story about me, because I'm one of the people I'm writing about. I'm not a power shopper, but I love malls. I love them for all the obvious reasons. I love the color and the crowds. I love looking at commercial art, because it is, in fact, beautiful. I love people watching: seeing the wonder of children's eyes and the animated conversations of teenagers. I like the oasis of pedestrianism in a car culture: I like walking, and I like to walk in malls. But I also love malls because in them, as geographer Jon Goss says, "I have learned a great deal about myself: about my humanity, the values and beliefs of 'my' culture, and my intimate desires."[12]

I appreciate malls more now than I did at the beginning of my research. When you look closely at their complexity, especially the intricate coordination needed to produce each day's consumption, it's a miracle that they work as well as they do. I have come to understand that shopping centers are part of a huge conspiracy, a conspiracy of customer satisfaction. The people who work in malls genuinely want to please the people who shop in malls. So I appreciate the ways that shopping center professionals study Americans to see just what, in fact, will please us, and I appreciate the many pleasures that are to be found at the mall, whether or not we ever buy anything.

But I also appreciate the ways that a shopping center can be a "social trap," an institution in which the sum total of perfectly good behavior is not so good. Still, my main complaint is not primarily with malls but with a larger commercial culture that characterizes us mainly as consumers. My main argument is with an America that sells itself short by buying into the cluster of values expressed so powerfully in our malls.[13]

One Nation under Goods is a collection of essays exploring the "dense facts" of the shopping center, those facts that "both reveal deeper meanings inside themselves, and point outward to other facts, other ideas, other meanings." Dense facts complexify seemingly simple phenomena. They invite people to use their "connecting mind" to discover and uncover patterns of belief and behavior in their everyday lives. Mannequins, mirrors, universal product codes, cash registers, credit cards, potted plants, escalators, and security cameras—each of these is a "dense fact" in itself and a powerful part of the culture that constructs malls architecturally, economically, socially, and politically.[14]

Each essay works by making sense of common sense, by making complex our first impressions of the mall. We already know about mannequins, for example, but this book can help us to think about mannequins in a more sophisticated way. *One Nation under Goods* studies what we buy and why, but it also explores what we buy into, and as such, it looks at the mall as an intersection of aesthetics, economics, ethics, and politics. The mall, explicitly about aesthetics and economics, is also implicitly about ethics and politics.

This book focuses on the practices of the larger malls of America—regional malls, superregionals, and megamalls—because they dominate the imagery of shopping centers. For that reason, the emphasis is mainly on the malls of the middle class. A lot of retailing takes place in strip centers and community centers, in power centers and outlet malls, but those are stories for other people and other books.

Shopping centers are big, and they are a big part of American culture. They are also a big topic, so I have by necessity left out a lot. I think I could have written a whole book about any of the topics treated here, but I have chosen instead to synthesize, assembling a lot of ideas all in one place. Like the shopping center itself, this book stacks and displays ideas in some semblance of order. It's not comprehensive, but I hope it's comprehensible.

This book can make you a better shopper, and I hope it does. If you detest shopping centers, I hope that this book will make you think twice about the good among the goods. If you love shopping and shopping centers, I hope this book will make you think twice about the hidden costs of consumption. If you are indifferent, I hope you will see how shopping centers make a difference in American lives. At the very least, I hope it gets you in a questioning frame of mind, because, as James Thurber once said, "it is better to know some of the questions than all of the answers."

PART ONE

Producing Consumption
How Malls Prepare for Us

ONE

Inventing Malls

In his 1862 essay "Walking," Henry David Thoreau asked, "What would become of us, if we walked only in a garden or a mall?" Despite his deep suspicions about commercial culture, Thoreau wasn't worried about shopping centers. In his day, a mall was a particular sort of pedestrian environment, a more or less formal garden. The National Mall in Washington, D.C., is a mall in this historic sense—a public promenade, an outdoor space sometimes lined with shops.

When developers began to build shopping centers in the twentieth century, they often included a mall like this between the shops, and this grassy area was a novel part of the shopping experience. Early community shopping centers such as J. C. Nichols's pioneering Country Club Plaza in Kansas City or Cleveland's Shaker Square often included a space that resembled the public square of small-town America. With its evocation of the urban park, this grassy space helped to make shopping seem recreational as well as commercial, public as well as private, natural as well as cultural.

Modern malls retain very little of this original mallness. The enclosed shopping center eliminated the grassy mall even as it took its name. Beginning with architect Victor Gruen's Southdale in 1956, shopping centers have put nature in the mall instead of locating stores on the mall. Modern malls remain pedestrian environments, but, as we shall see, nature serves different purposes *in* the mall than *as* a mall. Since the 1950s, the mallness of malls has involved a different set of characteristics: a shared parking lot, common ownership and management, uniform and aesthetically pleasing design, clear and consistent marketing goals, a carefully controlled commercial environment, a tenant mix designed to provide variety, and a wide range of consumer goods. The new "introverted" mall wasn't a random conglomeration of stores as in a city's downtown; it was an intentional community of commerce. To understand the evolution of shopping centers, we need to take a short walk in the mall of history.[1]

Even though we commonly call them "malls," modern shopping centers owe more to department stores and to urban "galleria" than to the domesticated nature that worried Henry Thoreau. Beginning with the establishments of Alexander Stewart, John Wanamaker, and others, urban department stores created a monumental commercial environment that reflected and affected an emerging "land of desire." Department stores synthesized and symbolized their era. As historian Susan Porter Benson suggests, "The congestion, the liveliness, the anonymity, the grand scale, the material promise, and the class divisions of the city were all distilled into the great stores." Americans built department stores, and the department stores, in turn, helped construct American consumer culture.[2]

Department stores depended, of course, on the prior development of shopping itself. At the time of the American Revolution, about 95 percent of Americans lived on farms and made most of what they consumed. In a subsistence economy, people bartered with neighbors and visited markets in town, but except for city dwellers, they did not shop much. Shopping derives from a profound Declaration of Interdependence, from the economic revolution declared in 1776 by Adam Smith in *The Wealth of Nations*. As each of us specializes, we become dependent on others to supply the things we don't produce ourselves. So shopping is both the price of our specialization and a benefit of it. In America, shops and general stores grew up at country crossroads and in towns. In larger settlements, specialty shops proliferated. And eventually, the department store housed a collection of specialty shops in a single building. Thus department stores were both an architectural expression of Americans' commercial interdependence and a seductive invitation to shopping. As "anchors," department stores would become a prime catalyst in the development of malls.

The "galleria" or "arcade" was another urban innovation, designed to create a uniform environment for the smaller specialty shops that would eventually become tenants in the modern mall. Arcades began as glass-covered passageways between streets in European cities, with shops on either side. The Victor Emmanuel Arcade in Milan, Italy, was the most famous and influential, but arcades also appeared in America. The Cleveland Arcade, for example, with a three-hundred-foot glass dome covering five floors of retail shops and offices, was the world's largest when it was completed in 1890. In America, arcades never seriously challenged department stores, but they influenced the design of suburban malls.[3]

By the 1920s, when shopping centers began to develop in the suburbs, America's central cities were often dirty, congested, chaotic, and (occasionally) dangerous. If you came by car, traffic and parking posed real problems; if you did not come by car, carrying your purchases home on crowded public transportation could be a substantial feat. Mall critics sometimes imagine that malls have always been a problem. In fact, over time malls have been the solution to some urban (and suburban) problems. The department store and the galleria worked well in the central city, but the decentralization of the city called for different commercial solutions.

Shopping centers grew out of the convergence of several historical trends: cars and the new concentrations of population that cars made possible, commercial media (movies, magazines and radio) and the new consumer dreams that media made possible, and national brands and advertising. They were part of the socio-spatial segmentation of the city, as people decided that there should be a separate place for everything. Instead of integrating industry and commerce and residential life, Americans in the twentieth century decided to separate them, thus maintaining the purity of home life. So when people with consuming passions moved to suburbs specializing in residential life, America's developers tried to respond to their real needs with shopping centers.

Country Club Plaza: Mediterranean Kansas (Photo courtesy of Wilborn and Associates)

The first new retail response was the strip mall, a small collection of stores with a common parking lot. Located along the main thoroughfares of America's expanding metropolitan areas, these strips appealed to the car commuters of the 1910s, 1920s, and 1930s. Such strips included groceries, pharmacies, and hardware stores and service shops specializing in, among other things, laundry and shoe repair. With a limited clientele, they appealed more to efficiency than style. Designed to service suburban commuters, they quickly succumbed to many of the same problems as central business districts: heavy traffic, random placement, and visual chaos. Although they were convenient, quick stops in a car culture, they did not make a customer want to linger. They allowed suburbanites to pick up purchases without encountering the full experience of shopping.[4]

The second suburban innovation was the community shopping center, designed by architects to express the character of new communities sprouting up on the urban periphery. The first significant mall of America, J. C. Nichols's Country Club Plaza in Kansas City, which opened in 1922, was meant to meet the needs of a new suburban community located four miles south of Kansas City. Although most residential real estate developers ignored the commercial needs of new suburban homeowners, Nichols promoted the synergy of his residential and commercial projects.[5]

Nichols pioneered a wide variety of techniques that created a new commercial, and community, environment. Architecturally themed, the plaza's buildings brought a Mediterranean look to Kansas. At the same time, drawing on the English garden city ideal, Nichols equipped Country Club Plaza with small parks, fountains, benches, public art, and a schedule of community activities. Such innovations instilled civic pride as much as they assured commercial success. Other community shopping centers of the 1920s and 1930s were also designed as selling points (in both senses of the term) for planned residential districts. They, too, began to feature community activities such as art shows, band concerts, square dancing, fashion shows, pet parades, and holiday fireworks. Such innovations might have had a profound impact on the history of American shopping centers, but the Depression and World War II dampened their diffusion. After World War II, however, a booming economy permitted the application of Nichols's ideas in a substantially different form. In 1950, there were only about one hundred neighborhood and community centers in America; by 1953, that number had tripled.[6]

The most significant postwar innovation was the regional shopping center, the community center, such as it is, of the modern suburbs. Regional malls reflect and affect the power of metropolitan deconcentration—the movement of population, business, and retail from city centers to peripheral places. The regional shopping center developed in America's new Edge Cities, amid many new developments, residential, social, economic, and political. After the enforced savings of World War II, Americans had money to spend. An urban housing shortage, coupled with cheap suburban land and low-cost loans from government mortgage programs, pushed residential development into farmers' fields. Between 1947 and 1957, Veterans Administration and Federal Housing Administration mortgages accounted for almost half of all homes sold, and these agencies heavily favored the suburbs. New interstate highways provided easy access to the suburbs and offered intersections ideal for the placement of shopping centers, and starting in 1954, Federal tax policy allowed "accelerated depreciation" of new commercial buildings. Further, the people who moved to the suburbs were prime consumers, with median incomes well above the national average, and they had both houses and children to outfit.[7]

The 1950s saw the first shopping centers anchored by major department stores, which moved to the suburbs with their customers. In Seattle, Northgate

7

Southdale Center in Edina, Minnesota: new city in the suburbs
(Photo courtesy of Southdale Center; reprinted by permission)

(1950) pioneered parallel strip centers anchored by a department store and facing a central pedestrian mall. Shoppers World (1951) in Framingham, Massachusetts, offered the first two-tier center. In 1954, Victor Gruen's North-land Center in Detroit featured a "cluster plan" and parking for ten thousand cars. The first mall with central heating and air conditioning, Northland's plan also included 80 acres of trees and gardens. But Southdale Center in suburban Edina, Minnesota, was the most influential design of the decade. Created by Victor Gruen, whose 1960 *Shopping Towns USA: The Planning of Shopping Centers* would become the Bible of mall developers, Southdale included competing department stores to anchor the specialty shops, a two-tiered design, a strict separation of car and pedestrian movement, a central interior courtyard, and complete climate control. As Gruen discovered, air conditioning was the key to larger introverted shopping centers, because it removed the need for doors and windows for ventilation. With fewer elements exposed to the outside, the mall was also cheaper to build and cheaper to heat, even in a Minnesota winter. And with fewer reminders of the outside, it was easier to keep people inside.[8]

Southdale's technical solutions also offered aesthetic and commercial advantages. The problem of two-tiered shopping centers had always been how to get customers to move from floor to floor. Gruen solved this problem with parking lots at both levels and escalators in a central court equipped with public art accenting the verticality of the design. People in this signature courtyard could see the bustle of business on the other floor, and they were visually drawn to move there. In addition, because businesses in the enclosed center no longer had to advertise to passing car traffic, their storefronts could be more subdued and harmonious.[9]

An Austrian refugee from nazism, Gruen considered shopping centers a centripetal counterbalance to the centrifugal forces of cars and suburbs, an "urban" oasis in the suburban sprawl, a "middle landscape" between the chaos of the city and the segmentation of the suburbs. In a 1956 *New Yorker* interview, Gruen expressed his pride as the planner of Northland Center: "In Detroit, six or seven thousand people make their way to Northland on Sunday afternoons. The stores are closed, so what are they doing there? Looking for open space. They window-shop and stroll through the gardens and sit on benches and soak up the sun and enjoy the fountains and sculpture. What Northland teaches us is this—that it's the merchants who will save our urban civilization." Gruen thought that public amenities were part of the price, and the purpose, of private shopping centers. Southdale, therefore, included fifty thousand dollars' worth of public art, and it was equipped with an auditorium for meetings and performances of community groups. "Sometimes," Gruen said, "self-interest has remarkable spiritual consequences. As art patrons, merchants can be to our time what the Church and the nobility were to the middle ages."[10]

Gruen thought that shopping centers could be catalysts for a civic revolution. "By affording opportunities for social life and recreation in a protected pedestrian environment, by incorporating civic and educational facilities, shopping centers can fill an existing void," he wrote. "They can provide the needed place and opportunity for participation in modern community life that the ancient Greek Agora, the Medieval Market Place and our own Town Squares provided in the past." Gruen's suburban work wasn't opposed to the city; in fact, it was inspired by the city. "For Gruen," one observer claimed, "the mall *was* the new city."[11]

Other regional shopping centers also rationalized and romanticized shopping, making the experience easy, efficient, comfortable, and aesthetically pleasing. Planned parking lots and good security made shopping easier, and a wide variety of stores made shopping more efficient. Enclosed malls and air conditioning comforted customers, and architectural and graphic designs harmonized with Muzak to convey messages of fun and modernity. The halls of enclosed malls echoed idealized urban streetscapes; indeed, *Architectural Forum* described Southdale as "more like downtown than downtown itself."[12]

The success of Southdale and other regional shopping centers threatened local downtowns, many of which promptly made themselves over into malls. Impressed by the pedestrianism of the enclosed shopping center, many towns closed or narrowed their main streets to make the streetscape seem more like the common area of the mall. Early regional malls had often imitated an idealized Main Street (à la Disney) inside their halls, so now Main Street imitated the mall imitating Disneyland. The 1954 Housing Act and the 1956 Federal Highway Act provided funds for urban renewal, including the improvement of commercial districts, and many small towns took the opportunity to compete with the mall by becoming a mall. With grassy landscaped gardens replacing the main streets, these malls were often malls in the original sense of the word.[13]

Even architects like Victor Gruen, devoted to civic communitarianism, eagerly applied mall solutions to city problems. Gruen, in fact, influenced the malling of America's downtowns with his pioneering 1959 design for a downtown mall in Kalamazoo, Michigan. Still, although it was relatively easy to get federal funds for urban rejuvenation, it was harder to get a group of independent downtown merchants to coordinate their activities as efficiently as mall retailers in a merchants association and under the direction of a mall manager. And such projects proved difficult, because it was easier to renew the face of downtown than it was to renew its circulatory system. The chamber of commerce and Main Street merchants might try to compete with an outlying mall, but demographically and institutionally, the mall had significant advantages. Increasingly, residential segregation (and market segmentation) located malls near people with money and left downtowns with poorer populations. As early as 1954, malls passed metropolitan downtowns in total retail sales. And by 1976, the suburban branches of major department stores were ringing up 78 percent of department store receipts.[14]

Small towns were not the only places to respond to the malling of suburban America. Cities, too, felt the pressure from suburban mall developments, and they responded with mall developments of two kinds. The first, the festival marketplace, renovated historic industrial and commercial buildings by making them into malls. The second, the vertical mall, set malls into skyscrapers and invited suburban residents to find the familiar mall in the city center. Against suburban malls that were supposedly "more downtown than downtown itself," these projects provided the one thing the suburbs could not: downtown's demographics, that lively mix of people who came to the city not just to shop, but for hundreds of different purposes.[15]

The festival marketplace renovated historic buildings to create retail theme parks in the inner city. The first of these, San Francisco's Ghirardelli Square, restored a block of old industrial buildings near Fisherman's Wharf in 1964. According to Carole Rifkind, "Dirty old brick was scraped clean, enticing shoppers to explore the complex's odd nooks, unexpected spaces, and multiple levels, all enlivened by a fountain, plantings, decorative lighting, craft shops, fashion boutiques, innovative displays, and unique product lines." Such retail restoration increased impulse buying, especially by tourists. At the festival marketplace, notes essayist David Bosworth, "history becomes shopping, as shopping becomes touring, the seat of old commerce replacing the art museum, civic building, or nation-forming battle site as the favorite attraction of the out-of-towner."[16]

Boston's Faneuil Hall Marketplace, designed by the influential James Rouse, opened in 1976, combining food and specialty retail in historic buildings. Baltimore's Harborplace (1980), New York's South Street Seaport (1983–85), Washington's Union Station (1988), and other festival marketplaces also used many of the techniques of the suburban mall to create an urban ambiance. Developer Rouse echoed Gruen by calling for the confluence of retail, restaurants, and recreation, creating downtown districts that became "destinations" for America's shoppers. Like Gruen, Rouse was what might be called a "commercial idealist" or a "retail reformer" or "commercial communitarian." A longtime member of both the Institute for World Order and the Urban Coalition, Rouse felt that "there is no

Faneuil Hall Marketplace in Boston: the mall moves downtown
(Courtesy of the Rouse Company)

place where a shopping center is worse than on the outskirts of town. Walking
down the streets, meeting people—that's what a small town is all about. When you
lose that, you lose everything." Shopping centers, especially in America's cities, he
believed, could provide a socializing and humanizing influence. Capitalizing (literally) on the newfound popularity of historic preservation and adaptation, the
new festival marketplaces transformed the age of the city from a disadvantage to
an advantage. Making the old-fashioned avant-garde, this commercial gentrifica-
tion made the open-air market fashionable again.[17]

Many festival marketplaces have been commercial successes. But they have
not lived up to Rouse's communitarian ideals, because a community of tourists
is not really a community and urban shopping is not exactly urbanity. Festival
marketplaces commodify the "authenticity" of historic places, but tourism itself
affects that apparent authenticity, because the essence of community is not simply casual and commercial. At the festival marketplace, tourists and townspeo-
ple both buy into the ideas of community and continuity without committing to
a real community and its complex traditions.[18]

The second urban innovation, the vertical mall, also brought many "mallpractices" to the central city. Like the regional mall, vertical malls used leasing

12

arrangements to establish economic and aesthetic control over the chaos of urban retailing. In Chicago, Water Tower Place (1976) brought a shopping center to Michigan Avenue, the premier retail artery of the city. Featuring stores, a hotel, offices, condominiums, and on-site underground parking, Water Tower Place is still one of the best mixed-use projects in the country. By exploring the synergies of residential, retail, office and hotel activity, developers minimized the risks of inner-city development.[19]

Since 1976, there have been still more developments in the malling of America. A new type of store, the category killer, has inverted the appeal of the department store. Instead of offering products in a wide variety of departments, big-box retailers like Office Depot and Office Max, Best Buy and Circuit City, or Toys "R" Us offer a wide variety of products in a very few departments— computers, electronics, office supplies, toys, and so on. The power center, usually an immense strip mall anchored by these category killers, often profits from its proximity to regional or superregional malls.

Factory outlet malls, which create space for manufacturers to sell their own merchandise at discount prices, have also established themselves as popular shopping places for bargain hunters. Sometimes, as at Ontario Mills in California, they are places where upscale merchants sell their goods at downscale prices. And sometimes, as at Sawgrass Mills in Florida, these projects are immense— more than two million square feet of sale stuff. More often, though, outlet malls are essentially large strip malls with common parking. Often, too, they are more exurban than suburban, both because low land prices keep prices low, and because they don't compete as much with the full-price centers downtown and in the suburbs.[20]

Faced with competition from home shopping networks and the Internet, the most recent trend in malls has been "shoppertainment," the combination of entertainment with a heightened sense of a shopping "experience." The best examples are the new megamalls, West Edmonton Mall in Canada and Mall of America in Minnesota. West Edmonton's 5.5 million square feet include a water park, and Mall of America includes a seven-acre amusement park, a Lego Imagination Center, a two-level miniature golf course, several theme restaurants, and a walk-through aquarium called Underwater World. ("Ocean under construction," the signs said modestly as the attraction was being built.)[21]

Even with all these new developments, since 1990 the greatest growth in shopping centers has come from renovation and redevelopment. The malls built in the boom years of the 1960s and 1970s are aging, but because they still occupy important space in their trade areas, owners have repositioned and retenanted many of them to keep them competitive. Some centers are "de-malling," opening up enclosed spaces to easier access from cars. Others move upscale or downscale to attract a new demographic mix. And still others cease to be malls altogether, converting to office or housing uses.[22]

Despite the good intentions of Victor Gruen, James Rouse, and other leaders in mall architecture, virtually all of these shopping centers were better for commerce than for civic life. By 1978, even Gruen was disgusted with the shape of the contemporary shopping center. Like Thoreau, he wondered what would become of people who walked only in the modern mall. In a loud lament at the third annual conference of the International Council of Shopping Centers, Gruen complained that the prophets of shopping centers had given way to the profiteers. A new generation of real estate developers, many of whom "just wanted to make a fast buck," had ignored the civic dimensions of the pioneering plans and had created instead "single function ghettos." In an article titled "The Sad Story of Shopping Centres," Gruen charged that "the environmental and humane ideas underlying . . . the original centres were not only not improved upon—they were completely forgotten. Only those features which had proved profitable were copied." Therefore, he predicted, "the shopping centre in its conventional meaning has no future at all." As it turned out, of course, Gruen was wrong: the malls of America did have a future. And they still feature community programs, even though they don't remotely approach the ideals of pioneers like Gruen who created the very mallness of modern malls.[23]

TWO

Designing Malls

When Americans go shopping, we are usually thinking about the stuff we hope to buy, the food we hope to eat, or the people we plan to meet. We're not usually thinking about the system or structure of the mall, even though it has a significant impact on our shopping. And as Kenneth Clark said, you can "tell more about a civilization from its architecture than from anything else it leaves behind. Painting and literature depend largely on unpredictable individuals. But architecture is to some extent a communal art—at least it depends upon a relationship between the user and the maker much more closely than in the other arts." So the architecture of malls is especially revealing.[1]

Malls are designed to make money. But malls only make money if they make sense to consumers, so the design of shopping centers begins with market research— the art of finding money that's not yet being spent.

Finding out what people want so that you can sell them stuff is basically a way of shopping for shoppers. When you know what prospective customers value, all you have to do is attach their values to your product—or vice versa. That way, people get to buy their own values in the form of a commodity or service. Consequently, mall developers and managers use a lot of market research.[2]

Mall planners use market research to imagine the customer, and then to imagine the mall that will keep the customer satisfied. Shopping center design is both science and art. As architect Charles Kober suggests, good retail design "addresses the task of attracting a fickle consumer, keeping that person at the center longer, stimulating impulse purchases, appealing to the consumer's self-image and aspirations, and making the shopping experience safe, convenient, and fun to ensure a return visit." If the architects and designers do their jobs well, the result is customer satisfaction and increased market share.[3]

The mall, therefore, is a planned society, building structures and structuring relationships—social and economic and political—among the people who populate it. Cultural critic Richard Keller Simon contends that "visitors learn the meaning of a consumer society at the mall, not only in the choices they make in their purchases, but also in the symbol systems they walk through." This chapter explores the design and development of those symbol systems.[4]

Designing the Market

One of the most important parts of mall design is market research. In Iowa baseball, it may be true that "if you build it, they will come." But in shopping centers, if you build it in the wrong place, they will only come to the going-out-of-business sale. Shopping center managers depend on market research to tell them who will shop at the mall and why. They need to know how we think and how we shop. They need to know our dreams in order to make their dreams come true. And researchers employ increasingly sophisticated tools to teach mall managers how to make their sales.

Market research begins with area research (usually quantitative) and then turns to consumer research (usually surveys). Area research focuses on the demographic possibilities of different general regions or specific sites. It includes population, income, employment, and retail sales data. A more specific trade-area analysis looks

Producing Consumption

at population, transportation, physical or psychological barriers to particular sites, and competing retailers. Such research helps a developer decide where to build a center, what size it should be, which tenant mix will attract the most dollars, and how to improve mall performance through operational decisions.[5]

Consumer research consists primarily of surveys—phone surveys, mail surveys, and interviews in the shopping center. These surveys ask respondents demographic questions (regarding age, sex, marital status, zip code, income, education, etc.), but they also ask about consumers' favorite shops, TV and radio stations, newspapers, and magazines—and about other shopping centers they visit. On-site surveys also ask which stores customers patronize, how much they spend, what they like or dislike about the mall, and what types of stores they would like to see in the future. Combined with sales receipts sorted by zip codes, this survey data can tell mall management exactly where their money is coming from. Such research is used both for minor adjustments (new tenants or services, new advertising outlets, etc.) and for more extensive renovations. It can also be helpful in determining a project's feasibility, in attracting particular tenants, and in planning advertising and marketing campaigns.[6]

When Minnesota's Eden Prairie Center planned a 2000–2001 renovation at the southwest corner of the Twin Cities metro area, they depended on such market research to justify upscaling the mall with a new mix of retailers. Projections for the trade area included a population of 324,605 with an aggregate annual income of $10.9 billion. The average income of the 128,499 households was $84,745, with the compound annual growth in incomes a projected 5.5 percent. Almost 65 percent of households had incomes over $50,000, and 24 percent made $100,000 or more. Further, nearly half of the population was concentrated in the prime spending years, ages twenty-five to fifty-four. Two-thirds of adults had some college experience, and 72 percent enjoyed white-collar employment. In terms of life-style, 47 percent were "affluent," 17 percent were "upscale," and 13.5 percent were defined as "up and coming singles." In short, the research showed that these people had both money and the motivation to spend it.[7]

When we go to the mall, we generally think that shopping centers are selling stuff to us, and they are. But we're also sold to shopping center developers. Increasingly, communities compete to get good shopping properties. In a recent issue of *Shopping Center World*, for example, an ad for Corona, California, informed

Designing Malls

readers "why we should be your retail target." Evidence included population growth, household income and education statistics, and a "high traffic corridor of 350,000 cars daily." In the same issue, Rancho Cucamonga's ad promised that "our Rancho shoppers have the demographics you want and they're at the center of a $3 billion economy in one of the fastest growing MSAs [metropolitan statistical area] in the nation."[8]

In a similar way, shopping centers compete for retailers by selling them the profit possibilities of the trade area. When shopping centers advertise space to prospective retailers in journals like *Shopping Center World*, they emphasize features like the number of people in an twenty-mile radius, the number of tourists or visitors to the area, the prosperity of those prospective shoppers ("$115,000 average household income in trade area"), the quality of the job market ("#1 fastest growing job market in America"), and any special facilities, like an entertainment zone, that make the mall particularly attractive. Retailers and regional shopping centers like to be placed in the vicinity of money. Just as television networks are in the business of selling audiences to sponsors, shopping center professionals are in the business of selling markets to retailers, who then sell merchandise to customers. And market research helps everybody make the sale.[9]

Values and Life-Styles

Shopping center developers and managers can also commission proprietary research from some impressive national firms, including Claritas, VALS, and Yankelovich. This market research goes beyond people's income and spending to determine their values and life-styles. Demographic research indicates *how* people spend money; psychographic research tells *why* they spend it. Such research wasn't necessary when the retail trade was a local phenomenon and people were known as customers instead of consumers. A customer is a person who regularly takes their custom to a particular place, becoming accustomed to a neighborhood shop or shopkeeper. A customer is a person with an economic relationship to a business, but also with a personal relationship to a businessman or businesswomen.[10]

At the mom-and-pop stores of the past, retailers didn't need market research to determine a customer's values and life-style—they already knew. But as stores

Producing Consumption

became larger and larger, and as trade areas expanded, customers became consumers. And as the professional, full-time sales staff was replaced by minimum-wage workers, the chances of maintaining a relationship with a businessperson declined. The customer became a consumer, who needed other reasons to shop at a particular place.

Values have been around a long time, but life-style is a relatively recent word, invented to describe the lives we make for ourselves as consumers. In the past, people had a life, but not a life-style. Some living people had style, but style wasn't deemed essential to life. People admired character and competence, who you were and what you could do. They didn't care particularly what car you drove, or what clothes you wore, or how many appliances you owned. Over the course of the twentieth century, however, character and competence were increasingly challenged by personality and personal style. Character implied values rooted in community and tradition, a life lived in conformity to goals sustained in groups. But personality is more an individual attribute, more a matter of style. People with personality possess interpersonal competence even if they can't do anything productive particularly well.[11]

Some national research firms, like Claritas, depend on residential segregation for their power and predictability. These market researchers profit from the fact that Americans like to live next to people who look and act pretty much the same. Historically, we have chosen to locate ourselves in what sociologist Robert Bellah calls "lifestyle enclaves," clusters and subdivisions of housing that express uniform tastes and, to some extent, values. This means that zip codes actually provide a fairly good predictor of wealth, values, and commercial behavior. The PRIZM system, for example, shows that Northfield, Minnesota's most common clusters are "God's Country" (executive exurban households with an average income of $65,300), "Big Fish, Small Pond" (small-town executives who watch *ER*, read *Country Living*, and shop at Ann Taylor), "New Homesteaders" (younger white-collar families with Sears charge cards who shop by direct mail), "Golden Ponds" (retirement town seniors who shop at Wal-Mart and go bowling and golfing), and "Agri-Business" (farm families who ride horses, watch nostalgia TV, and read romance novels). This sort of statistical sorting means that malls can choose locations and retailers to appeal to particular segments of the population. They can profitably engage in "niche

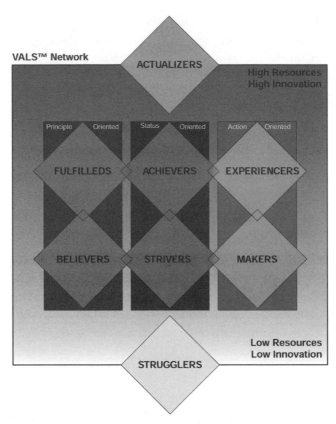

ACTUALIZERS

High Resources
High Innovation

Principle Oriented   Status   Oriented   Action   Oriented

FULFILLEDS   ACHIEVERS   EXPERIENCERS

BELIEVERS   STRIVERS   MAKERS

Low Resources
Low Innovation

STRUGGLERS

The VALS network (Source: SRI Consulting Business Intelligence)

marketing" or segmentation, selling to specific slices of a consumer demographic. The irony of niche marketing is that it also makes the niche it markets. Having identified a cluster of consumers, the marketing reinforces that identity, and curtails other imaginative possibilities. So the market segmentation of mall developers both reflects and reinforces our patterns of residential segregation—and patterns of race and class stratification.[12]

Other market research tools are more sophisticated, and depend on extensive survey research. One of the most popular is VALS. As early as the 1970s, the VALS researchers at the Stanford Research Institute (now called SRI International) were trying to figure out how the new social values stirred up by the Sixties would affect consumption. Many of the 1960s generation had negative feelings about money, consumption, corporations, and capitalism. They rejected conformity, conventional measures of success, and "materialism in its flamboyant forms." The question was how to sell products and services to people who didn't want to "sell out" by buying into the system. In a 1974 report on "Consumer Values," VALS developer Arnold Mitchell suggested that "the central problem in advertising will be how to sell values increasingly geared to processes, not things. Sales appeals directed toward the values of individualism, experimentalism, person-centeredness, direct experience, and some forms of pleasure and escape will need to tap intangibles—human relationships, feelings, dreams, and hopes—rather than tangible things or explicit actions."[13]

SRI Consulting Business Intelligence promises that "the VALS team can help you apply VALS most effectively for your specific projects." VALS can help shopping centers and retailers (1) identify *who* to target, (2) uncover *what* your target group buys and does, (3) locate *where* concentrations of your target group lives, (4) identify *how* best to communicate with your target group, and (5) gain insight into *why* your target group acts the way it does.[14]

VALS research divides the American population into eight consumer groups: Actualizers, Fulfilleds, Achievers, Experiencers, Believers, Strivers, Makers, and Strugglers. The main dimensions of difference in the profiles are self-orientation and level of resources. Self-orientation describes the way consumers relate their purchases to themselves. "Principle-oriented consumers" use "abstract, idealized criteria" to make consumer choices; they're not much interested in the approval and opinions of others, because, in fact, they are often opinion leaders. "Status-oriented consumers" seem less secure and look for goods and services that say "Success!" to their colleagues, friends, and neighbors. "Action-oriented consumers" buy stuff for the experience, thrills, variety, and social or physical activity.[15]

Each of the eight psychographic profiles comes with what we might call a "buy-ography," a shopping pattern that matches the life-style. Actualizers, sophisticated people with abundant resources, enjoy "the finer things" in life. Their own security makes them open to new products, technologies, and shopping ideas. Highly educated, they read a wide variety of publications and tend to be light TV watchers. Actualizers are skeptical of advertising, which means that advertising directed at them needs to be qualitatively different—tasteful, understated, coded to acknowledge their highly developed tastes—and placed in upscale media such as *Architectural Digest* and the *New Yorker.*[16]

Strivers tend to be image conscious. They have limited discretionary income, which they often extend with credit-card purchases, they spend a lot on clothing and personal care products that enhance their appearance, and they prefer watching TV to reading. Strugglers have fewer resources than those in the other seven groups, and as a result, they tend to use coupons and watch for sales. They're more brand loyal than wealthier consumers who can afford and appreciate more stimulation and variety. Strugglers watch TV often, perhaps because it's cheap entertainment, and they read tabloids and women's magazines.[17]

Advertisers use VALS all the time, but shopping center developers can also use such psychographic tools to choose which department stores should anchor a mall, and which specialty shops can complement the anchors. They know that Brooks Brothers and Ann Taylor shops work well in areas populated by Achievers and Strivers (generally young, hard-working, status-conscious yuppie types), while Believers and Makers (middle-class conservatives and conformists with fewer resources) prefer the value of Kmart or J. C. Penney. Mindful that shopping is mainly in the mind, psychographics is a way of "minding the store" so that it makes the most money.[18]

Malls and retailers and their trade associations also generate their own research, conducting "customer intercept surveys" to learn more about shoppers' life-styles and preferences. Such surveys show that mall shoppers are younger than other Americans—and make more money too. Women dominate malls, outnumbering men almost two to one. In 2000, shoppers averaged thirty-eight mall visits a year, averaging seventy-five minutes and two or three store visits each time. That means we spend roughly a whole work week every year in shopping centers. In the mall, we buy stuff at about half of the stores we enter, spending an average of $71.40 each time we visit the shopping center.[19]

The ICSC's 1997 Mall Customer Shopping Patterns Report also shows that most of us are destination shoppers—coming to the mall to go to a specific store or for a specific purchase. But for a third of us, the mall itself is the destination; we go just to browse, happy to be socializing or shopping for nothing in particular. When we just go to the mall, not for any particular purpose, we tend to linger longer, averaging twenty minutes more than destination shoppers.[20]

By the time we're ready to shop, market research has the mall ready for us.

Building Malls of America

Malls are designed to please us. "With the exception of the film industry," says Stafford Cliff in *Trade Secrets of Great Design*, "I cannot think of any other profession in which so many people display so much talent and energy to entertain us, to educate us, to enrich our lives and to continually push back the boundaries of what is possible." Mall designers know that Americans are shopping, not just for goods, but for shopping centers, and that if this mall doesn't please us, a competitor will.[21]

Good mall design begins even before we enter the parking lot. Outside the mall, designers and developers work on location, visibility, signage, traffic control, landscaping, and parking. Mall developers follow the three cardinal rules of American real estate: location, location, location. Good location for a mall includes a concentrated target population and easy access by car. Shopping centers thus reflect widespread American values about land, operating on the common assumption that the best use of land is the most profitable. If a shopping center makes more money than a cornfield, then you ought to build a shopping center. A shopping center is an adaptation to place, but the place is defined demographically and economically, not ecologically or aesthetically. In this calculus, the primary value of land is its market value. Realty becomes reality.[22]

In the business of mall location, the economies of sale determine the economies of scale. According to Reilly's law of retail gravitation, "all other things being equal, shoppers will patronize the largest shopping center they can get to easily." Strip malls don't require a large population to succeed, but regional malls operate on a different scale. A book on *Shopping Center Management* estimates that a regional center with one to three department store anchors and a total gross leasable area (GLA) between 400,000 and 1,000,000 square feet needs 150,000 to 300,000 people in a trade area of seven to ten miles. And superregional malls need an even larger trade area to get a concentrated population poised to spend their earnings.[23]

In either case, access and visibility are absolutely essential to the success of a mall, so malls are often located at the intersection of interstate highways—called a "golden link" in the trade—or of busy thoroughfares. Inside and out, malls are in the business of trafficking: in the mid-1980s, developers preferred locations passed by at least fifty thousand cars a day. Especially at the beginning of a project, the traffic engineering consultant is one of the most significant designers, especially in planning the traffic flow at peak periods—evening rush hour (roughly 5:00–6:00 P.M.), evening rush to the shopping center (7:00–8:00 P.M.), and closing time (8:30–9:30).[24]

Mall developers know that shopping is a matter of seeing and being seen, and they make sure the mall itself can be seen from the highway. First impressions are important, because if they're not good, they can be last impressions. So "curb appeal" is an essential element of mall design. Usually, the mall serves as a sign for itself, its own bulk a mark of its magnificence. Anchor tenants (also called "magnets") also negotiate for positions in the mall that involve maximum visibility from the highway. The anchor stores announce their name and logo on the sides of their buildings, but other tenants depend on the magnets to draw traffic past their storefronts.

The first shopping centers made money without a lot of distinctive design. But with the proliferation of shopping centers, it's become more important to distinguish one shopping center from another. One way to distinction is a different story, and one way to tell a story is with a visual theme. "Today, more than ever before," Charles Kober wrote in 1988, "a center must have individuality. A theme can give a center uniqueness and curb appeal."[25]

Malls are built for people with cars, and people with cars expect malls with parking, so malls provide lots of parking that's quick and convenient. Mall designers try to get almost all the parking places within three hundred feet of an entrance, because they know that Americans hate to walk (at least in parking lots).[26]

Once we've found a parking place, we're ready to look at the mall itself. Since nothing is for sale outside, there's no reason for the exterior to be fancy. The building is basically a fortress designed to protect us from the trials and tribulations of the world we're coming from. Indeed, this "architecture of introversion" offers no reason to linger outside and many reasons to go in. Regional malls generally don't have windows, because we're not supposed to think about the world outside the mall. "I don't want the public to see the real world they live in while

24

Setting the stage for something significant (Image by Wernher Krutein)

they're in the park," said the influential developer Walt Disney, speaking of Disneyland. "I want them to feel they are in another world." The same is true of shopping centers.[27]

The mall's entrance is an important point of transition between "out there" and "in here." It should let us know that we've arrived at someplace momentous, a place with enough power to solve our problems. It's usually an imposing edifice, a triumphal arch, a grand gateway to our getaway. It gets us in the door, but it also gets us in the mood for something significant—like shopping.[28]

Inside, other features emphasize the consequence of the mall. Skylights in tall courtyards draw our eyes upward, just like the stained glass windows of medieval cathedrals. Rich materials like marble or burnished metals or polished wood elevate our emotions. Works of art make the stores seem like galleries. And the spic-and-span cleanliness of the center makes us feel like honored guests. As we come through the entrance, advised one expert, "the elements of this new environment should provide such exciting interest that the shopper's first feeling

25

Designing Malls

is one of a satisfying emotional uplift." If a mall is well designed, customer satisfaction begins before a shopper buys anything.[29]

Upscale malls are even more impressive, because they need to create a context for the consumption of luxury. You can't sell Gucci in a garage or Prada in a pole barn; it violates the fitness of things. People pay high prices for designer items, in part because the malls' refined atmosphere reinforces the refinement of the goods—and of the people who purchase them. As the *Shopping Center Development Handbook* suggests, "granite or marble signals upscale shops, specialty tenants, an orientation toward fashion, and expensive merchandise." Stucco or synthetic plaster usually go with outlet and off-price centers, and brick buildings with slate roofs often suggest a more conservative community orientation.[30]

But even in the most modest of regional malls, there's an aesthetic impression that comes from the sheer proliferation of space and stuff. This is what we might call "the commercial sublime" or "the shopping sublime"—the sense of awe and amazement that comes from the cornucopia of commodities that are stacked, packed, hung, folded, and displayed in the stores and shops of the mall. Americans get used to this astounding affluence, and we tend to take it for granted. Immigrants to America more realistically appreciate the astounding superfluity of our shopping centers. But whether or not it still amazes us, it *is* amazing, both historically and commercially.

Shopping centers are basically in the business of renting space to retailers, restaurants, and service providers. They usually charge a fixed rental per square foot of floor space, plus an "overage"—a small percentage of profits on sales above the base rent. At the malls of Simon Property Group, the largest publicly-traded retail real estate company in North America, base rents in the year 2000 averaged $28.31 per square foot, and retailers averaged $384.00 in sales for each square foot of rented space. At America's malls, percentage rents range from about 2 percent for department stores to 8–10 percent for fast-food tenants. Most shops pay in the 5–8 percent range. The rent structure means that shopping centers have an interest in designs and promotions that help retailers satisfy customers. It also means that retailers in the mall are engaged in "coopetition"—competing with each other by cooperating with each other to promote the success of the mall.[31]

For the last fifty years, the main structuring principle of malls has been "magnets," the large department stores with names and reputations that attract most of the customers and most of the financing for the project. These anchor stores pay for advertising and promotion, but they benefit from favorable rents and, sometimes, from a substantial say in the mix of specialty shops. Designers locate the magnets at opposite ends of corridors lined with specialty shops. To get from one magnet to another, people must pass all the other storefronts. Designers hope to achieve what's called "the Gruen transfer," the transformation of a "destination shopper" looking for a particular item into an "impulse shopper," open to other suggestions. Basically, then, a mall design is a highly calculated plan to stimulate unplanned purchases, a rational system for the promotion of impulse buying.[32]

Leasing agents also carefully arrange the specialty shops to maximize traffic for mall retailers. According to the *Shopping Center Development Handbook*, "The amount of sales space for each category should be based on the estimated sales volume that can be captured in each retail segment, based on the market analysis." Specific stores may be chosen based on life-style marketing, brand identity, and merchandising procedures. Specialty stores add variety to the shopping center, and good specialty stores generate traffic of their own. Sometimes called "intercept stores," their job is to intercept consumers passing by. For that reason, they need to pay particular attention to their window displays and the first ten feet of their floorspace. Specialty stores pay higher rents than the anchors, and they usually provide a good profit margin for the mall.[33]

Still, some specialty shops never make it to the mall. Although we think that the mall has "everything," it doesn't. Malls need shops with high turnover and impressive profits, retailers who can afford the premium rents for mall space. Shopping centers can't afford many stores (like furniture stores) that need a lot of floor space, because success is calculated by sales per square foot. They can't afford shops that sell perishable goods, because then shoppers go home instead of spending more time (and money) in the mall. Malls prefer shops that sell portable items so that consumers can carry their purchases from one store to another. Other shops end up outside the shopping center, in the strip malls and power centers that surround the mall itself.[34]

Mall managers also can't afford stores that can't predictably pay the rent, which means that they are more likely to lease space to a national chain with a TV and fashion-magazine advertising budget than to a local shop with less brand equity and consumer clout. The national tenants, sometimes called "credit tenants" because they help developers get loans for their projects, are essential for regional malls. As a consequence, many of the different stores in the mall are just variations on a theme by a larger retail conglomerate. The Gap shows up in hundreds of malls, but Gap, Inc. is also the parent company of Banana Republic and Old Navy. The Limited is a retailer, but it's just one part of Limited Brands, which also operates Express, Aura Science, and Henri Bendel. Limited Brands also controls about 80 percent of Intimate Brands, which includes Victoria's Secret, Bath and Bodyworks, and White Barn Candle Company. When Gap or Limited Brands commits to a mall, therefore, it makes a leasing manager's job a lot easier. On the theory that nothing succeeds like success, malls come to be populated by the same stores nationwide. About 80 percent of sales space in regional shopping centers is occupied by national chains; in superregional malls, it's 90 percent.[35]

Because successful stores draw traffic, they also draw other specialty shops. Thus mall managers try to profit from "adjacent attractions," two or more retailers that make a mini-magnet of their own. If you're going to the Gap, the theory goes, you're likely to be attracted to the fashions in The Limited. Customers of the Pottery Barn will also shop at Williams-Sonoma, which (not coincidentally) is operated by the same company. Men looking for shoes might be tempted to stop in the sporting goods store. Children's clothes and toy stores profit from a location near women's apparel and shoe stores. Some leasing agents try to create adjacencies that form little "merchandise worlds" within the larger world of the mall. Using an aesthetic of aggregation and juxtaposition, the mall arranges its compositions artistically, according to the aesthetic properties of commercial art, in which beauty is not just in the eye of the beholder but also in the vault at the bank.[36]

Beyond the "magnetic" layout of the mall, designers keep people moving with a variety of techniques. Focal attractions, which Walt Disney called "wienies," draw people to them. Water features like fountains are particularly effective. Courtyards can also be a draw for crowds, providing a dramatic oasis in the desert of retailing. In the courtyards, too, light itself can be an attraction. People feel good about light that comes from above, like the sun, so skylights and clerestory windows are popular in newer designs.

Even subtle elements can keep us moving in the mall. Escalators, for example, are "a primary mechanism to generate traffic flow to every part of every store

Upward mobility: the mall's escalator clause (Image by Wernher Krutein)

level." Architects discovered that Americans wouldn't climb many stairs to get to the upper levels of a mall or a department store. Elevators moved people up and down, but they worked best for "destination shoppers" who skipped whole floors of purchase possibilities. Escalators, on the other hand, take customers to every floor, and they escalate the profits of the upper floors. An early ad for Otis escalators noted that "the Escalator beckons to the customer and assures him that he can travel upward quickly and without effort. No waiting, no crowding. This induces casual shoppers to visit the upper floors . . . [and] look at merchandise they would otherwise never have noticed."[37]

In the last twenty years, escalators have increasingly become a signature design element, the central focus of an atrium awash in light and space and style. Less functional than the courtyards of early department stores, which furnished daylight and natural ventilation to a large building, today's escalator atriums function as "an iconographic center of the store" and "a compelling feature that increases storewide sales." Dramatic light streaming from vaulted ceilings or

29

Designing Malls

domes draws people to the atrium, where they are shown the multiple shopping levels that await their exploration. Accordingly, store planner Lawrence Israel contends that "the escalator is the unquestioned center of the selling plan. Because it is the focus of vertical traffic throughout a multifloor facility, it generates that traffic and becomes the 100 percent location." When people can see the escalator from all around the shopping center, and the expanse of the shopping center from the escalator, they know there's more to explore.[38]

Other elements also induce exploration in malls. Linear designs and contrasts of color and light can lure people in certain directions, and signs and waymarkers can pique a person's curiosity. Within the halls, benches, planters, fountains, trash bins, and freestanding promotions serve not just their single purpose but also the purpose of channeling traffic closer to the storefronts. Like television, which is basically an institution devised to rent eyeballs to advertisers, the mall is an institution designed to parade eyes past a cornucopia of stuff. As one prominent mall architect said, "We want people to get lost [and] to discover new things."[39]

As consumer preferences change, so do malls. "For the same reason that fashion changes," notes Charles Kober, "a retail center must also change in order to keep the interest of its market." All malls change slowly by replacing tenants that can't meet the expected "tenant profile"—the average sales per square foot in its retail category in the center. Often tenant turnover runs about 10 percent a year. Sometimes, too, malls change dramatically. The *Shopping Center Development Handbook* recommends updates every five to ten years "because of the intense competition and the fickleness of American consumers, who demand the most up-to-date retail formats, tenant mix, and physical environment." Like aging people, aging malls get facelifts and makeovers. Demographic transitions, changing life-styles, increasing emphasis on entertainment, new merchandising techniques, old-fashioned buildings—all of these things invite renovations. Such "mall morphing" suggests how much mall managers listen to their customers' preferences, trying to reflect (and affect) evolving tastes.[40]

Shopping center architecture is basically commercial art you can shop in. "Shopping architecture is not meant to be seen," says designer Daniel Herman in *The Harvard Design School Guide to Shopping*. "It is not gauged by the eye, but by the *statistic*. The numerical demands of the market—volume, turnover, expansion, gain—give architectural form to shopping." Good design is design that is profitable.[41]

Once you understand mall designs, a shopping center can seem like a trap for the unwary—and, of course, it is. But it's a trap that we help set for ourselves. Investors, developers, architects, managers, and retailers make the mall, but we make it too by the way we occupy the space and respond to the designing minds of mall marketers. Because malls pay attention to the life-styles and preferences of their customers, it's fair to say that we, too, are the architects of America's shopping centers.

These issues of design and control are important in thinking about American consumer culture. Early scholars of shopping and consumption often argued that America's materialism developed as a result of corporate control, usually through advertising. They used the concept of "hegemony" to show how some groups, especially "captains of consciousness" in adverstising and marketing, influenced others and how commercial ideas and assumptions gained more power than others. They suggested that common people were often duped by the power of the mass media. Lured into a "false consciousness," Americans acted in ways contrary to their own best interests.[42]

There is some truth in this analysis, but recent scholars have challenged the view of the passive consumer. They contend that popular culture is powerful not because it exerts power over us but because it's one place where power is contested in this society. Media critic John Fiske especially argues against what he calls the "cultural dope" theory, contending instead that people make their own meanings out of the materials they're given. Scholars such as Fiske contend that people's pleasures in popular culture are real and substantial. We might wish that consumers, including ourselves, had more uplifting pleasures, but we ought not to minimize the ones we actually have. When scholars suggest that shoppers' experience isn't real or authentic, it clouds the issue of who is qualified to decide what's real and authentic. I think it's safest to assume that if people think they're having fun, they probably are.[43]

Corporations, elites, and advertisers exercise enormous influence on American life, but it's not uncontested influence. They can't make us act the way they want. We make ourselves act the way they want, which is often also the way that we want. Sometimes, we consumers *conform* to social and corporate expectations;

sometimes we *transform* them. Sometimes, we even consume to resist or evade the dominant ideas and institutions of our culture, including the culture of consumption. At times, we may be foolish, but it's not always because we've been fooled.

Shopping and shopping centers are forms of popular culture, which the people make, but not absolutely freely. Popular culture is creative, not in the way God is creative (making something out of nothing), but in the ways that people are creative, making something out of the materials at hand. It's making it up as we go along. In American culture, we make meanings out of the objects and ideas—and spaces—provided by commercial culture. We may not plan to design shopping centers, but, in the course of our daily lives, we play an important part in the social construction of malls of America.

THREE

The Nature of Malls

Malls are obviously a cultural construction, built of steel and concrete, values and expectations. But malls are also an American *natural* phenomenon. We first see nature in the landscaping outside the mall. Inside, we see it in potted plants and ornamental gardens. It operates as a symbol system in settings as diverse as department stores, cosmetics counters, and bath and body shops—and in products as diverse as clothing and Beanie Babies. In many malls, we find nature at the outfitters or the nature stores. In a few malls, we can encounter nature in simulations. And, of course, the mall itself, and its contents, is nature converted to commodity. The shopping center is powered by nature; it takes nature to sustain consumer culture. This chapter explores the nature of malls and the nature of American retailing.[1]

As we know, malls were originally pedestrian pleasure grounds like the National Mall in Washington, D.C.

Most regional malls turn this concept literally inside out—or more precisely, outside in. An enclosed shopping center is a way of boxing the Great Outdoors, which becomes, by virtue of being boxed, the Great Indoors. Modern malls are, in fact, a celebration of American interiority, a controlled environment that manages heat and light, and eliminates weeds and bugs and snakes and rodents (at least most of them). But there's still nature inside America's malls, and it performs a lot of cultural work. Indeed, the nature of the mall can tell us a great deal about American culture, including our consumer culture.

Nature as Landscaping

Nature appears at the mall in a variety of guises. As we drive in, we see the landscaping that accents the mall exterior. Trees and bushes relieve the flat expanses of parking lots and the mall's exterior walls. The *Shopping Center Development Handbook* advises that "creative landscaping can help produce the type of memorable environment that will draw customers back again and again, while inappropriate landscaping can badly damage a shopping center's image." The handbook suggests "indigenous plants" around the mall, both for survivability and because they "add to the local character and authenticity of the shopping environment."[2]

The American practice of outdoor landscaping comes from a long tradition of presuppositions and practices concerning nature and culture, seen in the very language of "landscape" and "landscaping." As a noun, a landscape is a view or vista of scenery on land, or a painting or picture representing such a view. A landscape is not land; it's a look at land. It's a visual phenomenon, the sight of a site. As a verb, though, landscape becomes more cultural than natural. To landscape something is to adorn or improve the land by contouring it and by planting it artfully with flowers, shrubs, and trees. A landscape painter may or may not idealize nature, but a landscaper who doesn't improve the landscape won't be in business long.

At most malls, landscaping is largely a beautification project. Trees and shrubbery and flowers can act as a form of impression management, helping a shopping center to make its guests feel at home. Outside the mall, as at home, we tend to like the look of the manicured lawn or landscaped trees. When wild nature asserts itself, we spray it or trim it or cut it to conform to our tastes. Similarly, the nature of the mall tells customers about its fashionability. The artful arrangement of nature at the mall reinforces our trust in the aesthetic judgment of mall retailers. If they know the cultural codes of "natural" beautification, they probably know the codes of fashion and interior decoration. If they can make the mall look this good, maybe they can help us look good too.

The Garden in the Machine

There is also landscaping inside America's malls. In department store and shopping center courtyards, nature often takes the form of a garden, and the mall can be seen as a giant greenhouse or conservatory. Kenneth Clark contends that gardens are an attempt to make dreams come true. Landscape gardeners try to create "the most enchanting dream which has ever consoled mankind, the myth of a Golden Age in which man lived on the fruits of the earth, peacefully, piously, and with primitive simplicity." The artful mall garden is a variation on that dream, operating as an air-conditioned, climate-controlled middle landscape where nature and commercial culture coexist in a different sort of Gilded Age.[3]

Many characteristics of traditional gardens have their counterparts in the modern mall. As Richard Keller Simon suggests, lakes and ponds have been miniaturized but fountains have been retained, since falling water attracts the eye, the ear, and the customer. The garden mount that presented a vista has been replaced by the escalator. The garden's labyrinth remains in the aisles of department stores, designed to move the shopper past the maximum number of attractions. The traditional kitchen garden takes the form of the food court, and the classical statues have become mannequins. The garden's architectural antiquities are reproduced in department stores and neoclassical storefronts. In the mall, however, the purposes of the garden are inverted. No longer a place of rest and contemplation, the modern garden of Eden focuses more on earthly delights than on primitive virtue or simplicity. As Simon notes, "Conspicuous consumption has replaced quiet repose."[4]

Mall designers also arrange plants and props like benches, light poles, and wastebaskets to make shopping centers feel like parks. Like Central Park and other designs of nineteenth-century landscape architects such as Frederick Law Olmsted, these "parks" suggest a counterpoint of nature and culture and a space for recreation and (perhaps) contemplation. Like Olmsted's work, they engineer nature for culture, but unlike Olmsted's parks, there's no public input or oversight at the shopping center. In this instance, in fact, nature is the sign that helps to make a private enterprise feel like public space.

These complex (and sometimes contradictory) combinations are part of the peculiar pleasures of the mall. We're in the mall, but we're still in nature. We're in a social construction, but we still feel like a free individual because the freedom of nature complements the freedom of consumption. We're in a private space, but it feels public. We're in a commercial institution, but it feels natural.[5]

Mall designers call their garden plantings "softscapes" because they look softer than the steel and concrete of the construction. But they also serve to soften our resistance to the commercial character of the mall. Greenery seems to increase the amounts of green that consumers spend at the mall, as nature "naturalizes" the transactions at the cash register. A postcard from Minnesota's Mall of America, for example, claims that "nature's beauty flows through Mall of America year-round. Fountains, streams, live plants and trees flourish in the department store courtyards, in Knott's Camp Snoopy, along every avenue, and at Golf Mountain, an 18-hole miniature golf course. Sunshine through the many skylights adds an outdoors radiance to this natural, indoors setting." Ask yourself, just what does the word "natural" mean in that last sentence? What is natural about any indoors setting? In fact, in this situation, nature is the face that culture (and especially the culture of commerce) wears at the mall, as these plantings make us feel like we're in a natural place where we're not being manipulated—which is, of course, exactly where we're not.[6]

But if the mall sets us in place, what place is it? The nature of the mall is usually not local. The unique characteristics of different places disappear in the climate-controlled interiors of malls. So the plants in the mall are not usually native species but species easily adapted to indoor environments. Trees tend to be tropical—black olive, oleanders, hibiscus, southern species of pine. Even at the Mall of America, most of the flora are natives of Florida and other summery climes. These specimens tell us something about plant life, but not much about the local plant community. Outside, native plants are adapted to their environment. Inside the shopping center, plants are also adapted to their environment, but it's a commercial rather than an ecological environment.[7]

The harvest of the mall garden, synthetic or photosynthetic, is greatly different from all previous gardens. "The eighteenth-century garden," Simon sug-

Potted plants: the nature of the mall (Photograph by the author)

gests, "was designed as an aid to reflection—recollection, introspection, worship—but, after all, it was quite consciously created as an elaboration of the pleasures of individual liberty, with vistas of open space, places to make choices, and secluded bowers to be alone." Simon contends that "in contrast, the mall was quite consciously created as an elaboration of the pleasures of consumption, with enclosed space, places to make economic choices, but no bowers to be alone. Introspection and reflection are discouraged, but education, nevertheless, is taking place, for visitors to the mall are constantly confronted with information about the meanings of the space and their role in it."[8]

The Nature of Potted Plants

Inside malls, nature grows most often in pots. But why? What's the precise purpose of a ficus tree in a twenty-gallon ceramic container? What functions are fulfilled by flowers in planter boxes? Although almost every mall has potted plants, very little shopping center literature is devoted to them. The *Shopping Center Development Handbook* suggests that "plants and seasonal floral displays appropriately placed inside the center make it much more appealing to customers, and plantings, water displays, and sculptures can transform an interior pedestrian space into a focal point for the community." But what exactly is the appeal?[9]

The appeal isn't agricultural. Except for errant children, we don't eat the produce of these potted farms. The appeal of potted plants isn't health, even though organizations like the Plants for Clean Air Council and many landscapers promote indoor planting as a cure for "sick-building syndrome," the health problems that can result from stale indoor air. Generally speaking, potted plants are therapeutic in a different way, and the plants can be considered medicinal, even though they're not ingested. Indeed, the final harvest of potted plants is more symbolic than substantive. They function pretty much like houseplants; they're a way of domesticating the mall, of making us feel at home. They're not necessary for shopping or for living, but they're a grace note, a touch of nature in the house of culture. They tell us that we can live in harmony with nature because nature is under control. Like our indoor and outdoor landscaping, these plants suggest that nature is primarily scenic and visual, and that nature is not substantially disturbed by the activities of the household or the mall. In this scenario, the potted plants are literally a "plant," which the dictionary defines as "a misleading piece of evidence placed so as to be discovered."[10]

Nature as Art(ifice)

Like the plants in the walled gardens of the past, the organic plants in today's malled garden require special care. But some mall plants, the flora of *natura artificia*, require considerably less care. Preserved Treescapes International, for example, manufactures preserved trees. Harvesting palm leaves in the deserts of California, the company uses a proprietary process to preserve them and then attaches them to tree trunks made of natural palm trunk material combined with urethane and fiberglass. Such specimens, vice president Vito Milano contends, are better than "those sickly looking six-foot ficus trees" because "God didn't create indoor plants." Even though they cost twice as much as the real thing, Milano attributes the success of unnatural trees to changing customer tastes. "As the theming aspect has become more and more popular, it is no longer acceptable for a mall to put a 6-foot ficus in a decorative container. Consumers are demanding that commercial space be far more interesting."[11]

There are also some practical reasons for these trees. Milano touts the advantages of installing "a 35-foot palm tree that doesn't require light, doesn't require soil, and doesn't need watering or spraying of pesticides." The only maintenance needed is occasional dusting. Artificial trees are fire resistant, and an inorganic tree never dies. Artificial trees can hide unsightly columns or structural features, and they can house a security system, or a staircase, or an elevator shaft.[12]

Another firm, modestly called NatureMaker, also manufactures nature for commerce. They shipped a sixty-two-foot redwood to Scheels Allsports in Coralville, Iowa, and a walk-through sequoia tree to the Ontario Mills shopping center in California. Their trees go all over the world, and clients pay up to quarter of a million dollars for larger specimens. "Only God can grow a tree," they admit. But, they add, "only NatureMaker can make one this realistic."[13]

NatureMaker's trees grow quickly, reaching full maturity in two months to two years. That's because they're grown "from seed—the seed of inspiration" and because NatureMaker's trees are assembled by construction teams. Welders build steel frames, which are wrapped in wire mesh and then covered with foam. Some trees are coated with real wood cured to prevent rot; others are sheathed with a proprietary composite material molded to replicate real bark patterns. Trees are hand-painted. Branches sprout next, along with polyester-silk leaves. The result is, as they say, "one-of-a-kind masterworks [that] embody the beauty, tenacity, and individual character of arboreal specimens at their peak."[14]

As the word "masterwork" suggests, NatureMaker emphasizes the art of their nature. Partner Gary Hanick says, "Our goal here is to offer museum-quality work at prices affordable to high-end architects and developers." Americans have long included trees in their landscape painting. But NatureMaker celebrates the trees themselves as art. "Every tree a work of art," claims their web page. "Literally." There's no messy reliance on natural selection, or organic processes. These designer trees are "the art of nature. Recreated by man." So they can be perfect every time.[15]

NatureMaker's Gary Hanick justifies these faux trees as an encounter with nature, noting that "people's interactions with nature are becoming less and less.

The Nature of Malls

This might be their only interaction with nature." Yet even NatureMaker knows that you can't really see the forest in these trees. Still, you can see something, and that's the point. Functionally, these steel monsters aren't trees. They don't do anything that trees do, except look like trees. But in the land of looks, what you see is what you get—or at least what gets you. In American culture, trees say "nature" and nature means good. According to the company, NatureMaker trees can "capture the serenity of the Alps, the rugged outdoor spirit of the West, or the awe of the Rockies" with carefully crafted evergreens. This creates feelings that are both comforting and stimulating, and now we can have those feelings wherever we happen to be. In an age of multitasking, we can conveniently experience the pleasures of nature while we eat or shop in the mall.[16]

Nature as Experience

Occasionally shopping center simulations go beyond single trees, creating nature "experiences" that bring people to the mall. The now-extinct American Wilderness Experience, for example, allowed people to visit five California ecosystems inside the Ontario Mills shopping center. A creation of the Ogden Corporation, the American Wilderness Experience was a "concept" that brought the wilderness experience indoors. The brochure for the attraction invited shoppers "to step inside the great outdoors" and "go wild in the mall!" After purchasing tickets, guests were escorted to "the outpost," a clearing in the woods where they were welcomed to a "half-million-mile hike" in the wilderness by hosts dressed like park rangers. The hike began with a video about Jonathan, a boy who wanted to be an architect and urban planner. In the video, Jonathan imagines the construction of a great city, an image not unlike the standard fare of World's Fairs. But an owl appears, and wisely advises Jonathan that his vision of the built environment "does not include animals." The owl invites the boy to "see the world through our eyes."[17]

Luckily, this possibility is not just a figment of Jonathan's imagination, as the doors open up to the Wild Ride Theater, a movie/motion simulator that permits people like us to feel what it would be like to be "a mountain lion bounding through the forest, a dolphin swimming through the sea, or a bee zipping through the trees. Through the magic of animation and motion seats, you'll experience adventures man has never known before . . . learn nature's most valuable lessons . . . and have loads of fun along the way. All at no extra charge."[18]

At the end of our experience as an animal, we exit into the first of five "indoor recreations of . . . natural ecosystems." In the Redwood Forest, "the spirit of the wilderness" speaks to us. This spirit, a hologram that looks a good deal like John Muir, tells us, "There's nothing like the wilderness to calm your soul." As we "wander through this magical forest," we smell the scent of redwoods and see small exhibits of king snakes, rubber boas, and tiger salamanders. According to the brochure, we also ask, "Can this really be in a mall?"[19]

Within minutes, we can "trek the high Sierras," "explore the harsh [Mojave] desert," "stroll along the Pacific shore," and "venture into Yosemite Valley." In each ecosystem, we see examples of the fauna displayed in dioramas that evoke the sublimity of nature. Bobcats, roadrunners, seals, salamanders, and snakes inhabit this small zoo, offering a vision of wild nature tamed—or at least confined. "Your five-region tour is complete," the brochure concludes. "You've covered almost a half million square miles of California wilderness and hardly broken a sweat." Still, after all that exertion, we might be hungry, and luckily there's the Wilderness Grill, where we can eat "under a canopy of redwoods as the sound of crickets and the smell of hickory tease your senses." We can even order s'mores for that authentic campfire experience.[20]

Last but not least, we'll need a souvenir of our sojourn in the wilderness of the mall. And so the gift shop, Naturally Untamed, has just the thing: books, CDs and videos; plastic and plush animals; jewelry, gifts and "an exclusive line of outdoor clothing." We can also visit an official California Welcome Center, in case we want to see some of the state that's not enclosed in the mall.

Such nature "experiences" now provide us with what Umberto Eco calls "adventures in hyperreality." This nature is a real version of our imaginative fictions. It's relatively easy, of course, for environmentalists and other nature lovers to decry these fake flora, but if we go to nature for scenery and psychological relief, and we can get those effects in the mall, who cares? People don't generally criticize landscape painters for their fakery and fabrications. And landscape art is generally thought to be a measure of people's love of nature. So what's different about the nature of the mall, except that it's in a mall and not a museum? If fake nature makes us feel as good as real nature, why not celebrate that fact? The scenery may be fake, but the pleasure can be real.

At the mall, nature, both real and fake, is under control, the garden in the machine. "At its core," Michael Sorkin says, "the greenhouse—or Disneyland—offers a view of alien nature, edited, a better version, a kind of sublime. Indeed, the abiding theme of every park is nature's transformation from civilization's antithesis to its playground." Like the greenhouse or the conservatory, it's a place where homo sapiens demonstrate their control of other species.[21]

Nature as Souvenir

Not every mall has NatureMaker trees or an American Wilderness Experience. But virtually every mall offers a nature experience of its own, because nature serves as a prominent symbol system in the shopping center. Malls cultivate natural images to sell us nature in the form of commodities, and to naturalize shopping and commercial culture. A fashion retailer tells us that its designs are "inspired by nature." Cosmetics counters help us to achieve "the natural look." One new Colorado mall, FlatIron Crossing, promotes itself as "the natural place to shop."

In some malls, nature is for sale at specialty stores like Naturally Untamed, Animal Lover, the Zoo Store, Forever Green, Natural Wonders, and Rhythm of the Earth. Nature stores fit a particular ecological niche in the mall environment. They tend to thrive in markets densely populated by middle- to upper-middle-class families who value education for their kids. Nature stores aren't usually destination stores; they're impulse gift stores, so they thrive in proximity to toy stores or life-style stores like Banana Republic, the Gap, or Williams-Sonoma.[22]

In a brilliant essay titled "Looking for Nature at the Mall," Jennifer Price explores the nature of these nature stores. She notes that such stores promote their wares as a direct connection to nature, but, in fact, they market "the meanings we've invested in nature." At such stores, we can buy rocks, wildflower seeds, and replicas of animals (typically the wilder forms of fish and fowl and reptiles and mammals). They also sell maps, star charts, and books that explain the wonders of nature. We can buy microscopes and telescopes and other implements for scoping nature. We can buy books about science and nature, CDs of the surf

Producing Consumption

and the wind, and posters of the sublime wilderness. And inside these stores, the sounds of nature are often used as mood music for merchandising.[23]

With our purchases in these stores, we buy into middle-class conceptions of nature. We invest in nature as wilderness, as unspoiled, exotic, remote, and romantic. It's also usually peaceful; among the plush animals in the mall's nature store, there's not much Darwinian "nature red in tooth and claw." It's not so much the state of nature as a state of mind that appeals to busy Americans. According to Price, we buy into nature as "an exterior world that fosters an interior world of feelings and emotions." We put our money on conceptions of nature as counterpoint, as "a palliative for urbanism, anonymity, commercialism, white-collar work, artifice, alienation, and the power of technology." Nature stores are in the business of stress relief for the middle class; they market antimodern medicines to help us cope with the symptoms of modernity. As Price suggests, "Developers install nature like a sign to middle-class shoppers, saying this place is a real place, and it's for you." Consuming conceptions of nature that are opposed to a consumption society, we become "anticonsumer consumers." We invest in nature as we invest in stock—for peace of mind. And so we get "a mall version of a Thoreauvian encounter."[24]

In some stores, we buy into a conception of nature naturally disappearing, so our connection with nature is a kind of salvage project. The Endangered Species Store, for example, highlights the fragility of nature but implies that a souvenir purchase is the best we can do to preserve it. The store capitalizes on our genuine affection for nature, selling gorgeous t-shirts bearing the logo "Extinction is Forever." Jon Goss contends that such t-shirts perfectly deconstruct "the nature-commodity aesthetic: buy one before it goes out of style." At the Endangered Species Store, we can acknowledge our awareness of the loss of biodiversity by engaging in our own buy-o-diversity.[25]

Nature as Elsewhere

Many Americans hope to experience the real wilderness, and fortunately, there are stores in the mall for that too. In *The Dream Society*, Rolf Jensen suggests that "nature is part of the adventure market. Nature has moved from being merely a source of food and raw materials in the late twentieth century, toward becoming—

in the affluent countries—a source of stories." One of the stories we like to tell is "my adventures in nature." "Whether it's to unwind after a frantic workweek or to find some solace in Mother Nature," *American Demographics* reports, "the outdoors is becoming increasingly appealing to every demographic." So while outfitters sell us tents and sleeping bags and freeze-dried foods, they also sell us stories in which we are the primary protagonists.[26]

Outfitters such as Eddie Bauer, REI, and Galyan's equip us for ventures into nature—outside the mall. As retail consultant Martin Pegler says in a book called *Lifestyle Shopping*, "Communing with nature also calls for special clothes. Companies like Eddie Bauer and The North Face cater to the nature-loving lifestyle with clothes, accessories, and even home furnishings to complete a domestic environment in keeping with that lifestyle." Converting the outdoor life into a consumption experience, they try to convince us that we can't really go hiking or camping without the proper, specialized (and expensive) "gear." Often we also wear these clothes and accessories at home, at school, or in the neighborhood to show that, even though we're currently here, we would prefer to be there. "I may be an accountant," we say sartorially to people around us, "but at heart I'm really a mountain man."[27]

Outfitters provide gear, but they also gear our minds for the experience of nature. If we can get back to nature, we think, we can get back to our roots—to a genuine place, authentic life, our inner self. Outfitters also influence which nature we see fit to experience. The outfitters, for example, fit us for hiking and back-packing in the western wilderness, the open spaces supposedly untouched by human hands. They sell us a specialized West, the recreational West—not the West where many westerners really live. Going to Boulder, for example, wouldn't be the same as trekking through boulders. Even the wildness is commodified—modified by being offered for sale.

Much of the marketing of nature by the outfitters of the mall invites us to get "back to nature," which suggests that we're not in nature here and now. But we *are* nature, and we are *in* nature now, so a conception of nature that obscures this fact also obscures important natural (and cultural) relationships. Historian William Cronon criticizes the American obsession with wilderness, especially when it leads us to think that our affection for wild nature absolves us from responsibility for the rest of it. Cronon suggests that we are stewards of nature, both wild and domesticated, and invites us to think of nature—all of it—as home. "If wildness can stop being (just) out there and start being (also) in here, if it can start being as humane as it is natural," he states, "then perhaps we can get on with the unending task of struggling to live rightly in the world—not just in the garden, not just in the wilderness, but in the home that encompasses them both."[28]

In malls, the success of the nature stores and outfitters is measured not by ecological literacy, or living lightly, or even landscape appreciation. When *Shopping Centers Today* reports on the performance of a store like Natural Wonders, the performance is measured by the same criterion as all the other stores—in sales per square foot: "Natural Wonders performed very well last year and its stores remain strong, running up sales of $400 per square foot in the average 2,400-square-foot store." The nature of the mall depends entirely on the nature of business.[29]

Nature as Product

"Can we find nature at the mall?" asks Jennifer Price. "It would be impossible not to. Nature provides the raw materials the mall is made from." As Price perceptively points out, all of the products of the mall are manufactured from the manufactures of nature. So every time we buy something at the mall, even if it doesn't have a nature logo, we're buying nature transformed and transported for our benefit.[30]

Indeed, even the t-shirt we buy at the Endangered Species store has a story that's more complex than we usually imagine. In *Stuff: The Secret Lives of Everyday Things*, John Ryan and Alan Durning trace the steps involved in making a generic cotton-polyester t-shirt. Producing polyester involves oil exploration, drilling, piping, refining, and transportation to make a petrochemical fiber. The process causes air pollution: one-fourth the polyester's weight in nitrogen and sulfur oxides, hydrocarbons, particulates, and carbon monoxide, and ten times the polyester's weight in carbon dioxide, which causes global warming. The cotton is also complicated. Cotton seed is dipped in a fungicide and planted in a Mississippi field sprayed with aldicarb, one of the most toxic chemicals applied in the United States. Then, as the seeds germinate, the ground is sprayed with a soil sterilant to kill everything that might compete with cotton, including earthworms. This in turn affects the absorptive quality of the soil, which in turn requires irrigation. As the cotton grows, it's sprayed four or five more times with organophosphates, which can damage the central nervous system of human beings. And just before harvesting, the crop is sprayed with paraquat (a defoliant). Then a single human being driving a diesel-powered cotton stripper made in the United States from parts produced in twenty countries picks the cotton. The cotton goes to be ginned, but the chemicals stay in the soil or wash off into lakes or streams.[31]

In a North Carolina textile mill, the fibers are carded and spun into yarn. Another textile mill weaves the fabric then washes, bleaches, and dyes it to specifications, finishing it with industrial chemicals like chlorine, chromium, and formaldehyde. Some of the dyes, which are toxic substances, run off into the wastewater. In Honduras, women cut and sew the t-shirt, mount it on cardboard made from Georgia pinewood pulp, wrap it in a polyethylene bag made in Mexico, and stack it in a corrugated box from Maine. The box goes by freighter to Baltimore, by train to San Francisco, and by truck to Seattle. It shows up in the local shopping center, where this story, its environmental history, is largely ignored.[32]

Each of the products at the mall has a similar story, a narrative of nature becoming culture, and (often) of nature being degraded in the process. These stories are an integral part of the story of consumer culture, and an important chapter in the story of our own lives. But in general, these are stories we don't know and don't tell. Indeed, we usually think less about the meaning of these stories than about the meanings added to the shirt by advertising.

Nature as Season

In 1952, announcing the plans for Southdale, the world's first fully enclosed shopping center, department store magnate Donald Dayton said "we plan to make our own weather at Southdale. Every day will be fair and mild." At the center's opening in 1956, architect Victor Gruen said that "it can be one hundred degrees above or twenty degrees below zero—things which I understand happen in Minnesota. But here flowers will grow, birds will sing, and it's going to be spring." Since 1956, enclosed malls have given us a perpetual spring, excising the heat of summer, the color and the sere beauty of fall, and the chill of winter.[33]

As this suggests, malls have an interesting relationship to the seasons of nature. The Western tradition overflows with celebrations of seasonal change. But in contemporary American culture, the change of season seems to be determined almost as much by the cant of retail marketing as by the cant of the sun. There are spring and summer fashions and fall and winter collections. The retail seasons may suggest that we're still attuned to the solar seasons. But often, in fact, we're not preparing for different *weather*. Indeed, since many of us commute from an attached garage to a parking garage, we don't really need as many different clothes as the changing seasons once required. Instead, as table 3 suggests, we're often preparing for a different *whether*: whether or not we get approval from our families, friends, and colleagues for being up-to-date, "in season."

In an article ironically titled "The Changing Nature of Retail Seasons," researchers for the International Council of Shopping Centers suggest how retail seasons interact with the natural seasons. Their analysis of Commerce Department statistics reveals that four basic retail seasons parallel the natural seasons: Easter (spring), Memorial Day (summer), back-to-school (fall), and Christmas (winter). These four seasons are used as cultural cues to tell us that it's time to shop. In *Visual Merchandising and Display*, Martin Pegler suggests that in a window display, "a few actual plants can also add a particular color or seasonal note." The seasonal note in such displays says basically, "It's time to buy the items we're featuring now." So these plants are not just a mark of solar seasons, but a mark of commercial seasons.[34]

The four seasons of the retail year make us into seasoned shoppers as these cultural seasons continue to supplant those of nature. But ICSC researchers also found that with the notable exception of Christmas, retail sales are smoothing out. The seasons are getting longer, so that there's almost a single shopping season from the first of January to the end of December. Increasingly, we seem to believe that shopping is perfectly seasonable any time of the year.[35]

Nature as System

One nature that we usually don't see in the mall is nature as system. Inside, we're comforted by constant temperatures and by the recurring seasons of the fashion year. Sometimes, though, we forget that shopping centers have natural connections beyond the ones they want us to see. Enclosed malls, for example, like

Table 3

Monthly Mall Sales and Promotions, by Event

	Sales	Promotions	Events
January	Christmas clearance, inventory sale white sales, foundations, lingerie	Bridal showings, resort and cruises, Valentine's Day preparation	Football bowl games, Martin Luther King Day, Super Bowl, Chinese New Year (sometimes in February)
February	Winter clearance, President's Day, housewares, spring pre-season	Valentine's Day, spring fashions/colors	Groundhog Day, Valentine's Day, Bachelor's Day, Mardi Gras, Black History Month
March	Pre-Easter spring and Easter sales, seasonal accessories	Summer bridal, home and garden, spring housecleaning	St. Patrick's Day, NCAA Final Four, Academy Awards
April	After Easter sales, sleepwear and lingerie	Easter summerwear, early swimwear	April Fool's Day, income tax deadline, Easter
May	Baby week, home furnishings, spring apparel clearance, barbecue supplies, Memorial Day	Mother's Day, bridal, summer sportswear, luggage, vacation accessories, outdoor living, graduation	Cinco de Mayo, Mother's Day, Kentucky Derby, Memorial Day
June	Home furnishings, bedding, furniture	Graduation, Father's Day, Flag Day menswear, camping, outdoor summer activewear	Father's Day,

July	July Fourth, summer clearance, white sales		Independence Day, Bastille Day
August	Summer clearance 2, furniture and bedding, fur sales	Back-to-school clothes, school supplies, career fashions	
September	Labor Day	Fall fashions, sporting and hunting, new coats, outerwear, Christmas decorations	Labor Day
October	Columbus Day, anniversary sales, Halloween	Christmas gifts, (especially personalized),gifts layaway plans, furs	Columbus Day, World Series, Octoberfest, Halloween
November	Veterans Day, pre-Christmas, Thanksgiving, fur sales	Election themes, Santa arrives, Toyland opens, Thanksgiving, Christmas decorations, gifts	Election Day, Veterans Day, Sadie Hawkins Day, Thanksgiving
December	Holiday sales, Christmas clearance, New Year's sales	Christmas gifts, Christmas-themed fashions, New Year's party clothing and supplies	St. Nicholas Day, Christmas, New Year's Eve

Sources: Data from Pegler, *Visual Merchandising and Display,* 164–65; Mills and Paul, *Applied Visual Merchandising,* 136; Lusch, Dunne, and Gebhardt, *Retail Marketing,* 493.

to promote their "climate control," and air conditioning is, in fact, one of the essential elements of enclosed shopping centers. Inventor Willis Carrier called it "man-made air" or "manufactured weather," and claimed that it would increase the productivity of manufacturing workers. But it also increased the productivity of consumption, because air conditioning allowed larger floor spaces without the distractions of weather or windows. Until the advent of air conditioning, people stayed home in sizzling hot weather. But early air conditioning proved an attraction, as people came in for the cold. As Victor Gruen said of his enclosed mall designs, "the shopping center consciously pampers the shopper, who reacts gratefully by arriving from longer distances, visiting the center more frequently, staying longer, and in consequence contributing to higher sales figures."[36]

Despite the commercial advantages of conditioned air, malls don't really have climate control. What they have is heating and cooling systems, precisely because the climate *can't* be controlled. In the mall, climate is mostly metaphorical, although malls contribute, in a perverse way, to climate control. Like all enterprises that depend on the burning of fossil fuels, shopping centers stoke the fires of global warming. Keeping customers warm in the winter and cool in the summer has the unintended effect of making all of us warmer in the long run.

In the same way, too, while the products sold in nature stores may restore *us*, and make us feel good about our relationship to nature, they don't generally restore nature. Most nature stores tell us that "no habitats were damaged by harvesting in any way," but for most of our purchases as Americans, habitat *is* affected, and we don't much think about it. We forget that *every* store is a nature store, since they're all full of nature converted to commodities to be converted to cash. In this culture, though, such a process is "only natural."

Shopping centers also have proximate environmental impacts. The mall, for example, occupies a particular landscape, which has often been scraped clean of its indigenous vegetation. Where fields were once covered with a tallgrass prairie or planted with wheat and corn, they're now supplanted by a crop of money-producing retail hybrids. Topsoil builds about an inch every five hundred years, but not on the site of a mall. The mall is a place, therefore, where we're literally out of place—at least organically.

As these examples suggest, the shopping center can be seen as the center of a larger ecological web. In ecology, an ecotone is a place where two living biomes come together, a convergence characterized by a rich variety of vegetation and animal life. Malls are a commercial ecotone, a place where products composed of different ecosystems meet and mingle. In the malls of my area, Minnesota, the native ecological communities come in contact with commodities and communities from around the world. And like a natural ecotone, the commercial ecotone is unusually rich, with more cross-fertilization and variety than less diverse spaces. Imagine the mall as a system of flows: people in, people out; commodities in, purchases out; food in, sewage out; money in, and global flows of money out. The mall is a modern version of what Richard White calls "an organic machine," feeding on nature, ingesting materials and expelling wastes. At the mall, we too, are implicated in these flows, as human energy derived from the plant and animal calories in our food is expended working, walking, and trying on clothes and identities.[37]

The mall is also an essential part of its ecosystem, participating in all the essential cycles of nature. Malls and parking lots absorb and reflect solar radiation. They absorb and channel water, affecting soil conditions, water runoff, and water quality. Malls breathe in and out, affecting air quality and atmospheric conditions. Ventilation and air-conditioning systems act as the lungs of this bionic machine, conditioning fresh air and controlling the indoor climate to suit homo sapiens, the most powerful inhabitant of the range. By covering acres of ground, they affect the character of biotic activity, creating spaces with little species diversity and few organic interactions. Although malls are cultural constructions, they have substantial environmental impacts.

Some malls show some understanding of their connection to natural cycles. They highlight their recycling programs, which implicitly acknowledge our need to be resourceful about our use of resources. But shopping center publicity seldom talks about pre-cycling—the design of products that don't need to be recycled. And they don't talk much about repair or re-use. In the kingdom of novelty, you can't show secondhand goods. And you can't remind people that, ultimately, most of our goods are destined for the dumpster. The mall emphasizes affluence, not effluents.

The nature of the mall serves several different purposes. It's an attractive ornamentation, in landscaping both indoors and outdoors. It's an attraction, especially in the nature stores and the simulations. It's a marketing motif used throughout the mall. It's a resource, modified to make the commodities we buy. It's a force to be controlled, in climate control and in the control of natural resources. And it's an environment in which all of this activity occurs.

Each nature of the mall has its cultural consequences and its environmental impacts, but all together, too, the nature of the mall performs cultural work. It naturalizes the commercial environment and motivates people to purchase the products of the mall. Aestheticizing nature, it reinforces our disposition to think about nature more romantically than realistically. It undercuts genuine ecological thinking and keeps us thinking more about the meanings of nature than about nature itself. Looking at the images of nature in the Endangered Species Store, for example, we sometimes forget about all the species (including homo sapiens) actually endangered by American shopping. Malls, and the patterns of shopping they support, are unsustainable, but the nature of the mall doesn't remind us of that fact.

In a culture that systematically strips nature for its own benefit, the nature of the mall is a form of "imperialist nostalgia." It reminds us of what we destroy but maintains our innocence. In a world where culture often degrades nature, the culture of the mall "re-*stores* nature, and enacts its reconciliation with culture under the sign of the commodity." Confronted with a constant, but questionable, contrast between nature and culture, we symbolically take sides with nature by buying a cultural construction of it.[38]

As a result, the nature we learn most about in the mall is human nature.

FOUR

Retail Designs

Mall design gets people into the shopping center and into a shopping frame of mind, and retail design gets people into the stores and into serious shopping. Retail anthropologist Paco Underhill contends that "if we went into stores only when we needed to buy something, and if once there we bought only what we needed, the economy would collapse, boom." So retail design is designed to get us to spend time and money in the store, because in the retail trade, as in life, time is money. The goal of retail design is to increase the "conversion rate," the percentage of people who enter the store and buy something, and the "turnover rate," the number of times a merchant can sell (or "turn") the stock in a year. In their book *Designing to Sell*, designers Vilma Barr and Charles Broudy state that retail design is the art and science of creating spaces that move merchandise. "Store designers," they say, "are in the business of seduction as well as design." This chapter examines that seduction.[1]

Retail design wasn't particularly important when shopping involved telling a clerk what you wanted and then waiting while the salesperson got the goods for you. But when retailers shifted to a self-service system, the shopping interaction also shifted. Previously, the interaction was largely between two persons, as a salesperson "sold" the customer on the commodity. But increasingly the primary relationship is between the consumer and the product. When the salesperson no longer sells the product, the store and product packaging have to become silent salespersons. When roughly two-thirds of purchase decisions take place in the store, store design is no casual matter.[2]

Retail design tries to convert market research into market share, maintaining "image continuity" among advertising, marketing, and merchandising. It's an essential element of "integrated marketing," presenting a consistent image from web site to sales floor, from entrance to dressing room, from mannequins to sales staff. At stores that emphasize integrated marketing, like the Gap, every retail detail contributes to a consistent style and life-style message. Barr and Broudy assert that "the benchmark of success in store design is how effectively the environment and the merchandise are integrated. The measurement of such success starts at the front door and ends at the bottom line." As this suggests, the purpose is profits. "It is not sufficient to just please the observer," affirms one text in visual merchandising; "the objective is to sell the merchandise. Therefore, an impulsive desire for the merchandise must be aroused." So a good designer uses the elements of design to tell stories with stores. As Dik Glass, vice president of store planning and construction for FAO Schwarz, says, "Design will always be the genius required to tell the product's story."[3]

The goal is, in part, theatrical. As Barr and Broudy suggest, "Designing a retail store is like creating a stage set. Shopping is an experience in which people act out their innermost hopes, dreams, aspirations, and desires. A shopping excursion can be a personal minidrama for customers; their imaginations are going full tilt while they are in the store, visualizing how attractive they will be in a new skirt, how a new chair will look in the living room, or how much a gift will be appreciated." Life-style retailers especially—stores such as Pottery Barn, Orvis, Cybersmith, Bath and Bodyworks—make connections between their goods and their consumers' interests and avocations. Good store design creates an imaginative space for the daily dramas of our lives, the soap operas that occur on our side of the television screen. When we walk into a store, we're looking for a setting that helps us to act the part we're scripting for ourselves. And we're looking for the store(y) with a happy ending.[4]

Retail design influences both the retailer's "market position image," which attracts people to the store, and "sales productivity," what they spend in the store. Retail design "gives the store its visual personality," a personality that either invites customers or puts them off. A designer can create a store that says "Stay out unless you've got lots of money to spend" or a store that says "Come on in— we're just folks here." It's a challenging job, because each retail design in a shopping center is in competition with every other design—and with every other use of a customer's time. So retail design can be an important "strategic differentiation element" in a coordinated identity program. Even when a store carries essentially the same merchandise as a competitor, it can be designed to feel substantially different to a shopper. The average customer stops in two or three stores on each mall visit, and retail planners hope that it's entirely by design.[5]

Retail design and visual merchandising are forms of commercial art. Commercial art isn't art for art's sake (a curious idea in itself), but it *is* art; all of the aesthetic conventions apply. It's meant to be appreciated, and there's no reason to ignore the genuine aesthetic pleasures in malls. At its best, commercial art is both beautiful and profitable. Still, the commercial character of commercial art shouldn't affect its artistic evaluation. It's not bad art because it makes money; it's bad art if it's bad art. We don't think that Rembrandt's paintings are aesthetically compromised because collectors pay for them, so it makes sense for us to learn how to appreciate both the commercial and the artistic elements of commercial art.[6]

Often retail design takes its cues from the color, graphics, and arrangements of catalogues and TV ads, so that the store is the three-dimensional version of the advertisement. In such instances, a customer needs to know certain texts to fully understand the store "text" in front of them. Such "intertextuality" can be quite pleasurable, because things fall into place in a patterned way that excites us. At Victoria's Secret, for example, retail designers can label their slinky fashions as "hot off the runway" because they assume that customers will know about the Victoria's Secret fashion show and the supermodels on the posters in the store. Stores often reinforce their media advertising through the medium of retail design.[7]

Elements of Retail Design

Retail design is a complex art because it encompasses many different elements. Display windows, storefronts, and entrances begin the seduction. Mirrors and mannequins and props offer reflections of American culture, especially material culture. Layout, flooring, fixturing, and architectural details also establish a mood for our relationship with the goods. Sightlines and traffic patterns establish how we'll encounter the merchandise. Fixtures (including display cases, platforms, shadowboxes, ledges, islands, or environmental settings) reinforce the character of the place and create spaces to dramatize the merchandise. We notice, consciously or unconsciously, the finishes and materials used in the store and react accordingly. Light and color and music and aroma also seduce our senses. Even signs send different messages. All of these elements combine to affect our perception of the merchandise and our affection for a purchase. As the authors of *Applied Visual Merchandising* note, "Visual merchandising means glamorizing the everyday."[8]

Retail design begins even before the customer enters the retail establishment. The store itself is a part of a retailer's "image engineering." If it looks like a palace, it suggests one thing; if it looks like a warehouse, it suggests another. Stores are often themed to fit their target market, attracting either men or women or both, inviting upscale shoppers but excluding the riffraff, or vice versa. Certain themes and decorations can make a space literally into a "no-man's land," as Victoria's Secret does with its aggressively pink boudoir theme. Other items, like canoe paddles and fishnet or bicycles, can give a store the L. L. Bean feel. Radio Shack attracts men by featuring computers and components, and women by focusing displays on telephones and toys. NikeTown's "old gym" theme invited both men and women with a reworking of cinematic scenes that were at one time mostly masculine.

Even before we enter the store, display windows, signage, and entrances all express the image of the store and begin to get a person thinking like a consumer. In *Windows: The Art of Retail Display*, Mary Portas suggests that "if eyes are the window to the soul, so shop windows reveal the soul of the store." In trying to "turn a pedestrian into a customer," the windows make a visual statement about the store and the character of its customers. The windows are a preview of the attractions inside, so they're designed to catch the eye and, eventually, the rest of the customer. They capitalize on what's current and trendy in American culture, and they appeal to our desires, both deep and shallow.[9]

Windows often operate on what retailers call the "price-point-to-aperture-ratio": the pricier the item, the smaller the window. Big windows and big displays suggest lower prices. That's why "high-priced jewelry is particularly effective shown in small cube windows, precisely illuminated and artfully arranged." Designers agree that window displays should be changed frequently so the average customer sees a new set of merchandise every time he or she enters.[10]

Even the props make a difference in window dressing. Mary Portas suggests that "props are the key players in the window because you can use them to create a language, a drama, that is unique to your business. Think of your props as the product's DNA—they fashion its character and identity, and render it unique." She also contends that good props can speak as seductively as the stuff that's for sale, propping up the message about the merchandise: "Props can be used to attach specific values to the product to underpin the brand message and speak to the consumer. Look at what polo boots did for Ralph Lauren; remember how Levi's latched onto a great old mahogany rocking chair to make their point that some things improve with age."[11]

In many cases, brand names also appear in the window, because stores are branded by their brands. "Brands are what give you credibility," says retail consultant Robert Gibbs. If you carry designer brands, you carry all the clout that comes with them. Brands assist customers with life-styling, helping people to identify with the symbolic functions of the merchandise. Brands also help create "life-style stores," stores that are identified by the nationally advertised brands that imply certain life-styles and aspirations. Inside the store, too, designers often feature brand names and logos as an organizing principle of store design.[12]

The storefront—the structure that surrounds and supports the windows—also affects a consumer's perception of the store. Barr and Broudy argue that "the storefront can be considered a sales stimulating, long-lived advertisement, like a lively architectural billboard." Storefronts range from classical architecture to metallic techno, and their common message is great expectations. But each storefront also speaks to a specific market niche, inviting particular people to enter as

The elements of retail design (Courtesy of Vilma Barr, *Designing to Sell* © 1990 by McGraw-Hill, Inc.; reprinted by permission)

special customers. A good storefront helps a retailer "achieve a critical edge over competition by pre-selling customers before they walk in."[13]

Attracted by the storefront or the window displays, customers turn to the entrance, which also tells a story about who's welcome inside. To some extent, the bigger the entrance, the lower the prices: exclusive stores often use smaller entrances to discourage unqualified customers. In either case, from a retail designer's perspective, the entry is an "attitudinal adjustment space" intended to help the customer get comfortable in the store before having to make a buying decision. Paco Underhill calls this space "the transition zone." Some stores now employ greeters in the transition zone, both because a greeter allows the store to "start the seduction" and because "security experts say that the easiest way to discourage shoplifting is to make sure staffers acknowledge the presence of every shopper with a simple hello."[14]

As customers enter the store, designers direct their eyes in a flow from "the

The Elements of a Store Interior

1 Non-skid carpet treads recessed in wood

2 Stairway with landings to permit easy access to lower levels

3 Open vista encourages shoppers to use stairway to lower level

4 Natural wood floor adds warmth to the color and materials scheme, a counterpoint to white fixtures and trim

5 See-through glass railing provides unobstructed view between levels

6 Two- and three-way movable merchandise display fixtures

7 Merchandise display table

8 Wall lighting to supplement accent lighting and ambient lighting

9 Slatwall for display flexibility

10 Directional accent lighting

11 Low brightness fluorescent lighting lens for ambient lighting

12 Drywall dropped lighting trough and beam highlights ceiling

13 Lights, sprinklers, and grilles are integrated into the ceiling layout

14 The armoire is a multi-purpose cabinet for merchandise presentation: hanging, shelving, face-outs, and display

Design:
Charles E. Broudy
& Associates

front line" to "the departmental center" to "the Wall," three zones with different, but complementary, purposes. The front line usually includes feature presentations based on seasonal, monthly or promotional themes or new selections. Sometimes this means a "power display" right at the entrance; such a display works as a kind of speed bump to slow the transition, and it often suggests some new, fashionable things to buy. Another strategy is to put basics in the front of the store so people know they can come back to them.[15]

The departmental center is the meat of the marketing, and it can be designed to feel like a single department or a collection of boutiques. Subtle changes in layout, lighting, flooring, and fixturing can signal the boundaries between one area and another. Designers will plan primary and secondary focal points, and primary and secondary routes to guide people to the merchandise. Even a change in ceiling height, which would normally just go over our head, can make us feel differently about the spaces of the store.[16]

Within a store, merchandise is often segregated by brands, and, therefore, brand names and designer logos often appear on valances over shelves or on the wall behind a life-style group of mannequins. When Ralph Lauren sells his merchandise in department stores and specialty retailers, he adjusts the image of that section of the store to fit with the identity of the Lauren and Polo names.[17]

"The wall" marks the back of the store, but not the end of the marketing. Merchandisers often use the back wall as a magnet, because it means that people have to walk through the whole store. Getting a customer to walk the perimeter is a good thing because "distance traveled relates more directly to sales per entering customer than any other measurable consumer variable." Sometimes, the wall's attraction is simply sensual, a wall hanging or a graphic that catches the eye or a sound that catches the ear. Sometimes the lure is specific merchandise. In supermarkets, the dairy is often at the back, because people frequently come just for milk. In drugstores, it's usually the pharmacy. At Blockbuster Video, it's the new releases (with impulse items, and high-margin items, in the center aisle).[18]

Sometimes the wall can be a media wall with a bank of television screens to attract attention. In American culture, we're trained to watch TV, to look at moving images. A media wall capitalizes on that training. At the very least, it says that the store is dynamic and contemporary. In many cases, as when a store is designed for the youth market, MTV images can be used to complete the cross-marketing that begins on cable TV. Studies show that video walls in retail stores can increase traffic by up to sixty percent. In any case, retail designers often use the wall to give customers a focal point that arouses interest and attracts traffic.[19]

Retail design works best when it's invisible to consumers, when it guides us to merchandise without our knowing we're being assisted. For that reason, sight lines are crucial; it's important to focus shoppers' eyes on the merchandise as much as possible. Designers try to help us see merchandise from afar and then appreciate it more as we approach. "If you don't see a display from a distance—say, ten or twenty feet—then you won't approach it except by accident," says Paco Underhill. "That's why architects have to design stores with sight lines in mind." According to Underhill, the goal is to achieve a "pinball effect" where "the felicitous dispersal of merchandise bounces shoppers through the entire store."[20]

Retail designers also have to consider how customers move through the stores, designing traffic patterns that maximize the amount of merchandise seen, and minimize the difficulty of establishing a relationship with the merchandise. They utilize consumer psychology and behavior in their designs. They know that time-deprived shoppers appreciate a clear visual order in the store, whereas teenagers might prefer the stimulation of a denser design. They know, for example, that customers, women especially, don't like to be touched from behind. Paco Underhill calls this "the butt-brush factor." If the aisles aren't wide enough to allow people to look at stuff without being "butted," they won't stay in the store.[21]

Designers also understand the "rightness" of retail design. They know, for example, that they can capitalize on the fact that most Americans move through stores counterclockwise. "Because American shoppers automatically move to the right, the front right of any store is its prime real estate," explains Underhill. "That's where the most important goods should go, the make or break merchandise that needs 100 percent shopper exposure." For the same reason, because most people are right-handed, merchants stock store shelves with the most popular brand straight ahead, and the brand a retailer's trying to "build" just to the right.[22]

A store's interior architecture and fixtures can also send marketing messages. A retail designer decides whether a store will be classic or modern, muted or colorful, traditional or rebellious. Even structural supports can be utilized in telling stories. Upscale shops, for example, sometimes use classical columns to emphasize classic merchandise and underscore the sense of aesthetic exclusivity. The same intentionality carries over to the sales floor. In apparel stores, roughly 85 percent of the floor space is devoted to racks and shelves that display the merchandise. So designers must choose well. As Barr and Broudy say, "A display does its job when it draws customers to the merchandise and then invites product investigation." Front-facing merchandise attracts more involvement than side views; handbags on pedestals and platforms draw more response than bunches of bags hung on hooks. The racks are not just to hold the merchandise; they're to hold the customer.[23]

Both inside and outside the stores, materials are a material witness to the quality of the merchandise and the quality of the shopping experience. Woods give a warm, natural look. "Light woods have a casual feel and indicate affordable, good quality," says one expert. "Dark woods project higher cost and quality." Pine suggests an outdoor, camp theme, and cherry and mahogany convey a message of class. Bronze and brass are expensive, and they need polish to maintain their luster, so they're "appropriate for jewelry or fine apparel stores that require a quality appearance." Aluminum gives a contemporary look, appealing to cutting-edge consumers. Brick and stone facades convey solidity and timelessness, and stone, especially limestone, imparts the feel of the great outdoors. Even glass, which is transparent, can convey messages, as etched glass lends a subtle and elegant look to upscale stores.[24]

Fixtures—the shelves and racks that display merchandise—also help with merchandising. One designer likes fixtures at a forty-five-degree angle near the front of the store because this "induces penetration," leading customers in a more indirect path through more of the store than a straight front-to-back arrangement does. Other designers advise fixtures that get as much merchandise as possible in "the zone," the area between a customer's eyes and knees, because stuff above and below isn't seen as much. Virtually all retail designers like fixtures flexible, so that they can be changed by the time of the average customer's next visit.[25]

Individual displays are also designed to transform shoppers into stoppers— people who will pause to look at a product, touch it, and consider how it might enhance their lives. Visual merchandisers combine mannequins and props, color and light, and a variety of visual techniques to make merchandise both attractive and seductive. In one case, the addition of a simple background and a floral arrangement behind a set of mannequins modeling dresses had a dramatic effect, increasing "lookers" by 60 percent and "stoppers" by 80 percent, even though 75 percent of the shoppers later revealed that they hadn't come to the store for dresses at all. If all goes well, "the display person is the creator of the final, all-important phase of advertising, the one who ultimately transforms the potential customer's semi-conscious interest into desire for possession, breaking down inhibiting barriers and directing the final steps toward the sales counter."[26]

One element of effective displays is a mannequin, a model American who models clothes for us. Visual merchandisers use the fashions and the mannequins

Producing Consumption

Model American (Image by Wernher Krutein)

to make life-style statements and show us "how looks are put together"—how different pieces of clothing can be artfully combined as an "outfit." They get us thinking about more than one purchase. Visual merchandiser Martin Pegler says that "if you are trying to sell a 'look' or an overall effect, then the mannequin with the proper physique . . . will do it faster and better than any other form of merchandise display."[27]

Although we usually think of mannequins as figures for the display of clothing, they are also figures for the display of figures. While fashions come and go, the *infrastructure* of fashion, the mannequin itself, stands firm. Its representation of the human body is re-presented with each new set of clothes. Mannequins work, Pegler says, because "the mannequin is the dream image of the young shopper who may have more chest than is in vogue or more hip than is hep. . . . In her mind's eye, she sees herself recreated in the mannequin's proportions. So what if she lumps and bumps where the form is lean and lithe—she 'knows' that's how she will look in that outfit." Mannequins combine the power of suggestion and the power of self-deception.[28]

In women's fashion, more clothes are designed for mannequins than for people. Most American mannequins are a very long-legged size eight. Although mannequins come in different sizes, the industry standard stands between five feet eight inches and six feet tall, with measurements approximately 34-24-34. The Census Bureau shows that 55 percent of American women over age fifteen wear a size fourteen or larger. So fashion lines designed specifically for "large" or "full-proportioned" women are designed, in fact, to fit the average woman. What is "normal" is not, unfortunately, the norm for American fashion.[29]

Mannequins could be designed to display a wide variety of human shapeliness: short *and* tall, slim *and* fat, full *and* flat, soft *and* muscular, rounded *and* angular. They could be a gallery of gracefulness, a testimonial to the varieties of beauty, but instead they offer a model of hard-bodied uniformity, a Barbie and Ken for adults.

Like Barbie, these dolls don't reflect the shapes of Americans; instead, ironically, the shape of mannequins often shapes us. Instead of manufacturing mannequins that look like us, we try to manufacture ourselves to look like them. Like Pinocchio in reverse, we want a magical transformation from the real to an ideal. From diets to liposuction, from exercise programs to plastic surgery, we sculpt our bodies to look like these sculptures. When we get in shape, this is often the shape we're aiming for. It makes you wonder who's the dummy now.

Mannequins make sense by themselves, but they make more sense within a whole set of cultural meanings that Joan Brumberg calls "the body project." Within that project, getting in shape can often mean getting in trouble. Young girls try to fit in by getting fit, or at least by getting skinny. Dying to be thin, thousands of girls succumb to anorexia and bulimia, eating disorders that come from a hunger for control, especially control of the body. Mannequin manufacturers and advertisers who cultivate the cult of thinness seem to assume that it's an individual's responsibility to resist social pressures and live a healthy life. They litter the social landscape with cultural messages about body image then disclaim their responsibility for the results.[30]

Without ever speaking, mannequins echo other messages of America's malls. Racially, they suggest the normative whiteness of the social world. Mannequins come in different colors, but their facial characteristics remain pretty much the same. What does it do to an African American woman to see Caucasian facial structure as the essence of beauty? What does it do to an Asian American boy to find that most of the models look like somebody else?

Mannequins model the wearing of clothes, but they implicitly model a number of other skills. These human forms teach us how to see and be seen. Like human models, they also teach us about attitude, the way we carry and display the body, the way we pose in the drama of everyday life. Mannequins are literally a form of posturing. We learn early in life to read body language, and retail designers use their knowledge of our knowledge to teach their mannequins how to tell stories that appeal to us. Mannequins don't just show us clothes; they show us how to wear clothes and how to be a part of the social scene.

Mannequin faces offer a look that is at once wooden and plastic and vacuous: they embody the kind of cool that is aloof, indifferent, and distant, the kind of designer detachment that's increasingly cool in contemporary American culture. They embody what Mark Crispin Miller calls "the hipness unto death." There's seldom any excitement, or enthusiasm, or wonder. The mannequins are too cool for the expression of any emotion except superiority.[31]

When store personnel are required to wear the retailer's wares, they serve as living mannequins who enliven the shopping experience of customers. "All our research shows this direct relationship," says Paco Underhill. "The more shopper-employee contacts that take place, the greater the average sale. Talking with an employee has a way of drawing a customer in closer." People like to shop where they feel wanted. They appreciate the recognition that good salespeople give them. Any human contact increases the likelihood of sales, and any suggestions from sales associates increase it even more. As we shall see, even the sales staff is designed to help make the sale.[32]

Retail designers also deal in atmospherics, the elements of design that give a store and its merchandise a certain cachet. Mary Portas contends that "the shopping environment is a tightly controlled arena which launches an assault, on a subconscious level, on the customer's senses—from choices of music and background noise levels, to merchandising to encourage touch, and even the use of aroma." Atmospheric elements contribute not only to the seduction of customers but also to the cash flow of a store.[33]

Retail designers use light to move people and merchandise. Light draws shoppers into the store, and "lighting can influence traffic flow to specific displays or to sections of the store, particularly to the back and perimeter walls." According to Barr and Broudy, a good lighting plan attracts shoppers, dramatizes space, flatters customers, and sells merchandise. Good retail designers tell stories about merchandise with light. Joseph Weishar, for example, notes that fluorescent lighting is perfectly functional, but "incandescent lighting says fashion and a certain exclusiveness." It's not enough to make the merchandise visible; retail designers use light to make it desirable. Designers have traditionally used light to highlight fabric quality and color. In a clothing store, for example, focal point and display lighting—with spotlights and other accents—help to draw shoppers to the newest and best merchandise, and to the dramatic displays that teach people how to mix and match coordinates. Spotlights also add a theatrical touch to a display, and focus our attention on the attributes of the merchandise that are most attractive. Spotlights can make an outfit dramatic or jewelry dazzling, adding value to the merchandise. Light tells us where to look and how to feel about looking. It creates a hierarchy of attention, directing the eyes to the most compelling displays and merchandise.[34]

Once we've chosen an outfit to try on, the light changes. In a well-designed store, the light in the dressing rooms is different from the light of the sales floor. The light that makes fabrics speak most eloquently, Portas notes, is "a very cool, high-colour-rendering light." But the light that enhances the look of people is like candlelight—a warm incandescent light. So retailers need to use one light with the merchandise and another one in the dressing rooms. "In retail," she says, "flattery will get you everywhere."[35]

Color also affects a customer's perception of a store and its stock. In *Design for Effective Selling Space*, Joseph Weishar contends that "by tapping into the mind of the customer through the eminently powerful tool of color, we can orchestrate much of their response." A simple change of background colors, for example, can move the customer from one part of the store to another. Color has both physiological and psychological effects. Our eyes react most quickly to bold reds and yellows and oranges, so these colors can be used to attract people to different displays and parts of the store. White, one the other hand, is a "clean" color and a good background for the color of clothes. Black radiates sophistication, but on the down side, it absorbs light. A good designer also considers the interaction of color and lighting. Weishar notes that fluorescent lights make colors blue-green, a color negatively associated with hospitals and institutions. Conversely, the lights used in dressing areas emphasize red, orange and yellow, thereby enhancing a white person's skin tones.[36]

Color also sets the stage in different departments. Weishar says that "people prefer the primary and secondary colors—deep shades of red, blue, yellow, green, orange, and violet. Intense color also goes with seasonal merchandise, or merchandise that is being featured." But if bright colors overpower the merchandise, muted colors are the solution. Barr and Broudy recommend neutral colors in fabric and women's apparel stores, where the designer wants the colors of the merchandise to be the focus of attention. They recommend conservative, cool colors—gray, blue-green, gray-violet—for home furnishing and men's wear. Pastels are a selling aid with lingerie, cosmetics, and jewelry—and near mirrors—because peach and mauve and lavender are flattering to white women's complexions. Bright colors work well with toys, children's wear, or housewares, conveying a lively, upbeat mood. Color colors our perception, and our reception of the retailer's storyline.[37]

Music also functions as part of retail architecture, as the history of Muzak suggests. It began in the early 1920s and earned its reputation as "elevator music" because it was used to calm people's nerves on elevators. In 1939, Muzak moved into the workplace, where it increased morale and productivity. Today, Muzak is ubiquitous. The company claims that its harmonic convergences are heard by 100 million people a day in at least 300,000 stores and restaurants. Its five hundred cassette programs and sixty satellite channels provide diverse sounds for a single purpose: to make spending more pleasurable. Muzak is often the price we pay for being in places that want us to pay their prices.[38]

Muzak and other music programs help define the ambience of the store. It's audio merchandising. Shoppers think of it as "incidental music," but it's seldom incidental. It's intensely intentional music, and it's intended to make us better consumers. "You can look away from many things in a store," says John Baugher of AEI Music, a music designer specializing in retail environments. "You can look away from video monitors and store signs. You may not notice the fixturing. But sound is always there." The essence of the mall's "muzak-ality" is not musicological, but psychological; not aesthetic, but commercial. It's the music that puts us in tune with American consumer culture, increasing our productivity as consumers by increasing our proclivity to purchase products.[39]

When it works well, music programming works with merchandising and retail design to create a distinctive brand image for a store. As AEI says on its web site, quoting the Grateful Dead's Jerry Garcia, "Magic is what we do. Music is how we do it." Classical music, for example, tells us that we're upscale and refined. String renditions of classic rock make an appeal to mature baby boomers, country music tells us that we're down-home and authentic, and avant-garde music confirms that we're cool. Retailers use each of these formats to set the tempo for our shopping.[40]

Muzak is the five-hundred-pound gorilla of programmed response music, but it's also the inspiration for other music formats. Muzak is basically "background music," but many stores now feature "foreground music"—music meant to be actively engaged. Foreground music associates the store with particular sounds and artists and succeeds even more than Muzak in creating a distinctive brand image for the store. Founded in 1971 by people who liked rock music more than elevator music, AEI Music Network occupies the foreground of "targeted music programming" with tunes in over sixty thousand stores, including the Gap, The Limited, Eddie Bauer, Abercrombie & Fitch, Banana Republic, Express, and Starbucks. In 1997, retailers paid sixty-five dollars a month per outlet for a four-hour custom mix that both establishes and standardizes the store's brand identity from coast to coast.[41]

Signs are another way of telling stories about a store. Although retail designers agree that "it's more effective to speak with merchandise than with signs," they also know that signs convey more than words can say. Without even reading a sign's message, customers can tell if they're in Wal-Mart or Saks Fifth Avenue. "Make sure the sign reflects the store," says retail designer Joseph Weishar. "Small signs—and small entrances—suggest exclusiveness; large signs—and large entrances—communicate the message of a price-conscious retailer that offers basic stock and nonexclusive fashions." Similarly, both the number and colors of signs carry messages of their own. Customers read lots of signs as an indication of self-service and an absence of signs as a mark of personal service. They read black-on-yellow (the easiest combination to read) or other garish colors as signs of discount stores and clearance racks, while they read understated signs as a mark of distinction. Standard typefaces are seen as a sign of standard service and selection, while elaborate scripts and calligraphy (even when mass-produced) serve as signs of a personal touch. At their best, signs act as a "silent salesperson" in the retail establishment.[42]

The placement of signs is almost important as the script, because if they're in the wrong place, people won't read the message. Signs ought to be within popular sightlines, and they need to fit people's movement: just a few words when people are moving into the store and more details at the point-of-purchase. Moving signs will slow moving customers: kinetic elements attract attention and interactive designs invite involvement. Both increase the chances that people will really look at a product. Once a person focuses on an item, point-of-purchase signs need to tell the whole story, unless there's a salesperson to serve as storyteller.[43]

Of course, retail design can only go so far. It can enhance the merchandise, but it can't transform it. You can't sell crap for long, even in mahogany boxes. In a retail store, the merchandise itself needs to tell a story of quality and value, style and sophistication. Empty shelves irritate customers, who expect to find their size in whatever style and color attracts their eye. Customers especially expect to find the basics in stock. The Gap, for example, would go broke if it didn't always have a full range of jeans and khakis and t-shirts. Full shelves inspire customers' confidence, which is why sales associates restock continually. Generally speaking, merchandise needs to be in reach so customers can touch the goods. As Paco Underhill says, "We buy things today more than ever based on trial and touch." Samples can also increase customers' involvement and their eventual purchases. That's why Bath and Bodyworks is so free with its lotions and potions. If we try it, we're more likely to buy it.[44]

Retail design can also help with the "add-ons" that sales associates promote with "suggestion selling." Sometimes called "cross-merchandising," such a strategy is designed to increase sales of so-called accessories. Belts should be located near the pants, hats and scarves near coats, purses and pocketbooks near the appropriate clothing, and so on. Mannequins and other displays should show the organic connections between these things: if things are presented together, it's possible the customer will buy the ensemble.[45]

Once we've shopped a store and chosen an item, we proceed to another essential element of good retail design—the checkout, called "the cash/wrap" in the trade. "In many ways," says Paco Underhill, "the cash/wrap area is the most important part of any store. If the transactions aren't crisp, if the organization isn't clear at a glance, shoppers get frustrated or turned off. Many times they won't even enter a store if the line to pay looks long or chaotic." At the cash/wrap, the clerk completes the sale and then places the item in a shopping bag that advertises the store's success to other mall customers.[46]

Finally, retail design promotes security—of both customers and the store. As designers lay out the store, they need to be mindful of maintaining the sightlines that allow surveillance. They need to make it difficult to slip small valuables into a purse or pants pocket, and they need to place the cash/wrap so that checkers can check out both the paying and unpaying customers as they leave. They need to integrate electronic devices to catch shoplifters as they pass through an electromagnetic field as part of electronic article surveillance (EAS). Part of retail design is making sure that merchandise stays in the store until it's sold. These design elements are usually invisible to shoppers but visible to professional thieves.

A good retail designer influences consumer behavior, but all of the seduction takes place in a context of other considerations as well. The design needs to work on the customer, but it also needs to work for the sales staff. They need to be able to see the entrances (which are also exits) and the different departments of the store. They need comfortable places to stand and fold clothes, and they need an efficient cash/wrap. The "back of the house," too, needs to support the sales floor. Offices, lunch rooms, locker rooms, and rest rooms need to be conveniently located, and spaces for receiving, marking, and shipping merchandise need to be easily accessible. The designer also needs to be mindful of the store budget as she proceeds. Low-maintenance materials and fixtures and energy-efficient lights are both essential (but invisible) elements of store design.[47]

These are some of the elements of retail design—windows, storefronts, entries, layout, light, color, sound, smell, display—that good designers have in mind. All of them are intended to provide "value-added benefits to shoppers," making it literally worth our while to shop in one store instead of another.[48]

But there are other elements of design that are so fundamental that we seldom think about them. Some of the most essential elements of retail design can be found in the basic classifications that structure the store. Over time, retailers have decided that stores need separate spheres for men's and women's clothes, thus reinforcing the gender differences that are so prominent in American culture. Retailers also reproduce society's age segregation, using different spaces for goods targeted to different developmental stages. Baby items often appear in specialty stores, but larger

70

stores often separate the men from the boys, and the women from the girls. In clothing departments, business dress is usually segregated from sportswear, just as work and leisure are opposed in our minds. Cosmetics, which are what you wear *on* your skin, are sold in a different place than clothes, which are what you wear *over* your skin. In the men's department, retailers separate suits from sweatsuits, but not business shirts from sport shirts. Shoes often get a department of their own, in part because of the practicalities of stocking. So retail design reveals and reflects the deeper design of our culture, the way we see the world and act in it.

Even more deeply, retail design is meant to school us in a particular way of seeing, providing a vision in which perception is infused with desire. Retail design is meant to design minds as well as stores. It's meant to show us what beauty and status look like and how they can be embodied in products that we can possess. In the long run, like a good art museum, it teaches people commercial art appreciation. It also teaches us many of the complex pleasures of shopping. Unfortunately, even the best retail designs get old. Even classic store architecture needs to be updated to fit with consumer moods and expectations. The cycle of renovation seems to get shorter and shorter—currently, retailers remodel about every five years—but according to one prominent interior designer, remodeling a store increases sales by 20 to 30 percent. And so the cycle of retail design begins again, along with a new cycle of consumption.[49]

PART TWO

Producing Consumers

How We Learn to Shop

FIVE

Home Shopping

At many malls, you can find a t-shirt or a bumper sticker bearing the cheerful message "Born to Shop," a message that, on reflection, seems demonstrably false. Indeed, despite its omnipresence in American society, shopping is neither a natural nor instinctual act. In the Bible, American culture's main religious account of creation, there's not much evidence that people were created to shop. Even on the seventh day, when God rested, He didn't go shopping with his human creatures. In Genesis, of course, after the Fall, Adam and Eve clothed themselves because they were ashamed. But there's no textual evidence that they shopped for their apparel.

And there's little scientific evidence for the proposition that people are genetically wired for consumerism. Indeed, anybody who has seen a newborn baby can testify that they're not yet equipped for shopping. They have desires, an essential element of shopping, but they're not ready for malls of America. Nor is there much historical evidence that people are congenital shoppers. Although many Americans consider shopping almost a birthright, history shows that people lived fully human lives for thousands of years without shopping.

"Born to Shop" t-shirts to the contrary, shopping is a social construction, and we *learn* to shop as we learn to speak and write and dine and drive. As Barbara Kingsolver suggests, "Human young are not born with the knowledge that wearing somebody's name in huge letters on a T-shirt is a thrilling privilege for which they should pay eighty dollars. It takes several years of careful instruction to arrive at that piece of logic." The instruction begins early: the average American child makes a first trip to a mall at two months of age. By two years, American kids can name a product. By four, they can evaluate a product, and at six they've internalized the idea that "better brands cost more." At the relatively late age of eleven, they begin to understand that some claims are misleading. In this culture, growing up means growing to be shoppers.[1]

Our kids need this education, because few American malls provide detailed instructions for shopping. For the most part, malls are merely warehouses—huge spaces filled with stuff displayed for our delectation. When you march into the mall from the parking lot, there's no sign with the rules or etiquette of shopping. There's precious little information about items at the mall. Clothes are piled on tables, or hang from racks, and signs indicate only the brand name or the price. Occasionally a sign screams "Sale" or "Clearance," but generally speaking, the mall keeps its secrets. It gives us precious little information about the process of shopping. Malls presume that we already know. And we do. But *how* do we know? How do we learn to shop?

Before we actually go to the mall on our own, we learn how to act when we're there. Called "consumer socialization," this learning is basically the preparatory course for malls of America. We learn where to park and where to enter. We learn about longing and desire, about the difference between window shopping and shoplifting. We learn what to say when the salesperson asks, "May I help you?" We learn about money and credit cards, and how to make a transaction at the cash register. In short, we learn the "common sense" of shopping. Einstein said that "common sense is the collection of prejudices acquired by age eighteen," and most of us have acquired our consumer's common sense by that age. This chapter, therefore, begins to explore the epistemology of malls—how we know what we know. It looks at how we acquire the knowledge that lets us productively and pleasurably navigate malls that offer few explicit directions. It also looks at shopping as an imaginative act, probing the ways that malls help us to put what's in our minds into our shopping bags.[2]

Bringing Up Baby

Although we *go* to the mall, we learn to shop at home. Home is where the heart is, but it's also the heartbeat of consumer culture. Home is, after all, where most of the commodities we buy at the mall end up. It makes sense, therefore, to explore the ways that home life prepares us for a life of shopping, the ways that we Americans teach our children to become consumers.

We teach our children to shop, but we have help from shopping centers, and from more than two million advertisers, marketers, retailers, service suppliers, and media magnates who work in the children's market. In America, commerce comes home all the time. A man's home may be his castle, but its defenses against commercial culture are generally weak. Television, telemarketers, newspapers, magazines, catalogues, family, and friends all march across the moat with impunity. And the Internet, with its easy invitation to a different kind of Windows shopping, is increasingly wired into American homes. These institutions help to manufacture desire, supplying the demand that's subsequently satisfied in shopping centers.[3]

So even though Americans aren't born to shop, the preparation for shopping begins early. In America, especially in the large middle class, we make a house a home by filling it up with stuff that's ours. We go to the mall to buy carpets and curtains, furniture and appliances, antiques and accents, shelves and knickknacks to fill the shelves. We need pictures and paintings and posters; we need an entertainment center. We need these things to "make ourselves at home," and we need them to express ourselves to others. In India, this relationship is different, according to researchers Raj Mehta and Russell Belk. "While an Indian home is considered rich if it is filled with people," they note, "an American home is considered rich if it is filled with things, and especially things regarded as expressing individual identity." The American home, therefore, depends on virtually every

department of the department store, and many of the shops in the mall. And the relentless commercial emphasis on "home improvement" keeps us focused on the home as both symbol and substance of "the good life."[4]

Even before our babies come home from the hospital, we've begun the process of teaching them how to consume. We've often prepared a nursery, for example, by decorating a room or corner with new paint or wallpaper, a crib and changing table, a mobile and assorted plush toys. We don't do these things for the baby, who isn't yet looking at things with a critical consumer's eye, we do them to tell our friends and relatives how we feel about children and about the child's relationship to the world of goods. The baby just got home and already she has a life-style. She's too young to appreciate it, but she'll breathe it in like air. The nursery nurses a child's sense of the meaning of goods.[5]

It's a parent's responsibility to feed and clothe and shelter children, and we do this—as parents always have—in the world of goods. Most American parents fulfill these parental responsibilities in the world of branded consumer commodities. We have to decide between Pampers and Huggies, Cheerios and Frosted Flakes, Gymboree and Baby Gap. We choose the colonial house over the contemporary home, the Chevrolet over the Ford, the private over the public school. In raising children responsibly, we teach them to respond to the world of consumer culture. Because we love our kids, we provide things for them to consume. And in the process, we teach them that shopping and brands matter to people who matter.

The things we buy our kids are, in many ways, an expression of our hopes and fears for them. We buy them clothes that fit them and help them fit in. We buy books and videos and toys and computers to stimulate their imagination and teach them about the world. We buy food and drink to nourish them (and candy and ice cream to please them). We buy museum memberships and souvenirs to help them make cultural attachments. We buy bicycles and sporting goods that enable them to develop skills of play and teamwork. Often, we make substantial sacrifices to make these purchases. In America, we love our children by shopping for them.[6]

Kids are also a way we express our own taste and status. Increasingly, we clothe middle-class children not just in garments, but in assumptions about the cachet of the clothes. A baby doesn't care if it's dressed in Baby Gap, but many parents do. So many American merchandisers, and many fashion designers, have extended their product lines to include clothes for kids. Tommy Hilfiger even licenses a designer-dressed doll that's sold at FAO Schwarz. Ralph Lauren markets clothes for girls at a web site called ralphlaurengirls.com. The name implies that the kids may own the clothes but Ralph Lauren owns the girls. When we dress our children in such fashions, we make them into designer kids—kids designed in part by professional fashion designers and kids designed to be designer-conscious.

By our own purchases and participation in the commercial economy, we teach kids a set of assumptions about home as the preeminent site of consumption. We pass on our conception of "home, sweet home"—our belief that the home should be a haven in a heartless world and that it's a sweet haven because it's where we get to enjoy the stuff we've earned in the workplace. But we generally don't teach kids that the home, which is our respite from the world, rests on the world's foundation. We don't show them how our home, through its consumption patterns, is interconnected with hundreds of other homes throughout the world.

Home Schooling (in Consumption)

From birth we teach our children how to be consumers. We teach them that, in our culture, everything is possessed; everything belongs to someone. We teach our kids the concepts of ownership and property by showing them how to say "Mine!" and we teach them how to make things "Mine!" by buying them. As journalist Constantine Von Hoffman suggests, "An honest look reveals us as happy and willing participants in indoctrinating our child in consumerism." We try to teach our children family values, but we often forget that our families *value* commercial goods, and that kids know it. To most American children, consumption *is* a family value.[7]

Kids learn the pleasures of consumption before they learn any of its costs. As dependents of adults, they can be independent of the responsibilities of consumption. So kids' first encounters with the culture of consumption give them a taste of gratification without any aftertaste. They are oblivious to the consequences of consumption, and, as protective parents, we try to maintain that oblivion as long as possible. Many Americans never figure out the consequences of consumption. Having learned to think narrowly about the costs and benefits of consumerism, we maintain our myopia into adulthood and middle age.

As soon as kids can count, we teach them simple mathematics by teaching them to count money. A nickel is five pennies, a dime is two nickels, a quarter is two dimes and a nickel, and so on. We also teach them addition and subtraction by offering retail story problems: if apples are two for a quarter, and you have a dollar, how many apples can you buy (assuming, of course, that there's no sales tax on food)? Both at home and at school, we teach our kids how to make change, as if they might someday work at the mall. By second grade, we've generally succeeded: most American children know the value of coins and bills and how to use money in the marketplace. The manifest function of such teaching is a mastery of numbers and mathematical operations, but the latent function is the naturalization of money and market exchange. By teaching kids to make change, therefore, we teach them not to make any significant changes in our market economy.

80

Later, allowances and other sources of income allow kids to participate as consumers in the commercial economy. In a country with strict child labor laws, American children usually make money only with parental consent. Between the ages of four and twelve, they make about fifteen dollars a week, and they spend two-thirds of it immediately. James McNeal suggests that the dramatic increase in children's income in the last twenty years shows that "parents want their children—expect their children—to be practicing consumers." Most of us understand an allowance as training in money management, an essential skill for a maturing American. We hope that kids will learn to save their money and, in some cases, make contributions to churches and charities. But an allowance also introduces children to autonomous consumption, and it usually privileges individual choices over group choices.[8]

When money is given to children as a payment for work performed, for household chores or for academic grades, it also teaches children responsibility, even as it frees parents to work longer hours. Kids now perform about 10 percent of household work in America, and they make about $5 billion a year performing housework. Payment for that work introduces children to wage labor, and to the pattern of accepting extrinsic rewards for their work. It also teaches children that consumption is the standard reward for productive activity.[9]

The rituals of family life also inevitably immerse children in the commercial economy. Some families read the Sunday paper together in preparation for a weekly shopping excursion. Many of us go out to eat on special occasions. We teach kids how to participate in the gift rituals of American life, those occasions when we define relationships with meaningful things. We celebrate birthdays, for example, by giving gifts—often purchased in America's malls. As kids invite friends to their birthday parties, and, even more important, when they go to birthday parties, they learn about the commodification of care. They learn how to express their feelings for friends by buying them "cool" toys or fashionable clothes. They know that, in general, the more expensive the gift, the better. Within the family, kids know that they can make gifts for their parents and siblings up to a certain age. But after that, they're often expected to buy manufactured goods to express their personal feelings.

Americans also use the religious festival of Christmas to deepen our children's home schooling in consumption. During the Christmas season, we may or may not

attend religious observances, but we almost certainly will be in attendance at the mall. During the Christmas season, we teach our children how to express their own desires by making lists and communicating them to Santa Claus, either in person or by mail. We teach them to express affection, or at least to feign affection, by buying appropriate gifts for the special people in their lives. We teach them the rules of American gift giving. We show them how social relationships can be reinforced by the exchange of things. As we shall see, Christmas, perhaps the preeminent public ritual of American life, is suffused with consumption.[10]

Some of us mentor our children carefully in the practices of consumption. We talk to them about purchases and prices. We teach them how to clip coupons, how to wait for a sale, how to determine the quality of products. We pass our shopping patterns, retail preferences, and brand loyalties from generation to generation, making consumption both familiar and familial. Some of us read advice books to help us teach our children well. In *Piggy Bank to Credit Card: Teach Your Child the Financial Facts of Life*, for example, Linda Barbanel offers a detailed road map to consumer education for kids. But most American parents "appear to have few educational goals in mind and make limited attempts to teach consumer skills." In general, we leave consumption to the informal curriculum of life. We seem to expect children to learn consumption on their own. Of course, to a great degree, they do.[11]

We raise our children in families, but even at home, we teach them more than family values. We channel them into TV, which often subverts family values. Even *Sesame Street*, which is a part of noncommercial public television, teaches children about consumer culture. The show itself naturalizes money and commercial exchange by treating them as an ordinary element of everyday life. The products associated with the show—books, tapes, CDs, and plush toys—also teach children about consumption, and the virtues of cross-promotion. Commercial television also targets children as influential consumers, teaching them both what they want and how to get what they want. "Indeed," says environmentalist David Orr, "capitalism works best when children stay indoors in malls and in front of televisions and computer screens. It loses its access to the minds of the young when they discover pleasures that cannot be bought."[12]

Advertisers spend more than a billion dollars a year advertising to children, mostly on television. This is supplemented by $4.5 billion of promotions (including retailers' coupons, contests, and clubs), $2 billion of public relations, and $3 billion of packaging especially designed for kids. These sellers see children as a primary market, as an influence market, and as a future market, so they're making an important investment in the future of consumption. As a primary market, children between the ages of four and twelve spend about $35 billion a year on stuff they like. As a persuasive market, kids now influence purchases worth $290 billion annually, so corporations naturally hope that they'll use their "pester power" to influence family consumption. Their spending as a future market is literally incalculable. As sociologist Dan Cook observes, American marketers believe that "childhood makes capitalism hum over the long haul."[13]

As the American home changes, its consumption practices also change. Long-term trends—like two-career households, a lower birth rate, older parents, more involved grandparents, single-parent households, broken and blended families, and even the size of the average new house—affect the way we think about the home and home shopping. Often the two-career household trades increased discretionary income for decreased time together, with several consequences. Kids are in daycare and latchkey programs longer and, therefore, are more susceptible to peer pressures than they would be at home. Working parents can't always supervise their children's consumption choices, but they can often afford to indulge kids to make up for time deficits. Indeed, as children's marketing expert James McNeal suggests, "Quality time often means giving kids more when parents are away and doing more with them when they are together." Divorced parents often buy children what McNeal calls "DWI gifts"—gifts to help kids "deal with it"—and distant dads also use consumption to compensate for custody issues. Fractured families and blended families provide kids with more adults to buy stuff for them. In many of these situations, grandparents have become more involved in kids' lives, adding an income source for kids, and a pair of doting adults who spend even more per toy than parents do. Houses themselves have changed, doubling in size in the last fifty years, creating more space for our consumer goods.[14]

Kids also teach their parents how to buy. We teach our kids to ask for what they want, and they do. Ninety percent of their requests involve a brand name, and parents like to learn their kids' favorite brands. So ads and promotions, and parents, aim to make children into parental pickpockets. They teach kids how to use the "gimmes" to get what they want. Young kids teach each other effective strategies for "getting to yes," and even young teenagers who go to the mall to shop with friends often need to come back with parents for big purchases. As Deborah Roedder John notes, these kids have mastered a full repertoire of influence strategies: "(1) bargaining strategies, including reasoning and offers to pay for part of the purchase; (2) persuasion strategies, including expressions of opinions, persistent requesting, and begging; (3) request strategies, including straightforward requests and expressions of needs or wants; and (4) emotional strategies, including anger, pouting, guilt trips, and sweet talk." Every negotiation between parent and child over a purchase is a lesson in the issues of consumption.[15]

But kids also fuel our consumption patterns in other ways. Parents who want "the best" for their children often find that it means both more work and more shopping. Economist Juliet Schor refers to this as "keeping up for the kids." It means thinking about what to buy to maintain Johnny's popularity or Jill's fragile confidence. According to the Center for a New American Dream, two-thirds of American parents say their kids define their self-worth through stuff, and a majority of American parents confess that they buy things they don't approve for their kids because the kids say they "need" them to fit in with their friends. "Keeping up for the kids" sometimes means buying a computer to make sure that kids become comfortable with the technologies of the future. It means paying for private education, so that kids can go to Harvard or Yale or Stanford and earn an income that will allow them to provide "the best" for their kids. And it means, for parents without as much money, watching other people's kids enjoy advantages that your kids can't have.[16]

Home Shopping at the Supermarket

We raise our children at home, but we don't keep them at home during childhood. We also introduce our kids to consumption by introducing them to other institutions in American culture. We send them to school. We take them grocery shopping when they're young, and we drive them to the mall when they're older. We teach them that one sign of autonomy is the ability to buy things yourself.

Kids learn from what we do as well as from what we say, and one of the things we do is shop. We take them to the supermarket and the mall almost as soon as they can sit in the cart, usually by the age of two months, in part because "grocery stores and malls are among the few places where mothers accompanied by their children can go and find that they are welcome." Eventually the kids become the family purchasing experts for items like cereals and snack foods and desserts and toys. Even in the cart, kids are learning about brands and products, purchasing skills and pricing, and the shopping scripts needed to successfully complete a transaction. By the age of two, children have learned enough to make a first request, usually for a sweet cereal or snack, and they enter the "gimme" stage of consumption, having learned that they can be agents in their own satisfaction. In a retail world that emphasizes self-service and self-selection, children can become shoppers early on. By forty-two months, toddlers will pick out a product for themselves, bringing a colorful brand-name box to the cart. In societies like China, where self-service is less evident, the process is often delayed. Because we want our children to be consumers, and because we want our food shopping to go smoothly, we tend to indulge children in supermarkets, buying some of their favorite products or rewarding them for good behavior with a purchase or two. Even when our children misbehave, we often buy them a product that retailers call "a shut-up" to quiet them down.[17]

Between the ages of four and six years, we help our kids to make their first purchase, handing a fistful of coins to the clerk in exchange for a product. By this time, mass merchandisers such as Kmart, Wal-Mart, or Target have replaced grocery stores as the primary site of kids' consumer socialization. Children also begin to buy more toys than foods, suggesting that their attention is shifting from eating to playing. When they get to be about eight years old, we send kids around the corner to the convenience store to make their first solo purchase—milk or bread or bananas—and we reward them, of course, with a treat for themselves. By this time, they have mastered the essential concepts of consumer competence. It seems simple, but that's just because, in most cases, consumer socialization works so well.[18]

All in the Family

Like the supermarket, shopping centers assist with our home shopping by helping us supply the needs of family members. We go to the mall for back-to-school sales and for electronics and appliances. We visit Santa Claus in the shopping center courtyard and do our Christmas shopping in the mall's stores. We help our kids shop for birthday gifts in the mall toy stores. We go to the food court for a quick meal on a harried evening, and we go to the movies at the mall cineplex. By the time American kids reach age ten, they are going to more than five stores a week and making more than 270 shopping visits a year. Like our supermarkets and schools, the mall is a place for children to learn about the characteristics of consumer culture.[19]

Shopping centers play an increasingly important part in this early training, but they aren't the center of consumer socialization. Malls account for 7 percent of children's first shopping experiences but only 3 percent of their first in-store requests. Shopping centers are home to 7 percent of kids' first requests, 9 percent of first assisted purchases, and 12 percent of first independent purchases. One study of small-town teenagers showed that common mass merchandisers like Kmart and Wal-Mart were their favorite stores, even when such stores weren't close to home. Another study asked kids where they would spend a hundred-dollar windfall. Almost half named a discount store, and only a quarter of kids named a mall. Until they get to be teenagers, kids are bound by the shopping strategies of their parents, and these more often involve routine provisioning at supermarkets and discount stores rather than shopping trips to the mall. But when they get to be teenagers, as we shall see, the mall assumes a new importance.[20]

At first, the mall is just a jumble of perceptions to a child, because that's all their cognitive development permits. For small children, the mall is like an amusement park. They like riding the escalators, playing hide-and-seek in the clothes racks, peering over the balconies, and eating in the food court. They like to play on kiddie rides (race cars, airplanes, helicopters, motorcycles, etc.) placed in malls by companies such as Impulse, Inc. Attracted by the lively shapes and colors, seductive sounds and smells, and particular products and displays, they tug at parents to "Come see this!" But their brains are only equipped to see the mall one thing at a time. After age seven, they can begin to make sense of the mall, reading it with more sophisticated skills, filtering discrete perceptions and analyzing them in a relatively coherent way. Still, not until the age of eleven or twelve, just when we begin to drop them off at the mall on their own, do they have the cognitive skills to understand the mall as well as an American adult, which is still not saying very much. After all, it doesn't take as much cognitive ability to spend money as it does to spend it wisely.[21]

America's malls share an interest in the welfare of our children, not just because the mall is a place of consumer socialization, but because children come to the mall with adults who carry cash and credit cards. "Shopping center operators know that nothing can shorten a shopping trip faster than a restless or unhappy child," notes a writer in *Shopping Centers Today*. "That's why those trying to lure families to their malls consider kids' leisure more than just child's play." To keep kids happy at the mall, shopping center owners supply play areas, kiddie rides, carousels, babysitting services, and so on. If they're done well, these juvenile attractions become an anchor for the kids. "Kids want to go to a mall where they can play, and then parents stay to shop."[22]

Malls also try to be family friendly because they like the authority that parents bring to consumption. Some malls even celebrate family days, encouraging young mothers (usually) to take advantage of mall facilities for family outings. And some shopping centers also sponsor kids' clubs that offer weekly entertainments like puppetry, petting zoos, concerts, and magic shows. A club in Canoga Park, California, offers events at least once a week, including puppet shows twice a month. It sponsors joint promotions with mall tenants and recognizes kids' birthdays with coupons and gifts that help in "getting families to the mall and into stores." Often kids' clubs are connected to media partners. The WellsPark Group of shopping centers ties its kids' clubs to PBS stations, and TV characters from popular shows make appearances at these events.[23]

Kids' clubs are a form of commercial symbiosis, a kind of commodified child care in which the parents of children raised in the relative isolation of American single-family homes can expose their kids to the interactions that used to be freely available in the neighborhood. They're a play group where someone else does the planning and where playmates are not neighbors from home but neighbors from a consumption community. Kids in these clubs develop ties not just to the other children, but to their commercial sponsors. So the clubs can be good for their sponsors too. "Done right," James McNeal suggests, "a kids' club can capture the purchasing power of the right children at precisely the right time."[24]

Such "free" shows please kids (and their parents), but this "freedom" is illusory. The shows work on the same principle as free samples at the grocery store or the free shows on network TV: the payment is deferred but not in doubt. We don't buy the sample or the free entertainment, but we eventually pay for it by paying a higher price for the product. It's a kind of socialism for capitalist institutions. If these "free" shows didn't pay off, they'd be turned off. But they do pay off, and therefore they please retailers, whose coupons and promotions can become a part of the show. In an article on kids clubs in *Shopping Centers Today*, Hilary Townsend notes that "just about every marketing director considers it a cost-effective way to build traffic in off-peak time slots." Such clubs also build customer loyalty, as appreciative parents express their appreciation in the shops and food courts of the mall. And the membership rolls of mall clubs provide a convenient customer database, allowing malls and retailers to make marketing appeals directly to young children and their parents.[25]

In larger malls, the appeal to children can be even more extravagant. At Minnesota's Mall of America, General Mills has opened a "Cereal Adventure" for children ages two to twelve. Inspired by Hershey's Chocolate World, the adventure is a fifteen-thousand-square-foot theme park designed to build brand equity in Trix, Lucky Charms, and other General Mills cereals. The different pavilions of the park teach kids about the production and processing of cereals, and the attractions associate the company's brand names with fun and games. In the Wheaties pavilion, kids are immersed in the culture of celebrity by learning about the sports heroes who promote these wheat flakes; but they can also *become* a celebrity, with their own pictures on a Wheaties box. A playground features a Honeynut Hive and a cereal spoon slide that drops into a Cheerios bowl.

Cartoon characters like the Trix Rabbit, Lucky the Leprechaun, and Sonny the Cuckoo Bird bridge the gap between television ads and this architectural advertisement. The attraction may also give General Mills a chance to test kids' preferences and improve sluggish cereal sales.[26]

Smaller malls can't afford a full-time cereal adventure, but they do sponsor "events" like the Scholastic Magic School Bus tour or the Scooby-Doo Mall-O-Ween promotion. Such tours and appearances feature celebrities and cartoon characters, creating promotional tie-ins between TV and movies and retail merchandise and appealing to kids by giving them "the chance to interact with a product." They give mall management free entertainment that lures customers and moves merchandise, and they create a buzz for the particular products promoted and the specific retailers sponsoring the tour. The value of such events even led General Growth Properties to create the National Mall Network, a coalition of more than six hundred malls that makes it easier for marketers to coordinate promotional events at a nationwide selection of shopping centers.[27]

Some malls also offer parents a place to park their children while they shop. Filled with mazes and playgrounds, Barbies and Legos, interactive toys and TV screens, these indoor playgrounds allow parents to bring kids to the mall without shopping with them. As one child-care manager says, they "target parents of young children to help them have more quality time shopping." So far, few child-care facilities have been able to meet mall management's expectations for sales per square foot, but as some operators point out, you have to think of it "as an amenity that draws more people into the mall and lets them spend more time in the mall. You have to look beyond the rent."[28]

As a result of kids' direct and indirect purchasing power, almost two-thirds of American retailers have made some effort to target the kids' market. In the mall, the trend of "keeping up for the kids" has resulted in many kid versions of retail stores. GapKids, Children's Place, Gymboree, Gadzooks, Abercrombie, and Pottery Barn Kids have all focused on the children's market, appealing to the desires of kids and their parents. Pottery Barn Kids, for example, offers furnishings, bedding, toys and decorations specifically for children. At the same time, it offers early lessons in branding, status, and store personality, teaching kids and their parents that upscale specialty goods are superior to the products procured

Mannekid: the quintessence of cool (Photo by the author)

at discount stores. Such stores and promotions are also good at helping youngsters make the transition from mass merchandisers to mall stores.[29]

Home shopping (and not just the TV shopping channels) is the heart of American consumer culture. We learn to shop *at* home, and we learn to shop *for* home. We experience shopping as both getting stuff and giving love, as both an act of pleasure and an act of devotion, a practice of commitment to the people we care for most. When we go to malls, we go with the implicit endorsement of home. Sometimes, as parents, we accuse TV and advertising and other media of making our children more materialistic than we would like, and their messages are certainly influential, but they build on a solid foundation of consumerism constructed in our homes, and we are the architects of that shopping center.

If there were standardized tests for consumer competence, American kids would pass with flying colors. By the time they turn nine, most American kids have made at least 750 store visits (with and without parents), as many as ten thousand purchase requests to parents, between three and five thousand of their own selections, and several hundred assisted and unassisted purchases with their own money for their own choices. By sixth grade at the latest, therefore, most Americans have succeeded in teaching their children to be materialistic consumers. Other institutions, like American malls, have helped with this arduous process, so that our kids know the standard operating procedures of the mall, the scripts for exchanges between shoppers and salespeople, and the general rules of mall etiquette. As a result, half of American parents say their kids would rather go to the mall than go hiking or on a family outing. And so the life-cycle of consumption continues, with a new generation primed to assume its spending responsibilities in the halls of the mall.[30]

SIX

Hanging Out at the Mall

In the first few years of childhood, our families teach us the rudiments of shopping, but after that, kids begin to teach one another the lessons of consumption and shopping. Choosing specific reference groups, they begin to compare their behavior to others around them. This peer socialization takes place at home and at school, in cars and in corner stores, and in malls. American adolescents have a lot of things on their minds, and malls help them deal with some of them.

Peer socialization doesn't end with adolescence. Even after we're teenagers, we still pay attention to peers, comparing our lives and possessions to those of people around us. We, too, adopt a peculiar "peerspective" on life, and we use the material world to negotiate our social worlds. As we age, we may not be able to keep up with what's "cool," but we still teach others how to consume appropriately, and most of us take part, in one way or another, in keeping up with the Joneses. So when we come to the mall, we come with a head full of images and ideas affected by our peers.

Cool School

In a culture of possessive individualism, it doesn't take kids very long to learn that some things are "Mine! Mine!" and it doesn't take much longer for them to begin to compare their possessions with those of other people. Even toddlers notice the differences between their toys and those of their friends.

Kids especially develop this "compeerative" perspective when they leave home for daycare programs and kindergarten. We send our kids to school to learn a variety of subjects. They master (we hope) reading, writing, and mathematics. They learn some history and politics, and something about the sciences. If they're lucky, they can participate in art and music and dance and theater. But they may actually learn less *in* classes than *between* classes, where they imbibe the hidden curriculum of school, including its essential lessons in consumption. They learn, over time, that education is meant to prepare them for success in a commercial economy. They learn to accept the idea that school is work, and to accept extrinsic rewards like grades for their work. They learn the value of consumption as a counterpoint to the drudgery of everyday life. Away from home, they learn the importance of the right clothes, the right toys, and the right attitude toward the material world. They learn to use the back-to-school sale to get parents to buy the right supplies for social promotion within their peer group.

Schools themselves are no longer commercial-free zones. Coke and Pepsi compete for exclusive rights to sell soft drinks on campus; school cafeterias lease space to fast-food companies. Other companies develop "educational materials" designed to teach kids about important issues, including which brand to buy. In some schools, Channel One supplies television sets and news programming in return for the opportunity to advertise to kids who can't turn off the TV or leave the room. "We have the undivided attention of millions of teenagers for 12 minutes a day," trumpeted Channel One in a 1998 ad. "8.1 million teenagers in classrooms nationwide watch Channel One's award-winning daily news program. And since they're not channel surfing, talking on the phone or getting snacks from the kitchen, they're tuning in to the world and to you [the advertiser]." The ad's tag line is "Channel One. Where Teens Get What's Going On." Schools are not malls (although a few of them are located in malls), but schools increasingly share commercial characteristics with malls.[1]

Especially as they enter junior high school, kids begin to teach each other the rudiments of "cool." Between classes, in the cafeteria, and in the schoolyard, conversations center on styles and fashions in music, movies, magazines, TV, clothes, hair, sports, and video games—the stuff of "real life" that doesn't get treated in the classroom. For many students, if not most of them, these are the vital topics of their lives. Students show and tell and share and trade things, and in the process, they make their own meanings with things. "Look what I got!" is often a way of showing our belongings in order to belong.[2]

Cool is, according to the dictionary, "moderately cold." But cool isn't merely meteorological; it's also a social state. In the social world, cool carries two related meanings. Cool is "having a quiet, indifferent, and aloof attitude," but it's also "excellent; first-rate, superior." The causal connections between the two are remarkably complex and sometimes contradictory.

People who are cool are autonomous. They do their own thing. In a society that believes in self-made men and women, their self-possession is a mark of merit. Because they embody American values of individualism and independence, we really warm up to people who are cool. Ironically, their indifference to the opinion of others is an attraction to others. Because they don't depend on us for their cool, we often want to depend on them for ours.

Cool people are charismatic. Even though they don't seem to care about people outside their clique, cool kids are often socially graceful. They have a good sense of humor and lots of friends. They're good-looking and attractive to the opposite sex. If you're cool, you can't be caught sucking up to people, in part because you're the one who's already up. Even without any leadership training, cool people are natural-born leaders. They're not trailblazers because they want to lead particularly, but because they seem to be going in their own direction and other people want to follow.[3]

Real cool, of course, is effortless. You might maintain your appearance and pay attention to the currency of your clothes. You might be smart, or an athlete, but you don't have to be. If you're cool, you don't have to work very hard at it. It just comes naturally, even though the criteria of cool are entirely cultural.

Producing Consumers

And real cool is relatively rare. Most kids *aren't* cool and they know it. In this way, the adolescent culture of cool teaches kids about the "haves" and the "have-nots" and trains them for a market economy that systematically values status objects that most people can't have.

For young people, cool is partly defined in opposition to adults and author-ity figures. It's a generational thing. And it's ironic that some of the authority of cool comes from its indifference to authority and authority's indifference to teenagers. So cool is also a cause, and a consequence, of generational segrega-tion in America, the process by which we regularly abandon young people to the pressures of their peers. A few parents and teachers are allowed to be cool, but it's not generally because of their own independence and individuality. When adults are cool, it's not because they're in tune with the cosmos—it's because they're in tune with teenagers, or at least seem to be.

Who's cool helps people to think about *what's* cool. Cool people have their own style, individually and collectively, but cool people don't necessarily buy cool things. Quite the contrary. When cool people buy things, the things *become* cool. In some magical way, the cool person transmutes mere objects into cool things. And this, of course, is where marketing comes in. If a company can fig-ure out *what's* cool to kids who *are* cool, they can sell a lot of stuff to other kids who would like to *look* cool.

Coolhunting

American teenagers have a lot of money, and America's malls would like to earn some of it. Developers, designers, managers and marketers know that American teenagers are wealthy, spending $172 billion in the year 2001. The average teenager spends $104 per week, about two-thirds of it on themselves. And the teen population is growing: there will be 35 million teenagers in 2010. These young people are tomorrow's customers, but they're also a significant market niche today.[4]

To capture the teen market, malls and manufacturers need to know what teens want. "Cool" is obviously one of those things. In fact, there's a niche of market researchers called "coolhunters" who do precisely that: hunt American kids by researching the bait kids will bite—and buy—on. Coolhunters hang out with cool kids, the ones who are called "early adopters" in the marketing trade. They go to concerts and basketball courts and skateparks, where they observe the cool kids and videotape them. They talk with these coolsters. They visit teens at home to study their "ensemble" of goods, and they pay kids to participate in focus groups. They watch MTV, which is basically "Market Television" for teens, and they lurk in chat rooms (sometimes they even create chat rooms on web sites where unsuspecting teens offer their opinions to market researchers). Coolhunters look for the "new look" that might define a trend and the new music or new slang that might help to sell the new look. All the while, they're hunting for attitude and mindset, so that they can set other minds on that mindset— or at least on the commercial expression of it. They're looking for charisma to commodify.[5]

The firm Look-Look exemplifies the practice of coolhunting, providing "information and research connecting you [the merchandiser or media merchant] to youth culture." Sometimes the research is fairly standard. During the summer of 2000, Look-Look's coolhunters interviewed about five hundred teenagers at four California malls with special "teen zones" to see how much of their mall experience was shopping and how much was "hanging out." They found that shopping predominated, with kids spending money on apparel and shoes (34 percent), entertainment (22 percent), and food and drink (16 percent). They asked about favorite hangouts at the mall (the mall in general, restaurants, and outdoor spots were most popular), about spending per visit (46 percent spent between twenty and forty-nine dollars), and about boredom as a cause for coming to the mall (56 percent of teens said they came when they were bored).[6]

Look-Look also employs thousands of "cultural correspondents" or "culture spies," including teens themselves, to talk to teens and film them. Their reports are collated and presented on the Look-Look web site, where businesses pay a huge annual fee for the assembled information and for the ability to ask the "correspondents" marketing questions in real time. The idea is to capture a trend and commercialize it quickly, before it shifts from "cool" to "so over."[7]

Another firm, Teenage Research Unlimited (TRU), conducts two surveys of teenagers a year, asking about brand preferences, products purchased, words that are "in" and "out," and activities. Survey results go to a list of clients that includes the Defense Department; a host of advertising, marketing, and media firms; several credit card companies; and mall brands and retailers such as Nike and Foot Locker, Abercrombie and the Gap, Calvin Klein and Tommy Hilfiger, and Gadzooks and Wet Seal. Teenage Research Unlimited also calculates TRU*Scores for athletes and celebrities to guide advertisers about which stars to place in ads. In addition, TRU conducts over a thousand focus groups a year for its clients, and their researchers even accompany teens to malls to see how they actually shop.[8]

TRU also uses their Coolest Brand Meter survey to establish America's "coolest brands." Nike has claimed the top spot for every year of the poll's existence, but Sony is now a strong second, with Abercrombie & Fitch, Tommy Hilfiger, Old Navy, American Eagle, and the Gap also in the top ten. The top characteristics of cool are quality, age appropriateness, and appealing advertising. Next are uniqueness and its opposite—the number of cool people and friends who use it. About one in ten teens think that the coolness of things comes from the coolness of the store. It's interesting to note, too, that four of the top five cool brands are shoe or apparel brands—the "badge" items that express the self to other teens.[9]

TRU researchers classify teenagers into four groups. The Influencers are the good-looking, sociable teenagers who establish trends. Disproportionately African American and Latino, these confident kids lead high-energy life-styles that other kids consider "cool." About half of teenagers are Conformers, kids who depend on cool brand names to maintain their fragile confidence. The Passives are passionate about achievement but impassive to consumption; they think they have better things to do, so they may well be "nerds." And the Edge kids are the outsiders—punks, goths, skaters—who often inspire fashion trends but wouldn't be caught dead in something widely considered cool. Coolhunters often go to the Edge to predict what the Influencers will want next, but marketers don't generally try to sell to Edgers—they try to leverage the authority of the Influencers to sell to the more numerous Conformers. As TRU president Peter Zollo suggests, Conformers are "the group from which marketers profit."[10]

Except, perhaps, for the Passives, who are too intent on achievement, American teenagers characterize themselves as focused on fun. From a list of fifteen statements, TRU researchers asked a sample of two thousand teens to choose the three that best described their generation. "We're about fun" was the

Hanging Out at the Mall

top choice, with half of all teens choosing it. In the same way, 70 percent of teenagers agree with the statement "I always try to have as much fun as I possibly can—I don't know what the future holds and I don't care what others think." Both guys and girls see their teenage years as an interval of fun in a life of work and obligation, and they put their money where the fun is. Facing an American adulthood that seems to emphasize responsibility more than fun, teenagers plan to make the most of their adolescent interlude. And malls can, of course, make the most by marketing to teenagers' desire for fun.[11]

Conversely, marketers can make money by combating boredom, the byproduct of fun morality. Two-thirds of American teenagers say that they're bored "some" or "all" of the time, probably because their expectations for fun and frolic are so high. "Boredom—or complaining about being bored—seems to be a natural part of this life stage," Peter Zollo explains. "Products, services, and messages that combat boredom may be especially welcomed by teens." So if advertisers can cast school or church or home or adulthood as boring—and they do—they can sell teens the magical antidote: Dr. Pepper, a pizza, or a new pair of pants. It's no wonder that teenagers wonder whether they want to grow up.[12]

The commercial economy often invites Americans in their teen years to define their individuality (and their cliques and communities) by their consumption choices. Ads and magazines present teenagers with stories of singularity and conformity (sometimes combined) expressed by spending. They also introduce teens to different reference groups who may influence their consumption—the Pepsi generation, MTV models and music mavens, TV and movie

Producing Consumers

stars, the "in" crowd of kids who share *Seventeen* or *YM* or *Maxim* or *Stuff* for tips on how to look and act—and spend. Impressionable teens who want to make an impression with their friends often copy the seemingly successful styles of celebrities like Britney Spears, Christina Aguilera, Michael Jordan, or Alan Iverson. As a sixth grade boy revealed, "I wear what I wear because it is in style. . . . It also makes me feel real cool. Some of the kinds of clothes I like are Nike, Guess, Levi's, and Reebok. When I wear my clothes, it makes me feel real cool. I also blend in with all the other people at school and everywhere else I go."[13]

These commercial suggestions come just at the time when teenagers' social development makes them particularly vulnerable to the seductive interpersonal appeals of advertising. Not until age 10 or so can American kids seriously even contemplate another person's perspective. But very quickly, between the ages of twelve and fifteen, kids learn how to understand other people's perspectives as a function of social groups or social systems. At exactly the same time, their understanding of impression formation, and of the symbolic meanings of products and brand names, gets considerably more complex. Together, these psychological developments help kids make sense of the social meanings of the consumer marketplace. But they are also a recipe for peer pressure, as individual kids begin the process of impression management by their participation is the system of consumption. And such peer perspectives are a foundation of American materialism, which also crystallizes about fifth or sixth grade, as kids begin to value things for their social worth.[14]

Although teenagers dislike the peer pressures imposed on them, they still respond, and they impose pressure on each other. Fifty-eight percent of teenagers think that peer labeling is "stupid," but an even greater percentage considers the labeling inevitable. When asked what they dislike about being teens, the number one answer is "peer pressure." Still, almost half of teens admit to bowing to peer pressure. In fact, in some ways, the smartest way to deal with peer pressure is to succumb to it. Peer pressure influences consumption choices, but it also influences kids' use of alcohol and drugs and their sexual activity.[15]

Because market researchers understand teenagers better than most Americans do, ads are an integral part of teenage peer culture. As Peter Zollo suggests, "To teens, advertising is more than product information. . . . To teens, advertising is popular culture." Like many Americans, therefore, teenagers respond to ads not just by buying things but by making them a part of their own lives. Advertisers use teenagers, but teenagers use ads for their own purposes. In fact, about 80 percent of teenagers talk about commercials with their friends. In doing so, they transform a medium with commercial purposes into a medium of social uses—a topic of conversation, a sign of values, and a mark of relevant knowledge ever so much more important than the dry facts of American history. Many teenagers even collect ads and promotional posters to hang on their walls and in their lockers. For an advertiser, therefore, success can be measured by the amount of word of mouth generated within schools and other teen communities. In a commercial culture, talking about what we like in ads is a way of revealing what we're like, and whether or not we want to be liked in a particular crowd. Kids know they can appreciate the ad without buying the product, but it's not surprising that cool ads and cool brands are strongly linked in the teenage brain. And Nike is coolest of all. "To teens," note authors Mark Ritson and Richard Elliott, "Nike *is* sports. Nike communicates desire, grittiness, empowerment, and even humor. And no brand has leveraged celebrity better than Nike."[16]

In many ways, American teenagers define growing up in terms of consumption choices. In a commercial culture, you know you're growing up when you can choose your own clothes and your own entertainment. Somewhat later, you know you're growing up when you can drive a car or drink alcohol. Young teens especially like to be called teenagers and like to buy stuff that makes them seem older than they are. Older teenagers prefer to be called "young adults" and are less likely to buy products advertised with the word "teen." Retailers such as Abercrombie & Fitch make millions of dollars by pitching their marketing to older teens, because in addition they get the younger teens who aspire to be older. And because teenagers think that sex and sexiness are an important part of growing up, the adult content of their controversial catalogues is like honey to flies.[17]

In a commercial culture, too, it's a sign of independence when you can make your own "spending money," without depending on Mom and Dad for a handout or an allowance. As soon as teenagers are old enough, therefore, they often get jobs to support their newfound spending habits. More often than not, the jobs are in retail, where kids may be routinely exposed to the attractions of the mall. At an age when teenagers could be learning a lot of different things, many of them are learning to fold t-shirts at the Gap so they can buy the t-shirts or cargo pants or cars that will establish both their independence from adults and their "cool" standing among their friends. Ironically, even at an early age, we depend on the consumption economy for the signs of our independence, even as we're apprenticed to the pattern of work-and-spend that characterizes so much of American life.

The term "spending money" is instructive. We don't usually use the term "savings money," even though some portion of it might be diverted to saving for a college education. In the past, child labor, or a child's labor, supported the family. But especially in middle-class America, a teenager's earnings are meant to support consumption above and beyond the necessities of life, because that consumption is increasingly seen to be a necessity of teenage social life.

Mall Rats and Mall Bunnies

Going to the mall is a rite of passage in American adolescence. "Teens love to shop," Peter Zollo contends. "It is an experience rather than an errand, an event rather than a chore. What teens buy reflects what they think of themselves and how they wish others to perceive them." Jon Berry and Selina Gruber note that "as they get older, kids gain more independence to go shopping on their own. The primary hangout and shopping place for kids once they gain their independence is the shopping mall."[18]

Shopping centers have not always been excited about this "hanging out." As late as 1990, an article in *Shopping Center Age* interpreted this teen socialization mainly as loitering and discussed appropriate measures to deal with the apprehensions of merchants and other customers. Locating teen attractions in "side malls" and corners of the plan, beefing up security and surveillance in the common areas adjacent to teen attractions, and banning unescorted youths on Friday and Saturday nights were some of the solutions. While these measures still persist in malls, the sheer size of the youth market has made shopping centers more inviting to kids.[19]

For tweenagers (ages eight to twelve) and young teenagers (ages twelve to fifteen) especially, the mall is an oasis of freedom in a world of apparent restrictions. In a culture that celebrates independence and autonomy and freedom of choice, the life of a pre-teen can feel pretty constrained. The mall is nothing if not a large space with lots of choices. The mall honors youth's power and potential, or at least its potential purchasing power. And despite mall surveillance, it's a different sort of eye than the eyes of parents and neighbors.

For parents, the mall is an oasis of security in a world of seeming dangers. Parents let their kids hang out at the mall because they think the mall is a safe space—and it is, if you think that consumer culture is safe for children. The mall tries to shield shoppers from beggars and drug dealers and gangs. In the mall, kids don't generally drink or do drugs or copulate, although they might be planning for such activities. Mall security can be a hassle for some teenagers, but mall security *is* security for parents. And the relatively small cost of hanging out at the mall makes the mall seem like a good deal for parents.[20]

The mall is an important place for American adolescents to work out their identity and community. Market researchers know that "at a point where peer approval is critical, the mall serves its purpose well by providing kids with a support network of other kids." Hanging out at the mall is a group activity, an occasion for talking about individuality and social acceptance by talking about things. But the shopping center is a different space for girls and guys, who buy different things to establish their identity and community.[21]

"For girls," says Peter Zollo, "fashion rules. Apparel is the most important product category to teen girls, consuming both the greatest proportion of their disposable income and their greatest parent-campaigning efforts. Next to fashion, girls spend the most on personal-grooming items from mousse to mascara." Girls teach each other about norms of acceptability and popularity by engaging in what Elise Braaten calls "cute talk." "That looks really cute on you," they say, confirming the importance of looks for women. "That's adorable" or "It fits well," they say, acting like mirrors who talk for their friends. "She's kind of pretty, but she dresses cute," they say of another girl, affirming the possibility of remaking the self through consumption. At this age, it's more important to be "clothes cute" than physically beautiful, because "clothes cute" confirms your adherence to cultural norms. Pressuring each other to focus on good looks, these girls surely look good to retailers in America's malls.[22]

Girls create their own cultures of fashion, but they do so in conversation with American magazines and advertisers. As Zollo notes, "girls bond with their

Producing Consumers

Cute talk (Photo courtesy of Herman Krieger)

favorite magazines, depending upon them for critical information about the key questions and issues of their lives—from boys, beauty, and fashion to parents, school and community." Almost half of all girls, for example, read *Seventeen*, and more than a third also read *YM* and *Teen* faithfully. So peer pressure is reflected and affected by commercial pressure, and retailers like Buckle, Wet Seal, PacSun, Old Navy, Gadzooks, J. C. Penney, Kohl's, and Lady Foot Locker use ads to invite girls to malls of America to buy clothes, colognes, perfumes, cosmetics, lipsticks, shampoos, hair colors, moisturizers and the other "necessities" of teen life. These ads have an impact on girls. When asked where they prefer to hang out after school, 20 percent of girls chose the mall. When asked about weekends, the figure was 49 percent.[23]

Guys care about their looks, but their identity doesn't depend on it, so they spend more on food, gas, music, and movies. They spend a lot on sound systems to show off their musical tastes, and on TVs and DVD players, to provide for their entertainment needs. Guys don't read as much as girls, and their magazine reading tends toward sports and gaming journals. *Maxim* and *Gear* and *Stuff* are trying to become life-style magazines for guys, but so far they've been less successful than *Seventeen*. Still, teenage guys also like to hang out at the mall, which is the preferred choice for 15 percent of them after school and 40 percent of them on weekends.[24]

Although guys and girls in America's malls are shopping for different stuff, they're also shopping for each other. "Scoping" each other and "just looking" in mall stores, teenagers tell each other what's "cool" and what's "hot." At the same time, of course, they define "nerdy" and "deviant." Checking out other people, especially the opposite sex, is important; it defines a self not just as a personality but as an assemblage of products and attitude. Even "just looking" is not just looking, because it involves a constant conversation about values and virtues and appearances. When a group of girls talks about tank tops or lipsticks or "sex pants," or when a group of guys talks about their video games or rock bands, they're also talking about the norms of acceptability. And when teens gossip about each other, they create peer pressure that drives both consumption and life-style choices. Both their personal compliments and put-downs are ways of sanctioning certain behavior.

The mall also allows teenagers to play with their attractiveness and sexuality, especially their heterosexuality. For both guys and girls, one of the main attractions of commercial culture is its sexiness—its promise to make the self "sexy." Guys sometimes go to the mall to "pick up girls." And girls go to meet guys. Sometimes it's just a game, as a group of girls might try to see how many guys they can get to say "Hi." Sometimes the encounter ends with a conversation or a movie date. Occasionally, it leads to an exchange of telephone numbers and a later date. But the play itself is important, as it allows teens to try out the costumes and scripts of their emerging social roles.

Mall managers know how teenagers spend their time and their money, so they try to provide spaces for that spending. Teenage girls spend $4 billion a year on cosmetics, so a mall will want a tenant like Claire's who can attend to their beauty issues. Both guys and girls define themselves by their preferences in popular music, so a music store like Sam Goody will attract teenagers to the mall. Because teens spend more on clothes than other Americans, specialty retailers who sell to teens suffer less in economic downturns than chains selling to adults. And because teenagers appreciate a good deal, it helps to have a Dollar Store on the mall premises.[25]

Specialty retailers have also targeted our kids and their peers. The Limited Too, for example, began with stores targeting girls from infancy through adulthood, but they refined their concept to focus on "tween" girls aged eight to thirteen. They recognized that these girls were reading *Seventeen*, watching music videos, and becoming fashion-conscious. "What Britney Spears wears, that's what [our customer] buys," acknowledged a Limited Too spokesman. So the stores feature apparel and adornments to reinforce their customers' sense of coming of age as young women.[26]

Charlotte Russe, Inc. targets the same tween girls with a new concept called Charlotte's Room, a boutique offering accessories and gifts, along with sleepwear and novelty t-shirts. "Our target customer is 11 to 17 years old," says Harriet Sustaric, president of Charlotte Russe. "She's the hip girl who is looking for special gifts and home and room décor—everything from her bedroom to her college dorm to her locker décor." Stores are designed to make girls feel at home, by developing themes and accents that remind them of the personal space of their own bedroom. A custom soundtrack plays Top 40, techno, or club music. "We feel music is critically important to creating the entire shopping experience, especially for this age group," says Nancy Mamann, Charlotte Russe's vice president of marketing.[27]

Old Navy's success with teenagers comes from the fact that "Shopping is Fun Again," and from their ability to provide individualistic conformity with simple styles, like t-shirts, in a wide variety of colors. Buying the t-shirt helps Conformers fit in; buying it in their own color helps them stand out.[28]

Given their penchant for fun, teenagers also have an appetite for entertainment. Ninety-two percent of teenagers think that going to the movies is "in," and they show it. Although kids ages twelve to twenty are only 16 percent of the American population, they buy 26 percent of the movie tickets. Sixty-two percent of teenagers watch a videotape movie at least once a week. Between seventh and twelfth grade, the average teenager listens to more than ten thousand hours of rock music, occupying almost as much time as classroom experience. Eighty percent of teens watch music videos, and they buy billions of music CDs. Teenage boys spend almost twice as much time watching MTV as reading for pleasure, and girls watch even more. And this affects consumption choices. "Teens, both black and white, look to music videos for the latest in music but also for the latest in fashion and language." Growing up with Sam Goody, or maturing at the movies, these young Americans are teaching one another the essential assumptions of consumption, in part because these media offer inspiration for more stuff to buy.[29]

One of the newest developments in America's major malls is teen zones designed to appeal to "Generation Y," a "generation that is very comfortable in malls and has money to spend," according to retail consultant Sid Doolittle. California's Glendale Galleria pioneered this concept and won a 2001 Maxi Award for "Center Productivity" from the International Council of Shopping Centers. The mall began with a focus group of area teenagers called "the Z team" that revealed their desire for "hot retailers, plus video screens, Internet terminals, a lounge, message boards, and a broadcast booth from which L.A.'s most popular radio station would air." The Galleria then added a cluster of stores called "the Zone" for shoppers age eight to eighteen, with hip, street-smart clothes and disc jockeys on Friday and Saturday nights. Merchants like Hot Topic, Cat Walk, Van's, and Juxtapose occupied an upper-level area that had been a relatively dead space in the mall. And the Zone sponsored live events that began to draw teens from a larger trade area.[30]

The Galleria won a second Maxi from the ICSC for its promotion of the Zone, an ad campaign with the theme "It's Your Thing." Seven different TV spots featured area teen performers showcasing talents from juggling to extreme BMX bike tricks. Radio promotions featured a popular KIIS disc jockey. The ads ran on radio and on teen-oriented cable networks like MTV and VH1. They were supplemented by a web site at thezone-online.com, and a "guerrilla" marketing effort in which teens distributed flyers at area teen hangouts and schools. The results were impressive. Six thousand teens attended the grand opening, and the web site registered sixteen thousand hits a month. Sales in Galleria II, the section of the mall hosting the Zone, increased 25 percent, and sales at stores focused on Gen Y customers increased 21 percent. In addition, the mall secured more than $500,000 in outside sponsorships for promotions in the Zone. At the same time, the marketing staff compiled an e-mail database of nine thousand teens who get notices of upcoming events and promotions.[31]

The 2001 Maxi Awards also honored General Growth Properties, a shopping center chain, for "sales promotion and merchandising." ICSC's web site notes that "General Growth Properties wanted to persuade teens to visit its centers in person, spend their cash there, and remain loyal customers." To do this, it needed to update its image, so it settled on a "Rock the Mall" promotion that included a concert tour, in-school performances, a sweepstakes, and volunteer opportunities. General Growth sponsored day-long teen festivals in the common areas of eleven malls, featuring two "girl bands" with new CD releases. They engaged corporate sponsors like Pepsi and Sam Goody to distribute freebies and sell stuff. They gave space to a nonprofit called Do Something to solicit volunteer pledges from teens, and they gathered teen e-mail addresses in an enter-to-win promotion. Before the concerts, Do Something organized assemblies at twenty-one schools to pitch their volunteer message; the bands played in the schools and encouraged kids to attend the mall festival later in the day. In addition, a sweepstakes called "Shop.Rock.Win" in seventy-seven shopping centers rewarded teens for shopping with prizes including CDs, soft drinks, and a one-thousand-dollar shopping spree. Appealing both to teenagers' fixation on fun and their social consciousness, the promotion resulted in a 10 percent increase in traffic and a 73 percent increase in sales during the promotion.[32]

Growing Up at the Mall

American adolescents have a lot of serious thinking to do. They need to think about the standard stuff of school and jobs and family and friends. But in the process, they have to consider some bigger questions, such as what they're good at and what they're good for. They need to consider both their bodies and their brains, their sexuality and their sex lives. They need to think about what they mean by love, and how they mean to love. They need to think about their place in the world, both geographically and socially, and how they might be good for the world. They need to think about nature, and how their culture and consumption affects nature. They need to consider the question of God, and their own spirituality. They need to think about self and society and how individuals make communities (or avoid them). They need to think about what it means to grow up, and how growing up affects their growth as full human beings.

Malls don't help much with these questions, and generally we don't expect them to. We assume that the business of retailing is sales, not personal growth or maturity. Coolhunters capture the cool that's commodifiable, but they approach teenagers more as consumers than as whole persons. Surveys, for example, show that philanthropy and spirituality are important to teenagers. About two-thirds of American teenagers say "It's very important to me to get involved in things that help others and help make the world better." And about 60 percent of teens acknowledge the importance of religious faith in their lives. But faith and idealism are hard to sell, so the mall sells style and cynicism instead. American culture doesn't always fulfill teenagers' idealistic expectations, and teens, therefore, are left to drift to the mall.[33]

Malls often trivialize teenagers' issues by transforming them into purchase decisions. Instead of thinking carefully about the meaning and morality of love, a teenager can simply engage in the commercial rituals and exchanges that, in part, constitute love in this culture. Instead of worrying about the competences that make them good for other people, teenagers can show their competence as shoppers. The mall sometimes makes life easy for us by converting the complexities of our lives into the simplicity of a purchase.

In a culture of specialization, we assume that teenagers will answer life's big questions in places other than malls, and, of course, they do. Parents, pastors, teachers, and peers help kids come to a sense of themselves and life's purposes. But shopping centers also have an effect, complicating the work of our other educational institutions. Sometimes shopping centers are just a distraction, a place to go when you're procrastinating or just playing around. They give kids a break from serious questions, and a space for socialization and fun. This is a good thing, because it's as important to live life as to ponder life's meaning all the time. But sometimes shopping centers seem to suggest that distraction *is* the purpose of life, and that questions of consumption—"What movie should we see?" "Which prom dress should I buy?" "Do I want the Xbox or the PlayStation?"— *are* life's big questions.

As a primary institution of American consumer culture, shopping centers are more than a mere distraction. Like our families and schools and churches, they offer interpretations of the good life. Often, they suggest that you have to buy something to be somebody. Shopping centers celebrate the pleasure principle, while

Producing Consumers

parents and pastors and teachers generally support principled pleasure, the deeper joy that comes from doing good. Malls reward desire and money more than character and competence. Shopping centers encourage a passion for possessions more than a compassion for others. Shopping centers invite us to focus on the present instead of the future or important cultural traditions. Shopping centers help socialize our kids to some of the dominant values of American culture.

Shopping centers understand the pressures (and the peer pressures) of adolescence, and they try to capitalize on them. Commercializing the dreams and desires of America's youth, they subtly skew those dreams and desires. The kid who wanted more freedom finds himself with a t-shirt that reads "Fuck Authority." The girl who wanted responsibility finds herself with responsibility for credit card debt that she didn't need. The teenager looking for intimacy now owns a sexy perfume called Lolita Lempicka. As America's adolescents wrestle with the difficult questions of growing up, America's shopping centers sell them the answers that are marketable. And in doing so, they reshape the peer pressures that help teach teenagers how—and why—to shop.

SEVEN

Christmas Shopping

Ecclesiastes tells us that "to every thing there is a season," but in America's malls, it's always the shopping season. From New Year's Day to New Year's Eve, shopping centers tell us that now is the time to buy. "We are invited to buy to honor Abe Lincoln and George Washington, to get ready for Easter, to celebrate summer, and to prepare for school," note authors Robert Holsworth and J. Harry Wray. And, of course, our biggest shopping spree is the Christmas holiday season.[1]

Christmas is a time of joy and merriment. It's the season of Santa and his elves, of Christmas trees and toys, of mistletoe and holly. And Christmas is the season of shopping centers, the time when we ritually count the number of shopping days left. These shopping days are the most important to the American economy. Although Christmas decorations appear earlier every year, the season of commerce opens officially on the day after

Thanksgiving. In these few weeks, Americans spend about $200 billion, more than $800 a family. Although this gift giving originated as a tribute to a savior, today the gifts are also a savior to our economy, which depends on consumer spending for two-thirds of its volume. General retail stores do 25 percent of their business on Christmas shopping days, and many specialty stores log almost half of their sales during the holiday season. We buy a lot of our Christmas gifts and supplies at America's malls.[2]

"The holiday season for most people inevitably revolves around going to the mall," notes the International Council of Shopping Centers. Given the centrality of shopping centers in our celebrations of Christmas, malls try to create a context that's conducive to shopping and spending. Most malls begin decorating for the holidays on November first, replacing the Halloween displays with Christmas decorations. About the same time, retailers begin to mail Christmas catalogues to get people's minds focused on what they want—both for themselves and for others. The ad blitz intensifies around Thanksgiving, as malls work to produce sales by producing the Christmas spirit in Americans. Santa Claus also arrives at American shopping centers in November, usually about a week before Thanksgiving. By Turkey Day, too, the mall begins to play its Christmas theme music—the Christmas carols that boost our holiday spirit. These stories—commercial Christmas decorations, Christmas promotions, and shopping center Santas—are the main story of this chapter. There's also a counternarrative about "the true spirit of Christmas" that contributes to the cultural work of a shopping center Christmas.[3]

History

Shopping centers have been a part of America's Christmas for less than a hundred years. And "America's Christmas," the traditions we know now, is less than two hundred years old. In fact, the American Christmas is an "invented tradition" dating to the mid-nineteenth century. The earliest Americans, Indians, didn't celebrate Christmas because they weren't Christians, and the earliest Englishmen, often Puritan refugees, believed that the celebration of Christmas desecrated the day. In Massachusetts, for example, a 1659 ordinance threatened fines for people who treated Christmas as a holiday from their normal work.[4]

During the nineteenth century, as American industrial capitalism transformed American social life, a "battle for Christmas" broke out, pitting middle-class Victorians against an unruly working class that believed in Christmas as a time of drinking, carousing, and revels. In some cities, mobs of young men would practice a kind of Christmas "trick-or-treat," appearing at the homes of the wealthy to demand gifts of food or drink. In 1828, New York City outfitted its first professional police force in response to a violent Christmas riot. The middle class countered this working-class carousing with a new "tradition," the American family Christmas. Texts like the 1822 poem "A Visit from St. Nicholas," Charles Dickens's *Christmas Carol*, and Thomas Nast's cartoons of Santa Claus began to create an iconography and rituals for the holiday, which would celebrate the family as a "haven in a heartless world." By 1836, American states began to recognize Christmas as a legal holiday; by 1890, it was a national holiday. Within a short time, it was *the* American holiday, both religious and secular. And virtually from the beginning, it was a commercial holiday. In fact, the commercial character of Christmas helped to make the holiday national: in a country characterized by geographical regionalism and religious denominationalism, the marketplace was one place where diverse people could come together. Sometimes Americans of different faiths even adapted their celebrations to conform to the commercialism of the secular Christmas. By the end of the nineteenth century, the middle class and their merchants had transformed an antimaterialist's birthday into "a grand festival of consumption."[5]

It's Beginning to Look a Lot Like Christmas

In a revealing book called *Christmas Displays and Promotions*, visual merchandiser Martin Pegler contends that "Christmas is more than a religious holiday—more than the eagerly awaited gift-giving and gift-getting time that closes one year and opens a new one." Christmas is, he continues, "a state of mind—and the most important selling season in the retailer's calendar. Though there are many who want the true meaning of Christmas returned to the holiday—they want to de-commercialize it—it has already gone way beyond a religious celebration to become a national and international event." In his lavishly illustrated book, Pegler shows retailers how to use "the old familiar and lovable motifs" in merchandising windows, store interiors

Producing Consumers

and store-wide promotions, bags, and banners. Such displays, he concludes, are "what the Christmas retail season is all about. So, may all your Christmas displays be merry and bright—and may all your Christmas sales be right—and green."[6]

Pegler reminds retailers that they need to keep customers in the mood for spending money: "Filled with the spirit of giving, the shopper steps into the store ready, willing, and hopefully able, to get into the spirit of getting; getting the right presents for all the people on the Christmas list." The shopping center needs to keep that spirit alive and well. According to James Zielinski, director of field marketing for Chicago's Heitman Retail Properties, good displays help to "enhance the shopping environment during the season, and to basically put [people] in the mood to shop."[7]

On average, America's malls spend just over twenty thousand dollars on Christmas decorating, although regional malls may spend as much as one hundred thousand dollars for a major display. The average mall adds one full-time employee and four part-timers to help them with holiday preparations. So if "it's beginning to look a lot like Christmas," it's largely because America's shopping centers are setting the stage for the season. No other institution, except perhaps the American home, does so much to establish the look of the holiday. The "old and lovable" motifs and mall decorations include light strings, stars, poinsettias, snowflakes, snowmen, Christmas trees, wreaths, pine cones, cardinals, ornaments, Santa Claus, elves, reindeer (especially red-nosed ones), sleighs, gift boxes, bows, and nutcrackers. Each of these motifs has a story of its own, and each works within the larger narrative of an American Christmas.[8]

One important motif in mall displays and promotions is children. Christmas is a holiday for children, and for adults who wish to recall the wonder of their own childhood. At Christmas, therefore, shopping centers love to cater to children, whose acquisitive instincts are presumed to be innocent. Store designers use fairy tales and folk stories, and their commercialized equivalents—like Disney movie motifs—to attract the attention of the juvenile mind. Stores create magical Toylands to appeal to the younger set and often tie in a proprietary stuffed animal with a storewide promotion. Malls bring in Santa Claus to get children thinking about their unmet material desires.

But there aren't enough real children to make Christmas really profitable, so one of the functions of Christmas displays is to make metaphorical children out

Christmas Shopping

of all of us. "How better to 'Celebrate the Season,'" Martin Pegler says, "than through the eyes—the mind—and the heart of a child." For a child, Pegler says, Christmas "is a time to celebrate and to thoroughly enjoy being young and innocent and being the receiver of the many good things Christmas promises to bring." In this formulation, being young and innocent is connected to the "joy of getting." And, of course, childish innocence also means being oblivious to the commercial causes of our joy.[9]

A related theme of commercial Christmas displays is the family. As Pegler suggests, "Home for the Holidays strikes a deep responsive chord in many viewers' hearts." Even though Christians go both to church and the mall during the holiday season, the holy place of the holiday is the home. So designers evoke our family feelings then sell them back to us in material form. In a society with millions of homeless people, and with millions more whose homes are a mere rest stop between frenetic activities, the ideal of home is still a potent one. In a society where 70 percent of us don't know our neighbors, the promise of home entertaining at Christmas is a way of dealing with our astonishing loss of social capital.[10]

While Pegler develops a long list of contemporary themes that keep Christmas ever green—childhood and the family, lights and evergreens, Santa Claus and his bag of gifts, reindeer and elves, and the North Pole—he also highlights a few important traditional themes. Pegler notes, for example, that many store displays use Renaissance and Victorian motifs to promote their products. These motifs work in several ways. The Renaissance motif usually involves reproductions of paintings of the Madonna and Child, the three kings, or the manger scene. It hints at the religious meanings that cannot be foregrounded in a mall, as religious art allows a secular culture to display beliefs it has largely banished from public life. The Renaissance motif also helps to make the occasion more sublimely aesthetic. When store designers invoke classic artwork, they associate the department store with the museum, with established aesthetic traditions, and with the refined taste that can appreciate art that's not painted on black velvet. Renaissance motifs make it seem like all our commercial activity is somehow aesthetic as well as materialistic, religious as well as economic. The process basically makes advertising spokesmen of Renaissance artists, transforming their paintings into contemporary commercial art, and suggesting that if an all-American Christmas was good enough for Michelangelo, it should be good enough for us.[11]

Producing Consumers

Victorian motifs work a little differently, evoking "the good olde days" of the nineteenth century, when Christmas was a holiday unsullied by commercial activity. As Martin Pegler says, "Old-fashioned seems to be synonymous with Christmas." Although one of Victoria's secrets is that the contemporary American Christmas was invented by Victorians and that it was *always* commercial, we conveniently forget this history in our nostalgia for the warm feeling of a family like the Cratchits. By identifying our Christmas with the prim and proper Victorians, we can perhaps displace the doubts we feel about participating in the new-fashioned Christmas that violates so many old-fashioned values.[12]

It's not just visual merchandisers who help to create the spirit of Christmas in the shopping center: aural merchandisers also loop their tracks. We shop to the beat of our favorite Christmas carols and novelty songs. AEI Music, a Muzak competitor, suggests, for example, that "seasonal music can strengthen all your efforts and bring the holiday to life for customers. Create an atmosphere that promotes gift-buying and merry celebrating with a smart assortment of AEI's Holiday programs."[13]

The American shopping center sets the stage for an American family Christmas. But shopping centers elsewhere also get dressed up for the holidays. As Melanie Conty suggests in *Shopping Centers Today*, "Because American culture has spread around the globe, North American-based holiday designers are finding their services needed in Europe, Africa, Asia, and South America, where Christmas is also a big deal." During the 1990s, one Brazilian mall spent more than $3 million on Christmas decor. And a mall in Kobe, Japan—a country with only a handful of Christians—employed Center Stage Design of Paterson, New Jersey to create their Christmas look. So it's beginning to look a lot like Christmas around the world, with evergreens and holiday lights helping to keep people in the spirit of shopping.[14]

Adventures in Advent

The mall's decorative preparations for Christmas are supplemented by the TV specials and ad supplements that help to prepare *us* for Christmas. The first big batch arrives with the newspaper on Thanksgiving Day, and the rest accompany the subsequent Sunday papers. With all the catalogues that have been coming

since September, these ads put the "ad" in "Advent," and they're filled with phrases so clichéd that we've ceased to think about them. And yet these ads are carefully researched and designed. So a little scrutiny helps us to think twice about several themes of the contemporary American culture of Christmas.

Retail stores and catalogue companies deluge consumers with attractive advertising designed to convert Christmas customs into customers. One retailer claims to be "Where Christmas Begins"; another contends that it's "Your Holiday Gift Headquarters." One store promises that it is "making the holidays merry," as if merriment were inextricably associated with the hundreds of items in the circular. All of this publicity is filled with pictures of products, a few words of descriptive copy, a price, and some sort of hype. Two things make these circulars seasonal: the decorative detail that evokes the holiday season, and an emphasis on commodities as gifts.

Each year, one of the main themes in these circulars is wishful thinking. One department store presents its ads as a book of stuff called "The Wish List," a list to help people "make wishes come true." Most of the ads of the commercial Advent focus on helping us find the right gifts to fulfill the wishes of the loved ones in our lives, but one store asks candidly, "What are *you* wishing for?" Such establishments understand that Christmas is a season of wishful thinking *and* wish fulfillment—that we go Christmas shopping not just to fulfill the wishes of others, but our own wishes too.

Some retailers refer to their circulars as Christmas "gift books." This tactic transforms the products they've been selling all year long into something special and unselfish—a gift. Throughout our malls, retailers offer what are called "gift

Producing Consumers

solutions," as if giving were somehow a problem for Americans. The problem can be solved, the flyers suggest, if we purchase "the perfect gift." If you read the circulars carefully, you'll soon see that the gift's perfection occurs when the gift the recipient wants *most* coincides with the commodity the retailer *most* wants to sell. One store even offers the "perfect gift guarantee," which basically means that purchases are returnable.

Other circulars promise "great gift ideas for everyone on your list." This common phrase does double duty. First, it reminds us that Christmas shopping is an act of imagination, matching personal preferences with impersonal commodities to produce "the perfect gift." It's hard work, and we ritually complain about it all season long. Second, this phrase normalizes the idea of the Christmas list, the roster of people to be coordinated with a list of commodities in this seasonal game of matchmaking. Such phrases emphasize the planning and preparation involved in Christmas shopping, and the amount of work that goes into it.

Newspapers and magazines join their supplements in the promotion of a commercial Christmas with stories about "what's hot this season" and advice for good gift selection. The ICSC publishes a list of "what's hot" on the "Holiday Watch" section of its web site. The "hot" items for a cold season are a cultural curiosity, in part because they become hot even before they begin to sell. This anticipatory "hotness" is a kind of prospective peer pressure, letting us know what we need to buy to be up-to-date.

Trade magazines and the business press approach the season differently, making Christmas shopping into news. The ICSC publishes a weekly "Holiday Watch," and other business groups also track holiday sales with eager anticipation. As the season approaches, commentators rehearse predictions of analysts and experts. After the first weekend, they take stock again. In 2001, for example, a *New York Times* story reported, "Shoppers' Solid Start Gives Hope to U.S. Retailers": "Deep discounts on items from CDs to turtleneck sweaters lured shoppers to the mall during the Thanksgiving weekend, but consumers did not turn out in the way they did last year. And it is still unclear whether they will spend robustly enough to help pull the economy out of its downturn." Such ritual stories report what's happened, but also suggest that consumers are shopping not just for the perfect gift but also for the perfect economy—a perpetually growing gross domestic product."[15]

Sometimes the stories are more specific. Each year, for example, there are stories on toys. In 2001, a story titled "Toy Firms Bank on Harry Potter Holiday Magic" described the new line of licensed toys and the strategy of Warner Worldwide Consumer Products in producing toys for each and every age group. Pointing out that half of America's $23 billion expenditure on toys falls during the final quarter of the year, it described toy retailers' hope that movie tie-in toys would "produce a bit of magic themselves: a profitable holiday season." A few days later, another article on "scarce commodities" reported on toys that were selling out quickly, including the Harry Potter Hogwarts castle, the Babbling Boo doll, and toys connected with the Disney hit *Monsters, Inc.* A few days after that, as if to console parents for their presumed failure to get the hottest toys for their children, a third article listed the "classic toys"—Legos, Lincoln Logs, Silly Putty, Yo-Yos, Slinky, Monopoly, and so on—that "have fascinated kids generation after generation." All of these stories are written within an interpretive frame that presumes that parents should buy Christmas toys for their children: no articles question that commercial presumption.[16]

Each year, too, there are articles on extravagant gifts. Often, these report on the new Neiman Marcus offerings: his and her miniature submarines or hot air balloons or matching camels. Besides being great publicity for the upscale Texas department store chain, these articles assure us that even though we're spending a small fortune on our Christmas gifts, other people are spending a large fortune. In a culture of relative morality, their extravagance helps to make our extravagance seem like prudence, or even wisdom.[17]

The outcome of all this advertising and promotion is not exactly known, since most of us already intend to buy Christmas gifts. These ads may point us to particular stores and products, and prices and promotions might convince us to "Act now!" instead of later. More broadly, the presence of these ads certainly reinforces our desire to buy presents, and they legitimize the commercialization of Christmas. At the same time, these ads both reflect and affect our American histories of love, and family, and gift giving, and Christianity.

Santa Claus

When "'Tis the season to be jolly," nobody is more jolly than Santa Claus, the central character in the American folk celebration of Christmas. Every

November, Santa appears in most of America's malls, where the nation's children wait in line to speak to him. They climb on his lap, and, if they're not too terrified, they tell him if they've been naughty or nice. Like religious penitents, they confess their transgressions, ask for absolution, emphasize their special graces, and then plead for indulgences—or at least indulgence.

Santa Claus was the most important element of the "invented tradition" of an American family Christmas. Loosely connected to his European ancestors Saint Nicholas, Sinterklaas, Father Christmas, and Pere Noel, the American Santa Claus "is more than an amalgam of these characters and is instead uniquely American." Unlike all Santa's ancestors, the American Santa has no religious associations, no bishop's robe or staff or mitre. Unlike the other Clauses, Santa is a tangible figure, more visible than invisible, appearing all over the holiday landscape. And while the Clauses in other countries usually bring fruit and nuts and homemade toys for children's stockings, the American Santa is a profligate giver of brand-name commercial items. And finally, even though Santa claims to be discriminating between the naughty and nice, he's not really a punitive figure.[18]

The American Santa Claus is also a quintessentially commercial icon, drafted by merchants and advertising agencies into the service of increased sales. As early as 1845, Santa could be seen in a New York candy store. By the 1870s and 1880s, he often appeared on merchants' holiday trade cards. During the 1880s and 1890s, American department stores installed Santa in their stores, first as an icon in the display windows, then as a living presence in Toyland. Beginning in 1924, he began to appear in Macy's Thanksgiving Day Parade. And as soon as there were shopping centers, Santa became a fixture in their seasonal sales. At one level, this commercial Santa is the Christmas counterpoint to Christ. "While Christ reigns in the realm of the spirit," notes anthropologist Russell Belk, "Santa's realm is that of material abundance. . . . Santa is first and foremost a symbol of material abundance and hedonistic pleasures."[19]

These days, Santa Claus is brought to us by the merchants of the mall, who hope that parents will purchase Santa's presents at their shops. "Santa is very big business," says Diana Leone, marketing manager for a Michigan mall. The ICSC also keeps track of Santa. At 86 percent of American malls, Santa's arrival is marked by a special ceremony—usually a parade. And according to the ICSC, mall Santas average 8,750 visits by children per mall per season.[20]

The Santa Clause (Image by Wernher Krutein)

There's only one Santa, of course, but every regional mall in America needs one, so the demand is generally greater than the natural supply. Fortunately, several companies provide Santas for America's shopping centers. The oldest, Santa Plus, dates to the 1920s, when *Chicago Sun-Times* photographer Sid Samuels began using his flash camera to take Santa photos at department stores. Today, Santa Plus places over fifteen hundred Santas at about four hundred malls.[21]

Santa Plus and other Claus suppliers select people for looks, personality, people skills, voice, eyes, and endurance. Most companies pay a premium, up to ten thousand dollars a season, for portly men with real white whiskers. People who need wigs and padding get paid a lot less, usually less than ten dollars an hour. Not surprisingly, the Santa suppliers like people who like people. "We look for a congenial Santa with a twinkle in his eye," says one company executive. "He must have stamina, patience, and love the spirit of Christmas." And most of their Santas do: over 80 percent of Santas come back for another year because they enjoy the interactions with kids.[22]

The prospective Santas must pass a criminal background check before they

Producing Consumers

begin training in the art of impersonation. At one company, applicants must attend Santa Claus University, where they spend a day learning the "do's and don'ts" of their role as Santa. Santas are warned to bathe daily and use a good deodorant. They learn how to dress, how to apply makeup, and how to lift children without straining muscles. The actors are told to keep in character, and to refer to the customers as "folks." Santa doesn't refer to "boys" and girls"—it's "young men" and "young women." And he only speaks of himself in the third person. In training, Santas learn to be subordinate Clauses, asking questions, and listening to kids. They practice answering hard questions, including the names of the reindeer and the perennial question "Are you real?" They learn all the season's hot toys and become conversant with the contemporary culture of children, including favorite games, TV shows, and so on. They learn never to promise anything but to say, "Santa will take that into consideration." And they learn to excuse themselves by "going to feed the reindeer."[23]

One Santa manufacturer, Cherry Hill Photo, announces on its web site that "no one believes in Santa more than we do. Last year alone we placed more than 180 naturally bearded Santas in malls and department stores throughout the country. Our Santas have even reached celebrity status, appearing on television programs such as CBS's '48 Hours' and in advertisements around the world. It is easy to see why. Our selection process and intensive training assures that not only do our Santas look the part, they become the part. If you would like more information on how a 'real' Santa can bring 'real' success to your next Christmas photo promotion, please call."[24]

As this suggests, even a child's visit with Santa has been commercialized as a photo opportunity. The sign in front of Santa's castle announces "Photos of Santa with Your Little Elves." You can get a five-by-seven-inch photo for $10.99, with additional prints for just $5.99. You can buy an eight-by-ten for 15.99 or a five-by-seven and four wallet photos for $19.99. Families aren't forced to buy a photo, but "suggestion selling" by Santa's helpers makes sure that most of them do. Both Santa Plus and Cherry Hill Photo Enterprises are in the business of selling photographs, and they're quite successful, averaging 10,250 photographs per mall for the holiday season. With their many happy returns, the companies pay Santa and his helpers, and they pay the mall a fixed percentage of sales. The rest is profit.[25]

But even though he's a commercial invention, Santa is also a social construction. His is a story that most Americans tell, and so the characteristics of the American Santa Claus can tell us something about our own character. Santa Claus, for example, is supernatural. Like the traditional God, Santa is omniscient, knowing all about our every activity. Like God, Santa is theoretically a judge, separating the good from the evil and assigning appropriate rewards for good behavior. Thankfully, however, Santa Claus is more merciful than just. Like God, Santa works miracles—like flying reindeer—to present gifts to people. Unlike the Deity, however, Santa is also a god who laughs. As one writer says, Santa has all of the advantages of Jesus without any of the hang-ups. In malls of America, he's probably more congenial than Jesus would be. Santa's a god who blesses the American Christmas. Willing to give people as much as they can afford—and then some—he's an appropriate icon for an affluent society.[26]

Like God, too, Santa is a guy, and, with Mrs. Claus, he often reinforces gender roles of American culture. Indeed, it's ironic that an old man is the chief symbol of a holiday orchestrated mainly by America's women. Still, as a guy, Santa plays the stereotypically masculine role of provider, bringing home the metaphorical bacon to households throughout the nation. He also teaches boys and girls to be men and women, as do the gifts he brings in his bag. Western Temporary Services, a California company that hires more than thirty-six hundred Santas a year, tells their Clauses to greet boys by saying "You're growing tall." But the suggested line for girls is "What a pretty dress!" Boys will be boys, as we say, and girls will be attractive. Boys will want action toys, and girls will get Barbie. And Americans will get another generation of traditional gender roles.

With his white hair and beard, Santa is also an old guy. He's been around the block once or twice, and he understands the privileges of age. Like a grandparent, for example, he's allowed to spoil kids more than the parents who have their children's moral development in mind. Santa's indulgence of children is related to his own self-indulgence; his round little belly makes him a fitting figure for an American culture of obesity. A slim Santa would be too judgmental, too much in control. Better the jolly gentleman who indulges himself, and hopefully us, a little too much.

In the American mythology, Santa's main job is the distribution of presents on Christmas Eve. In reality, Santa's prominent role in our rituals confirms the

Producing Consumers

centrality of secular exchanges, both commercial and personal, to the American Christmas. He disassociates the presents he distributes from their commercial contexts and decontaminates them by magically transforming commercial commodities into a thought that counts. Santa's loaded sack obscures the actual origins of our gifts. The myth of Santa's workshop obscures the reality of workshops in the Third World. And the Santa myth also obscures the social and ecological costs of Christmas consumption. The Great Decontaminator, Santa allows American businesses to sell indulgence religiously. Originally the patron saint of children and fishermen, our secular Saint Nicholas is now the patron saint of shopping centers.

As the Great Decontaminator, Santa also allows parents to indulge children more than they should. Santa's devotion to children makes Christmas a celebration of childhood and youthful innocence. As such, Christmas is a dramatic counterpoint to broad cultural patterns of child neglect and children's poverty. One out of four American children are born in poverty, and one in five is poor now: one of every eleven kids lives at less than half the poverty level. One of three American children is born to unmarried parents, and one in four lives with just one parent. One out of five children is born to a mother who received no prenatal care in the crucial first three months of pregnancy, and one out of seven American children has no health insurance. One of three American kids is a year or more behind in school, and one out of every two will never complete a single year of college. Americans love children, it seems, but mainly in their own families. We contribute generously to Toys for Tots, but we seem incapable of extending the spirit of Christmas much beyond the Christmas season.[27]

It should be no surprise, of course, that Santa Claus reflects American cultural values. It's important to remember that he exemplifies a spirit of unselfish generosity that's increasingly rare in a commercial and contractual society. But if the true spirit of Christmas is not just generosity, but justice, we may want to rethink our conceptions of Santa.

The Perfect Gift

Shopping centers and retailers advertise their Christmas specials; they decorate for the holidays; and they play host to Santa Claus—all to help us focus on

Christmas Shopping

Christmas gifts. With a gift list in hand (or in head), we traipse off to the mall in search of "the perfect gift" for spouses, children, relatives, friends, colleagues, and (sometimes) acquaintances. And we shop intensely. As sociologist Theodore Caplow notes, Christmas shopping "mobilizes almost the entire population for several weeks, accounts for about 4% of its total annual expenditure, and takes precedence over ordinary forms of work and leisure." Christmas shopping and gift giving are a complex cultural activity, a blend of personal preferences and cultural rules, a combination of generosity and greed, a mix of spirit and materialism. Still it's possible to unwrap at least some of the cultural meanings of the gifts we buy at the mall.[28]

Like other elements of the "invented tradition" of an American family Christmas, shopping and gift giving haven't been stable elements of the celebration. Early English settlers to America brought their tradition of giving gifts, not to each other, but to servants and the poor. In this incarnation, gift giving was a part of a carnival inversion in which standard social roles were suspended and reversed for a day. By the 1870s, charitable "fancy" fairs sold homemade gifts created by women. But commercial commodities and "Christmas shopping" still played just a small part in a "traditional" American Christmas.[29]

In 1874, Macy's initiated the promotion of manufactured goods with a window display containing ten thousand dollars' worth of imported dolls. Between 1880 and 1920, department stores intensified this publicity, both with advertising and store displays. But Americans remained uneasy about the message of materialism in these self-serving promotions. So the department stores began to offer strategies for sacralizing materialism. Offering a commodity as a "Christmas gift" changed its character, because it blanketed impersonal manufactures with a cloak of personal generosity. Newly popular wrapping paper also covered the commodification of Christmas, especially if gift givers removed the price tags that marked the commercial exchange. And, of course, Santa Claus also served to decontaminate the commercial character of commodities. Together, these promotions helped Americans get into "the spirit of giving."[30]

Over time, Americans have developed clear patterns of gift exchange. We generally think that we are following personal preferences in selecting our Christmas gifts, but Caplow suggests that there are *social* rules to Christmas gift giving, with lots of complicated corollaries. For example, the "rule of relativity" says that gifts are not given randomly, but to express and reproduce social relationships. We give gifts to people we relate to: sometimes these people are relatives, sometimes they're friends; occasionally, they're people we work with. Sometimes families or offices draw names to channel gift giving, but even such a lottery is an expression of the familial bond and boundaries.[31]

The "scaling rules" demand that gifts be scaled to the emotional value of the relationship. During this holy season, feelings and sentiments are converted into commodities, and vice versa. The gift is both a way of pleasing the recipient, *and* a way of reinforcing social status hierarchies. The size of your gift has less to do, in fact, with your actual affection for people than it does with social expectations of affection in these relationships. Spouses come first, then children. Parents of adults are less important than immediate family, but more important than siblings. You can't give a bigger gift to your secretary than to your husband; you can't favor one child over the others; you can't exchange with one set of in-laws but not the other. Most disputes over gifts can be traced to differing estimations of the value of relationships.[32]

"Fitness rules" determine who may give what to whom. You can't give underwear to business associates. You can't give alcohol to minors or to alcoholics. You can't give pink to men. Adults may give money to children, but not vice versa. Men can't give diamonds or intimate apparel to every woman they know. Women can't give flowers to men. You shouldn't give clothing that doesn't fit, and you especially shouldn't give women clothing that's too large. You can't give things that are *too* practical or utilitarian. Indeed, we often say that a gift should be something that a person wouldn't buy themselves, which means, in practice, that a gift should be, by definition, something we don't need, something in excess of enough, somewhere in the range of too much.[33]

The "reciprocity rule" says basically that, unless you are a child, if someone gives you a gift, you have to return the favor. Conversely, if you give a gift, you can expect to get one, thus providing an ulterior motive for generosity. There is one complicated clause in the reciprocity rule, and that is, of course, "the Santa clause." The Santa clause permits parents to spoil their children with too many gifts, especially if the gifts come from the season's symbol of generosity and indulgence, jolly old Saint Nick. Santa Claus also allows parents to escape from their own principles. One couple, for example, refused to buy their children toy guns, but, using the Santa clause—the escape clause from principle and consistency—they managed to arm their youngster without violating their own opposition to violence.[34]

The "surprise rule" suggests that gifts should surprise the recipient, either by their generosity, or by some creative variation on an established theme. You can get Dad another tie, but if you do it right, you'll get a tie that's different without, of course, being too different. The "publicity rule" suggests that gifts should be public, opened in front of the family or community, so that everyone can judge the gift giver's skill in interpreting and applying the rules of giving. Paralleling the surprise rule and the publicity rule is the "Kodak corollary," which specifies that people should be photographed at the exact moment they open a gift, thus documenting our relationship with things, and the person's reaction to this personal gift. Even if you don't like the gift you've received, the rules of Christmas mandate that you should act pleased.[35]

The "rule of personal touch" suggests that gifts must be personalized, if not actually personal, showing some understanding of the recipient's taste and life-style. Except in unusual circumstances, you can't actually give adults money for Christmas, because that would be too crassly economic. Instead, you can launder the money by buying a gift certificate, which at least shows your personal awareness of the recipient's shopping preferences.

All of these rules imply that we're buying gifts for someone else, but increasingly Americans are also buying gifts for themselves. These "self-gifts" are interesting, justified not by our relation to the recipient (as other gifts are), but by our own sense that "we deserve it." We seem to think that if Santa no longer rewards our good behavior, perhaps we should reward ourselves. A national chain that understands this new pattern of gift giving advertises its stock as "All *You* Want for Christmas."

Sometimes, of course, these "self-gifts" are disguised as exchanges. When we tell each other precisely what we want for Christmas, we essentially become members of a mutual acquisition society. As Russell Belk suggests, one function of such pseudo-exchanges is to "acquire luxuries (as gifts) without suffering the concomitant guilt of self-indulgence that might accrue from buying these same things for ourselves."[36]

Gift certificates also try to hide the materialistic aspects of gift exchange. They operate on the presumption that the person with the best sense of a gift's personal

Producing Consumers

fitness is the person him/herself. More and more, therefore, Americans seem to believe that the perfect gift is a gift certificate—because then everybody gets exactly what they want. B. Dalton Books highlights the B. Dalton gift card, and advises us to "let them choose their favorite things." Kohl's promises "more gift giving pleasure" from its "Make the Season Bright" gift card, because "the choice is theirs—the value is yours." With our gift certificates, we become, in effect, our own Santas. In these cases, "self-gifts" stretch both the fitness and the personal touch rules by implying that a gift is not so much an act of altruism and affirmation as the presentation of a particular product. We still tell ourselves that it's the thought that counts, but we often act as if it's the thing that counts more.[37]

The rules of Christmas giving are complicated because gift giving is a complex social task. Structurally speaking, too, Christmas gifts fulfill complex purposes. They help us to deal with the fact that we are persons, human beings, living in a global economy characterized by competition, calculation, and human exploitation. In fact, according to James Carrier, Christmas shopping is the way we domesticate the global economy. Carrier contends that shopping for gifts is an essential component of an American family Christmas, because such shopping is not entirely materialistic—it's also a protest against materialism. If globalization is the economic trend of the early twenty-first century, domestication is its counterpoint.[38]

Carrier suggests that we know, at some level, that commercial capitalism is inadequate to the task of being fully human. We know that if we ask "What are people for?" commercial capitalism doesn't have the answer. Christmas, he says, is the time when we ritually prove to ourselves that we can control the capitalism that mostly controls us. We do this by shopping, by transforming the cold commodities of an impersonal economy into something both personal and meaningful: we make things into gifts. In malls of America, the objects of our desire are still just objects. "They are manufactured in the world of work and express only the impersonal desire for profit by the company that made them and the impersonal acting out of work roles lightly adopted and in return for money, by the unknown people who produced them." When we buy these objects, we engage in an impersonal exchange of money for commodity. But we also engage in an act of personal selection. We have chosen *this* item with *that* person in mind. When we present these gifts, wrapped with the price tags removed, we transmute them into expressions of personal affection and relationship. In the process, we personalize the impersonal; we domesticate the market.[39]

This is why handmade gifts aren't as popular as store-bought goods for Christmas giving. Only 2 percent of American Christmas gifts are homemade, and it isn't just because we're lazy or unskilled. It's because homemade gifts can't convey this important cultural message. They show us how to opt out of the commercial economy, but purchased gifts, and the rituals that accompany them, show us how to appropriate the commodities of American capitalism to our own purposes all year long.[40]

In this way, Christmas shopping itself is as important as the family gift exchange. Malls are as important to Christmas as the family living room, because shopping is how we demonstrate that we can make personal meanings using the impersonal objects of the market. As Carrier explains, "Americans see family and friendship as surrounded by the impersonal world 'out there,' the world of work and alienated commodities. It is the Christmas shopping that proves to them that they can create a sphere of familial love in the face of a world of money. Shopping is a key part of Christmas." Christmas shopping reassures us that even though we live in a market economy, we're not yet reduced to mere market relationships. It tells us that we can still carve out a community that operates according to different values. Paradoxically, Christmas shopping is the antimaterialist appropriation of American materialism—and vice versa.[41]

It's an irony, of course, that we transform commercialism mainly in the market with money. We *transform* commercial capitalism just for the holiday season, instead of *re*forming it for good. But perhaps Christmas and our Christmas shopping point us in the direction of a better world, a world redeemed in part by our own efforts to incarnate the virtues and values that redeem us as human beings.

The True Spirit of Christmas

One venerable Christmas tradition in America is complaining about the commercialism of many holiday customs. Some Americans don't participate in Christmas at all, and sometimes they complain about the extraordinary cultured power of the holiday. Sometimes the criticism is religious. Even though not all Americans are Christian, critics often claim that commercialism has taken Christ

128

out of Christmas, and, in fact, there's plenty of evidence to support their claim. A 1999 poll found that 61 percent of Americans think Christmas has less religious significance than it did when they were growing up, and 54 percent attributed that decline to increased emphasis on shopping and gift giving. And, of course, the time we spend shopping is time not spent in religious observation or church festivities.[42]

By connecting shopping to Christmas, critics contend, Americans have almost made shopping a spiritual obligation. The mall becomes our cathedral of consumption and Santa our patron saint. We all join the repeated processional and recessional throughout the season. Muzak carols are our sacred hymns; the food court is our communion table. We pray for bargains, and if we find them, the sale is our salvation. While the church doesn't sell indulgences any more, the mall does sell indulgence, and many of us buy. The cash register is the tabernacle that contains the Holy of Holies, the Almighty Dollar, and the sales counter is the altar upon which we sacrifice our money and our lives for the redemption that consumption promises to bring.

Since 1973, a nonprofit organization called Alternatives for Simple Living has tried to "equip people of faith to challenge consumerism, live justly, and celebrate responsibly." Alternatives began as a protest against the commercialization of Christmas, and currently focuses "on encouraging celebrations that reflect conscientious ways of living." Working mainly with Christian churches, the organization publishes a book called *Whose Birthday Is It, Anyway?* suggesting that Americans should focus less on the gospel of consumption and more on the gospel of justice. The book is intended for people of faith and comes in several different denominational editions. It includes scripture suggestions and reflections on Biblical passages, some of them written by social critic and environmentalist Bill McKibben. It also suggests "alternative giving"—Christmas gifts to charities and relief organizations—as an option for Christmas. Each year the organization puts out a Christmas kit to help people celebrate the true spirit of Christmas; the 2001 kit includes one greeting card that reads, "Buy me nothing. I'll still love you." Distinguishing the gifts of the Magi from the gifts of an American commercial Christmas, another card reminds us that "bearing gifts doesn't make us wise." The organization also acts as a clearinghouse for resources on simple living and voluntary simplicity.[43]

Secular critics of Christmas offer an additional litany of problems: seasonal stress; excess and extravagance; credit-card debt and bankruptcies; advertising that suggests that you can buy a person's love; rampant materialism; and opportunity costs (both economic and spiritual). They often use shopping centers as a symbol of the things that are wrong with the holiday. An organization called SCROOGE—the Society to Curtail Ridiculous, Outrageous, and Ostentatious Gift Exchanges—criticizes our lavish expenditures on impractical and conspicuous gifts. The society asks members to avoid expensive purchases, especially heavily promoted fad and status items. They suggest exchanging gifts that involve thought and originality, including handmade, homemade items, and in general they encourage people to experience the joys of the season by avoiding its commercial excesses.[44]

The critics of Christmas also worry about the scope of the traditional American Christmas. They admit that America's gift rules help us to negotiate the Christmas season in the social space of our families, but they argue that these rules don't extend far enough. The rules of relativity and reciprocity organize our giving, but they confine its scope to people we know and love. They're part and parcels of the increasing privatism of American life. It's good to love our families, of course, but the challenge of Christianity, they say, is to give to people we don't know and don't love. To critics, the surprise rule is like the bumper sticker that asks us to practice random acts of kindness. Surprise and spontaneity are fine, they say, but critics contend that we are also called to *institutional* acts of kindness and generosity—and justice.

Christian critics like McKibben suggest that sometimes our focus on Christmas shopping and gift exchanges keep us from focusing on more significant gifts. At their best, they say, our rules for gift giving should remind people of the gift of Creation. They should challenge us to think about the global economy as a gift economy, and to think twice about our cultural patterns of getting and getting ahead. Further, they should remind us that, as gifted people, we have responsibilities to give ourselves, not just to family and friends, but to all of God's Creation.[45]

As these critics show, it's easy to be critical of Christmas shopping. It's important, however, to be thoughtful too, even about the criticism. Some of the criticism of our Christmas customs is dualistic, suggesting that we're either Christians

Producing Consumers

or consumers, even though Americans have lived with the tensions of both for more than a century. Some of the criticism is nostalgic rather than historical, based on a mythical "Christmas Past" undefiled by commercial concerns. Some of the criticism is almost sectarian, a fear that other traditions, such as Hanukkah or Kwanza, dilute the "true spirit" of Christmas. Of course, many of the criticisms are just plain right. Sometimes our Christmas customs, including our Christmas shopping, do feature the worst aspects of our consumption culture.

Yet while there's a lot to criticize in the American consumer's Christmas, there's also much to praise. It's important to remember, for example, that shopping centers already practice the true spirit of Christmas. They serve as collection points for the Salvation Army's bell ringers and for programs like Toys for Tots, which make Christmas happier for kids whose families can't afford the whole Christmas package. Many malls make holiday contributions to charities. Some malls even provide space for people who sell certificates for charitable donations. Southdale Center, for example, houses a kiosk that sells gift certificates for "alternative gifts" to charities and nonprofit groups.[46]

It's also important to remember that commercialism makes Christmas a bigger deal than it could ever possibly be as the exclusive provenance of church or family. At the same time that commercialism detracts from the "true spirit" of the holiday, it also contributes to it. As historian Leigh Eric Schmidt suggests, "the commercial aggrandizement of Christmas only served to make religious symbols all that much more public and pervasive." At least until the Supreme Court rulings of the 1980s, and our increasing pride in our rich multiculturalism, a commercial Christmas could support the "true spirit" of Christmas. And it's still true, according to Schmidt, that "the marketplace helps raise, for a few days at least, the tattered remnants of the old banner of a Christian America." Shopping centers may be focused on the "false spirit" of a commercial Christmas, but they seem to promote the "true spirit" at the same time.[47]

Americans who shop at malls also practice the "true spirit" even in the midst of their materialism. It's not an either/or situation. At the holidays, Americans spend profligately, but we also tuck our coins and bills in the Salvation Army's kettles, and we increase our charitable contributions significantly. It's no accident that charities and nonprofits send us their solicitations during the holiday season. Organizations like UNICEF and Heifer International encourage us to

131

extend our giving beyond the boundaries of family, and church groups teach children to focus not just on the gifts they get, but on the gifts they have to share with the world. As odd as it may sound, our Christmas shopping seems to get us in the mood for Christmas caring too.

In some ways, after all, materialism *is* the message of the "true" Christmas. For Christians, Christmas commemorates the feast of the incarnation, the time when the Word was made flesh, the season when God put the skin on love. Christmas is the season in which embodied people celebrate the embodiment, the materialization, of God. Unfortunately, when critics get to thinking about the true spirit of Christmas, they sometimes forget the flesh that's being celebrated. Indeed, the "true-spirit" protesters often tend to disembody Jesus. But the message of a religious Christmas is the delightful dance of spirit *and* flesh, of spirit *in* flesh, of the spirit *of* flesh. Christmas tells people that there's holiness in the world as well as out of it.[48]

If we ever did de-commercialize Christmas, contends historian Penne Restad, "we probably wouldn't keep it as a society." Eric Schmidt agrees, noting that the commercialization of Christmas does important cultural work "by taking in diverse, local traditions and creating relatively common ones." A Christmas without commercialism wouldn't be nearly as powerful, in part because the new observance "would lack the cultural resonance and impact of a holiday rooted in the marketplace."[49]

Malls serve as official sponsors of the American family Christmas. They serve several basic functions for us. They set the stage for the holiday season, using commercial art to create one spirit of Christmas. They play carols and novelty songs that may lift our spirits, and they sell many of the gifts we give to each other. They provide a place for Santa Claus. When we do our Christmas shopping at the mall, we are paying for these practical services.

But we're also paying for cultural work that supersedes the simple transactions of the shopping center. At Christmas, shopping centers (and Santa) socialize our children for consumption. By connecting consumption to family and religion, they legitimize a consuming culture. The American mall Christmas keeps retailers and the economy in the black, reinforcing an economic system that depends on consumer spending.

Shopping centers aren't, in fact, the center of an American Christmas. If all the malls disappeared tomorrow, it would complicate Christmas, but it would-n't compromise the celebration. The real center of an American Christmas isn't the mall or even the church; it's the living room. Still, even though shopping centers aren't the main course of an American Christmas, they apply a lot of the seasoning for the season. Shopping centers set the stage for the celebrations that embody the true spirit of Christmas.

And shopping centers probably help explain the fact that Christmas is our favorite holiday, even though it's the most commercial. Indeed, these two facts are likely related. Seventy-seven percent of us exchange gifts for Christmas, and 63 percent attend a church service during the holiday season. We expect Christmas shopping to take about sixteen hours each year—two full workdays—but we expect to spend about the same amount of time at religious services. Two-thirds of us tell pollsters that we focus on "the material aspects of Christmas" instead of the spiritual aspects. Eighty percent of us say that Christmas is more a commercial holiday than a religious observance, and about 80 percent of us dislike the commercialism. Only 3 percent of us list shopping as our favorite activity. Increasing numbers of us would eliminate gift giving as a part of the Christmas ritual, but if we had more money, 30 percent of us would spend significantly more on gifts. Bah, humbug![50]

But we still like Christmas. Although most of us think that Santa Claus and gift giving detract from the true spirit of Christmas, almost half of us think that our secular customs actually enhance the religious celebration. We may not like gift giving, but we persist in giving gifts. Indeed, more than 60 percent of cat and dog owners give their pets a Christmas present. About 80 percent of us agree that "Christmas brings out the best in people," and about the same percentage say that "Christmas is a time of reflection for me" and that the holiday "rejuvenates me." We may be suspicious about the shopping center's sponsorship of Santa, but 95 percent of us believed in Mr. Claus, and most of us will teach our children about the jolly old elf.[51]

The commercialism of Christmas may be overdone, but it provides a way for Americans to do important personal and cultural work, especially concerning our ambivalence about consumption and materialism. For many Americans, Christmas ties consumption to religion and the family. It defines the circles of family and friends in American culture and socializes children for consumption. It provides an outlet for traditional winter festivals of light and, with New Year's Day, provides twin celebrations—one retrospective, the other prospective. Christmas is a grand American complexity, and shopping centers are a complex part of the holiday. Despite the commercialism of the season—and perhaps because of it—we Americans still get "Santa-mental" about Christmas.

Producing Consumers

PART THREE

Mallpractices

What We Do at the Mall

EIGHT

Just Looking

You know the situation. You're in a store in your local mall. A clerk approaches and asks, "May I help you?" And you say, "No thanks, I'm just looking."

Of course, when store clerks ask if they can help us, they don't mean it literally or comprehensively. They don't plan to help us with our work, our children, or our emotional distress. Instead, the question "May I help you?" means "Can I say something that will entice you to buy something?" Similarly, our standard reply means more than it says. When we tell a store clerk we're just looking, we basically mean "Don't bother me." We mean "I don't *want* you to influence my decision. I can make up my own mind."

In this scenario, we often assume that a person who is just looking is a person who is not buying, a person who, perhaps, is not even really shopping. But, in fact, nothing could be further from the truth. Looking is actually an integral aspect of shopping and American culture, as even a cursory look at the consumption cycle suggests.

"Just looking" begins long before we go to the shopping center, often with a "wish list." In "An Emerald Green Jaguar, a House on Nantucket, and an African Safari," Susan Fournier and Michael Guiry explore "wish lists and consumption dreams in materialist society." They find that Americans routinely fantasize about things that we might purchase some day: bigger homes, faster cars, luxuries, and exotic vacations. We like to imagine ourselves with things we don't have, whether or not we have any likelihood of owning them. While these American dreams are about the pleasures of our future consumption, they bring us real pleasure right now. And these "pre-acquisition fantasies" also get us ready for the shopping center.[1]

Once we get to the mall, "just looking" is still more than just looking; it is what we might call "cognitive acquisition," a process by which we "try on" the actual and imputed characteristics of an object to see how it fits. When we look at the clothing on display, for example, we think about how we might look in an outfit of that cut and color and texture. We wonder if that logo will make us seem too preppy or what our co-workers will think if we show up in a designer suit. "Just looking," therefore, involves both inspection and introspection. And its effects go far beyond the specific commodities we see. As mall analyst Margaret Crawford suggests, "Mentally 'trying on' products teaches shoppers not only what they want and what they can buy, but also, more importantly, what they don't have, and what they therefore need." Just looking tells us, effectively, what we are just lacking.[2]

One variation of "just looking" is window shopping. Essayist Phyllis Rose suggests that window shopping is superior to actual purchasing because you get "the same high without the distressing commitment, the material encumbrance." Window shopping is different because no commercial exchange occurs. The shopper, in this case, gazes through a window—real or metaphorical—at the goods displayed, a materialistic voyeur. To a shopping center manager, though, window shopping is just the first step toward spending. Indeed, we might actually call window shopping *winnow* shopping because it helps a person sort through the number of objects considered for purchase.[3]

Usually when we say we're "just looking," we're looking for stuff to buy. But the process of looking at the mall is considerably more complex than a search for commodities, in part because that search involves so much of our lives. When we go to malls, we are of course looking for stuff, but we're also looking for ourselves, for our communities and relationships, for novelty and convenience, and—last but not least—for a bargain. Just looking involves an assessment of our identity and relationships, and their relationship to the material world, which is why shopping can be so involving. In many ways, as it turns out, we shop to get a life.

Looking

In America's shopping centers, one of the primary pleasures is looking at the mall; it is, in fact, designed to be a visual spectacle. From the soaring arches at the entrance to the intricate tilework in the restrooms, the mall is meant to impress us. As we have seen, designers play with light and space to catch the eye, and retailers craft window displays that beckon us invitingly. Colorful banners often festoon the food court, and seasonal decorations attract the eye. Architects and retail designers know that shopping centers need to look good to be good, so they prepare a visual feast for our daily delectation.

The visual merchandising of malls is a case study of American culture's emphasis on seeing. Human beings have five senses, but Americans tend to privilege the sense of sight. For example, we routinely equate visual perception with understanding by saying things like "I *see*." We pride ourselves on *seeing* different points of *view*, and on *seeing* things for ourselves. When we doubt a proposition, we say, "I'll believe it when I *see* it," not "I'll believe it when I smell it." We speak of "the mind's *eye*," not the mind's ears. While we do use all of our senses in the mall, we respond most to displays that catch our *eye*, and we scrutinize items carefully to *see through* any misrepresentations. Shopping centers, therefore, do the cultural work of reinforcing a certain kind of visual consciousness. In the land of looks, they're among the institutions that teach us to look carefully. They not only give us things to see but also show us how to see them. So "just looking" is not just a way of shopping, it's an American way of life.[4]

Looking for Stuff

Usually, however, we don't go to the mall just to gawk at it. We go looking for stuff. Sometimes we go with a shopping list, but just as often we go with a wish list. Sometimes we're just *doing the shopping;* other times we're *going shopping,* envisioning the possibilities of our lives. Sometimes we're shopping for stuff, which can be a chore; other times we're *shopping around,* which is more of a pleasure. Sometimes we're shopping to buy something, and other times we're buying something as an excuse for shopping. In both cases, we're often looking for more than mere merchandise or services: we're looking for meaning. And America's malls are well stocked with meaning.[5]

When we're *doing the shopping,* we're often just buying provisions. An unglamorous form of shopping, provisioning is simply the process of getting what we need. Supermarkets, drug stores, hardware stores, and convenience stores are the primary sites of American provisioning, but shopping centers also sell the necessities of life. Hubby needs underwear and a bigger blue Oxford shirt to fit his new fat. Mom needs a hairbrush to replace the one that Junior microwaved. Jack and Jill both need school supplies, and Jill needs new shoes for soccer. We can buy all these things at the mall, and so we do the shopping. There's not much that's romantic about this shopping trip, except the love that underlies it. It's about supplying our needs, but it's essential to malls, especially as the "frontier of necessity" moves forward.[6]

Sometimes we shop for stuff to go with our other stuff, acting out what's known in consumer sociology as the "Diderot effect." In a famous essay, Enlightenment philosopher Denis Diderot expressed his "Regrets on Parting with My Old Dressing Gown." Diderot found that buying a new dressing gown made his other possessions seem outdated, so he needed to replace his desk and curtains to fit with his new gown. Because we routinely use possessions to express the coherence in our lives, many of us are also affected by the Diderot effect. Once we buy a new sofa, we need a new coffee table. Once we get a new suit, we need the new tie. That new outfit just demands a new purse or a pair of shoes. Each purchase is an end in itself, but it can also be the beginning of a new round of consumption. Thankfully, the mall is stuffed with stuff to fulfill both our needs and desires.[7]

Looking for Self

Often we're looking for stuff that helps us define and express ourselves. In traditional cultures, the self was socially determined: as the son or daughter of a per-

Mallpractices

son of a certain rank, you didn't have a lot of choices. But Americans don't believe in such determinism. We know that parents influence our character and personality, and we expect to learn a lot about ourselves in school and at church. But we also believe in the self-made man and (finally) the self-made woman. We believe that we make ourselves by making choices, and that some of our most significant choices are in the realm of consumption. As sociologist Alan Warde suggests, "People define themselves through the messages and practices that they possess and display. They manipulate and manage appearances and thereby create and sustain a 'self-identity.' In a world where there is an increasing number of commodities available to act as props in this process, identity becomes more then ever a matter of the personal selection of self-image."[8]

The stuff we buy helps us make sense of who we are. Artist Barbara Kruger captured the relationship between shopping and identity with the Cartesian paraphrase "I shop, therefore I am." It's witty, but not strictly true. We shop both to express who we are and to *become* who we are. We produce the self by consuming stuff and experiences. I know I'm a scholar because I buy a lot of books (and read some of them). My wife knows she's an artist because she buys colorful materials for making quilts. My son knows he's a sportsman because he has the equipment for the experience. And consumption doesn't just confirm a preexistent self; it can help fashion a new self. Dressing more professionally can affect our sense of professionalism and our professional behavior. We can become healthier by buying exercise equipment, and we can grow wiser (or at least more knowledgeable) by reading the books we buy. We can become better parents by selecting good toys for our children, and we can become more relaxed by soaking up a session at the spa. Commodities don't usually make us what we are, but they can confirm our current sense of self, and help to develop it. In the process, commercial culture helps us to create a "commodity self." First, it helps us to construct a self defined by commodities, a self brought to life by the lifeless things we own. Second, ads and other promotions accustom us to the idea that the self itself is a commodity, constantly "sold" to other people.

"Life-style shopping" and "life-style advertising" appeal to this commercial practice of self-fashioning. Buying things at the mall, we construct life-styles for ourselves. The kitchen stuff from Williams-Sonoma and Pottery Barn inclines us to fine dining and dinner parties. The new home entertainment center from

Sears predisposes us to entertain ourselves at home. The running shoes we got at Sportsmart help to make us more sporting. There's no determinism of commodities—we could let our kids use the Williams-Sonoma pans in the sandbox—but what we buy often affects how we act (and vice versa).

Often at the mall, we're just looking at mirrors to assess our self-fashioning. We use mirrors to see if a suit or an outfit looks good on us or, more precisely, if we look good in it. A mirror reflects the images of objects, but it also reflects patterns of culture. It's a visual echo, and, like television, a mirror is a way of seeing. Malls are often halls of mirrors, with all of the fusions and confusions that mirrors can cause.

Mirrors are almost omnipresent in shopping centers, especially in apparel stores and at cosmetics counters. From a designer's point of view, mirrors serve several purposes. Because they reflect light without any additional electricity, mirrors can be an efficient way to bring light to space. They duplicate what faces them, so they can double the apparent size of a room or the drama of an engaging merchandise display. Because they multiply our normal lines of sight, mirrors keep store spaces visually interesting. They make it hard for people to pass by a storefront or store display without looking.[9]

As a matter of physics, mirrors reflect exactly the patterns of light and shade that hit them, but as a matter of culture, there can be significant distortions, because mirrors reflect not just the way we are but also the way we're trained to see. Mirrors reflect light to the eye, but they also reflect images to the I—the culturally conditioned self. For example, when we look at the mirror in the mall, we're trained by years of advice and advertising to see not just our own reflection, but its relationship to the ideal images we see on TV. The reflections in the mirror remind us that we live in a visual culture, and that looks and looking count.

In the mall, a mirror is a commercial form of self-consciousness. The mirror is where we try on different clothes and identities, preening, posing and pirouetting to see how we look. Mirrors permit self-scrutiny, self-absorption, and a kind of narcissism. This makes sense, because the word "mirror" comes from the same Latin root as the word "admire." Looking in the mirror, we can become a mutual admiration society all on our own.[10]

Mirrors support a kind of psychic schizophrenia. A mirror distances us

Reflections of America (Image by Wernher Krutein)

from ourselves, and lets us see the self as others do. For a few minutes, we are both see-er and seen, both *in* our body and (apparently) *out* of it. We become a sight to ourselves. Mirrors permit us to objectify ourselves, to look at ourselves from the outside. We each become what sociologist Charles Cooley called "the looking-glass self."[11]

Mirrors are also an essential prop in what analyst Erving Goffman calls "the presentation of self in everyday life." Mirrors help us with "impression management," as we manage our appearance to manage the response of others. American culture teaches us to be attractive and to dress for success, and the mirror allows us to see if we've succeeded. Image value is as important as use value, because image is useful. As contemporary philosopher (and tennis star) Andre Agassi reminds us, "Image is everything."[12]

Mirrors reinforce Americans' satisfaction with the surface of life. They are reflective, but they don't seem to make us reflective. For example, mirrors help us to think about what *looks* good, but not about what *is* good. We generally examine the surface of the self, but not the substantial self. We engage in self-inspection, but not examination of conscience. We gaze at ourselves, the reflections of modern American culture.

The United States is a country of expressive individualism, where we learn to let other people know who we are. So at the mall, we're often just looking at ourselves by looking at commodities. We're looking for ways to improve our lives, which means that we're looking at our lives while we're looking at athletic shoes and dresses. So when my local mall tells me that it's "a perfect reflection of you," I know that I can become myself in its shops and stores.

Looking for Community

At our local malls, we're just looking for ourselves, but we're also looking for a sense of belonging. We use shopping to think about our social life, the ways we fit, or don't fit, in the communities of our lives. We do this in several ways. When we shop with other people, we simultaneously explore our relationship with them. When we engage in "people watching," we play with the possibilities of belonging to different groups. And when we buy stuff, sometimes we buy belongings that help us to belong to a particular group.[13]

We can get a sense of belonging if somebody shops with us. So sometimes the quest for community is satisfied by the sociability of the people we came with. As we look at stuff and other people in the mall, we carry on a conversation that moves from things to human needs and back again. Because our lives are so tied up with things, things offer a way of talking about our lives, and vice versa. Shopping with a friend for a new outfit for our daughter, we naturally end up talking about how she's doing—in sports, in school, and in her social life. When we stop looking for the daughter's outfits a few years later, our companion knows it's because she's grown old enough to shop for herself. We may not buy anything on any particular trip to the mall, but if we're with a friend, we get something significant for the money we don't spend. Shopping can be about spending time instead of spending money. So "just looking" can be a way of looking at the nature of our relationships.

We can get a sense of belonging in malls even if we shop alone, because we're usually accompanied to the mall by hundreds or thousands of people. So we often practice people watching, which is a pleasure in itself. People watching

Shopping for sociability (Image by Wernher Krutein)

supplements looking for stuff; as we evaluate other people, our judgments tell us about what we value and why. "Look at that old guy," we think to ourselves. "He looks ridiculous in those tight jeans." Or "That outfit looks nice on her. I think I saw one like it at Ann Taylor." In looking at other people, we evaluate their looks so we can decide which "look" looks just right for us. We imagine ourselves as a sight, as the object of other people's attention, because we know that how we are seen determines, in part, whether we're ready to make the social scene. In comparison shopping, we not only compare commodities, but our own possibilities as people. People watching offers us examples of how to dress and live, as does the shopping center itself.

Malls cater to people's pleasure in seeing and being seen. They are designed not just so that we can see the merchandise, but so that we can see what other people do with merchandise. The mall, and the people who inhabit it, are literally exemplary, providing examples of how to live well. The department store shows furniture, but it also shows how furniture can be arranged. The apparel store sells pants, but also a conception of what to wear on which occasions. The gift shop is a school for interior decoration. The mall and its shoppers help us to learn the codes of culture and commodities.[14]

When we buy certain things, we sometimes become members of what historian Daniel Boorstin calls a "consumption community," a group bound together by their common belongings. We're members of the club, and our Air Jordans, or Armani handbags, or Department 56 collectibles are our badge of membership. Retailers try to promote such consumption communities with their loyalty programs. At Barnes & Noble, for example, a program called *Readers' Advantage* offers discounts and benefits to "members." For an annual membership fee of twenty-five dollars, customers get discounts at Barnes & Noble stores and at www.barnesandnoble.com, a one-year subscription to *Book* magazine, and a free canvas tote bag. The program also includes invitations to "members-only" events.[15]

Sometimes we need the stuff we buy at the mall to belong to a more proximate consumption community. If we're going to hang out with the cool crowd at school, we're going to need to dress like them. If we're going to join the group with season tickets to the opera, we'll need dressier clothes. If we're going to play on the softball team, we'll need the equipment. Even the book club depends on the purchase of books (or a good library).

Finally, sometimes we're shopping *for* a community. When Mom goes out to buy school clothes for the kids, or when Dad buys an entertainment center, shopping is an expression of family. We often use stuff to express the bonds and bounds or our communities. In fact, a lot of shopping is for gifts, which are enactments of generosity and relationship. Malls are full of gift shops, and the calendar of commercial culture includes several seasons of gift giving. Gifts are a practice of community and a way of ritualizing relationships. They let us see and feel and touch and smell some sense of what a person means to us, because gifts can embody care or love or passion. Gifts are one way that individualists choose to express their need for community and their membership in one another.

While we look for a sense of belonging in the mall, shopping centers love to suggest that we belong there. Whatever our social status, whatever the quality of our social life, we are welcome as members of the mall's community of consumers. And that's the final purpose of people watching: confirming that consuming in these common places is absolutely commonplace. If we ever went to

146

the mall and found it totally empty, we would probably be nervous; crowds corroborate our sense that shopping is natural and normal.

Looking for Distinction

Sometimes, at the mall, we're also looking for distinction. America's regional and superregional malls try to provide "a touch of class" for their clientele. In their shops and hallways, we can read the telltale signs of an upscale aesthetic. Artistic touches like classical architecture or sleek modernism (like Scandinavian design) tell people that they need taste to appreciate this place. Fine dark woods like teak and mahogany assert that you need real money to shop here. Leather chairs or sofas convey the exclusivity associated with dead cow skin. Upholstered chairs flanking a table topped with a floral arrangement suggest the leisure, and the taste, of the leisure class. Rich finishes make plain materials seem special, while glass cases make even the most plebeian of goods seem collectible. A grand piano or classical music provides a soundtrack for good taste. In this way, an upscale mall suggests that life could be better than it is, and beckons us both to home improvement and self-improvement. "A touch of class" could refer to any class, but it doesn't. It's not about the working class or the underclass; it's about the upper class, and the privileges of class.

Upscale consumers also get different service than their downscale compatriots. In upscale malls, the service desk is staffed by a "concierge" instead of a clerk. In stores like Lord & Taylor and Saks Fifth Avenue, the sales staff doesn't wear t-shirts and tennis shoes; they don't chew gum or spike their hair. Instead, they wear attire that makes them seem patrician or professional. Upscale stores train their staff to be polite and deferential, like servants. They're trained to recognize regular customers (the "guests"), and they learn to develop "friendly" relationships with them. Upscale stores often offer amenities like valet parking, free adjustments, and free delivery. This touch of class is not the Midas touch that turns everything to gold, it's the touch that turns gold to everything else.

Occasionally, upscale retail verges on sheer luxury, a word that comes from a Latin root connoting excess, extravagance—even a stench of overripe rankness. These days, it means "something inessential but conducive to pleasure or comfort." "To luxuriate" is "to take luxurious pleasure, to indulge oneself." Luxury is almost always about the self, and not a community, because luxury is priced out of the range of the community. Luxury is "over and above" sufficiency; it may possess intrinsic value, but its luxuriousness comes from its positional value.

It's one of the luxuries of luxury, of course, that rich people seldom have to confront poverty face to face. Shopping centers assist with this separation: they're different for the classes and the masses. There's no Saks Fifth Avenue in the strip mall, and no pawn shops on the premises of the regional mall. Within individual malls, too, there's often additional commercial segregation. In many malls, upscale stores are clustered together so the affluent shopper can drift from one to the other, looking not just for the good life but for the better life. The democracy of goods isn't entirely democratic. All malls are open to everybody, but not everybody comes.

Upscale shopping is functional for people with money (and people with credit cards), but upscale retailing performs cultural work for all of us, regardless of income. On the positive side, the production and distribution of luxuries produces jobs. And investments in luxury goods often lead to the general improvement of goods and services in society. In effect, the wealthy pay for the prototypes of commodities that are then cheapened into general circulation.

Luxury, however, also has its social costs. Both classy shops and upscale shopping centers reinforce the reality of class in the United States—a system in which the rich live luxuriously and the poor live poorly. Such stores reinforce the privileges of the powerful, but they also reinforce the "internalized oppression" of poor people. On the outside looking in the lavish display window, poor people have to explain their exclusion somehow. And American culture teaches all of us, rich and poor, to explain our condition the same way: "I earned it" or "I deserve it," we say. In an individualistic culture, we learn that we're responsible for our own status, so poor people at the mall—and elsewhere—get the message that their poverty is their own fault. If they were better people, they could afford better things. Upscale stores can have downbeat results.

Surveys of mall shoppers show that over half of mall visitors earn more than forty thousand dollars a year, and 37 percent of shoppers make more than fifty thousand dollars annually. The Yankelovich Partners remind us that "affluence is not mainstream." Among those making less than thirty thousand dollars a year, 63 percent are concerned about making ends meet, and 58 percent are living from payday to payday. Many of us are just making do, and some of us aren't even making that.[16]

Possessed by possessions
(Copyright Andrew B. Singer, www.andysinger.com)

Although poor people don't often come to upscale shops, they still have their uses in malls. Their constricted choices serve to make upscale shopping sweeter, because they remind us of our middle-class virtue compared to their supposed laziness and lack of ambition. If we can categorize them as the undeserving poor, we can think of ourselves as deserving consumers, people who have earned the right to buy anything we want. The "unfreedom" of poor people is also the cautionary tale of our freedom. If we don't get a good job, if we get laid off, if we can't afford the good life we currently enjoy, then we'll be reduced to their state. So the poverty of the poor is a good motivator for the continued cycle of "work and spend."[17]

In America, we're trained to think of luxury as a life-style choice, an option for those who make big money or inherit a fortune. But luxury is also a social choice, with sobering cultural implications. The society that celebrates luxury sometimes forgets to honor virtues like thrift and prudence and conservation. The society that promotes "more than enough" sometimes forgets that enough *can* be enough. And the indulgence of wealth sometimes comes at the cost of commonwealth. Money spent on furs and finery, cuisine and crafted cars, is money not spent on broader social needs. Rich living can impoverish the society.

Upscale shopping also affects upscale people. Indeed, the poverty of luxury is precisely its exclusiveness, the way it can isolate people from human and natural communities. Luxury cars say to people on the streets, "I care more for this car than I do for you." Luxury distinguishes us; it sets us apart from the hoi polloi, the many. But sometimes, it seems, wealthy people get trapped by all the trappings. They're so busy preserving their status and the status quo that they don't have time for the simple pleasures of life. Luxury can cut people off from the contact and the compassion that could bring us together.

Still, many Americans aspire to the privileges of class and hope to enjoy the lives of the rich and famous. Seventy-two percent of us believe that even average people can become wealthy and well known. Thirty-eight percent of us, and 56 percent of young adults, expect to be rich. And 75 percent of us say that Americans can live any way they want to. In a culture of inequality, these aspirations to wealth are understandable. They're also increasing, as upscale tastes have not been confined to upscale stores. In the past twenty years, both retailers and the American people have engaged in a process that Juliet Schor calls "upscaling." Starting in the 1980s, Schor suggests, the upper middle class, the top 20 percent, became the reference group for an increasing number of Americans. By the early 1990s, 85 percent of Americans aspired to become members of the upper middle class of Americans. Only 15 percent of us would be happy to be middle class.[18]

In 1986, the Roper polling organization asked people how much income they would need to fulfill all their dreams. The answer was $50,000 a year. By 1994, the answer was $102,000. The more people already made, the more they thought they needed to fulfill all their dreams. This "upscaling" obviously affects shopping centers and retailers. Even discount stores such as Kmart and Target have upscaled through their licensing arrangements with Martha Stewart and Michael Graves. Even though most of us don't have much money, it seems like we're all touched by a touch of class.[19]

Sometimes, however, the distinctions we find at the mall aren't the ones we were looking for. As the United States becomes more multicultural, shopping centers have adapted to serve a new world of Americans. In 1997, for example, the ICSC commissioned two focus groups to study the shopping preferences of African American consumers. One of every eight Americans are African American, and African Americans' after-tax income was $469 billion in 1996. At the same time, both the African American population and their income are increasing faster than the white population and their income. So it made sense for the ICSC to see what people in this "submarket" thought about malls. They found that African Americans generally spend their money like other Americans do. African Americans in American malls spent slightly less on apparel, and somewhat more on entertainment, food, pets, toys, and playground equipment, in part because of expenditures on the kids in their larger families. As a result, African Americans look for shopping centers with a strong family orientation, and community recognition.[20]

The focus groups complained about the quality and selection of merchandise, especially in nearby malls, and confessed that they sometimes needed to drive to suburban malls to get the goods they wanted. They wanted stores that featured African and African American themes and stores that displayed mannequins and carried cosmetics with black consumers in mind. They wanted more entertainment venues (including movie theaters) in their local malls, and more time-saving businesses like banks, repair shops, and dry cleaners. They emphasized the importance of cleanliness in the mall, and of security, especially in the parking lot.[21]

"Perhaps the most strident complaint" of focus group members was the lack of respectful treatment by sales personnel. Shoppers thought that salespeople tended to be curt or condescending when they weren't suspicious or hostile. Not surprisingly, said the ICSC researchers, "African Americans place a higher emphasis on the perceived friendliness of sales personnel than do Caucasians."[22]

During the 1950s and 1960s, African Americans mobilized a civil rights movement to secure equal rights for all citizens. One essential demand was full participation in the commercial economy. African Americans creatively used the "sit-in" to dramatize the built-in racism they faced as consumers, and they boycotted retail businesses, theaters, motels, and restaurants that refused to provide service to all Americans. Martin Luther King Jr. came to national prominence as leader of a boycott organized to desegregate the Montgomery, Alabama, buses.[23]

These days, of course, thanks to the 1964 Civil Rights Act and a new generation of racial attitudes, people of color can shop wherever they like. Unfortunately, they still can't shop equally. Our malls show the state of the nation's race relations, and while we say we no longer believe in "separate but equal," we clearly still believe in difference. At the mall, people share the same physical space but not the same social space. Especially at the regional and super-regional malls that cater mainly to middle-class white Americans, people of color are still shopping for equality, as they are in the society as a whole. And they still receive discriminatory treatment in many retail establishments.

African American activists call it "shopping while black," and it's a venerable tradition. Although few incidents of retail racism are as pronounced as the infamous case of Denny's Restaurants, they still persist. In 2000, Children's Place, a chain of children's clothing stores, signed a consent decree to end discriminatory practices in its stores. An employee claimed that when she was hired, she was told to prevent theft by following black customers as they browsed and by not giving them large shopping bags. She was told not to tell African Americans about upcoming sales or to ask them to apply for store credit cards. The Massachusetts Commission Against Discrimination investigated and found what they called "a pattern of conduct targeting people based on the color of their skin."[24]

Even though company policy always prohibits it, such instances of "retail racism" are not unusual. People of color receive scrutiny that other people don't, and sometimes they get differential treatment. KayBee Toys has been sued for refusing to accept checks in black neighborhoods of Washington, D.C. Security guards working at an Eddie Bauer sale took the shirt from a customer's back because he didn't have his receipt with him. Worried about theft, security officers and store clerks often pay more attention to African Americans and other people who fit a so-called profile of suspicion. Even worse, black people get stopped disproportionately on a supposition of theft. To some extent, this discrimination takes place to please white customers. Middle-class white Americans often get nervous around groups of young black men, and so store employees and mall security are often more watchful around such young men. When this happens, black people suffer for white people's discomfort.[25]

A 2000 Gallup poll asked black Americans if they had been treated unfairly because of race in the last thirty days at work or in shopping, dining out, using public transportation, or dealing with police. Half of them said yes. That's a lot of perceived discrimination. According to American University Professor Lawrence Steinhorn, that's because we've achieved legal integration without achieving social integration. "Whites tend to believe that race relations have never been better and we have largely eliminated racism from mainstream American life," he says. "But black people know better. If skin color were just descriptive and not defining," Steinhorn suggests, then "economic discrimination would be randomly distributed. . . . it wouldn't be discrimination, it would just be impoliteness and rudeness."[26]

America's retailers have responded to this problem because it's bad business, because they believe in customer satisfaction, and because they believe in equality. A recent essay by the editor-in-chief of *Stores* recounts the important steps that retailers like Denny's and Eddie Bauer have taken to get company practice in line with company philosophy, affirming a policy of no tolerance for intolerance. He acknowledges, however, that problems will continue, because the retail sales force is recruited from the American population and many Americans still harbor prejudices.[27]

"Shopping while black" is part of a broader system of color-coded consumption. In America, there's a long tradition of people asserting their personhood through material goods. Within the system of slavery, black people were the possessions of white people, and white owners decided how to feed and clothe and shelter this personal property. The difference between the races was marked not just by skin color but also by patterns of consumption, and white society ridiculed black people who dressed "up" because they refused to accept their place in the world. In such a situation, it was a mark of freedom and independence for slaves to earn their own money and buy goods that asserted their essential human dignity. Commodities as simple as a hat or a scarf, a pocket watch or a jackknife carried complex messages, criticizing the system that made commodities of people.[28]

Race is still performed through material goods, and freedom is still found in shopping and purchasing. And there's still a double standard of judgment about the appropriateness of consumption. The media still criticize the consumption of minority men in flashy fashions, or of welfare moms and ghetto kids, offering implicit standards of enoughness that aren't applied to the overconsumption of the white middle and upper classes. Even at the mall, with its explicit policy of color blindness, minorities are assaulted by stereotypes and moral judgments that keep the country's racial history alive.

Race also gets performed with commodities, some of which are implicitly color coded, and not just on the tags. Alex Kotlowitz suggests that "the inner-city poor equate classiness with suburban whites while those same suburban whites equate hipness with the inner-city poor." For young black kids in the ghetto, designer clothes are designed to "link them to a more secure, more prosperous world, a world in which they have not been able to participate—except as consumers." Even a discriminatory society doesn't discriminate against their dollars.[29]

Conversely, many young, hip styles come from the ghetto/gang mystique. Bored white teenagers emulate the styles of urban kids whose lives on the edge seem more authentic than theirs. This "romanticization of poverty by some white teens" involves invoking the life-styles of the poor and unfamous. White kids with no experience of discrimination or displacement identify, if only sartorially, with the dispossessed in American society. Yet, the connection is not even skin deep. It's just a style, a pose, a masquerade. Like other aspects of a consumer society, it's more about life-style than life, and it never seems to lead to any kind of personal or political connection. White kids could campaign to improve conditions in the ghetto; instead, they are sucked in by advertising campaigns selling them the "cool" of injustice. It's cool to adopt the look of poverty, but it's not cool to be passionate about ending poverty. It's cool to imitate imaginary ghetto kids, but it's not cool to care for the real ones.[30]

Sometimes, too, race gets performed with what Elizabeth Chin calls "market multiculturalism," the commodification of difference, the celebration of diversity in those forms that bring in dollars. Ethnically correct dolls, for example, make visible some important differences in American life. They remind us that Americans have different skin colors. But as Chin points out, they also help us forget that race is not a biological trait, but a social construction. And by featuring skin tones, they also allow a consumer forgetfulness of the intersections of race with class and gender and sexual preference, and residence and education and work. Ethnically correct dolls may be good for the self-esteem of ethnically correct people, and they are an immense improvement on "the unbearable whiteness of Barbie," but they don't address the complexities of race in America.[31]

The companies that market to ethnic pride are involved in what Chin calls "corporate nationalism." This segmentation of racial and ethnic markets parallels what Michael Weiss calls "the clustering of America." But this market segmentation may not ultimately be as important as the general homogenization of consumption. To a certain extent, diversity gets homogenized at malls because we can all buy the same stuff. That stuff identifies us as consumers, and our identity as consumers cuts across racial and ethnic identities. In his insightful survey titled *An All-Consuming Century*, Gary Cross suggests that consumerism has kept us from killing each other over other forms of identity politics. The stores at the mall may not always be equal opportunity employers, but they generally try to be equal opportunity sellers. They are color-conscious, but they're usually more conscious of the color of money than the color of customers.[32]

Looking for Novelty

At our local malls, we're also looking for stimulation. The mall itself, as we've seen, is a stimulating spectacle. And it's certainly stimulating to reinvent ourselves and our social relations. Psychologists contend that people need to keep their consciousness focused on goal-directed activity to maintain their happiness. Our minds are made for engagement, so when we feel like "there's nothing to do," we often become bored and depressed because we think about ourselves and the shortcomings in our lives. Shopping is a solution to this problem because, whether or not we buy anything, shopping is an activity that requires focus, mental energy, discrimination, and judgment. As psychologist Mihaly Csikszentmihalyi suggests, "It often does not matter what we are shopping for—the point is to shop for anything. It is a goal-directed activity, and thus it fills the experiential vacuum that leads to depression and despair." In a very real sense, the mental demands of shopping fulfill our experiential needs, making shopping a genuine form of retail therapy.[33]

Although it isn't on the classical list of seven deadly sins, boredom is one of the chief iniquities of the modern age. You can often get away with lust and greed and gluttony, but you better not be boring. You can be a clown or a counterfeit or a cad, but if you're boring, you're likely to be an outcast. So malls try to provide antidotes to boredom. They sell novelty and novelties in department stores and specialty shops, in the food court and at the movies. All of these novelties bring us into community, since we're often surrounded by other people who are also avoiding boredom by shopping—and shopping for the new. With friends and family, we discuss the new fashions, the new restaurants, the new cuisine, the new movies. They're literally conversation pieces. And we feel up-to-date if we can keep up our end of the conversation.

Most of all, shopping centers sell novelty in the form of fashion, which is one way of relieving boredom and providing the stimulation we crave. Fashion is a way of letting us play with modernity; it's a form of thinking in time and thinking about time. New fashions aren't really fashionable because they're new (especially since so many of them are really retro) but because they're *defined as new* by fashionistas. Fashion appeals to the avant-garde, the cutting edge. It's the nub of the new, the frontier of the future. When Mrs. Consumer appears in her Versace dress and handbag, she knows she's in tune with the times. To be fashionable is to be up-to-date, as if each date needed its own defining fashion, and as if human beings depended on freshness dating.

Fashion is a way of dressing up continuity to look like change. It's a predictable system of novelty. Despite the fact that there are new fashions every season, the average fashion trend lasts about seven years. Seasonal "theme trends" influence purchasing and visual merchandising, but the general shape of outfits is more stable than the seasonal variations of theme. Basically, the mall presents the new in a setting of familiarity. Indeed, the function of fashion and the mall is to domesticate the new, and to make sure that the new is never *substantively* new, since a genuine revolution could be a threat to commercial enterprises. This is why designers and promoters work so hard to commodify dissent: "commodifying the new" sucks the newness out of it. New styles are good for business, but a new system might not be.[34]

When we buy clothes and commodities, they're usually new. But the newness itself is old. Newness is one of the oldest sales pitches in the American marketplace. Newness is a venerable tradition, an essential part of our history. We were the New World on a new continent, a new nation with a new birth of liberty. We voted for the New Freedom, the New Deal, and the New Frontier. We live in New York, New Orleans, New Hampshire, and New Mexico. Even more important these days, we buy lots of new stuff, and we often buy it just because it's new.

We do this, of course, because over the course of the twentieth century, advertisers worked tirelessly to make "new" synonymous with "improved." Even though the root of "improvement" is "prove," there's often scant evidence that the new really is improved. Many times, the new is simply *un*proved. But the American ideology of progress absolutely depends on this linkage between novelty and betterment.

In fact, however, improvement depends on how we define it and what we really value. A product may be stylistically improved without being functionally improved. A commodity may be improved without the world being improved, and without people being any better. People can be materially improved without being spiritually improved, and individuals can be improved without society being better off. Often, it seems, "new and improved" means "modified just enough to sell a second one to someone who already has one."

One consequence of our fascination with novelty is disdain for the old and for tradition. In fact, the meaning of "new and improved" depends on the complementary definition of "old and established." As early as 1924, journalist Samuel Straus suggested that what he called "consumptionism" undercut respect for wisdom and established traditions. In what he called the "new age," Americans just accepted "the common belief that the world is for the young and that the old are merely clogs on the chariot wheels of triumphant Progress."[35]

This process is still at work. Many Americans suffer from what we might call "neophilia," the obsession with the new and the novel—not the literary novel, of course, since reading is hopelessly old-fashioned, but the commercial novelties of shopping centers and discount stores. Neophiliacs are always looking for the next new thing, the "new and improved" products that show up seasonally in the store windows.

Of course, it's the nature of novelty that it can't stay new. Inevitably, the new outfit becomes "the blue outfit" and then "that old thing." The new is, in fact, what makes the old old; in a commercial culture, this is what's called "obsolescence" (planned or not). The "new and improved" marginalizes the old and established, the tried and true. The new model or the new fashion doesn't make the old model less functional, except insofar as the function of the product is to mark our up-to-dateness. But this process also marginalizes wisdom, which comes with age and tradition. We don't speak of "new wisdom," because we know that wisdom usually requires that we become older and wiser. And you can't buy wisdom at the mall, although, if you're really paying attention, you can *get* wiser there.

Looking for Time

Increasingly we go shopping for time, one of the scarcest commodities in American life. Although time studies show that Americans enjoy a lot of leisure time, a significant number of us feel that we have little time for our own lives. We work what economist Juliet Schor calls "long-hour jobs," and we rush home to pursue one busy leisure activity after another. In her report on "The State of the Consumer 2000," Myra Stark notes that "the consumer's growing sense of time pressure has risen to epidemic proportions this year."[36]

The "time poverty" of affluent Americans is an essential element of modern retailing. More and more Americans feel rushed, living what corporate consultant Leslie Charles calls "just-in-time lifestyles." Ninety-one percent of us think that life is moving too fast, and three-quarters of the most affluent Americans (those making more than $100,000 a year) think that "managing time is harder than managing money." There are lots of ways to respond to the time crunch, including social and political activism. Unions once negotiated reductions in hours at work, and Americans used their government to enact laws concerning the workweek. But these days, it seems, we just don't have time for systemic approaches to time. Instead, we resort to individual "time management," which is to say, we take individual responsibility for the time pressures often imposed on us by others.[37]

Malls are affected by this time crunch, because people aren't lingering in shopping centers any longer. The average length of a mall visit declined by half between 1980 and 1990. In 2000, Americans made 3.2 trips to shopping centers but stayed only seventy-five minutes each time. In malls, the more time peo-

Mallpractices

ple spend, the more money they spend, so the time poverty of Americans directly affects the profitability of shopping centers.[38]

Shopping centers generally respond to the "time bind" of modern Americans in two different ways. They help us to "save time" by reducing the time we need for shopping, or they help us to "savor time" with more service and experience. When we save time at the mall, we often call it "convenience." A mall itself is a sort of convenience, a great variety of goods all in one place, but its shops and stores also offer other conveniences. Chain stores are a convenience because we know what to expect from coast-to-coast—and even overseas. Brand names are a convenience because we get an implicit promise of performance. "In effect," says marketing professor Roger Blackwell, "brand loyalty helps reduce people's shopping time." Given the time bind of our lives, retailers have also learned that we'll "pay a premium for the privilege of not being kept waiting." So shopping centers have tried to reduce the hassle of shopping so that we don't feel frustrated by the time we do have to spend.[39]

The other mall-adjustment to the time bind is to slow down time, to help consumers savor certain times. We often feel like we're "doing time" at work, and even at home, because other people make demands on us. So increasingly, malls help us to "un-do time," to let ourselves be directed by task-time instead of by clock-time. To some extent, malls have always done this by keeping clocks out of view. When we enter the mall, we enter a timeless environment. But now malls are incorporating attractions like sit-down restaurants and spas to help us make time to enjoy ourselves. The rituals of slow food, and the pleasures of conversation that often accompany such a meal, make restaurants a major force in time management. In our everyday lives, we're often too hurried and harried to really speak to each other, but a leisurely meal enforces a discipline of delay and creates a free space for the human intimacy that gets left behind in the rush of work and housework.

Spas are another way to alter our sense of time. "Spas are huge," said Art Spellmeyer of the Simon DeBartolo Group (now the Simon Property Group). "We're putting them in a lot of our malls." In the past, spas were often remote retreats where wealthy customers paid to be pampered for a day or a weekend. These days, however, many Americans don't have time for such distant and extended pampering. We're willing to savor a facial or a massage, but we want a quick pick-me-up, and we want it in a convenient location. The mall, which is just such a place, also benefits from the synergies of spas, because spas draw upscale Baby Boomers who are willing and able to indulge themselves. According to the *Shopping Center Development Handbook*, "Spas enhance a property's drawing power, helping to attract an upscale clientele. They are an antidote to the stress and strain of the fast-paced 1990s and hold appeal for overworked adults looking for a way to relax." The mall spa satisfies both of our time needs, letting us savor time while saving time at the same time.[40]

Looking for Bargains

As we've seen, just looking at the mall involves looking for a lot of things. But it almost always means looking for a bargain. Sometimes shopping is seen as wasteful extravagance—and, at times, it certainly is. But shoppers also love to practice the virtue of thrift. In a 1995 survey, 82 percent of Americans agreed with the statement "I am a sale shopper." And Roper surveys consistently show the pleasure we feel when we bag a bargain. We love to talk about the deals we got. "It was a 'best buy' in *Consumer Reports*," we tell our friends. "I compared prices on the web, and then I bought it on sale." Or we explain exuberantly, "It was $250 two weeks ago, but I got it for half price." The deal we got, the bargain we found, is material evidence for our thrift.[41]

In malls, of course, a bargain is seldom literally a bargain, because, even on sale, we don't actually haggle for things in our fixed-price retail culture. People in other cultures celebrate their skills in negotiating prices on merchandise. But in America, we long ago bargained away our bargaining power, ceding pricing to retailers. We may wait to buy something until the price goes down, but we don't generally ask for a lower price. But if you look closely at the mall, you'll notice that most of the signs announce sales of one sort or another. At Minnesota's Mall of America in August 2001, for example, writers for *Promo* magazine counted sixty-six sale signs visible from the hallway on the first floor alone. Such price reductionism might inspire public skepticism about pricing in general, but it doesn't. Instead, it tends to inspire increased shopping.[42]

In *A Theory of Shopping*, Daniel Miller suggests that routine shopping, or provisioning, is generally a practice of thrift, even when we're spending money. He

cathy

by Cathy Guisewite

contends that householders express their care for their families by spending wisely. When we are provisioning, we keep track of each family member's tastes and predilections, their clothing sizes and brand preferences. We buy stuff to please (and improve) the other people in our lives. And the more money we can save in the process, the more we can buy. Getting the most for our money is way of getting the most for our families. Further, taking care of our families makes shopping cosmologically significant, a practice of commitment to values of care and community. Miller argues, therefore, that shoppers can be "making love in supermarkets." We can also be making love in shopping centers.[43]

Retailers respond to our value for value by staging events that let us experience shopping as saving money. In shopping centers, we see seasonal sales (see table 3), but we also see clearance sales, dollar days, and inventory-reduction sales. We can "buy two for the price of one" or get "25 percent off our everyday low prices." We especially like "free" offers: "free installation," or "free with purchase" or "buy two, get one free." Many sales encourage us to "save more by spending more," helping us to forget that we also spend more by spending more.

Sales are good for business, both because they bring cost-conscious shoppers into the store and because they get costly merchandise out the door. A "Clearance" sign means "Help us clear our inventory and get rid of the stuff we couldn't sell at full price." And "40 percent off" means that the retailer has decided that they can't make the normal mark-up and the retail price has now been reduced almost to the wholesale price. Sometimes the signs say "Free installation" or "Free with rebate" or "Free with purchase," which is basically another way of saying "Not free." In any case, these off-price goods are always reduced from "our everyday low prices." Good sales marketing lets us think we're beating the system, but we're not. We're still in the system, and we're still in the mall.

But we are saving money. These sales allow us to practice thrift without visiting a thrift store. We can take pride in our judgment, our calculation, our perspicacity. It's interesting how much of our good judgment is invested in the purchase of consumer goods, and how much we judge each other's consuming abilities. Spending too much money on something can be a sign of vice or at least of mental instability. Buying an expensive shirt on sale is considered more virtuous than buying a moderately priced shirt. Sales are literally about discounts, but they're also about virtue and values. In some ways, our consumption is justified by our savings, and the sale becomes our salvation.

Like fashion, thrift is a way of thinking in time. If fashion is a method of living both in the present and on the cusp of the coming future, thrift is a method of exercising an old-fashioned virtue for the longer future. Money saved today can be spent tomorrow. Whether or not we actually deposit our savings in a bank account, but especially if we do, today's thrift is tomorrow's provision. Thrift isn't particularly fashionable—look at the negligible savings rate in the United States—but it can help us fashion lives we can afford.[44]

Despite our fascination with bargains, regional malls don't usually include second-hand stores or outlet stores. They may include off-price stores like Marshall's or TJ Maxx, which confirm the importance of high-priced brands even as they discount them. They occasionally include a discount store like Target, but they don't normally include Wal-Mart or Kmart in the tenant mix.

Some merchandisers don't even like the idea of sales, fearing that discounting will harm an upscale image. In *Windows: The Art of Retail Display*, Mary Portas responds to this fear. "Many retailers," she says, "are embarrassed by sales and try to get them over with as quickly as possible, which is a shame, I think, as customers enjoy them. They don't in any way undermine your brand as they are by definition simply the sale of leftover stock, not merchandise that is defective or cheap." Portas says that "psychology is a powerful tool in sales promotions. Red, for example, is uppermost in people's minds when they think of sales, so work with the power of the colour. Stop them with it. And give time to the stories you can depict with the merchandise." Portas also suggests that "the sale might be some of your customers' only opportunity to shop at your store, so make them feel as special as the last of the big spenders." Finally, she notes that "everybody loves a bargain, and there's a world of difference between a bargain and something cheap."[45]

"Just looking" at the mall, we look for identity and community, for novelty and convenience, and for bargains. Shopping can be satisfying precisely because it involves such important issues, inviting us to make complex intellectual, aesthetic, and ethical judgments in making our choices—judgments that may be more complex and pleasurable than the day-to-day demands of our jobs and home lives. Looking carefully at what we're really looking for, we can understand some of the considerable pleasures of our malls.

Ironically, while we are "just looking" at the mall, the mall is looking back. In this age of surveillance, videotape cameras keep an eye out for shoplifters. Most of the time, however, what the cameras record is people looking at commodities. They keep an eye on us as we eye the merchandise. It's one of the ironies of modern American life that we must be seen for merchants to be secure. And it's another irony that security cameras show us shopping for the personal security and stimulation that's apparently lacking in our everyday lives.

NINE

Shopping for the Fun of It

Americans go to malls for many reasons. We're "just looking" for stuff and the self, commodities and community, novelty and time, and, of course, a bargain. We're hoping to buy what we need and, occasionally, what we don't need. But sometimes we go to the mall just for the fun of it. "Entertainment is a major component of American culture, maybe the major component," says Michael Beyard, coauthor of the *Shopping Center Development Handbook.* It's no surprise, then, that shopping centers try to capitalize on their entertainment value, selling fun in addition to all the stuff.[1]

One year before Victor Gruen's landmark Southdale Center opened in the suburbs of Minneapolis, another influential mall opened its gates on the West Coast. Despite its official designation as a theme park, Disneyland was, and still is, a mall. It's a mall—in the original sense of a pedestrian promenade—and it's a shopping center too. An early visitor said that Main Street USA is "an ordinary shopping center where they sell souvenirs, film, . . . ice cream, have a movie house—all functioning as would any ordinary shopping center. Except for one thing. It's a stage set of Main Street circa 1900." From the beginning, this mix of merchandise and entertainment has made the Disney shops highly profitable, achieving some of the highest sales per square foot for retail properties in the United States.[2]

As a consequence, Disney's lands have greatly influenced the malling of America. "If malls influenced the design of Disneyland," suggests Karal Ann Marling, "the malls of the 1990s are being transformed by the theme park. . . . Since the mall is among the essential American public spaces of today, the application of Disneyland theming techniques and aesthetics to the shopping center has far-reaching consequences for architecture in the 'real' world." Coming full circle, a few megamalls, like West Edmonton Mall and Mall of America, have even incorporated amusement parks, in order to get the synergies of theme parks and themed retail.[3]

In recent years, Las Vegas casinos have also marketed retail entertainment in shopping centers like the Forum Shops at Caesar's Palace, the Grand Canal Shoppes at the Venetian, and Desert Passage near the Aladdin Casino. Like Disney's lands, these themed retail venues have mixed fun and merchandising, and have influenced other malls of America. Especially since 1990, American stores and shopping centers have made entertainment an essential element of the tenant mix. Like Disney's lands, these mall entertainment projects have tried to provide, in the words of Mall of America, "a place for fun in your life." In the process, they provide a way to think about the place of fun in American life, and the cultural work of fun.[4]

Disneylands

Disneyland opened in 1955, just twenty-seven years after the premiere of Walt Disney's first cartoon, *Steamboat Willie*. Disney World opened for business near Orlando, Florida, in 1971, with EPCOT Center following eleven years later. Disney-MGM Studios opened at Walt Disney World in 1989, and Disney's Animal Kingdom was added in 1998. Overseas, Tokyo Disneyland opened in 1983 and

Euro Disney in 1992. Despite enormous resistance when it was first proposed, Euro Disney has become the number one tourist attraction in France, and the largest restaurateur in that country of high cuisine, selling 30 million meals a year. Recently, Disney has committed to build a new theme park in Hong Kong.[5]

Since the mid-1980s, the Disney empire has extended beyond its parks and playgrounds. The Disney Store opened in 1987, the first of more than nine hundred retail outlets in malls of the United States and eight other countries. Disney's designs have also had an impact on the so-called real world. In 1994, the Disney company committed to renovating a Times Square theater, and participating in the renewal of the neighborhood. And in 1996, the company applied its "imagineering" to urban design with the town of Celebration, Florida.[6]

So what have mall developers learned from Disney's lands?

The first lesson of Disneyland was the positive effects of planning and careful placement. The Disney parks are planned down to the smallest detail. Unlike earlier amusement parks, which capitalized on the apparently random juxtaposition of rides, Disney's new park divided the attractions thematically. The rides provided not just the ups and downs of standard amusement park rides but also the ins and outs of a story. It matters that the Matterhorn is a mountain, for example, because it makes a simple roller coaster into a geographic adventure.[7]

Thanks to good planning, the Disney parks are an oasis of order in a chaotic world. The trains run on time, and the litter doesn't linger on the ground very long. The old buildings are newly painted, and even the vegetation is spruced up regularly for aesthetic effect. This environmental control helps with social control, as the built environment of the park affects the social order, with most people on their best behavior. Submitting to the order of the park, we become orderly without actually being ordered.

Part of the planning for the Disney parks was purely pedestrian. Walt Disney understood the value of walking in the age of the automobile. Although one of the most popular rides for children was the Autopia, Disney understood that adults would appreciate the pleasures of strolling in a pseudo-civic space. Drawing on the tradition of Copenhagen's Tivoli Gardens, he carefully crafted his park to appeal to adults with a sense of wonder.

If planning was the first Disney lesson, theming was the second. By theming the "lands" of Disneyland, Disney made his customers into characters in his

Mallpractices

stories. At a time when the theme of the International Style of architecture was the machine, or modernity itself, Disney offered more accessible stories. Summoning the same willing suspension of disbelief that makes books and movies work, the five lands of Disneyland were architecturally and ornamentally themed to evoke different American dreams. Main Street USA evoked the communitarian fantasy of the small town. Frontierland touted the significance of the frontier and the pioneer spirit. Adventureland updated the frontier story of domestic conquest for an international age by featuring exotic locales of the Third World. Fantasyland spun its own fantasies, mostly connected to the themes of Disney movies. And Tomorrowland launched all these dreams into the future, evoking the promise of a better world of advanced technology. Long before architect Robert Venturi learned anything from Las Vegas, Disney demonstrated that Americans love to play with architecture and imagination.[8]

Disney's theming led to the third lesson, what we might call cineplexity. He knew that people liked to watch movies, so he created three-dimensional movie sets and staffed them with "cast members" in supporting roles: the stars of the show were the "guests," the paying customers in the park. Designer John Hench, for example, explained that "in motion pictures, you start out with an establishing shot, a long shot, a wow." Main Street performs this function in Disneyland, with its forced perspective framing Sleeping Beauty Castle, the park's primary "wienie." Hench explains again: "Main Street is like scene one and then the castle is designed to pull you down Main Street toward what is next, just like a motion picture unfolding." Each area of the park had a wienie, and each of the rides, too, came complete with a story, often from a Disney film. It was, as Beth Dunlop suggests, "architecture with a plot."[9]

The theming and cineplexity of Disneyland's simulations combined to provide a fourth lesson—what Umberto Eco calls "adventures in hyperreality." Disney's theme parks presented real versions of imaginative fictions. The Disney parks are real, *and* they're synthetic; they're what architecture critic Beth Dunlop calls "totally authentic inauthenticity." But there's a deep pleasure in seeing the artificiality of it all. From the time of P. T. Barnum, Americans have enjoyed playing with fakery and foolishness. In places like Disneyland and Las Vegas—and malls—one of the most engaging questions for customers is, "Is it real or is it fake?" The answer, of course, is always "Yes!"[10]

The sensuality of Disneyland offers a fifth lesson. Many Americans work at desk jobs, which may be intellectually interesting, but which increasingly take place in cubicles that are basically sensory deprivation chambers. In an era when people no longer experience the everyday world with a heightened sensitivity, Disneyland gives us a place to wallow in sights and smells and sounds. From the confectioneries of Main Street to the restaurants in the rest of the park, it lets us taste the forbidden pleasures of fatty foods. We inhale the smells of fudge and french fries, cotton candy and caramel apples. We hear the sounds of music, the careening roller coasters, and children's laughter. And rides like Space Mountain give us a visceral experience that we don't often get in our desk chairs or car seats. We literally *feel* more at Disneyland than we usually feel at home.

Although he didn't invent it, Disney knew the power of family entertainment. For his sixth lesson, he showed how to capitalize on American family values and the value of family "togetherness." His deference to family values meant that the parks were literally familiar—both common and comfortable to the common people. Architect Robert Venturi contended that Disney World, inspired in part by Victor Gruen's *Heart of Our Cities*, was "nearer to what people really want than anything architects have given them. . . . . It's symbolic of American utopia."[11]

One of the family values that Walt Disney admitted to his films and parks was sentimentality, a characteristic much decried by critics. Like Norman Rockwell, who was also panned by highbrow critics, Disney celebrated the goodness of plain people and the maudlin pleasures of ordinary life. In an age when many critically acclaimed modern artists celebrated an aesthetics of abstraction or ugliness, Disney offered pleasing pictures in perspective. He understood the attraction (and the profitability) of living happily ever after.

Along with the values of familiarity and sentimentality, Disney's seventh lesson emphasized the value of both nostalgia and hope in the American narrative of progress. Nostalgia is basically wishful thinking about the past, and its main appeal, of course, is to adults, not children. Hope is also wishful thinking. If nostalgia is the wish that we were better than we *really* were, hope is the wish that we can *become* better than we really are. Disneyland and Disney World told a story of America as a land of progress and promise. Like Democracity at the 1939 World's Fair, the parks' Carousel of Progress (originally the GE exhibit at the 1964 World's Fair) expressed American expectations of "new and improved" technology and the improvement of family life. And EPCOT Center, originally the Experimental Prototype Community of Tomorrow, also features technological utopianism. Relentlessly optimistic, the parks were a form of wish fulfillment—past, present, and future. Providing the reassurance that we don't get everyday, Disney showed Americans the way we never were, and promised a future even better than his fiction of the past. The parks provided, as Marling says, "the architecture of reassurance."[12]

An eighth lesson of Disney's lands was the importance of providing a space for the inner child—and not just for children—to play. Childhood is a period of intense desire and not-so-intense restraint. By letting adults act childishly, Disney greatly increased the parks' appeal and profits. At the same time, Disneyland's appeal to children of all ages provided a oasis of innocence in a morally complex and compromised world. By "kidding" people, by letting them be kids, he made it possible for patrons to relive their own childhoods and reproduce romantic images of childhood as a time of innocence and play—and consumption. This "infantilization of the adult consumer" can be problematic, but it's also a release from the very real restraints of a bureaucratic culture. So it's not surprising that more adults than children visit Disney's lands.[13]

Disney's understanding of families and children led him to a ninth lesson, emphasizing the value of vacations—not just to the working people who needed them, but to the entrepreneurs (like Disney) who sold them. After the Depression and World War II, Americans needed a vacation, and labor contracts were increasingly providing them. By making Disneyland a vacation destination, Disney created an additional way of removing restraints from our billfolds and pocketbooks. He promoted the parks as an escape from everyday life—as *magic* kingdoms. And that they were. They celebrated the culture of consumption by hiding the production of fun. But they were (and are) indisputably entertaining.[14]

Disney also understood the power of the souvenir, the product that encapsulates the vacation experience and elicits memory. Visitors found, and still find, that the exits for rides and attractions are often the entrances to gift shops and you must pass the merchandise to reach the street again. Souvenir shops were also located strategically in each of Disneyland's lands, especially on Main Street, where everybody exits the park. The souvenirs are also literally conversation pieces, providing Disney and other retailers with word-of-mouth advertising as we describe our vacation to friends and neighbors and relatives.

Finally, Disneyland showed the promise of brand identity and cross-promotion. Disney had cross-marketed movies and toys since the 1930s and licensed its characters to other manufacturers, but the advent of Disneyland strengthened these commercial connections. The park came into existence as the physical manifestation of a TV show of the same name; it continually referred to the Disney movie archives; and it sold toys inspired by both big and little screen. Essentially, the park was an ad for the TV shows (including the wildly popular Mickey Mouse Club) and the movies. The TV shows were an ad for the park and the toys, and the toys were an ad for everything else. Further, people paid for all of these ads, becoming willing shills for the Disney corporation.[15]

More recently, the Disney company has moved Disney merchandise from its own malls into other malls. Karal Ann Marling suggests that these Disney stores and galleries "manipulate displays and spaces in a cinematic way unprecedented in retail circles." Their animated and expressive retail design inspired a generation of media-marketing combinations—the Warner Brothers Store, the Nickelodeon Store, the Discovery Channel Store, ESPN Sports Zones—and more lively storefronts and retail designs for a whole variety of mall retailers.[16]

In recent years, too, Las Vegas has also become a capital of shopping for fun. During the 1990s, Las Vegas entrepreneurs challenged Disney's worlds as a source of inspiration for retail design and entertainment. Architect Paul Jacob notes that "Las Vegas retail represents a unique testing lab for a new breed of projects where shopping, entertainment, tourism and food are bundled together in a themed environment. The successful projects so far reflect the notion that fantasy has become a highly sought commodity, even if that fantasy replicates a known and accessible reality."[17]

The Forum Shoppes at Caesar's Palace started the Vegas shopping revolution in 1992, with a retail theme park based on the ancient world of the Roman empire. Shoppers come off the Strip into an air-conditioned environment marked by classical columns, statuary, and piazzas surrounding lavish fountains. Overhead, clouds skitter across a "sky" that changes from dawn to dusk in a convenient, hourly cycle. Costumed characters roam the mall, staging skits for customers' enjoyment. At the far end of the arcade, so people have to walk past all the shops in the mall, the audio-animatronic stone statues of Bacchus and other Roman gods come to life every hour on the hour in a battle over the continent

170

Venice in Vegas: the Grand Canal Shoppes (Photo by the author; published with permission of the Grand Canal Shoppes, Las Vegas, Nevada)

of Atlantis. At the end of the show, visitors are invited into the Race for Atlantis, a 3-D Imax motion simulator. These attractions have made the Forum Shoppes a profitable destination, averaging over fourteen hundred dollars per square foot in sales, more than three times the national average for shopping centers.[18]

The Grand Canal Shoppes at the Venetian, which opened in 1999, evokes the city of Venice, with a fifteen-hundred-foot reproduction of the Grand Canal (complete with gondola rides and operatic gondoliers), St. Mark's Square, and assorted street scenes. Street vendors and performers interact with shoppers on the square and on the narrow, winding streets of the simulated city. With 500,000 square feet of retail space, the Grand Canal Shoppes offer high-end retailers and specialty restaurants to Vegas visitors seeking a unique shopping experience. In its first year in business, the mall averaged sales of one thousand dollars per square foot.[19]

Desert Passage, a 500,000-square-foot mall with 130 shops and restaurants, recreates the trade routes of the Middle East, with marketplaces from Spain to Northern Africa to the Arabian Sea. Winner of a 2001 Thea Award for "themed retail," Desert Passage celebrates the authenticity of its simulation. Spokesman Paul Beirnes claims, "We've taken authenticity to a whole new level. Every one of our lights and lamps and sconces were handmade in Morocco."[20]

Although this desert mall is enclosed and air conditioned, it still experiences the vagaries of weather. At Desert Passage, there's a sign that reads

Rainstorm Predicted
Monday–Thursday on the hour
Friday–Sunday on the half-hour

On cue, a thunder-and-lightning storm pours on a 155-foot freighter docked in a North African port. As fog rolls in, the temperature drops ten to fifteen degrees, and waves crash against rocks in the harbor. There's no merchandise directly associated with this act of nature, but it draws people through the shopping center like a magnet. Like the Rainforest Café, where a thunderstorm rolls through the restaurant every twenty minutes, Desert Passage celebrates its ability to predict (and produce) the weather that affects whether or not customers will spend time and money in the mall.[21]

Both the Disney parks and the Las Vegas malls are typically vacation experiences. At the Forum Shops in Las Vegas, 80 percent of customers are visitors; at the Grand Canal Shoppes, it's as much as 95 percent. Like Disney's lands, the Las Vegas ventures have taught other mall managers the profitability of the tourist trade. Increasingly, shopping center professionals understand that time-starved Americans shop on vacation, so they work hard to make even normal malls into destinations for tourists. According to the Travel Industry Association, shopping is the most popular vacation activity. Malls are among the top tourist attractions in at least ten states, and 77 percent of Americans go shopping on vacation. Half of Americans admit that shopping is a major feature of our vacation, and three percent consider shopping the primary purpose of the vacation. Tourists are good for mall business, because they spend four to ten times more than local shoppers, and they rarely return purchases.[22]

Mallpractices

Retail entertainment, then, is to some extent an attempt to bring the vacation into everyday life. Architect Gregory Rothweiler, who designed the Rainforest Café at the Mall of America, talks about providing customers with the "40-minute vacation, or a two-hour vacation." At Rainforest Café, he says, people get a chance "to take a little adventure. They get education, fun, satisfy their food needs, and the notion of a souvenir of the experience."[23]

The Disneyfication of Shopping Centers

Entertainment retail is not exactly a new thing. Early department stores sponsored all sorts of entertainment, and shopping centers have always been designed for fun. Malls have never been purely practical; from the Mediterranean theming of J. C. Nichols' Country Club Plaza, they've provided more than a simple place for buying and selling. The Plaza, in fact, was themed in two ways. First, the country club itself is a theme, connoting the life of the leisure class. Second, the Mediterranean architectural touches suggested a life more sensual, more radiant, more exotic than the routines of suburban Kansas City. "True entertainment retail is like good film, literature, art or music," a California consultant notes. "It moves people emotionally."[24]

Since 1955, Disney's impact on entertainment has been continuous. Main Street's success influenced the design of many early mall corridors, which also used street lamps and storefronts to evoke the "good old days" of a bygone America. "Like Disney's street," William Kowinski says in *The Malling of America*, "the shopping mall plans and carries out a consistent design so that the mall's street looks unified, quaint yet familiar. The mall also excludes the rougher elements of real downtowns—no dives or pool halls here—and like the Disney versions, the stores are smaller than stores on town streets." And the trend continues. In 1992, promoters for the Mall of America insisted that North Garden, one of four themed shopping areas in the megamall, "is Main Street U.S.A." In 1999, the International Council of Shopping Centers cosponsored a conference on "Bringing Main Street into the Mall." And newer "hybrid malls," regional centers with adjacent outdoor "streets," also emphasize their Main Street attractions.[25]

Disneyland's Main Street also influenced the malling of many real Main Streets in the 1960s, as cities converted their shopping streets to pedestrian promenades.

Starting with Victor Gruen's design for Kalamazoo, Michigan, many American towns themed their real commercial streets. If Main Street could be magical in Anaheim, they hoped, perhaps it would work also in their own hometown. Turning to the Main Street Program of the National Trust for Historic Preservation, merchants restored old buildings, and built new ones to look old, hoping to compete with the malls and Wal-Marts out on the edge of town.[26]

Disney's designs, architectural and otherwise, also influenced the design of festival marketplaces in urban centers. In 1963, for example, developer James Rouse told the Urban Design Conference at Harvard that "the greatest piece of urban design in the United States today is Disneyland." By 1976, Rouse had learned how to apply Disney's principles to the retail renewal of real cities, in festival marketplaces like Boston's Faneuil Hall, Baltimore's Harborplace, and New York's South Street Seaport, theming and malling the city at the same time.[27]

As early as 1971, as an essay in *Chain Store Age* contended, developers had "learned that today's shopper wants more than just merchandise. They want to be entertained. . . . The retailer competes for leisure time against other entertainment media, i.e., TV, radio. He must provide amusement in addition to merchandise." But the rapid mass production of malls in the 1970s and 1980s led to a sameness in shopping centers, and the novelty of malls wore off. Baby boomer females were spending time at work instead of at the mall, and their kids were also consuming time formerly devoted to shopping. In the 1990s, Internet sales began to offer a convenient alternative for time-pressed Americans. So observers began to speak about "the pall of the mall." "The mall as we know it," said one observer, "has almost become a thing of the past, a big lumbering dinosaur that stalks the suburban landscape offering an unending corridor of homogenous stores in an enclosed, atmospherically controlled environment of sameness." By the mid-1990s, the number of new shopping centers was falling, and managers realized that they would need to revitalize and reposition old centers to maintain or increase market share. In 1995, shopping center guru Melvin Simon told *Shopping Centers Today*, "We've found that sales in shopping centers have been flat [and] that people spend less time in the mall. We think that by the addition of entertainment and entertainment venues that they'll spend longer in the mall, therefore they'll spend more money and that will give us what we want, because the more exposure merchants get, the better off they are."[28]

In 2000, the International Council of Shopping Centers confirmed the importance of this emerging trend by sponsoring a pre-convention study tour of "entertainment-oriented shopping centers." The ICSC suggested that "entertainment is a hot topic in the shopping center industry and has become the necessary vocabulary of all professionals who own, manage and lease shopping centers. . . . . Shoppers now desire a versatile range of retail experiences that are exciting, playful, amusing or educational. They anticipate a distinctive social and personalized retail experience that will be impressive enough to return to the shopping center. Because entertainment creates excitement and generates interest, it attracts people to shopping centers to shop and to do things besides shopping. More and more the shopping experience is becoming an entertaining lifestyle trend."[29]

In recent years, malls have responded to America's fondness for fun in at least three different ways. First, drawing on Disney precedents and Las Vegas successes, individual stores and chains have tried to make shopping an "experience." Second, shopping centers have increasingly included entertainment and "eatertainment" in the tenant mix. Third, malls themselves have become entertainment attractions.

The Store Strikes Back

The first trend in mall entertainment is taking place at the level of the individual store. In 1999, a conference on "Bringing Main Street into the Mall" convened in Toronto, sponsored by the ICSC, the Canadian Urban Institute, and the Center for the Study of Commercial Activity. Speakers advised participants to "act like a theater, not a warehouse." Retailers and restaurateurs, they said, need to learn to "transform," not just "transact." The key to transformation is creating environments that elicit experiences, either a theatrical shopping experience or an experience evoking the theme of the merchandise. Retail designers can enhance the customer's shopping experience by making the store seem like a market, a streetscape, or a city square, returning customers to the urban experience of civic conviviality. They can enhance the thematic experience by designing specific sights and sounds. Such retail theater involves a plot imposed over the skeleton of mere purchasing.[30]

Shopping for the Fun of It

In a perceptive essay called "The Store Strikes Back," architectural critic Paul Goldberger describes how retailers have responded to the challenge of America's fascination with fun. Especially in an era of Internet sales and increasing time poverty, retailers realized that their unique selling proposition was not the product, which was easily available on line, but the experience of shopping itself. Writing about the NikeTown flagship store in New York, which won a 1997 Thea Award from the Themed Entertainment Association, Goldberger notes that "the first thing you think . . . is that this is not a store at all." The merchandise, he observes, "is secondary to the experience of being in this store, an experience that bears more than a passing resemblance to a visit to a theme park. NikeTown is a fantasy environment, one part nostalgia to two parts high tech, and it exists to bedazzle the consumer, to give its merchandise sex appeal, and establish Nike as the essence not just of athletic wear but also of our culture and way of life." Like a museum, NikeTown displays a history of athletic achievement, associating the shoes for sale with a culture of competition and victory, committing the consumer not just to a purchase but also to a life-style. In Boston, NikeTown features a Boston Marathon theme and benches from the Boston Garden, home of the NBA Celtics. Like tourists, we visit NikeTown for the experience; the shoes and sportswear are like souvenirs. In Chicago, within three months of its opening, Nike's Michigan Avenue flagship store was named one of Chicago's top tourist attractions.[31]

Increasingly, in our culture and way of life, people are screened from one another by computers and television, and by the cubicle culture of the modern workplace. "In a culture that is starved for public experience," Goldberger suggests, "stores entice us into their versions of a public realm, offering a Faustian bargain: step into our commercial world and we will give you the kind of communal excitement that is hard to find this side of Disneyland." Like early department stores, and like Disneyland, we pay for public experience that used to be free. And newer retail venues like NikeTown also offer "the pleasure of physically *being* somewhere, of going to a place that was bigger, grander and in every way more exhilarating than anything the consumer could experience at home." Retailers, Goldberger implies, can profit from the decline of civic culture by offering commercial substitutes for it.[32]

Other stores have also tried to become attractions. *Time* reports that "the idea that the store can be a destination, a pleasant rather than an off-putting experience, has been popularized by retailers such as Barnes & Noble, which added lounge chairs and coffee bars, turning the bookstore into a relaxed, meet-and-greet emporium." Williams-Sonoma and Pottery Barn offer demonstrations and classes that are as communal as they are educational. Sephora sells cosmetics and perfumes in bazaars full of touch-and-try products. Even coffee got themed, as Starbucks showed retailers how to make a cup of coffee an experience, not just a beverage. "What we've all learned from Disney," says John Ecklein, publisher of *The Entertainment Real Estate Report*, "is you have got to create a consistent feel, look, and attitude to create a high-energy environment."[33]

In an essay on "Themed Retail Design," Ronald Mendoza notes that you don't need themed retail designs for "needs merchandising." People will buy the things they need at gas stations, convenience stores, and discount stores. But people need more than things, and themed retail design reaps the "incremental revenues" that come from selling feelings. Mendoza suggests that "Themed Retail Design is an attempt to manage emotions" by creating contextual cues for role playing. The thematic context includes architectural and ornamental cues, but it also encompasses fixtures, lighting, sound, merchandise displays, and sales staff. According to Mendoza, when everybody and every thing plays a part in establishing the theme, themed designs cause "an emotional feeling that is positive and results in a sale." So whether the theme is the desert or the rainforest or Venice or Rome, the main theme is always money.[34]

Entertainment Venues

The second strategy for selling fun is to bring entertainment venues into the mall. Early regional malls often banished ventures like movie theaters to outparcels on the edge of the parking lot. They discovered, in fact, that such businesses were locating near the mall to profit from its traffic flow. So newer malls are integrating entertainment as an essential part of the program, trying to capture proceeds that had been proceeding elsewhere. Entertainment allows shopping centers to "generate free publicity, distinguish one center from another, boost traffic, extend shopper visits, generate repeat business and compete with entertainment venues like amusement parks."[35]

Carousel of fun (Courtesy of Simon Property Group)

"Entertainment," says Kevin Kenyon in *Shopping Centers Today*, "can reinvigorate a tired center, separate a property from its competition, attract much-needed traffic, and fill vacant spaces abandoned by apparel manufacturers." In a culture of amusement, mall managers have incorporated amusements into their tenant mix, hoping to promote "complementary uses" and "cross-shopping." "There's only one reason to bring entertainment into a mall," claims retail consultant William Haralson, "and that's because it will draw some people that otherwise wouldn't be there."[36]

Newer shopping centers can provide entertainment for all ages, from toddlers to grandparents, including people who previously didn't visit the mall much. Costumed characters, kiddie rides and indoor playgrounds appeal to little kids. Arcades and high-tech motion-simulation rides seduce teenagers and twenty-somethings. Cineplexes show movies from cartoons to chick flicks to action films to artsy dramas. Carousels are a magnet for youngsters and nostalgic oldsters too. "Carousels are a complete family attraction," says Rob Swinson of Chance Rides. "It can be experienced as a group, not just something that the parents watch." Sit-down theme restaurants attract older couples who don't think of themselves as shoppers, but who might shop at the mall if they're there for dinner and a movie. Although entertainment centers seldom produce the revenues that conventional retailers do, their ability to act as a magnet can increase revenues throughout a shopping center.[37]

Sometimes entertainment is occasional, part of a specific promotion designed to bring people into the mall. Starstruck Studios, for example, provides a small sound stage on which costumed shoppers can lip-sync songs in front of a video screen that makes them part of a movie. Typically, the Studios are set up for three to four days in the mall's common area, and customers who spend a certain amount at the mall get to sing for free and receive a souvenir video of their performance as a gift. Such shows, and there are a lot of variations, bring people into the mall, encourage them to spend more (to reach the threshold for the "free" gift), and pull other patrons through the mall to see the show.[38]

Sometimes entertainment comes in the form of a cineplex, or a family entertainment center. Americans like movies, and we spend both time and money at the movies. Seventy percent of Americans go to the movies, and young people see more movies than anybody else. Thirty-four percent of Americans aged eighteen to twenty-four go to the movies at least once a month, as opposed to 20 percent of all adults. This is, in part, because movies are considered a good date. Sixty-three percent of us go to the movies with just one other person, and only 6 percent go alone. Larger groups tend to be younger people, who pal around before and after the film.[39]

But movies have faced stiff competition from other entertainment venues, especially from home entertainment centers with their videotapes, video games, DVDs and Internet access. To some extent, this competition accounts for what one observer calls "the re-screening of America." Beginning in 1995, there's been a trend to make over movie houses into multiplexes that spread labor costs over a dozen films instead of just one or two. These multiplexes often offer perks like stadium seating and Dolby sound that appeal to the cineaste. They make movie-going a more memorable "experience" than watching the same film on the home entertainment center. "If you don't have the bells and whistles," warned Dave Sweetser at the 1998 ICSC Spring Convention, "you've either got to get in the game, or fall behind."[40]

Malls expect to capitalize on this movie mania because the multiplexes have become a destination in themselves. Like regional malls, multiplexes require an upscale trade area of 250,000 to 300,000 people. Sweetser explained: "The consumer makes a choice to go to the theater. People don't go to the Limited then say, 'By the way, let's catch a movie.' The theater is a destination anchor and should be treated as such." Reading *Shopping Centers Today* or *Shopping Center World*, you find that many mall renovations include multiplexes with ten to thirty screens. With so many screens, operators can qualify as a "district," which means that they can lock up first-run films first, and that they're unlikely to miss any blockbuster hits.[41]

Cineplexes and malls are often a good match, able to reduce costs by sharing parking and infrastructure. Movie theaters can occupy upper-level space that's hard to lease or space that's been left vacant by a department store closing. Movies increase mall traffic in off-peak hours, and mall managers hope to convert that flow to increased sales. Multiplexes also help draw customers in the mall's off seasons, summer and winter. It's hard to get people into the mall in summer's lovely weather, and it's hard to get them back again after the Christmas rush. But both summer and the holiday weekends of December and January are prime time for movies. A good multiplex, says Don Pollard, vice president of entertainment development at the Simon DeBartolo Group (now the Simon Property Group), "can bring in an extra 1 million or 2 million people annually, and those additional trips can translate into higher sales." Since movies change their offerings almost weekly, they also generate repeat business that's good for malls.[42]

Movie theaters depend not just on films but also on state-of-the-art concessions, which generate substantial profits. Even though only about a third of ticket buyers make a concession purchase, a good concession stand makes at least a dollar per movie patron, because mark-ups on popcorn, drinks, and candy can be as much as 500 percent. Popcorn, which is mostly air, and soft drinks, which are mostly water, are particularly profitable. But candy is sweet for movie theaters too. Concession stands stock candies like Milk Duds and Jujyfruits not because they're the most popular candies in America, but because they're the most profitable.[43]

Multiplexes increase business for bookstores, coffee shops, gift shops, and restaurants. They're especially good for the sit-down restaurant business, since "dinner and a movie" is a standard menu for fun in American culture. Pollard says that Simon studies show 20–40 percent sales increases at restaurants both in the mall and in outparcels. Cinema Grill Systems even arranges dinner and a movie in one place, targeting a market of adults between the ages of twenty-one and forty with cabaret seating and full food and beverage menus. "We have a sophisticated movie goer," says Vice President John Duffy. "Our market requires services."[44]

Family entertainment centers often include arcade games, motion simulators, kids' play areas, and redemption games like skee-ball. The family centers located on shopping center outparcels can add larger attractions, like carousels, indoor go-cart tracks, miniature golf, batting cages, and video golf. Both kinds of locations lure kids and their families, often for special events like birthday parties. Especially during the slower retail months after Christmas, these centers bring traffic to the mall. Inside many malls, new concepts like Gameworks (a joint production of Sega, Universal Studios, and Dreamworks) and DisneyQuest combine video games and virtual realities with bars and restaurants to expand the appeal of the teen and pre-teen arcades.[45]

Restaurants and food courts are an integral part of most mall entertainment venues. But going out to eat is increasingly an entertainment too. According to MasterCard's 1994 Dining Out Study, "Americans now view eating out as the No. 1 way to unwind and relax." As a result, malls have tried to include dining destinations among their attractions. Inspired by the worldwide success of themed restaurants such as the Hard Rock Café, shopping centers have increasingly opened their doors to themed and/or upscale restaurants to satisfy people's hunger for food, conviviality, and consumption.[46]

Theme restaurants were all the rage in the 1990s. Planet Hollywood, the Rainforest Café, House of Blues, Motown Café, Fashion Café, Dave and Buster's, and Dive! flourished as people took a first look (and a first bite). Many of these establishments served good food, but apparently not good enough to generate the repeat business that would keep them going in every city. In tourist locations, themed restaurants still work as a vacation destination, but around town, Americans don't seem to be eating up all these concepts.[47]

The entertainmentization of malls is part of a larger shift in commercial culture, as people have shifted from buying goods to buying experiences, some of them embedded in goods. As consultant Nina Gruen suggests, "Experiences have become more important to people—theater, sports, espresso at the neighborhood coffee shop—and less fixated on things."[48]

That's Entertainment! That's the Mall!

Some shopping center chains specialize in retail entertainment. The Mills Corporation has even trademarked the term "Shoppertainment" to describe its integrated mix of upscale discount shopping, bold graphics, and entertainment. CEO Larry Siegel claims that one inspiration for the mix was a fond memory of childhood, Wanamaker's department store, which sponsored a light-and-water show during the Christmas holidays.[49]

Projects like Riverwalk in San Antonio (1968), Faneuil Hall in Boston (1976), Horton Plaza in San Diego (1985), CocoWalk in Miami (1990), Mall of America in Minneapolis (1992), CityWalk at Universal City (1994), and Navy Pier in Chicago (1994) have used amusements to attract and contain a more diverse set of shoppers. More recently, San Francisco's Metreon, an $85 million "urban entertainment center" sponsored by Sony, opened with an IMAX theater, a cineplex, video arcade, and an interactive playground themed by Maurice Sendak's *Where the Wild Things Are*. "The attractions at Metreon are designed to have the visual impact of Hollywood sets combined with the elements of a theme park," says a spokesperson for Sony Development. In the stores, including a Sony Style store and a PlayStation store, the old rule of "do not touch" has been replaced by a "hands-on" ethic. Sales clerks encourage patrons to listen to CDs, and to play games on Sony's popular PlayStation to get a sense of "Sony's theme of technology and convenience." An integral part of downtown's Yerba Buena Center for the Arts, the Metreon complements (and helps to pay for) a theater, art museum, public park, and children's museum on the site. Early counts showed twenty thousand people a day visiting the entertainment center, about double original projections.[50]

The premier architect of the mall as entertainment is Jon Jerde. Jerde claims

Mallpractices

that he's not really interested in shopping, but he has designed some of the most interesting shopping spaces in the world, often reviving downtown districts in the process. After coordinating designs for the Los Angeles Olympics in 1984, Jerde's first blockbuster retail project was Horton Plaza (1985), a downtown redevelopment design that insinuated a shopping center into 10 blocks of central San Diego. He has followed that with Mall of America in Minneapolis (1992), Universal CityWalk in Los Angeles (1993), Canal City Hakata in Japan (1996), and both the Fremont Street Experience (1995) and Bellagio Casino (1998) in Las Vegas. Since founding the Jerde Partnership in 1977, he has designed 35 million square feet of commercial space, and he has another 29 million square feet programmed to open by the end of 2003. According to one observer, Jerde is probably "global capitalism's preeminent designer."[51]

Jerde began his career in architecture as a designer of enclosed shopping malls, applying the standard boom-time formula to one suburban location after another. "Malls were a tremendous education in humans," he says. "So even though it was a repulsive subject, I learned a lot." Because the cookie-cutter shopping centers of the 1960s and 1970s, including some of his own designs, had been designed as "machines for shopping," they often "lacked the kind of complex experience found in existing urban conditions." Consequently, Jerde decided that "shopping centers would be better designed for citizens, not just consumers." He believes that if you create spaces where people like to congregate, and you supplement the public spaces with stores, people will shop. But he's much more interested in the interactions of people than the transactions of the cash register. Unlike standard mall architects, who design shopping centers to feature merchandise, Jon Jerde designs them to feature the mall experience. "Shopping malls are considered the least honorable thing for an architect to work on," he admits. "But I'm working for the common man."[52]

Like Victor Gruen and James Rouse, Jerde is interested in what he calls "urban glue," the creation of community in commercial space. He contends that "communal experience is a designable event," and he tries to create spaces that bring people together. The web page of the Jerde Partnership says that "the firm's goal is to bring civility, continuity, and relatedness to the chaotic built environment of the late twentieth century." More specifically, it says, "Our adventure has been to reinvent the authentic urban experience." One appreciative critic notes that "his designs are fueled by the belief that the consumer public, though scattered

183

Shopping for the Fun of It

by sprawl, still hungers for the crowds and energy of cities." Another writer claims that "CityWalk is a shopping mall that refuses to be a shopping mall, where we're desperate consumers of one another's company."[53]

Unlike Mies van der Rohe, Jon Jerde believes that less is not more, so the more the merrier. Maintaining the "function and rationality" of the traditional mall, Jerde has "added moments of surprise and excitement. We created a magical quality utilizing intensity and activity; at our projects senses are stimulated." Unlike festival marketplaces, which often reproduce the authentic architecture around them, Jerde's urban experiments set older buildings in conversation with contemporary architecture. His designs have been animated by dramatic shapes, jutting facades, surprising twists and turns, bright lights, waving banners, colorful attractions, and occasional quiet interludes. "Orchestrating the level of drama," the Jerde Partnership designs not just space, but experience—or "aesthetic emotion." Like Walt Disney, Jerde tries to create a "visceral reality" in a world of increasing virtual reality, and in shopping spaces designed for selling.[54]

Like Disney, too, Jerde is an architectural populist. "We deal in the art of the ordinary," he says. "We yearn for a marriage between the magical and the banal. Our true client is the populace itself. We put people in a popular and collective environment in which they can be most truly and happily alive." It seems to work. One of the reasons that developers like Jerde's projects is, in fact, that they become tourist attractions. At a time when the average suburban mall was attracting 9 million customers annually, Horton Plaza drew 25 million in its first year. Mall of America attracts more shoppers every year than Disneyland and Disney World combined. In less than ten years, more than 70 million people have strolled through CityWalk. Initial sales at Canal City Hakata exceeded projections by 140 percent. All in all, a billion people a year visit Jerde projects.[55]

Critics accuse Jerde of prostituting architecture in the service of commercialism. Ada Louis Huxtable singles him out as a master builder of *Unreal America*. And the Museum of Contemporary Art included only one of his projects in its retrospective on twentieth-century architecture, in a gallery derisively labeled "Disneyfication." But Jerde contends that his work responds to real American problems, and that real Americans respond to his projects. After World War II, he says, "your realm became your backyard, so that the only possible public experience that you could have at all, ever, was in shopping. Consumption is the addiction of the American." Given the decline of city centers, the privatization of suburban life, and the historic associations of public space with the marketplace, it made sense to make malls serve broader purposes.[56]

In *The Harvard Design School Guide to Shopping*, Daniel Herman trivializes Jerde's work, claiming that it "has brought shopping to an environmental climax by taking the entire discarded repertoire of architecture and returning it as farce." Herman contends that "the Jerde mall physically dislocates the shopper by requiring all sorts of peregrinations through formless space. Such spatial gymnastics provoke a condition we might call the *Jerde Transfer*: the moment when a shopper's movements break down under excessive spatial stimulation. Shoppers become bewildered as to where they are, where they are going, and how they will get there."[57]

"The Jerde Transfer is akin to the operation of the fun house," Herman insightfully observes. "In the fun house, scale, orientation, and overall organization is rendered uncertain. The fun house uses sequential juxtapositions of spatial difference—expansion and contraction, vertiginous balconies, and claustrophobic corridors—to achieve its effect of dislocation." Herman sees the Jerde Transfer leading to confusion and bewilderment, but it's possible to see it differently. Such a judgment underestimates shoppers, who probably keep coming back not for confusion but for the satisfactions that good commercial architecture can bring. Putting it more generously, in fact, we might say that Jerde replaces the predictability and passivity of the typical mall with a sense of stimulation, sociability, and discovery. As Jerde says, "The shopping center is a pretty pathetic venue to deal with broad-based communalizing, but it's all we've got and it's the pump-primer in America." Critics might believe that Jerde's combination of commercialism and architecture is reprehensible, but a lot of ordinary Americans seem to think otherwise.[58]

The Cultural Work of Retail Entertainment

All of these innovations in our malls come from commercial concerns, but they have deep roots in American cultural patterns, especially the dialectics of work and play, boredom and fun. The reenchantment of the mall is just one element of a larger "entertainment economy," which is becoming an essential part of social and economic life and a cornerstone of consumer psychology.[59]

We often think of fun as trivial—what kids do, what we do in our spare time—not as anything significant. But fun is a fundamental construct of both modern and postmodern societies, and it's serious business. According to sociologist Martha Wolfenstein, fun has become a kind of fun-damental-ism in American society, as we have adopted a "fun morality" that makes fun an obligation. Some of us even feel guilty that we're not having enough fun. And fun performs cultural work for us. Anthropologist Clifford Geertz contends that "deep play" is a way that members of society learn their culture in leisure. "This too the mall does," according to Richard Keller Simon. "Funland is a place in which serious activities take place."[60]

People have always experienced pleasure and enjoyed themselves, but "fun" is a fairly recent invention, related to changing patterns of work and everyday life. For most of us, fun punctuates the life sentence of work. When we do things "just for fun," we think we are evading the instrumentalism and efficiency that structures our work lives; we think we are acting for pleasure and enjoyment— and we are. Fun is functional in a society that manufactures stress along with other mass productions. Fun dispels the funk that accompanies the vicissitudes of work and home. When we go *to* malls that promise "a place for fun in your life," we are going *from* the places for work in our lives.

This experience of fun, therefore, depends on cultural definitions of work that developed in the twentieth century. In 1900, Americans were in the midst of a great transformation from self-employment (usually in agriculture, but sometimes in trade and other occupations) to corporate employment. As people lost the autonomy of being their own bosses, or at least of knowing the boss as a person, not just as a functionary, they began to experience work as alienating. At home, too, work was redefined. The daily chores were relabeled drudgery, usually by people who hoped to sell housewives "labor-saving" appliances. Having culturally taken the pleasure out of work, Americans were poised to look for satisfactions elsewhere. And the emerging entertainment industry was willing to sell them new pleasures to replace the ones they had misplaced in their modernization.[61]

Mallpractices

When the mall is presented as a fun house, it acts as an escape from every-day life, which is not supposed to be fun. We go to the mall in order to get away from the daily discontents of our lives. But the mall is, in fact, a celebration of the structures of American life presented as an escape from them. Functionally speaking, then, one of the main purposes of fun is to get us back to work. We think we live for the fun of weekends, but weekends work best when they moti-vate us to work. As Witold Rybczynski says, "recreation is both a consequence of work and a preparation for more of it." So, structurally speaking, the system gets us going and coming. Mary Jo Deegan contends that "the seductive char-acter of fun emerges from its predictable capacity to generate short-lived, incom-plete escapes from mundane routine. In the process, fun simultaneously strength-ens and reproduces the core oppressions and repressions of everyday life." Instead of trying to change the structures of our alienation, we alleviate the alien-ation with fun. In escaping *from* the manifestations of modern capitalism, we escape *to* another manifestation of the same capitalism.[62]

In the same way, paradoxically, our desire for fun and leisure can actually increase our need to work. Economist Staffan Linder suggests that the develop-ment of commercial fun and leisure industries has increased the cost of leisure, converting "free time" into "consumption time," which has its workaday costs. For example, Rybczynski notes that Americans spend more than $13 billion annually on sports apparel, which means basically that we exchange leisure *time* for leisure *wear*. In the past, people might relax by doing nothing, or going for a walk in the woods, or having a conversation. They might read library books, or cook a meal together. We still do these things. But these days, when there's an implicit hierarchy of fun, such pastimes might seem too simple, with too little stimulation.[63]

"Are we having fun yet?" is a question we ask when we know we're not. It implies that fun is the standard by which we measure our activity, and increas-ingly it is. But as Thomas Pynchon suggests in *Gravity's Rainbow*, if they can get you asking the wrong questions, they don't have to worry about the answers. If we ask if something is fun, and not if it's fulfilling, we end up with different answers. Fun, for the most part, is episodic. We speak of a fun time, but not a fun life. We say we had fun at the concert, but not that all music is fun. Fulfillment, on the other hand, doesn't have to be episodic, nor is it necessarily fun.

Shopping for the Fun of It

Fulfillment describes the satisfaction that comes from living a good life—not "the good life" of consumer culture, but a life characterized by a right relation to the world. Fulfillment comes from going deep instead of skimming the surface of life. It comes from service, not from selfishness. Fulfillment satisfies the soul as well as the senses. Good relationships are fulfilling, because they challenge us to be good, which is not always fun. Raising children is fulfilling, but it's not always fun. Learning to write is fulfilling, but it isn't fun. And good work is fulfilling, even though it can be challenging. So the funny thing about fun morality is how much it keeps us distracted from other possibilities of deeper pleasure.

If fun is sold as an escape from our everyday lives, it's also sold as a break from boredom, which has its own cultural history. Boredom is the state or condition of being bored or uninterested; it's ennui. Twenty-one percent of Americans confess that they are regularly bored, and researchers expect that the real number is probably higher. A 1999 Yankelovich poll finds a "boredom boom," with more than 70 percent of Americans looking for more novelty in their lives.[64]

Boredom is a modern invention. In her lively book, *Boredom*, Patricia Spacks traces the historical development of boredom. The word "bore" first appeared in the 18th century, when individualism and ideas of leisure came to center stage. At that time, it described people who were uninteresting because of their own moral deficiency. By the nineteenth century, when the word "boredom" first appeared, it connoted a kind of sociological fatalism: groups, more than individuals, suffered from boredom. In the twentieth century, though, boredom changed again. It's no longer seen as a moral deficiency; it's understood as a poverty of stimulation. The responsibility for boredom has moved from the self to the society.[65]

To some extent, boredom is also a product of the people who want to sell us products. It's one of the consequences of an expanding consumer culture, because businesses need boredom to sell novelty. Fashion is not just a way of clothing ourselves, it's a way of covering up our boredom. And "new and improved" products are popular not just because they're better, but because they're literally novelties.

Historically speaking, boredom is the shadow side of amusement and entertainment. In his provocative book *Amusing Ourselves to Death*, cultural critic Neil

Postman suggests that we live in the Age of Show Business, and are socialized by the epistemology of TV, which makes entertainment "the natural format for the representation of all experience." TV also relentlessly stimulates our desire for novelty. Regional shopping centers were a novelty in the 1950s and 1960s, and immensely successful in the 1970s and 1980s. But their success formula led to a dull uniformity and "mall monotony"—the same basic stores in the same basic configurations all across the country. In 1999, then, it was no surprise when retail marketing consultant John Williams claimed that "shopping centers are the most boring places you'll ever find. Boredom is part of our problem."[66]

Ironically, boredom is also a side effect of novelty. The French say that the more things change, the more they stay the same. But Americans believe that the more things change, the more they *ought* to change. We believe in "the tradition of the new," and we have institutions devoted to the daily reporting of "the news." We often greet each other by asking "What's new?" So you might think that we wouldn't be bored. But in *Enchanting a Disenchanted World*, sociologist George Ritzer suggests that modern entertainment institutions, from Las Vegas casinos to amusement parks to shopping malls, raise the threshold of boredom: "spectacles tend to grow dated and boring quite quickly." The more stimulated we become, it seems, the more stimulation we need to be satisfied. Instead of appreciating what we already have, we look for the new and improved.[67]

"As a society," says Mary Catherine Bateson in her thoughtful book *Peripheral Visions: Learning Along the Way*, "we have become so addicted to entertainment that we have buried the capacity for awed experience of the ordinary. Perhaps the sense of the sacred is more threatened by learned patterns of boredom than it is by blasphemies." Instead of finding the extraordinary in the ordinary, we look for the extraordinary in entertainment. Bored or alienated, we go shopping for fun.[68]

American society manufactures a lot of alienation and boredom, and shopping is one way we deal with that. Malls build on this American fun morality. The shopping center becomes an entertainment center, with movies, restaurants, arcades, bowling alleys, and sometimes amusement parks. And the shopping center associates its fun with the holidays of American life. From New Year's to Christmas, malls offer us regular occasions for celebration. Inverting the function of the nineteenth-century world's fair, they convert "the celebration of production into the production of celebration."[69]

The Disneyfication of American consumer culture means that, thanks to Walt Disney (both person and corporation) "it's a mall world after all." Learning from Disney and learning from Las Vegas, shopping centers increasingly include entertainment in the tenant mix. In a culture where fun is fundamental, our malls reflect our fundamentalism. As Michael Sorkin asks, "Who doesn't live in Disney World?"[70]

TEN

Making a Purchase

At malls, we look around for what we want. We do our own personal dance of indecision, and finally we choose. Picking up the products we plan to purchase, we bring them to the cash/wrap, where a salesclerk scans the product code into the cash register. The computerized machine displays each price, calculates discounts and sales taxes, and shows a total. We pay for our purchases with cash or a credit card, and the sales associate puts them in a shopping bag emblazoned with the retailer's name and logo. When it goes well, the process is quick and simple. But it's also complex. The salesclerk is a person with a history—both individual and social. The clerk, the code, the cash, and the credit card all involve us in networks of change and exchange that affect both our shopping and shopping centers. Without them, our malls wouldn't work. But with them, we can learn a lot about shopping and American consumer culture.

Making the Sale

When we approach the checkout counter, most of us aren't thinking much about the sales clerk. But salespeople are essential fixtures of America's malls. Most Americans think of shopping centers as sites of consumption, but for more than 10 million Americans, the mall is the workplace. We come to the mall to take our minds off our work, but other people come specifically to work. While we consume consumption, they produce it. Both onstage and behind the scenes, they provide the customer service that enhances customer satisfaction. So if we're shopping for American culture, it's important to examine the work culture of America's malls, and no place is more important than the sales floor, where our American dreams meet commercial realities.

In upscale department stores and specialty shops, the salesperson is an active, engaged participant in the dance of decision. In this "class" merchandising, the salesperson doesn't just ring up the sale, he or she *makes* the sale. As consumers, we have experience buying things, but no formal training in selling things. Salespeople get formal training, and they sell things all day long. We think we know what we're doing, but in fact, the sales staff probably understands our behavior as well as we do, because they've studied the science of sales and we haven't. Shopping centers support this sales training: one major chain developed educational programs on "$elling," including a "$elling newsletter" and "$ell Star," a training video for temporary hires during the Christmas holiday season. They also employed "secret shoppers" to check up on how well retailers were applying the suggested sales strategies.[1]

Reading retail training manuals is a good way to get a sense of the complexity of this service work. Although it doesn't seem like a particularly difficult profession, the fine art of retail selling is challenging and increasingly rare. A good sales clerk maintains an appropriate appearance, greets customers cheerfully, explains the product line, gives advice, and efficiently makes the sale and bags the merchandise. A good sales clerk is an interdisciplinary scholar, a student of history, psychology, sociology, linguistics, aesthetics, and marketing. Because

Mallpractices

salespeople are dealing with complex human beings in a social setting that emphasizes aesthetics, they need to understand both the arts and social sciences.

In mass merchandising, however, the salesperson is more a clerk than a consultant. Many mall stores and chains compete primarily on price and need to keep labor costs low; the primary selling, therefore, is done not by people but by advertising, in-store videos, and point-of-purchase displays. The clerk can be more passive because the store itself is more active. The sales associate, therefore, spends more time tending the merchandise, maintaining its order and appearance. He or she answers questions when asked but doesn't try to sway customers' opinions. Once a person has decided to buy something, the clerk will handle the sale at the cash/wrap.

Compensation for the complex work of retail sales is minimal, often not much more than minimum wage. It used to be that salesmen and (as often) saleswomen were skilled professionals and paid by commission, but now retail service work pays little. In Minnesota, for example, the state Department of Economic Security found that "among employment sectors, the retail trade offered the worst wages. Retail makes up 19 percent of Minnesota jobs, but accounts for 38 percent, 313,000, of all low-wage workers in the state." Low-wage workers earn less than $10 an hour, or $20,800 before taxes, which is just barely above the 2001 poverty level. A person who works retail won't be buying much at retail.[2]

During the period of the most intense malling of America, a "retail revolution" occurred, affecting both the number of workers and the amount of their compensation. As late as 1958, there were only 2,900 malls in America; by 1980, there were 22,000. In 1947, about 6.5 million Americans worked retail; by 1980, the number had grown to almost 15 million. For every 100 people employed in manufacturing, 250 worked retail, but not all, of course, on the sales floor. As the country shifted from a production to a service economy, America became "a nation of salesmen."[3]

Beginning with labor shortages during World War II and continuing with competition from discount chains in the 1950s and 1960s, retailers revolutionized the sales force. Instead of depending on skilled people who might make a career in sales, they began to hire part-time help and youngsters to mind the store. Part of the pressure for part-time help was a result of extended store hours.

No longer could an employer cover the sales counters with a single shift, nor was it possible to cover peak hours efficiently without part-time assistance. Similarly, retailing is almost as seasonal as agriculture, with its primary peak during the Christmas season, when additional staff are needed. In addition, from an employer's perspective, one of the benefits of part-time workers is that they aren't always eligible for health insurance and other benefits.[4]

Especially as women entered the part-time work force, and as teenagers began to work for "spending money," retail employers reduced compensation and benefits and switched from commission sales to an hourly wage. No longer did sales positions pay enough to support a family; instead, they supplied housewives' so-called pin money or the wages of young people entering the work force. Willie Loman couldn't afford to work in modern retail; it may support the American economy, but it won't support the American Dream—the dream of a living wage to support a family. This meant, and still means, that turnover in retail sales is astronomical. A sales job is often a first job, a seasonal job, a temporary job after a layoff, or a part-time job in retirement. At the mall, one of the most prominent signs in store windows is the one advertising Help Wanted.[5]

With almost total turnover in the sales staff, and minimal compensation, the modern retail establishment can't generally count on sophisticated skills. Indeed, the sales force was systematically de-skilled in the self-service revolution, as retailers began to ask customers to perform the work formerly performed by the sales staff. Self-service is just that; the customer is an unpaid service worker. At the same time, discount retailers have invested in technologies that make retail sales almost idiot-proof. Computerized cash registers and scanning equipment make ringing up a sale a fairly simply matter of following a menu, and universal product codes make inventory and sales data instantly available.[6]

The turnover of labor in retail sales also makes unionization difficult. In an essay called "Sweatshopping," for example, Eyal Press points out that "the Gap has hundreds of outlets across America, employing thousands of workers, but not a single organized shop." The lack of unionization in retail work keeps hours unpredictable, wages minimal, and benefits poor. The lack of a decent wage makes turnover high. It's a vicious circle that keeps compensation low, and (the consumer hopes) prices low. It's one of the bargains that we don't generally bargain for at the mall.[7]

Mallpractices

As salespeople performed fewer persuasive sales functions, retailers began to advertise more. As Barry Bluestone notes in *The Retail Revolution*, "Retailers have turned to mass media to 'sell' the customer, leaving the less-skilled clerical/cash register tasks to store employees." Because of economies of scale, this advertising benefited department store and specialty chains and disadvantaged independent retailers, who couldn't afford full-page newspaper ads or full-color Sunday supplements. At the same time, because newer salespeople knew less about their merchandise, product packaging began to serve as both advertisement and informant on use and care.[8]

The result is that mall work, at least on the sales floor, is an entry-level job, a first employment possibility for teenagers trying to make money to buy their stuff at the mall, and for English-speaking immigrants who are trying to get a start in a new country. It's also an exit-level job, a way for retired people to keep a hand in the work force without the stress and time commitment of a full-time job. Retailers like senior citizens in sales positions because they were brought up with a service ethic that younger generations don't always have.

In either case, retail work is hard work. It's good to help people find what they need, it's even good to help them find what they want, but it's the same routine, over and over again. It's the infinity of folding clothes or stacking product. It's looking neat and acting chipper, even when you feel rumpled and resentful. It's assisting idiots and calming psychopaths. It's needing coverage on the floor for a bathroom break, a coffee break, or lunch. It's having to ask the manager to leave the sales floor. It's boredom from the tedium of the slow hours. It's sore feet from standing all day and jangled nerves from the constancy of the unexpected. It's working long hours for low pay and minimal benefits.

In both class merchandising and mass merchandising, customer service is an essential element of selling. As Judith Sains notes in "What Makes a Successful Salesperson," retail clerks need to "understand their role as the store's and the mall's representative to the customer." It's not good enough to have the goods; a retailer needs to have good service, too. A 2001 survey found that when we encounter bad service in a store, 20 percent of us walk out without a purchase, 20 percent stop shopping there altogether, and 26 percent of us tell our friends and warn them about shopping at that store. On the other hand, good service engenders repeat business, customer loyalty, and invaluable word-of-mouth advertising.[9]

Salespeople also have to deal with the disgruntled people from previous sales, people who have perhaps experienced the "dreaded buyer's remorse" and have come back to complain. With difficult customers, a salesclerk's psychological training really comes into play. And salespeople's acting abilities sometimes rise to the level of Academy Awards. A clerk may think that a customer is a jerk, but he can't say so. He may want to say, "It's not the product that's defective," but instead he's instructed to say, "I'm terribly sorry this product hasn't met your expectations." In *Calming Upset Customers*, consultant Rebecca Morgan stresses the importance of maintaining customer satisfaction. She points out that poor service is the leading cause of losing customers, and that the average angry customer tells eleven people about her dissatisfaction. Noting that it's much more expensive to prospect new customers than to maintain old ones, Morgan shows salespeople how to satisfy even unsatisfied customers.[10]

Appearances are an essential part of customer satisfaction. So in working retail, a person's own appearance and demeanor is a part of the package sold to customers. Salespeople are often selling "a look," so they know that appearances sell. In both dress and adornment, sellers need to make customers comfortable. Like the store itself, salesclerks are dressed and designed to respond to the target demographic. If you work at Nordstrom, you'll dress up. If you work at Old Navy, you'll dress down. If you work at Footlocker, you'll don the black-and-white-striped jersey for a day of officiating. At Hot Topic, you won't wear a suit, but you might have purple hair and a stud through your tongue. In some stores, employees are required to wear the brand they sell. In America's malls, a dress code really is a code, telling prospective customers what kind of service and merchandise to expect. So retail work begins at home, as salespeople work on personal grooming and appropriate dress.

In addition to appearance, attitude is part of the job. And acting is part of the job description. Retail marketers agree that "a little warmth goes along way toward making that sale." Successful clerks soon learn the payoff of "the commercial smile," the amiable affability that's expected in the stylized world of the store. Like secretaries, flight attendants, and other service workers, salespeople learn to feign—or even to feel—care for their customers. They're taught posture and body language, etiquette and self-effacement, because good customer service sometimes requires sales staff to act like servants. This emotional labor is what Arlie Hochschild calls "the managed heart," as clerks manage to show a friendly face for the benefit of both customers and management.[11]

In this way, retailing reinforces the general "friendliness" of American culture. The American social value of friendliness acknowledges American egalitarianism and the possibility of friendship with any person. But it's not friendship. Friendliness is less demanding than friendship. It's the *form* of friendship without the substance. Nevertheless, it's not an empty gesture, since we do feel obliged to give it and we expect to get it at the mall. "To act friend*ly*," notes anthropologist Michael Moffatt, "is to give regular abbreviated performances of the standard behaviors of real friendship." It's why we say, "Hello, how are you?" even when we don't want to know the answer. It's a social convention that keeps us apart by making us feel together. And it's a commercial convention that cloaks a business relationship in the guise of an interpersonal exchange.[12]

However insincere the smile we receive from salespeople, it still feels pretty good, and the absence of the smile is a telling omission. Whatever we might say about the sales staff at the mall, they're usually friendlier than the boss or an abusive spouse or ungrateful children. They don't nag and they don't whine. They're paid for good behavior. And the friendliness of the mall is increasingly important as we have less time for our real friends. Shoppers have become guests in malls as Americans have found it harder to entertain guests at home. In many ways, the sociability of the mall compensates for the declining social capital of the rest of society.[13]

From management's point of view, every person who comes in the door costs them money—in advertising, promotions, merchandise, fixtures, overhead, and so on—so they would like to make money from every customer. Consequently, retailers employ a variety of evaluation tools and retail workers perform their work under constant surveillance. The manager is watching, and so are the store's security cameras. Sometimes, too, "secret shoppers" are employed to check out the sales staff's skills. From a customer's perspective, good service involves getting what you want with a minimum of hassle. From a store's perspective, the same thing is true, because the goal is satisfied customers. But the store also has other goals, and these are reflected in the evaluation of sales staff. Sales per-

197

formance is measured, not just by individual satisfied customers but by more conventional economic measures. One measure of general sales performance is the "conversion rate," the percentage of people entering a store who make a purchase. Emphasis on the conversion rate helps prevent "walkouts," those who enter a store and leave without buying anything. "Without the conversion rate," says Paco Underhill, "you don't know if you're Mickey Mantle or Mickey Mouse." A second measure, for both individuals and the sales staff, is sales per hour. Since profit is the bottom line of business, and time is money, sales per hour is a quick measure of a salesperson's profitability to the company. A third measure is time allocation. Sales staff are expected to spend a specified proportion of their time in customer contact, with other time allocated to stocking, reshelving, and tidying the sales floor. Some stores also employ consultants to conduct a customer service and sales audit to determine exactly how specific elements of salesmanship affect sales. Such an audit measures actual behavior and shows the incremental sales benefits of acknowledging the customer's presence, initiating contact, answering questions, asking questions to clarify the customer's desires, active selling techniques, and suggestion selling.[14]

Sometimes, too, companies offer carrots to their employees. Top-selling salespeople can become "employee of the month," receiving recognition and, occasionally, prizes or special parking privileges. At the Gap, "super sales" will get your name in the company paper, the *Gap Rap*. Some retailers sponsor contests for employees. The Gapper with the most "units per transaction" in a particular store can win a Gap t-shirt.[15]

In addition to retail work, the salespeople at the mall are doing cultural work. The scripts and practices of retail sales reinforce a culture of consumption by reproducing it day by day. When sales associates treat us, the customer, as if we are always right, they reinforce the sense of power we feel in consumption and help us forget the more powerful forces at work on the sales floors of the mall. When they keep the conversation focused on us and our needs, they reinforce the individualism of American culture. When their sales presentations tie a product's features to social benefits, they reinforce the commodity fetishism that animates the culture of consumption. When they take our money and bag our purchases, they teach us by example about the importance of money in consumer capitalism, and about the propriety of private property. When they avoid mentioning politics or religion, because those topics may be too controversial, they reinforce the marginalization of important American institutions by the institution of the mall. Each part of their routine is a practice that routinizes consumption. In these and other ways, what's sold is more than what's purchased. We buy into a whole system of assumptions when we buy a t-shirt at the Gap, or a bra at Victoria's Secret. The work culture of the mall helps shoppers to find what they want (and what they don't want too), but it also reflects and reinforces the central values of American consumer culture.

Universal Product Code

The Universal Product Code, or UPC, is a system of marking merchandise so that it can be scanned by computers. According to the *Harvard Design School Guide to Shopping*, it's "the thumbprint of a good by which its identity is asserted in the realm of information, the wheels by which it travels the infobahn." In the olden days, before the UPC, clerks entered the price of each item by hand on a cash register, which then computed the total sale. This meant that clerks had to have brains, and that speed and accuracy depended on a checker's hand-eye coordination. With scanners, contemporary clerks can save their brains for something important, like television shows or computer games, and the customer's checkout proceeds, at least in theory, much more quickly.[16]

The UPC code assumes the omnipresence of computers in American business—and American life. In just a generation, computers have become an essential part of our lives, speeding tasks and streamlining processes so that we can have more time for family and friends, for TV and shopping. Many of us use computers at work and have personal computers at home. Some of us even carry portable computers, as laptops or Palm Pilots, so that we're never out of range of this artificial intelligence. When the computer is down, though, so is modern retail business. These days, a store without its computer scanners is a place where people are going nowhere fast.

The Universal Product Code speeds our progress through the checkout, and our happiness keeps the merchants happy, but the UPC serves other purposes too. On the sales floor and in the staging area, it eliminates retail workers once needed for pricing merchandise and inventory control and relieves checkout clerks of the

Escape from the bar code: an advertisement for Buy
Nothing Day (Image courtesy of www.adbusters.org)

task of punching in the price of an item. So the computerization of pricing is partly
responsible for the de-skilling and decline in status of retail work. These economies
of sale (and economies of scale) made computerized cash registers especially profitable for chain stores. The same could not be said for independent retail operations, which operated at a much higher payroll-to-sales ratio. "In this sense," contend the authors of *The Retail Revolution*, "the whirring and beeping of the computer
has been the death knell of the traditional independent."[17]

Bar codes are now used worldwide. In a postmodern, relativist age when few
people even believe in universals, it's reassuring to know that we can all agree on the
universality of products and prices. Besides its obvious functions, the UPC suggests
that, in this universe at least, everything is potentially a product and products have
a price. This means essentially that everything is convertible to money. The value
of groceries and sundries and clothes and cars can be expressed in cash; the value
of values can also be expressed in money. Companies talk about the cash value of
their good name; other companies spend cash for advertising that encourages our
trust. That trust, in turn, is worth a precise amount on the company's bottom line.
The equity of a brand name like Coca-Cola is more than $50 billion. In a market
economy, the universe is a commodity, and the UPC helps us to ring up the sale.

Mallpractices

Although it's keyed to report a product's price, the UPC is not a universal cost code. While it tells us what we must pay at the cash register, it doesn't register the full cost of the items we buy. The price of a particular product might be $5.99, but the cost can be substantially different, because manufacturers can ignore those costs of production that economists call externalities. Somebody sweats to produce this particular product, and they do get paid, but the price doesn't include the social costs of their work. Somebody pays for the roads that the shipment moves on, but that's not in the price of the product. Our children will pay later for the environmental costs of production and distribution, but that's not in the price we pay at the checkout. And often there are human and spiritual costs to production and consumption that are incalculable. At the cash register, we neglect to think about just how much the price tag we peruse puts a price on other people's lives and labor and land. Indeed, one of the tragedies of a consumption society is that we can enjoy unjust relationships with people we never see. Americans are a people, says environmentalist David Orr, who know the price of everything but the cost of nothing. Although it's easy to forget, the price is often *not* right![18]

The fact that everything can be converted to cash means that everything has a market value, even things we don't normally associate with the market. Wages put a price on people's labor, for example; some sweatshops put a price on child labor; prostitution puts a price on intimacy; in extreme cases, slavery puts a price on people themselves. All of these things are normal within the market. We may have moral objections to them, but in a market economy, the value of moral objections is also monetary. If we're mad enough about pollution or injustice, the marketeers tell us, we'll pay for a remedy.

Further, the more we adopt a market mentality, the more the world looks like the mall—an arrangement of objects arranged for sale. Conservatives tell environmentalists that there's no need for environmental protection because the market will protect the environment. When wilderness becomes truly valued, people will pay to preserve it. Until then, it's apparently not worth as much as the products we make from clear cutting forests and polluting water.

In *Nature's Metropolis*, historian William Cronon describes the industrial origins of this "consumer forgetfulness." Writing about the nineteenth-century triumph of meatpackers like Gustavus Swift and Philip Armour, he notes that "the packing plants distanced their customers most of all from the act of killing. . . . The more

Making a Purchase

people became accustomed to the attractively cut, cunningly displayed packages that Swift had introduced to the trade, the more easily they could fail to remember that their purchase had once pulsed and breathed with a life much like their own." The meatpackers converted the first nature of cattle and hogs to the second nature of steaks and roasts and chops and bacon. "In the packer's world," Cronon says, "it was easy not to remember that eating was a moral act inextricably bound to killing." Corporations made meat, but they also manufactured forgetfulness.[19]

Such forgetfulness, such ignorance, is the foundation of malls of America. As we shall see, it allows us to consume not just products but also people and the planet, without a second thought. It means that even when merchants are scrupulously honest, their prices can be dishonest. Caught in the social trap of retail pricing, we're often unable to see the wholesale impact of our purchasing. After a lifetime of paying for consumption on the cheap, we can become very anxious about paying the whole cost. When people try to tell us about the social and environmental impacts of our consumption, we often get "costophobia," a fear of knowing the real cost of a price system.

In the same way, we don't always consider the "opportunity costs" of our purchases when we are shopping. Economists use the concept of "opportunity costs" to describe the things we could have purchased but didn't. It's what you give up to get what you get. The opportunity cost of a luxury car might be a vacation, for example, or a year of college education, or contributions to church or charity, or a portion of a government nutrition program. Or the opportunity cost of a Nintendo game system might be time spent with our kids instead of working to pay for the product.[20]

When we buy a book at Barnes & Noble, when we pay for a t-shirt at the Gap, when we purchase a scented soap at Bath and Bodyworks, we confess our faith in the fetish of price. By exchanging a twenty-dollar bill for a Gap t-shirt and some change, we are *not* changing a system of pricing the planet. Indeed, we are reinforcing and reproducing the culture's emphasis on exchange values—values seen most clearly in the medium of money.

Money

There's still a lively academic debate about whether love or money makes the world go round, but it's pretty clear at the checkout that love alone won't get you past the security sensors. So we reach in our pockets or our purse, and we present the clerk with cash or a credit card. The credit card is a story in itself, so in this section, we'll just p(l)ay with cash. If we want to buy some pants, we give the clerk pieces of paper, or molded metal, and that does the trick. The clerk folds our purchases, puts them in a bag, and gives them to us. The commodity is now a possession—it's mine. The bills and coins we presented to the clerk, worth virtually nothing by themselves, have completed this exchange. We think of money as natural, but it's not. It's a cultural contrivance that makes shopping centers, and shopping itself, possible. Money is fiction in action, a story that we tell ourselves so convincingly that we come to believe it. It's one of a dozen social fictions being told at the mall, and all with the same result: a happy ending.

In a culture of convenience, we often forget the convenience of money. Instead of bartering goods and services, and depending on meeting the right person with the right stuff at the right time, we carry cash instead, cutting the time-and-toil cost of transactions considerably. The miracle of money is convertibility. With money, we find that we can, in fact, compare apples and oranges, because they're each just a certain price per pound. The bills and the coins have little or no intrinsic value; with the right equipment, you could manufacture them yourself, and that's exactly what counterfeiters do. Money is all extrinsic value, a pattern of belief and behavior that's every bit as mystical as most religions. In fact, the root of the word "religion" is the Latin "religare," "to bind together," and in many ways money *is* what binds us together in the modern world. We speak of "the almighty dollar" and think we're exaggerating. But it's hard to imagine a more powerful force on the planet today.[21]

American currency bears the motto "In God We Trust," and some of us do. But God is not who we trust to make money work. Faith in currency, Leah Hager Cohen says, "is really an extension of faith in everyone else—in your trading partners, in your neighbors—to collectively uphold and honor the notion of that currency." These days, our faith is strengthened by the American government: the U.S Treasury issues the currency, so at the checkout counter we're intimately involved with a government we increasingly detest. Taught by talk-show radio, we often think of government as a distant and dangerous force, but we carry its benefits in our pockets and pocketbooks every day. Whether or not we trust in God, we trust in money—and in the institutions behind our money.[22]

Money is both a time and space machine, a technology for making the world small and negotiable. When I give the clerk my $14.99 in exchange for a shirt, I am involved in a series of exchanges that span both space and time. I am involved with manufacturers in Indonesia, with shippers from Japan, and with wholesale and distribution chains throughout the United States. I pay my money to the clerk, but I am paying pennies to thousands of people coordinated by corporations. I pay the money today for work performed in a whole sequence of yesterdays, and I trust that tomorrow my dollar will still be worth a dollar. That's why inflation is so insidious—because it undercuts the constancy of money over time.

Money is a tool, a convenience, a means to an end. But sometimes it can become an end in itself, not because it *is* a means, but because it *means so much.* Manufacturers and merchants use money to assign value to things and experiences we buy, and then, oddly, we sometimes use the money value to convince ourselves of the product's value. If the suit is expensive, if the meal costs a lot, if the stereo is valuable, then it must be good. As economist Steffan Linder suggests, "If we spend money, it must be worthwhile."[23]

At the checkout, of course, I'm not meditating on money, and this speeds the transaction. But it also obscures the complexity of the transaction, and my complicity in a world of transactions and transformations.

Credit Cards

Sometimes we don't pay with cash; we "charge it" instead. Handing the clerk a plastic card, we set in motion another complex sequence of events.

The card itself is a small piece of plastic, about three and three-eighths inches long and two and one-eighth inches wide, weighing about a fifth of an ounce. These wafers of plastic may be charge cards, debit cards, ATM cards, or "smart cards," but most often they are credit cards. The front of the card displays the name of the bank or institution that issued the card and the logo of the card brand, usually Visa, MasterCard, Discover, or American Express.[24]

The back of the card is the business side: the magnetic stripe includes your name, account number, expiration date, PIN number, card class, and security code. When the clerk at Williams-Sonoma swipes my Visa card, for example, the card reader mixes this data with information about the merchant and the amount of the transaction and dials a computer maintained by the bank or firm that handles the merchant's credit card business. The computer processes the message, and dials Visa's computer, which checks with another computer at my bank to see if my credit line is sufficient. If it is, the bank's computer tells Visa's computer to tell the bank's computer to tell the merchant's computerized cash register to print a receipt, which I then sign. The store's computer then notifies Visa's computer, which bills my bank's computer, which debits my account. It's as simple as that—and infinitely more complex.[25]

Like money, a credit card is what Neil Postman calls an "invisible technology," a tool that shapes us even as we use it to shape our lives. Credit cards are a social practice intended to increase spending, and to make both convenience and indebtedness seem natural. These plastic passkeys are a way of making sure that the buck doesn't stop here, but keeps on circulating.

Credit cards are a relatively recent invention, barely more than fifty years old. In country stores and corner stores of the past, credit was available, but it was personal credit, afforded because the proprietor trusted you or your family. Oil companies and department stores offered "courtesy cards" to customers early in the twentieth century, but the first multipurpose charge card was introduced in 1950 by the Diner's Club. Charge cards allowed consumers to charge purchases to the card and pay off their bill at the end of the month. They offered consumers convenience and a small "float," the time between purchase and payment.[26]

Actual credit cards came later. Bank cards, most notably BankAmericard (now Visa) and MasterCharge, were established in the 1960s, a decade not generally known for its devotion to plastics. These bank cards offered several advantages. They were less bulky and less risky than cash, allowing people access to their money without having to carry it all around. They were more broadly accepted than checks, which were honored mostly within a local area. From a merchant's point of view, credit cards reduced the risk of bad checks and insured against customer defaults. Even though merchants pay for the privilege of letting their customers use credit cards, they profit from the payment. Customers like the convenience and credit of the cards, so they patronize merchants who are fully charged. The increased traffic into the store increases sales volume, which increases profitability. Cash-and-carry operations, which used to be the standard of American retailing, don't last very long.[27]

By 1997, Americans held more than 700 million payment cards, which we used to make more than 12 billion transactions worth $860 billion. By 2000, 158 million of us carried 1.5 billion cards, averaging ten cards apiece: four retail, three bank, one phone, one gas, and a travel and entertainment card (Diner's Club or American Express). About 20 percent of average household income goes out by payment card—the rest is still cash and checks. Our cards are honored by 4 million merchants in the United States, and 11 million more in 240 countries and territories worldwide.[28]

Credit cards allow consumers, the contemporary American equivalent of persons, to borrow money without applying for a loan each time. Some people in certain zip codes and socioeconomic locations are preapproved for such credit. After people are approved for a line of credit, they can charge purchases up to their credit limit. Credit cards permit us to make purchases "on time." In this case, however, on time doesn't mean on schedule or promptly; it means even before we have the money to pay for it. Instead of encouraging deferred gratification, credit cards are a form of deferred payment for incurred gratification. Buying on time means charging the present to the future, dissociating the pleasure from the responsibility and the buying from the billing.[29]

Credit cards change the economics of consumption, but they also change the psychology of shopping. When people paid with cash, they had to ask themselves, "Can I afford it? Is it worth it?" To some extent, we still do. Yet as Laura Pappano suggests, "Credit urges different questions, questions of desire and the opportunity for immediate gratification: Do I want it? Should I just get it now?"[30]

When we buy on time, we sometimes forget that we also buy *with* time— the time we need at work to make the money to pay the credit card bill. Even though he didn't carry Visa or MasterCard, Thoreau understood this. "The cost of a thing is the amount of what I will call life which is required to be exchanged for it, immediately or in the long run," he declared. He knew that we pay for our purchases with our lives, and that when we have to pay interest on our bills, we are spending our time to buy time.[31]

The dominant names in credit cards—Visa, Master Card, Discover, and American Express—promise freedom and security, control and mastery, discovery and travel, speed and nationalism. Ads for credit cards present them as necessities for being treated like celebrities all over the world: "American Express—don't leave home without it." "Visa—it's everywhere you want to be." Credit card ads show consumers parading in the paradise of consumption; they seldom show them opening the bill or writing the check. They show people on the verge of gratification, not on the verge of debt or bankruptcy, and they show us the benefits of credit cards over and over again. MasterCard, for example, repeatedly invited potential customers to "master the shopping possibilities" at featured upscale stores "and millions of other stores around the world." In 2000, credit card companies sent us 3.3 billion credit card solicitations and extended $17 trillion in credit to consumers.[32]

Credit card ads (more than $500 million a year) are in the business of generating business, for both credit card companies and the mall merchants. Visa and MasterCard don't care what we spend our money on as long as we spend it. They begin the process of generating our business very early, sending out solicitations to high school graduates and college students who have money to spend—or are willing to spend it anyway. Credit cards, like driver's licenses, are certificates of adulthood in American culture, a part of the rite of passage from adolescent to adult consumerism. They are one kind of obligation eagerly incurred by young Americans who seldom like to be obligated. These young people are the most profitable market niche for credit card companies, both because they haven't learned a lot of frugality and because they're likely to become card-carrying members of the consumption club for life. In the United States, more than 25 percent of teenagers have a credit card or easy access to one in their parents' name, and more than three-fourths of college students have a card. A 1998 solicitation for Visa told college students that they were "Free from parental rule at last. Now all you need is money." In 2000, student credit card debt averaged $2,748, up from $1,879 in 1998. John Waskin, president of the American Credit Counselors Corporation, says that young people "are accumulating debt because there is no stigma to it, nor is there a stigma to filing for bankruptcy." When these young people get caught in the cycle of consumer debt, it's a mess that belies the orderly aisles of the mall.[33]

Some credit card companies charge consumers an annual fee—an idea first introduced in 1980. Most companies also charge a small percentage for cash advances at ATMs. Bank card companies also charge merchants who allow the use of credit cards. When I pay for a purchase with my Visa card, the merchant gets 98 percent of the price. The other 2 percent, the "merchant discount," goes to the acquirer for providing its services. The acquirer pays 1.4 percent of the purchase price, the "interchange fee," to the issuer—in this case, my bank. Credit card companies made $17 billion on these charges in 1996. But they make the bulk of their money on the interest we pay when we don't pay off our debt; they depend on the not-so-juvenile delinquency of Americans young and old.[34]

There's a lot of interest in credit cards—literally. Interest is a cultural construction whereby some people make money by making money available to others. Credit card companies make money permanently by charging us rent for the temporary use of funds. The annual percentage rate is usually over 10 percent; on late payments, it may rise to over 20 percent. With rates like these, credit card companies make a lot of money: financing consumption in the form of credit-card lending is twice as profitable as any other banking activity. This profitability, furthermore, is not just economic, it's political. Many credit cards are issued in South Dakota, for example, because federal law permits lenders to circumvent state usury laws by issuing cards in other states, like South Dakota, that have no such laws. Likewise, in 1991, when the U.S. Senate passed a measure capping interest rate charges, the Dow Jones Industrial Average dropped 120 points in a day. Stocks for both Visa and MasterCard dropped, as did some of their associated banks.[35]

Doing our part to keep these companies in business, many of us do not pay off our debts at the end of each month, as people in "convenience households" do. Instead, more than 40 percent of us, the "revolver households," carry a balance from month to month. Credit card companies love these people, and they speak disdainfully of the "deadbeats" who avoid finance charges by paying their balances monthly. Fortunately for the companies, a lot of people can't afford to pay off their debts: at the end of 1997, Americans owed $453 billion on their credit cards, and the average household's credit card debt was more than $4,400. But averages don't tell the whole story: 33.5 million convenience households had no debt, leaving the revolver households with a much heftier average debt load of $11,575 in 2000. The total credit card indebtedness amounted to 43 percent of consumer debt, up from a mere 6 percent in 1972. The interest we pay on this

A HOUSE OF CARDS

(Copyright Andrew B. Singer, www.andysinger.com)

debt, generally about 7 or 8 percent of our disposable income, is money we can't spend on other things. We don't just pay back what we owe—we continue to pay for the privilege of owing.[36]

Even when we're revolving our indebtedness, of course, we can get benefits from our credit cards. College graduates call them "yuppie food stamps" because they provide necessities as long as you pay the minimum balance. People whose real earnings are in decline because of deindustrialization or downsizing can maintain their life-style by dancing the "credit card shuffle"—strategically transferring credit balances from one card to another. Employees who have been fired find that they can float on their credit card debt while looking for work, thus avoiding the stigma of downward social mobility. As long as we can pay the minimum balance, we can take advantage of the companies' interest in our interest.[37]

When we don't pay off our debt—when we *can't* pay off our debt—then many of us declare bankruptcy. In the year 2000, about 5 percent of credit card accounts were delinquent. And between 1980 and 2000, the number of personal bankruptcies tripled, rising from 288,000 to 1,217,972.[38]

The insolvency of cardholders affects the solvency of credit card companies. When people don't pay off their debts, the companies are left with "bad debt chargeoffs." Chargeoffs increased from $2,502,800,000 in 1987 to $17,356,200,000 in 1996, a time in which the economy generally improved. These losses caused credit card companies and retailers to push for changes in the bankruptcy laws, to make it more difficult for people in financial difficulties to escape their debts. This bankruptcy reform was passed to protect creditors from the negative effects of the "buy now, pay later" mentality that they market so effectively.[39]

But the spending spree caused by easy credit policies has consequences not just now, but in the future. As consumer spending rises, as Americans increase their shopping, our savings rate has plummeted. In the 1960s, the savings rate hovered around 8 percent; in 1998, it reached negative numbers. In the aggregate, people in the wealthiest nation on earth saved nothing at all. Perhaps we have no faith in the future. Perhaps we're hoping to be dead. But a society that has traditionally prided itself on striding confidently into the future is going forward with its pockets increasingly empty.

In a credit card culture, the economic landscape now is substantially different than fifty years ago. In the 1950s, only the wealthy held credit cards; in the twenty-first century, only the poor are without them, and paradoxically, their lack of credit can be critical. People who most need money are least able to secure it in the form of credit. In fact, people with poor credit basically subsidize people with better credit. The revolver households support the convenience households. While the upper classes get gold and platinum cards to distinguish themselves from the masses, the working classes are paying the cost of their credit. As Robert Manning says in *Credit Card Nation*, "Those who need credit the most ultimately subsidize the low-cost credit of those who need it least."[40]

Credit cards make it easier for us to buy stuff, but they also make it easier for others to sell us more stuff. When the clerk swipes our credit card, we're offering

Mallpractices

companies information that can be used to influence our consumption. Transactional Data Solutions, for example, combines MasterCard's transaction database with other market research to tell merchants more about their customers than customers would tell on their own. A joint venture of MasterCard and a market research firm, TDS can cluster consumers to tell retailers who shops at their store, how much they spend, how much money they make, where they live, and what they like to do. Without violating individual privacy, it reveals TV and radio habits, magazine reading, leisure activities, and products purchased—all information that helps marketers reach us with messages to increase our consumption. "Cool shop-a-lot" consumers, for example, like to shop at Banana Republic, Barnes & Noble, and Circuit City. They can be reached by newspaper or magazine, or on the Internet, and they tend to be brand loyalists, so it's more important in selling to them to emphasize brand value than to promote discounts or impulse buying. The American Express database includes a similar treasure trove of information on its members: "where they most like to shop, what and when they most frequently purchase, the destinations to which they travel on business or pleasure and their preferred means of transport, the restaurants they patronize, and even the economic conditions of their home countries." Such information allows the company to send targeted mailings to consumers that capitalize on our own expressed interests, and bring us back again to the mall.[41]

Because merchants like to make making a purchase as easy as possible, we don't generally spend much time at the checkout counter. We just pay for our purchases and take them with us. But this simple ritual is repeated regularly in our malls, and it involves us in some of our most important cultural patterns. Seen as dense facts, the quick scan, the exchange of money, and the swipe of the credit card illustrate our beliefs and behavior in the marketplace. They show both why we like to shop and why we need to think more carefully about our shopping.

PART FOUR

It's a Mall World,
After All

ELEVEN

The Politics of No Politics

The grand opening of a shopping center is a festive occasion. Shopping centers help put communities on the map, because good shopping is understood as an essential element of the good life; towns without a mall are the backwaters of a consumer society. So as a sign of civic boosterism, the mayor of Mall City comes to cut the ribbon. Other officials put in an appearance, too, giving public approval to the new venture. But when the mayor goes back to the office and the cleaning crew begins sweeping up the confetti, the mall reverts to a private enterprise. The mall is the town square of American suburban culture; some malls are even called Town Square. But this doesn't mean that the mall is public space. According to mall management, the shopping center is a center for shopping, not for politics.[1]

Yet even if there's no politics *in* the mall, there is a politics *of* the mall. Shopping centers are inevitably political places; in fact, shopping center executives exercise a lot of political power to maintain their malls' apolitical policy. Malls are intimately involved in a politics of free speech, a local politics of zoning and financing, a state politics of taxes and growth management, and a national politics of regulation and environmental issues. Finally, along with the cultural politics of race and gender and class and desire, malls reflect and affect America's politics of consumption and citizenship. As historian Lizabeth Cohen says, "The commercializing, privatizing, and segmenting of the physical gathering places that has accompanied mass consumption has made more precarious the shared public sphere upon which our democracy depends." This chapter traces the basic contours of the politics of no politics in American malls.[2]

The Politics of Public Places

As Americans started going to malls in the 1950s and 1960s, and malls celebrated themselves as community centers, they began to look like public spaces—a combination of park and village square. With their large common areas, they simply felt more public than a store on the street. People in malls acted as if they were in public. They took pleasure in visiting stores and shops, in people watching and pedestrianism. Like the seaside promenade or the city park, the mall provided a space to go public with friends.

As it happened, the crowds of shoppers were also crowds of citizens. If you wanted to reach the public in person, therefore, the mall was a good place to do it. Community organizations like the Red Cross held blood drives, and charities sponsored book and bake sales. In the early 1970s, some shopping center managers felt that shoppers "bring both their money and their civil rights. They expect to be accepted with both and to be treated fairly and equally. They also naturally think of the center as a forum and maybe it should be, for constructive social and political activism." But the complications of politics on the premises were problematic, because the exercise of activists' civil rights caused customers to complain about "infractions of their human rights (Consumerism)."[3]

Since the 1970s, shopping centers have fought legally to keep politics outside the shopping center. Like broadcasters who depend on the advertising dollars of the mall's retail chains, shopping centers have tried to avoid activities that

It's a Mall World, After All

might offend customers—and, in a relentlessly privatist era, politics can be offensive. It turned out that some ideas were more "malleable" than others. When unions tried to picket at the mall, when political activists tried to leaflet, when groups tried to assemble to hear a speaker, they discovered that mall managers considered the shopping center private property and prohibited such exercises of free speech. Court battles ensued. Over the last fifty years, as Lizabeth Cohen suggests, "American courts all the way up to the Supreme Court struggled with the political consequences of having moved public life off the street and into the privately owned shopping center."[4]

Legally, the malls argued that shopping centers were a private business and could be harmed by the practice of free speech. Mall managers opposed demonstrations not because they didn't care about politics but because they cared about the sensibilities of their customers. Mall managers often marketed shopping as an escape from everyday life, and they expected people to be left alone (at least politically) in the shopping center. Many shopping centers, therefore, banned what has come to be called "non-commercial expressive activity." In essence, mall managers contended that you could have any kind of community life you wanted, as long as it didn't interfere with sales.[5]

At first, the courts contended that free speech rights didn't end at the property line of the shopping center. But a series of Nixon appointees to the Supreme Court modified that rule, suggesting, for example, that antiwar leafleting was an unwarranted infringement of property rights, because leaflets could be distributed in other places without distracting mall customers from the distractions of shopping. A 1980 decision, *PruneYard Shopping Center v. Robbins*, affirmed both rights of free speech and private property, and essentially left the matter up to the states, where it remains. California and New Jersey have upheld the most liberal guidelines for free speech: according to attorney Suzanne Schiller, they decided that "a regional shopping center is the functional equivalent of a city street, and the free speech rights that people enjoy in a downtown area—to leaflet, for example—apply to shopping centers." But even states upholding the rights of free speech have given shopping centers a lot of discretion about where and when and how people may speak in the center. Mall management, for example, can determine where tables will be placed, how many people may be there, how they must be dressed, and what times are permissible.[6]

The Politics of No Politics

When we park our cars at the shopping center, therefore, we also park most of our rights to free speech, to assembly, and to privacy. We trade political rights for commercial opportunities. At one Colorado mall, a sign welcomes customers at the entrance by establishing the rules of dress and conduct. It requires "appropriate non-offensive attire" and requests that patrons "use trash receptacles located throughout the mall." It prohibits disorderly and disruptive conduct, including running, skateboarding, roller blading, and, less strenuously, loitering. It bans radios, pets (except seeing-eye dogs), and "dress that is commonly recognized as gang-related." And it asserts that "picketing, distributing handbills, soliciting and petitioning require the prior written consent of mall management." In some cases, when we enter the mall, we even give up our right to ask questions or take photographs. Basically, the rule is that we enter the mall to do what mall managers want us to do, and not much else.[7]

The result is that the primary political expression allowed at the mall is the politics of consumption, which is politically more powerful than any other politics. In fact, one of the latent functions of a shopping center is to create a space in which politics is seemingly suspended. In this way, shopping centers have been a part of the relentless privatization of American life, the *republican* agenda of the late twentieth century. Mall designs may evoke a feeling of public space, but it's primarily a simulation, meant to call up good feelings more than good citizenship.[8]

Local Politics

The pretense of no politics is itself political, but it's not the only political involvement of the shopping center. The politics of no politics often begins at the local level with zoning and tax-increment financing. Usually shopping centers locate on sites that have already been zoned for commercial development. But sometimes the mall displaces homeowners and other businesses, so the politics of zoning is part and parcel of developing shopping center parcels. In the search for a site, too, commercial developers can play one political jurisdiction against another, trying to get the best deal possible. And a good deal often comes from tax-increment financing.

You might think that people who believe in the privacy of shopping malls would insist on private capital markets for financing their projects, but you would

It's a Mall World, After All

be wrong. Tax-increment financing is a process that basically allows developers to build shopping centers now with the property taxes the malls will generate in the future. It's like a credit card for development costs, especially the costs of capital. A city or government agency sells bonds to provide money for infrastructure costs like land acquisition and clearance, and construction of roads and sewers. The bonds are secured by the promise of profits in the future, when the increased value of the land parcel generates increased property taxes for the city. The increased revenue is the "increment," and it constitutes the payoff to taxpayers.

Tax-increment financing is often used in special districts that need redevelopment, but it may also be used for new projects that seem to have a substantial future payoff. And malls often possess those payoffs. They generate jobs first in construction, and then in sales, and each of those jobs supports other jobs. They eventually generate tax revenues through real estate taxes and sales taxes. They often catalyze new construction and additional sales near the mall site, as restaurants and other retailers try to capitalize on the traffic flow to the mall. Shopping centers have important multiplier effects in the local economy.

But tax-increment financing isn't without its costs. Since the taxes generated by the new development go to paying off the bonds, they don't go to other projects, at least until the bonding is paid off. For the term of the bonds, the tax increment doesn't help school boards or counties or other governmental agencies that normally benefit from property taxes. Nor can the tax increment be used for the normal expenses of a city: police and fire protection, park and road construction, municipal programming or historic preservation. Those expenses are still paid by other businesses and taxpayers, some of whom could also use the sort of assistance the mall gets. And if the municipality overextends itself, its bond rating (which affects its borrowing costs) could be downgraded.

In general, tax increment financing favors the national chains of the shopping center over the independent mom-and-pop stores of the community. Independent merchants find it difficult to pay the increased rents in the vicinity of the mall, and they have a hard time, too, matching the advertising of the national chains. So the tax-increment financing of shopping centers can sacrifice the local character of retailing for the predictably larger incomes produced by national merchants. It can drive some shops off the tax rolls even as it adds others.[9]

The Politics of No Politics

Tax-increment financing often depends on unexamined assumptions about government responsibility for economic growth and ecological destruction. When City Hall considers whether to offer tax-increment financing for a development project, it seldom questions the assumption that more is better. It tends to focus on the financial benefits for the specific community, not on costs to other communities. It focuses more on economic considerations and less on social and cultural and familial consequences, and it focuses on the construction of a mall, not on the ecological consequences of consumption. It's politics in the service of private enterprise—and their privatized consumers.

State Politics and Sales Taxes

Shopping centers are not just a drain on public finances. Indeed, to the contrary, they are one of the primary sources of public finances, especially at the state and local level. Both sales taxes and real estate taxes are ways that shopping centers provide for the public treasury. The sales tax is a way of converting individual consumption to collective purposes. It's a way of making sure that a percentage of our private desire ends up in public projects. So even as we go to the private space of the mall, we're engaged in a public activity because in many states the sales clerk is also a tax collector. In 2000, shopping centers collected $46.6 billion in sales taxes.[10]

The sales tax is one of America's most regressive taxes. Poor people pay proportionately more in sales taxes than rich people do. With a 5 percent sales tax, a person who makes $300,000 a year pays ten times less (as a percentage of income) for the sales tax on a $30 pair of Levi's than a person in the same community making $30,000 a year. The tax, $1.50 on the jeans, is the same for both people, but the tax bite is very different. This doesn't sound like much for a single purchase, but since people with moderate incomes spend twice as much on clothes (as a percentage of income) as rich people do, the costs mount up quickly. The regressiveness of sales taxes is the main reason that progressive states exempt food and clothing from the sales tax. Localities that tax these items, and governments that depend on sales taxes, have made a political decision to let poor people pay proportionately more taxes than rich people.

The real estate tax is a levy on the assessed valuation of property. It's a way that people who have property, at least property of a certain sort, support the governments that protect their property and enhance its value with public improvements and services. Shopping centers aren't cheap, so they pay a lot in real estate taxes. They also tend to raise the value of land adjacent to the center, thus indirectly contributing more money to the public purse. Few types of retail development generate more money for communities than shopping centers.[11]

These contributions help our state and local governments, but they also amount to another example of government cooperation with commercialism and consumerism. With sales taxes, state and city income depends to some extent on consumer spending. As Ken Jones and Jim Simmons suggest, "State governments that depend on sales tax revenues have as large a stake in consumer spending as the K Mart Corporation." And it's not wise, presumably, to bite the hand that feeds you.[12]

The issue of suburban sprawl shows how the International Council of Shopping Centers gets involved in state and local politics. During the late 1990s, for example, the sprawl issue seemed to pose a threat to the shopping center industry. Vice President Al Gore proposed a "livability agenda" that included the regulation of suburban sprawl, and growth control referenda appeared on more than two hundred state and local election ballots in 1998. In an article "Antisprawl Raises PR Issues for Industry," Edmund Mander summarized the early responses. The ICSC responded with public relations releases reminding legislators that "people still want to live in a single-family home in the suburbs where there are new schools and there are new shopping centers, and they have a little more open space and they have a nice backyard." The organization also joined with the National Association of Homebuilders to publish a joint paper opposed to growth restrictions, and they worked with the American Legislative Exchange Council, a group of three thousand state legislators dedicated to free-market principles and limited government, to draft legislation to require economic impact studies before enacting limits to growth.[13]

National Politics

At the national level, there's not much direct support for malls. The Federal Interstate Highway Act indirectly supports suburbs and suburban institutions like shopping centers. Federal transportation policy helped create the infrastructure for malls, because highways attract the business of Americans who mainly get about in cars. There are not massive national subsidies for shopping centers, but the federal government still sets important parameters for America's malls.

Consequently, the ICSC also engages in Washington politics. "Politics is serious business," the council says. "The passage of one bill in the U.S. Congress alone can make a greater impact on the future of our industry than many decisions made by your own management." The ICSC web page thus includes a "Government" section that begins, "On behalf of our members, ICSC works with legislative offices and agencies on timely regulatory issues pertaining to the shopping center industry. ICSC operates a grassroots mobilization program, the Shopping Center Action Network, SCAN; an annual Congressional Contacts Meeting; and a Political Action Committee, ICSC PAC. Our Government Relations staff works closely with ICSC members who voluntarily serve on Committees and Subcommittees pertaining to their areas of interest."[14]

The ICSC Government Relations people monitor issues at both state and federal levels. At the national level, their primary issues are economic and environmental. Economically, the organization is interested in taxation of Internet sales, capital gains, the Americans with Disabilities Act, bankruptcy reform, and cost recovery of leasehold improvements. Environmentally, the shopping center industry worries about regulations that put undue restrictions on private property rights. So they support reforms of the Endangered Species Act and of wetlands regulations in the Clean Water Act. They also support regulatory relief in brownfields redevelopment, and promote restraint of "smart growth" initiatives that try to contain suburban sprawl.[15]

In addition, a "fast action" page on the organization's web site makes it easy for members to register their opinions with their legislators. In June 2000, the site instructed members to "Tell Congress You Want a Fair and Level Playing Field." Concerned that "the competitive tax advantage that Internet-based retailers currently enjoy could result in the loss of billions of dollars in future revenues to shopping centers, traditional merchants, and local communities," the ICSC advised its members to lobby for a sales tax on both Internet and catalogue sales.[16]

In addition to getting members involved in politics, the ICSC takes a part in electing and lobbying federal officials. Its political action committee, ICSC PAC, was established in 1988 "to help elect federal office candidates who favor the shopping center industry and its goals and initiatives." In the 1996 elections, the shopping center industry funded 120 campaigns, and "seventy per cent of Senate candidates and 84 percent of House candidates supported by ICSC PAC won their respective elections." Consequently, "visiting with ICSC staff and members has now become a routine stop for most federal candidates."[17]

The ICSC is assisted in the politics of shopping malls by organizations like the National Retail Federation (NRF) and the International Mass Retail Association (IMRA). The National Retail Federation asserts that "when NRF speaks, government listens. It listens because NRF is the world's largest retail trade association; a true federation made up of major nationally known retailers and independent stores, 50 state retail associations, and more than 30 national retail organizations." Recently, the NRF has lobbied for the elimination of the estate tax, for bankruptcy reform, for free trade with China, against new ergonomics standards for the workplace, and against increases in the minimum wage. Like the ICSC and NRF, the IMRA also supports "reasonable" regulation, defined generally as regulation with fewer restrictions on commercial enterprises. It also opposes increases in the minimum wage, supports free trade, and calls for civil justice reforms restricting class action and product liability lawsuits. There's a lot of politics in American commerce, and vice versa.[18]

Trade industry organizations set a political agenda that provides for the health of the industry, but other issues could also prove helpful to shopping centers. An end to poverty, for example, would be good business for America's malls. The ICSC's own statistics show that poor people make up almost 20 percent of the American population but only about 7 percent of mall shoppers. Still, poverty tends not to be a priority in ICSC political discussions. People who sell status apparently can't afford to mess too much with the status quo.[19]

The Politics of Consumption

Even though they prohibit politics on the premises, shopping centers are deeply involved in American politics at every level. They regularly use America's political institutions to support the politics of no politics at the mall, lobbying for legislation that makes selling stuff easier. But they also have a deeper influence on American politics because malls perform cultural work that helps to shape

American political culture. Shopping and consumption shape our assumptions about the place of politics in our lives, so that consumption itself becomes a political statement. We can see this in the creation of what Lizabeth Cohen calls "a consumer's republic" in the 1950s.[20]

During the 1950s, consumption was a political act. Jane Pavitt notes that "in the postwar West, against the backdrop of the Cold War, to be an active participant in a consumer society became increasingly regarded as a basic human right. The idea of citizenship [was] framed around the idea of consumership." Politicians in both parties heralded "the American way of life," and the material goods that symbolized American freedoms. At the Brussels World's Fair of 1958, the American pavilion included a fully stocked supermarket. At the Moscow trade show of 1959, the American exhibit featured even more consumer goods, including a fully furnished suburban home. Such exhibits praised Americans' freedom of choice in the supermarket and the shopping center, and implied (not inaccurately) that they were somehow related to American democracy. In the famous Kitchen Debate at the Moscow show, Vice President Nixon expressed this popular idea, making materialism a primary measurement of American cultural superiority. "The good life" was good political propaganda.[21]

Lizabeth Cohen notes that citizenship and consumption have always been essential elements of American political culture, but that the balance between them has shifted over time. During the early twentieth century, Progressives and New Dealers shaped a political system based on what Cohen calls "citizen consumers"—people who saw consumer issues as a catalyst for political reform. Citizen consumers believed that democracy offered a way to make capitalism work for the public good, and so they supported ideals like a living wage, the eight-hour day, minimum wages, workmen's compensation, pure food and drug acts, antitrust legislation, and, during World War II, price controls, rent regulations, and rationing restrictions. Both the Depression and World War II convinced Americans that they could act effectively as citizens to assure that they could act freely as consumers.[22]

After World War II, however, businesses attacked the restrictive regulations of the New Deal state and began to promote a new conception of citizenship and consumption: Cohen's "consumer's republic." In this "new and improved" political culture, "customer consumers" replaced "citizen consumers." The gov-

It's a Mall World, After All

ernment would be responsible for promoting economic growth and assuring elementary fairness in the marketplace, but decisions about the character of consumption would be shifted from democratic politics to the market. The consumer's republic promoted "a new post-war ideal of the *customer as citizen* who simultaneously fulfilled personal desire and civic obligation by consuming." In this social construction of reality, Americans hardly had to think about the public good, because it would be the inevitable result of private consumption. Indeed, consumption became one of the highest forms of citizenship. Immigrants had always come to America for both political and personal freedom. The consumer's republic continued to celebrate this combination. It still promoted American ideals of freedom, democracy, and equality, but it adapted these ideas to an increasingly commercial culture. In the consumer's republic, Americans voted for the pleasures of private life.[23]

During this period, Americans increasingly subscribed to what sociologist Richard Flacks calls "the postwar charter." This new social contract specified that Americans wouldn't bother the government as long as the government provided both security and economic growth. This "motivated disengagement" wasn't apathy: Americans freely chose not to participate in politics. Instead of fighting for the Four Freedoms, as they had in World War II, they chose to fight for the freedoms of private consumption. Experiencing freedom and choice in institutions like shopping centers and the home, they trusted the government to preserve their other freedoms. Instead of engaging in politics, they engaged in what Flacks calls "the politics of everyday commitment." Following that tradition, shoppers today don't want to be bothered by politics in malls, in part because Americans don't want to be bothered by politics, period.[24]

The "people's capitalism" of the postwar period seemingly solved the problem of the distribution of wealth; while it privileged present inequities (many the result of prior political decisions), its promise of growth assured increasing abundance for everybody. Proponents of the consumer's republic contended that American capitalism distributed goods better than Soviet socialism, and they conflated capitalism with democracy. Consequently, in the cold war world, when the United States attempted to "make the world safe for democracy," it usually made it safe for capitalism.[25]

Consumption was also a good answer to the crisis of democratic theory. As

Table 4

Coercive versus Seductive Cultures

	Coercive Culture	Seductive Culture
Center of Power	Military/party	Commerce
Expansive ambition	Global empire	Global market
Order of leadership	Centralized	Decentralized
	Highly visible and fixed	Invisible and mobile
	Dictator/general	Corporate board
Philosophical presumptions	RATIONAL Materialism	Rational MATERIALISM
	Commerce serving state	State serving commerce
	Science serving party line	Science serving bottom line
	Religion as enemy	Religion as commodity
Ultimate value	Power	Money
Social status	Proximity to power	Conspicuous consumption
	(Soviet May Day picture)	Lifestyles of the rich and famous
Cultural character	Repressive	Expressive
	Masculine	Feminine
	Patriotic	Self-centered
	Puritanical	Sexual
	Earnest	Sentimental
Cultural mythos	Ideology	Fantasy
	Party line	Pop culture
	State "hero"	Pop "star"
Modes of control	Command and conquer	Tempt and co-opt
	Conscription	Addiction
	Physical threat	Financial debt
	Party loyalty	Brand loyalty
	Fiat	Fashion
	Censorship	Saturation
	The Big Lie	The Big Top
Representative art form	Collage	Montage
Communication	Three-hour speech	Thirty-second ad
Structure	Berlin Wall	Mall of America
Profession	Apparatchik	Salesman/adman
Psychosis	Paranoia	Narcissism
Model world	Skinner box	Circe's Isle

Source: Bosworth, "Endangered Species," 224–45.

historian Edward Purcell has shown, American intellectuals increasingly doubted the capacity of the American people for deliberative politics. But the consumer's republic didn't require much deliberation about the public good. If people were smart enough to understand their own pleasure principle and self-interest, they would be choosing wisely for the political community. The politics of shopping fit perfectly with an "end of ideology" ideology, which counterpoised American pragmatism and practicality against Soviet ideological rigidity. Like abstract expressionism, which was celebrated as an expression of American freedom, the shopping center stood as a symbol of the promise of American politics.[26]

But even as Americans correctly contrasted the freedom of the American way of life with the coercive constraints of life in the Communist bloc, they often forgot the seductive constraints of their own seemingly apolitical system. Ideology hadn't really ended; it just took new forms in a culture of seduction (see table 4).

Under cover of this ideology of no ideology, American postwar consumption exploded. The pent-up demand of twenty years, coupled with the government's promotion of consumption with programs like the GI Bill and federal housing programs, led to unprecedented economic expansion. To people in the 1950s, of course, this abundance didn't seem extravagant. It seemed like a return to normalcy, a fulfillment of the promise of American life. In the process, though, the American standard of living came to substitute for the American way of life, with its social, political, and religious activities.

Shopping centers grew up in this materialistic milieu, and served, along with supermarkets, as symbols of American affluence. Although the first shopping centers were built during the 1920s and 1930s, the Depression and World War II delayed further development. Starting in the 1950s, however, malls mushroomed throughout the United States. In 1957, International Council of Shopping Centers was created to coordinate and promote the growth of the burgeoning industry. Although some shopping center pioneers expected malls to serve as centers of civic life, their plans fell victim to the cultural priorities of privatism and profit. The long-term decline in American political participation hasn't been caused by shopping centers, but America's malls have reinforced the politics of "customer consumers" in the postwar era.[27]

During the 1960s, radicals preached that "the personal is political," and celebrated the virtues of participatory democracy. Affirming the importance of consumption, they used economic tools like boycotts to pressure businesses to live up to the ideals of the consumer's republic. In 1960, for example, four civil rights activists sat down at the lunch counter at Woolworth's in Greensboro, North Carolina, and demanded the same service that white customers received. Their action inspired sit-ins and boycotts, both North and South, directed at retail stores that supported southern racial segregation, and at the laws that countenanced such discrimination. This political counterculture hoped to revolutionize the counter cultures of American retail establishments. "With their demands for more access to the stores, more respect inside them, and more African American employees working for them," historian Ted Ownby suggests, "protesters wanted full access to two central aspects of consumer culture. They saw shopping as a potentially democratic experience and hoped to find pleasure and dignity in the experience. Even if they did not emphasize the idea, they were defining the right to shop as a basic element in American freedom." African Americans demanded not just equal citizenship but also the equality of consumers. Shopping was part of their American Dream.[28]

American consumers supported other boycotts, too—like the boycott of grapes by Cesar Chavez and the United Farmworkers—to reform the market system. And antiwar activists asked Americans to boycott consumer goods produced by companies, like Dow Chemical, that also manufactured munitions for the Vietnam War. The market responded in two ways. In many cases, as in southern retail stores, companies acted to remedy wrongdoing, or at least to explain it with public relations. In the South, for example, the segregation of retail markets soon gave way to the segmentation of markets, as stores began to cater to the African American market.[29]

In other cases, the market responded by marketing the social revolution, turning a serious critique of profligate consumerism into a new style of consumerism. American commercial culture co-opted the counterculture of communes and simple living, commodifying dissent, and selling it back to the dissenters. Capitalists found that antimaterialism sold very well to selected customers. The more the counterculture could be construed as a life-style apart from politics, the more capitalists could sell the style without the substance. By marketing the outward signs of hippie life—music, psychedelic posters, clothes, beads, and drug paraphernalia—merchandisers found that they could make a profit on the ephemera of prophecy.[30]

Malls and their assumptions have increasingly defined other aspects of

The politics of consumption
(Copyright Andrew B. Singer, www.andysinger.com)

American life, including politics. "Liberal democracy still defines America," notes political scientist Alan Wolfe, "but liberty is coming more and more to mean that everything is, and ought to be, for sale; and democracy is being turned into the notion that whatever people want the most must be the best for them." Ironically, our "ideology of liberty" reinforces our liberty from politics. If we're really free, we should be free of politics too. So we still generally fulfill our duties to the polity by fulfilling ourselves.[31]

During the 1980s, the Reagan revolution reinforced the privatism of American political culture. When the government failed to uphold its side of the postwar charter, when real incomes failed to rise in the 1970s, American citizens got polit-

The Politics of No Politics

ical to preserve their private American dreams. They fueled the tax revolt, which was designed to give consumers the money they needed to fulfill their part of the postwar charter: self-fulfillment. Republicans used private consumption as a counter against public provision, and the Reagan administration guided this sentiment into an attack on Big Government and on politics itself. As the president spun fanciful stories about the shopping habits of welfare queens, he cut taxes so that Americans could go on a spending spree. And we did.[32]

Because conservatives like Ronald Reagan decided to conserve the free market more than anything else, they succeeded in conserving little else. As Alan Wolfe suggests, "By the time Reaganism finished working its way through American society, such quaint notions as uninterrrupted family meals, commerce-free Sundays, unspoiled places, and unindebted self-reliance had almost completely disappeared." And given the marketeers' penchant for putting a price tag on everything, market culture undermines "the ties of solidarity associated with friendship and family— ties that, if they are to endure through thick and thin, must be non-economic in nature." Conservatives believe that liberals have undermined American institutions and values, but the market is much more powerful than mere liberals.[33]

Unfortunately, as it happens, a consumer's republic is almost a contradiction in terms. The word "republic" derives from the Latin "res publica," the public things. In early America, republicanism worked because the culture itself encouraged restraint and self-government. Frugality was both an economic benefit and a political virtue, because it demonstrated the self-government that could restrain the desires of mass democracy. These days, however, the institutions that teach frugality and moderation are often overwhelmed by the market's emphasis on self-indulgent freedom.

During the last twenty-five years, conservatives have succeeded in convincing Americans about the evils of Big Government and high taxes. They have promoted and passed big tax cuts on the unproven theory that the American people can spend their money more wisely than our government can. They have repeatedly argued that you can't solve problems by throwing money at them. Such policies promote private enterprises like shopping centers, where, in fact, we go to throw money at our own problems.[34]

Shopping centers use politics to keep politics out of the mall and to keep the mall profitable. In the process, they also perform cultural work for Americans. The private consumption encouraged by shopping centers, for example, affects our taste for public goods. The more we can buy at the mall, the less we want to contribute to public projects. Why pay for good police protection when you can buy a private security system for your house and "the Club" for your car? Why pay for public playgrounds when you can buy one for your own backyard?

Indeed, shopping centers help to keep public issues out of sight and out of mind. They're just one institution that reinforces our penchant for political compartmentalization. It might affect the business of the food court if there were signs about hunger in the United States. It might be harder to buy toys for our children at KayBee if we were reminded about the scope of child poverty. We might think twice about a computer game if we were thinking about our school district's bond levy. Indeed, the shopping center is meant to center our attention on private spending, not public spending of any sort. We learn to satisfy our desires by buying individual "solutions" from private enterprise, instead of buying social solutions in the public sphere.[35]

Despite the claims of shopping center management, however, there's no such thing as "not political," there's just consciously or unconsciously political, intentionally and unintentionally political, and formally and informally political. Even the so-called free market is neither private nor free but the consequence of many prior public decisions. Shopping centers and retailers, for example, depend on currency, public roads, postal service, and police and fire departments. They depend on a legal system that defines and protects private property, enforces contracts, and prosecutes fraud and shoplifting. Corporations depend on the limited legal liability of investors and on the legal fiction that corporations are persons, able to sue and be sued. Corporations and credit card companies tend to do business in states that have structured their politics with loose regulations on taxes and interest rates. Lenders and developers depend on interest rates and tax incentives to motivate investments. As real estate investment trusts (REITs), shopping center companies can avoid paying corporate income taxes and still distribute quarterly dividends to stockholders. Manufacturers depend on tariff and trade laws, and they tend to do business in countries with minimal wages and environmental regulations. Once their product is made, they depend on the protections of patent and trademark law. Advertisers depend on the public airwaves, the post office, and minimal governmental oversight. Market researchers depend on the Census Bureau and the Commerce Department. We all depend on the confidence generated by specific pieces of protective legislation, especially involving consumer safety. And these companies also benefit from campaign finance laws that make it easy for businesses to assure that, as Calvin Coolidge once said, "the business of America is business." So despite the apparent politics of no politics, our shopping both affects and reflects American democracy and political culture.[36]

TWELVE

The World in a Shopping Mall

We go to the mall to shop, but we also go to encounter the world.[1] Americans have traditionally shopped for French fashions, Italian leather, and English refinement. More recently, we have shopped for German cars and Japanese electronics. We look for designer names with foreign cachet: Armani and Versace and Saint Laurent, or Chanel and Oscar de la Renta. We purchase products, but at the same time we purchase the foreign aura of products. And in virtually all the shops of the mall, we're also involved with the foreign origins of products. America's malls are, in fantasy and in fact, malls of the world.

Exotics at Home

One of the more interesting places for mall tourism in recent years is the Rainforest Café, which promotes itself as "a place for fun far away, that's just beyond your

The whole world in our hands
(Photo by the author; reprinted by permission)

doorstep." The "tour guide" calls, "Farrell, Safari of four? Your adventure is about to begin," hands us our "passport to adventure," which is prestamped with locations of the Rainforest Café worldwide, and directs us to follow the animal footprints until we're met by our intrepid "safari guide," who blazes a path through the rainforest all the way to our table.[2]

The café's menu is an inventory of puns and clichés, evoking images of the exotic from movies and cartoons, travel ads and travelogues. Kids can enjoy the Wild Bunch Munch, with a Banshee Screamer Sundae. Adults can order single appetizers or the complete Tribal Feast. Entrees include Jungle Safari Soup, Mogambo Shrimp, Rasta Pasta, and a Planet Earth Pasta. For dessert, there's Tortoise Ice Cream Pie, Gorillas in the Mist Banana Cheesecake, and Monkey Business Coconut Bread Pudding. No rainforest animals are actually served on the menu, but the food is generally quite good. The coffee is certified shade-grown and organic, which means that it helps preserve migratory birds that depend on coffee trees for shelter.

There's a Retail Village where we can buy souvenirs of our safari—clothing, toys, food, bath and body products, CDs, and collectibles. Staffed by assistants known as "pathfinders," this village has no permanent human inhabitants and few human connections. Its best-known residents are Cha!Cha! the tree frog, Tuki the elephant, Nile the crocodile, and five other characters who collectively make up "the Wild Bunch," an anthropomorphic crew featured in kids' books, videos, plush toys, and other souvenirs.

Now, it's not like people eat at the Rainforest Café instead of going to the rainforest. It's just a restaurant. But like *all* restaurants, it's also more than a restaurant. As a "dense fact," the Rainforest Café can be a starting point for a safari into a tangled landscape of ideas and assumptions about the exotic—and about America and the world. A safari, for example, is "an overland expedition, especially for hunting or exploring in East Africa," so most safaris take place in grasslands. But the café's logo, which includes species that don't inhabit the same ecosystem, suggests that this expedition is not really about the rainforest. It is virtual tourism, a postmodern pilgrimage, a way of going everywhere without going anywhere, except, of course, to the mall.

The Rainforest Café appeals in part to our genuine reverence for life and for unspoiled nature, but its central appeal, most likely, is to our sense of the exotic. The word "exotic" comes from the Greek *exo*, meaning "outside." The dictionary defines it as "from another part of the world; not indigenous; foreign," or as "having the charm of the unfamiliar; strikingly and intriguingly unusual or beautiful." The exotic, then, is "not us." But what especially attracts us to the exotic is our ability to shape it to our own ends. People and places get to be "exotic" not when we treat them on their own terms but when we treat them on ours. Despite its appearances, the exotic isn't "out there." Instead, it's in our minds and imaginations. The exotic is a mental category that provides a familiar place for difference.

The World in a Shopping Mall

What counts as exotic? As we look at images of the exotic in American ads and travel brochures, in TV programs and movies, we see a recurrent set of images that do not include all things foreign. We select particular symbols of the exotic to evoke the emotions we want, and we ignore other aspects of these places and peoples. The exotic is almost always picturesque. It's primarily visual, although other senses can be involved. So we see images of sand and sun and sea, picturesque pools of water or cascading waterfalls. We see palm trees, lush vegetation, a garden, or flowers—especially tropical flowers like orchids. We don't always see people: it seems as if the world's exotic paradises are largely unpopulated; perhaps that's why they remain paradises. When we do see people, they tend not to wear business suits but to appear in some sort of native dress. We prefer our natives in grass huts or tepees, not in ranch houses or colonial revival homes. We prefer primitives who slurp coconut milk instead of Coca-Cola because exotic authenticity is defined largely by an absence of modernism and commercialism. We portray them eating fruit straight from the trees, an Edenic image of natural plenty that suggests Zen affluence: having much by wanting little. We like to watch natives involved in activities—racing outrigger canoes, diving for pearls, singing, and dancing—that seem exotic to people like us whose primary leisure activity is watching television.

In a mall world, these images and expectations of the exotic come, in large part, from the history of tourism. Historian Daniel Boorstin suggests that in the nineteenth century, Western cultures substituted tourism for travel. According to Boorstin, tourism was a way of getting the benefits of travel without the travail, as travel agents and tour guides packaged transportation and accommodations, first creating and then accommodating the expectations of eager tourists. This touristic cosmopolitanism invited travelers to be at home not just at home, but in the whole world. And it gave people the illusion of encountering other cultures, without the difficult discipline of learning languages or customs.[3]

Such packaged tours had their pleasures, of course—and they still do. They permitted the pleasure of difference, and the stimulation of seeing something else. At its best, tourism provided a critical perspective on our own culture by offering "perspective by incongruity," the sight of ourselves seen through others' eyes. And even at its worst, tourism afforded new sights and sounds and tastes, all arranged to confirm the good taste of the tourist. Tourists enjoyed a sense of leisure, often in contrast to busy lives at home. And they often returned home with stories and photographs and souvenirs of their travels. Tourists consumed foreign cultures by consuming their sites and their stuff.[4]

Such tourism offered an entrée to commercial cosmopolitanism: a way of comparing and contrasting the civilization of tourists with other civilizations, or with the primitivism of natives. Indeed, the primitivism we still see as tourists has its attractions. "In the dominant modern imagination," notes geographer Jon Goss, "preindustrial peoples are modernity's children, closer to nature and their natural selves, and freely exhibiting values and behaviors that civilization has repressed." Primitives are "associated with stewardship relations with nature, a 'natural' economy, and innocent faith in the animate powers of the object world." We find such primitivism enchanting because it often evokes a people who really believe in magic. Its magic for us is the magic that our culture has systematically marginalized in the rational, scientific, secular, and bureaucratic disenchantment of the world.[5]

Still, despite the attractions, primitives are not us, and we—thank God—are not primitives. We love them because they show us the error of our ways, but also because they can't do anything about it. We buy books about the wisdom of native peoples, but they don't replace our guides to success in a commercial culture. We are aesthetically and emotionally drawn to primitivism, but not economically or politically. We might collect primitive art—that shows how civilized we are—but we don't intend to "go native." And we're shocked by people, like Marlowe in *Heart of Darkness*, who do. Oh, the horror!

The cultural benefits of tourism, the cultural capital it provided, didn't always require travel or actual encounters with the other. We think of virtual reality as a contemporary phenomenon, but virtual encounters with the world are not a new invention in Western culture. Books are a form of virtual reality, and travel narratives like Mark Twain's *Innocents Abroad* were popular in the nineteenth century. World's fairs were a way of displaying the world and exposing the exotic. Painting and photography often recorded scenes of other places. At the turn of the century, people purchased viewscopes and stereoscopes that let them see foreign pictures. In the twentieth century, magazines like *National Geographic* recorded and reproduced perceptions of the other world.[6]

By the mid-twentieth century, theme parks like Disneyland began to offer a variety of pseudo-safaris. At the original park, the Jungle Cruise (located in

Adventureland) took visitors on a boat ride down the rivers of the Third World. In just a few minutes, tourists could travel from the Nile Valley to the African savannah to the Amazon jungle to a Southeast Asian temple. At Disney World, EPCOT Center makes the globe into a theme park, allowing people to tour several different world civilizations in central Florida.[7]

Many of these places also offered "native" cuisine, giving visitors a literal taste of other worlds. Like the Rainforest Café, they promoted what might be called culinary cosmopolitanism. At home, too, more-or-less authentic ethnic cuisine could also be a sign of "good taste," and this culinary tourism—this going out for Chinese or Thai, or whatever taste was trendy today—could be another way of getting the benefits of tourism without going anywhere. In many ways, the Rainforest Café is Disney's Jungle Cruise as dining experience.

The Rainforest Café works within this tradition of virtual tourism, but it adds a new ecological overlay. In the nineteenth century, people talked about vanishing tribes or vanishing Indians and practiced what might be called "salvage ethnography" or "see-it-before-it's-gone tourism." But now we talk about vanishing nature and endangered species and engage in "see-it-before-it's-gone" eco-tourism.[8]

The Rainforest Café capitalizes on the rainforest chic at the turn of the millennium. Like Ben and Jerry's "Rainforest Crunch" ice cream, or like Caribou Coffee's organic Rainforest Blend, the Rainforest Café raises consciousness even as it raises revenue. Like the Endangered Species Store, or Disney's new Animal Kingdom, the Rainforest Café literally capitalizes on our affection for nature and our anxiety about its disappearance.

Such green marketing can be good business. In 1990, the Roper organization conducted research that found 78 percent of Americans in favor of "improving the environment." Other surveys show about one-third of Americans buy stuff because of ecological labeling, green advertising, or environmentalist endorsements. Ironically, it's possible to expand the culture of consumption by evoking the vulnerability of nature caused by expanding cultures of consumption.[9]

It's interesting that the endangered species and ecosystems that are featured in the mall are not generally the ones we live in. The Mall of America, for example, is located in a city, Bloomington, whose name suggests the blooming tallgrass prairie that has been virtually exterminated in the state of Minnesota. But the mall doesn't have a Prairie Café or a Corn-and-Soybeans Cabaret or a

Suburban Back-Yard Bistro. And there's nothing in places like the Rainforest Café to suggest that we, and not some other people, might be responsible for the extinctions we worry about, because we work by remote control, which is not just a feature of television, but a guiding principle of American civilization.

The popularity of the Rainforest Café doesn't come completely from the popularity of the rainforest, or the exotic or cosmopolitanism. It's also popular because it fits well with the rest of our lives. When we go *to* the Rainforest Café, the experience is conditioned by where we've come *from*. Its artificial jungle can tell us something about the tangled reality of our own lives. It tells us, I think, that we find our everyday lives boring—or at least that advertisers can appeal to us by promising to relieve our boredom. The mall's constant call to "adventure" suggests that our own lives lack adventure. The café calls itself "a *wild* place to shop and eat," suggesting that we need or want the wild in our lives. Thoreau said that "in wildness is the preservation of the world," but this is probably not precisely what he meant.

The *sensuousness* of the Rainforest Café and of malls of America, their appeal to sight and sound and smell and touch and taste, suggests that our everyday lives are not exactly sensual. In our malls, the tropics symbolize paradise, the garden of Eden, the primeval pleasure ground. The exotic can also be sexual, sensual, titillating: we call strippers "exotic dancers" because they provoke pleasures we're not always allowed to have. In the mall, the exotic image of the primitive, with its vitality and freedom from inhibitions, justifies impulse, desire, and immediate self-gratification. Evoking the exotic provides what historian William Leach calls "therapeutic release and excitement" for people normally restrained by puritanism and the work ethic.[10]

The *sensory overload* of the mall serves as counterpoint to the sensory underload of our everyday lives. One of the primary goals of American life is comfort, but once we've gotten comfortable, we discover that comfort can be problematic because it doesn't stimulate us very much. We take little pleasure in our comfort, because, as Bill McKibben suggests, "pleasure can only be had at the price of discomfort." Comfort is a steady-state of positive stimulation, but pleasure involves a sharp increase in our arousal level. In our everyday lives, we may be rushed most of the time, but the rush of the rat race doesn't give us the emotional rush we desire. We seem to want extra excitement and stimulation. And the mall is popular because it's willing to stimulate (or at least simulate) our senses.[11]

The World in a Shopping Mall

We like the exotic because it suggests an *authenticity* that we apparently don't find at home. Marilyn Halter notes that "the more artificiality, anonymity, and uncertainty apparent in a postmodern world, the more driven are the quests for authentic experiences and the more people long to feel connected to localized traditions seeking out the timeless and the true. . . . Increasingly, tourists want their travel agents to find sites to visit that offer fine weather *and* an authentic cultural encounter." Indeed, some cultural authenticity is created just for tourists who will pay for it. And in a mall world, artificial authenticity can also be evoked for paying customers. It seems that we find even artificial authenticity more authentic than our own postmodern lives.[12]

The Rainforest Café tells us, I think, that we don't generally find the here and now as fulfilling as the there and then. It capitalizes on the ubiquitous American theme of escape from the routines of our lives. At the Rainforest Café and other similar venues, we can "light out for the territory" and still get home in time to sleep in our own beds. For many of us, the escape comes packaged in the cultural institution of the vacation, when we vacate our homes and our regular responsibilities. Rainforest Café uses the safari trope to make eating out seem like a vacation. This is important to themed attractions because people on vacation spend more freely than they do at home.[13]

All of these imaginative deals—escape, vacation, safari, adventure—are counterpoints to our everyday lives, but they do little or nothing to affect the general quality of those lives. In fact, weekends, breaks, vacations, and escapes probably help us to put up with the stress and alienation of our normal lives. In this way, they operate as a safety valve for structural discontents and as a part of the powerful politics of no politics at the mall.

Banana Republics

Banana Republic was one of the first modern retail outlets to utilize exotic props and motifs in its stores. The company began in 1978 as a surplus clothing outlet. Entrepreneurs Mel and Patricia Ziegler opened a store in Mill Valley, California, stocked with fifteen hundred dollars' worth of Spanish paratrooper jackets. In an era of polyester disco-wear, Banana Republic offered natural-fiber clothes designed to appeal to outdoor adventure chic. But there weren't enough surplus clothes to supply the demand, so the Zieglers began to manufacture their own surplus, designing clothes—especially khakis with lots of practical pockets—based on the surplus *look*. They started to sell khakis just as khakis became the uniform of the 1980s. By 1983, they had five stores and total sales of $10 million. To finance additional growth, the Zieglers sold the firm to Gap, Inc., which expanded the chain to one hundred stores by 1988.[14]

Early stores were themed before the word "theme" became a verb. They included settings that looked like jungle hunting lodges, British officer clubs, and bush outposts. Thatched roofs and mosquito netting hung over props like Jeeps and Range Rovers. At some stores, a stuffed giraffe poked its long neck through the awning. Travel trunks, maps, and guidebooks evoked a peripatetic life of adventure, while bush jackets and pith helmets allowed customers to buy into the illusion. "It was," notes one author, "the place for people who wanted to go on safari—or just wanted to look the part."[15]

Changes in the American workplace resulted in a repositioning of the Banana Republic in the early 1990s. With the increasing informality of the American office, people were looking for something besides suits to suit them. Market research showed a gap in the clothing market between the Gap's laid-back look and Brooks Brothers' button-down look and predicted that it would be more profitable to sell business casual than casual clothes. Business casual began as "an appropriate uniform for casual Friday," but it has slowly colonized the other four workdays too.[16]

Established as a "life-style brand" in the mid-1990s, Banana Republic extended its product line to include personal care items, gifts, jewelry, intimate apparel, shoes, and tableware. "We kept hearing phrases such as 'I don't want to shop at Banana Republic; I want to live there'" CEO Jeanne Jackson explained. And so the chain expanded again, to almost three hundred stores, to serve a customer base that Jackson defines as the "worldly consumer."[17]

The new merchandise and stores have few references to the Banana Republic's early safari theme. But they still maintain connections to the history of banana republics, as do most mall apparel shops. At its founding, the Zieglers playfully chose a name rooted in the history of American imperialism, when American corporations like the United Fruit Company exercised their interests in the nations of Central America. In that era of world history, the Western powers often went

241

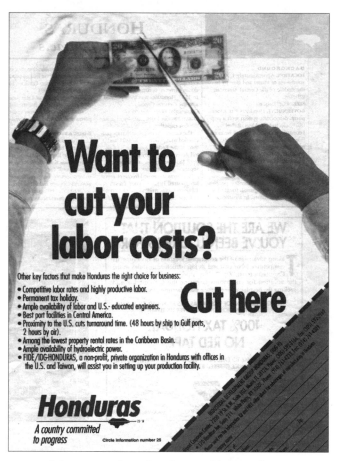

Want to cut your labor costs?

Other key factors that make Honduras the right choice for business:

- Competitive labor rates and highly productive labor.
- Permanent tax holiday.
- Ample availability of labor and U.S.- educated engineers.
- Best port facilities in Central America.
- Proximity to the U.S. cuts turnaround time. (48 hours by ship to Gulf ports, 2 hours by air).
- Among the lowest property rental rates in the Caribbean Basin.
- Ample availability of hydroelectric power.
- FIDE/IDG-HONDURAS, a non-profit, private organization in Honduras with offices in the U.S. and Taiwan, will assist you in setting up your production facility.

Cut here

Honduras

A country committed to progress

Circle Information number 25

Cutting labor costs: the value theory of labor (Photo courtesy of the National Labor Committee)

to banana republics for natural resources, for the produce—like bananas—that wouldn't grow on home ground.[18]

Although Americans still import bananas and other products of the Third World, we also exploit their human resources. If banana republics were once a place of resourcing, now they're a place for outsourcing. In the "bandana republics" of the modern world, workers toil not just to pick bananas and pack them, but to piece cloth and sew it into clothes. So we can encounter the world on the garment tags of American malls. One excursion to a local Banana Republic, for example, revealed clothing assembled in 20 different countries, including the Philippines, Malaysia, Macau, Brunei, Bahrain, Singapore, India, Hong Kong, Korea, China, Sri Lanka, Thailand, Turkey, Greece, Indonesia, Italy, Israel, Portugal, and the North Mariana Islands. A few t-shirts and shorts and socks were made in the United States, but everything else demonstrated the new geography of globalism in which relatively poor people produce consumer goods for the relatively rich. In America's malls, the "worldly consumer" is worldly in more ways than we normally imagine, because the stores are stocked with the productions of everywhere else. Indeed, counterfactually, it's hard to imagine what the mall would look like if we removed all the foreign-made products.[19]

The banana republics of the twentieth century have been replaced by the sweatshop republics of the twenty-first century. While American manufacturers focus on product development and brand management, they move the manufacturing of their stuff overseas. Not surprisingly, these factories and sweatshops are not featured in the exotic imagery of the mall. In fact, Third World manufactories are never depicted in American shopping centers. Such scenes don't qualify as exotic, because there's no "charm" in this unfamiliar sight. Although they're different, these factories are not "exotic" because they're not "strikingly and intriguingly unusual and beautiful."[20]

So the "business casual" of the contemporary American workplace has more than a casual connection to changing workplaces in the Third World. Until the 1970s, most American manufacturers made their own products or purchased them from importers who offered finished goods for sale. But in the last thirty years, the American companies have become "manufacturers without factories" by outsourcing production in order to concentrate on design, marketing, and sales. Because the World Bank and the International Monetary Fund have encouraged developing countries to create export sectors to bring in hard currency, Third World countries have created "free trade zones" offering tax, regulation, and infrastructure advantages, as well as development grants for corporations. Sometimes, as in the United States, these countries set the minimum wage well below the poverty level for their own country. At the expense of their own workers, nations began to compete with each other for the business and for the benefit of multinational corporations. American manufacturers, therefore, turned to offshore production to make things cheaply. By the end of the twentieth century, there were more than eight hundred export processing zones, with 27 million workers assembling more than $200 billion worth of products.[21]

Outsourcing offered significant advantages to companies like Gap, Nike, Disney, or Mattel. In a mall world, outsourcing gives companies manufacturing capacity without capital costs or labor problems. It provides flexibility in maintaining inventory, because the company isn't committed to the factory or its work force for longer than the term of the contract. It allows low-risk experimentation, letting a company try out a product line without steep start-up costs. It reduces the chances of labor problems by locating production in countries resistant to union organization. And outsourcing reduces costs by forcing suppliers to compete for contracts.[22]

Mall retailers are often intimately involved in such practices. Department stores, for example, know that if they create and promote their own private label brands, they reap more of the profit than if they sell other brand names. Even though most department store brands sell for about half the price of the cheapest designer lines, they net retailers between 2 and 8 percent more. And because of their sales volume, contracts from these chain stores can be lucrative to Third World agents and manufacturers. In Nicaragua, for example, the Chentex plant (owned and operated by the Nien-Hsing consortium of Taiwan) produces Sonoma jeans for Kohl's, Arizona jeans for J. C. Penney, Route 66 jeans for Kmart, Faded Glory jeans for Wal-Mart, as well as jeans for Bugle Boy, Cherokee, and Gloria Vanderbilt.[23]

Outsourcing also benefits people in the Third World. It benefits the brokers who contract the work and subcontract the manufacturing, and it benefits some government officials who are bribed. Outsourcing provides work for poor people in those countries, people often displaced by changes in the agricultural economy. Sweatshop supporters contend that people really want these jobs and note that they often pay better than the legal minimum wage in the country. In some cases, in cultures that devalue girls and women, factory work can be a needed source of independence for females.[24]

This is true, but it's not the whole story. Such rhetoric asks us to focus our attention on the individual's desire, rather than on the structural sources of that desire. It asks us to keep in mind the individual worker's benefit, while forgetting the history of underdevelopment and our complicity with the economic institutions that maintain it. It implies that these individuals have other practical options, that they are, in the tradition of *homo economicus,* free to choose a sweatshop or something better. In fact, workers in the world's export processing zones—usually young, unmarried women—are often slaving long hours for low pay in repressive conditions. Their living conditions are not much better. But the "trickle-down" rhetoric of globalism promises to let these people pull themselves up by making our bootstraps. It's what we might call "humanitarian imperialism."[25]

The sweatshop republics that support the bandana republics of the mall also offer advantages for American consumers. They promise economic advantages, because, theoretically, the consumer benefits from such corporate cost cutting. Within a purely economic framework focused on consumption and consumers, this is a good thing. If products are cheaper, prices are lower, and we can buy more goods. But such a "price-tag" analytical framework is a form of selective attention. A purely economic construction of the world of goods has its problems, because it omits so much. It misses the social dislocations in the host society, especially in urban-rural relations, and the uprooting of subsistence societies with traditional cultures of cooperation and collaboration. It undervalues the decline of agricultural production, as people move closer to these free-trade jobs, and it misses the ecological costs in societies without environmental protection agencies.[26]

At the same time, such analysis directs attention away from the deindustrialization of the United States. It ignores Americans who have lost jobs and ignores the impact on the labor movement. It doesn't count the cost of competition on small businesses and their ultimate absorption by larger companies. And, unfortunately, it may still be the case that cheaper production means higher profits but not lower prices. Companies that move their manufacturing offshore don't always drop their prices as a result.[27]

Economic advantages are, of course, important to consumers. Yet just as important are the psychological advantages of the new bandana republics. Indeed, sweatshops have therapeutic effects for American consumers because they keep such workers out of sight and out of mind. In 1996, Americans were scandalized to discover that clothes bearing the celebrity brand name of Kathie Lee Gifford were made in Honduran sweatshops where children as young as five made thirty-one cents an hour for working as much as a seventy-five hours a week. We would be horrified to see such sweatshops in our own neighborhoods, but somehow, in Indonesia or Honduras or China, these factories seem almost natural. We forget that the overdeveloped world profits from the underdevelopment of the rest of the world.[28]

In recent years, however, labor and human rights activists have reminded us of the development of underdevelopment by spotlighting the sweatshop practices of multinational corporations. Organizations like the National Labor Committee, the Asia Monitor Resource Center, Sweatshop Watch, Corporate Watch and others have interviewed workers and reported the results. College students have formed United Students Against Sweatshops, and pressured college bookstores to consider the sourcing of their sweatshirts and other logo apparel. "Without independent activists," says England's *Economist*, "the world would know much less about working conditions in the developing world."[29]

These revelations have had an impact. Many companies have adopted codes of conduct and employed independent monitors to inspect their plants. Nine companies—including Nike, Reebok, Adidas, Eddie Bauer, Levi's, Liz Claiborne, Phillips-Van Heusen, and Patagonia—have joined the Fair Labor Association, formed in the mid-1990s to create an independent monitoring system for labor abuses. The Gap, Banana Republic's parent company, has been an industry leader. After 1995 labor unrest at a subcontractor in El Salvador, Gap didn't desert the work force as other American firms did. Instead, it pressured the factory owners to improve working conditions and to work with local labor, religious, and academic leaders as independent monitors. More recently, American multinationals have been pressuring their international suppliers to tolerate unions.[30]

It's very difficult to effect change, however, and the Gap has not yet extricated itself from questionable practices. The *New York Times* reported that the lesson from Gap's experience in El Salvador is that "competing interests among factory owners, government officials, American managers, and middle-class consumers—all with their eyes on the lowest possible cost—make it difficult to achieve even basic standards, and even harder to maintain them." American mall shoppers are a primary part of the problem. Economists speak about a labor theory of value, which holds that goods acquire their worth because labor adds value to raw materials. Cotton in the fields isn't worth much, for example, until workers pick it, process it, spin it and dye it, assemble it as jeans or t-shirts, and package it for market. The labor theory of value asks us to value this "sweat equity"

It's a Mall World, After All

in our goods by paying workers adequately. And it asks us to notice that the profits accrued by capitalists and corporations come, in large part, from the "surplus
value" added by labor.[31]

But American shoppers seem to have a "value theory of labor," which suggests
implicitly that we can't get a good value unless we exploit foreign laborers. We
keep our prices low by keeping their wages low. Our interests as consumers apparently supersede their interests as producers. The beautiful thing about all this is
that we don't ever have to see the consequences of our actions; the free market and
multinational manufacturers take care of it for us. We understand consumption as
a matter of getting a good value at the mall, but not so much as a matter of maintaining good values in our economic institutions. We keep *our* values intact by
ignoring the fact that our preference for "a good value" is, in fact, a moral value.

Indeed, the invisibility of production makes consumption easier, because we
can purchase the illusions of marketing instead of the realities of manufacturing. As David Bosworth suggests, "These days, jeans can be sold as either
'ruggedly natural' or 'sexy and glamorous,' athletic shoes as 'high-tech wonders';
but none of these images could survive if the bleak reality of the real product's
manufacture were made visible somehow at the point of sale: these purportedly
'Western' goods are, typically, made in Asia, by impoverished women, in sweatshops reminiscent of Dickens' doleful London." In the manufacturing chain, retail
is where goods are decontaminated, because retail design is designed to disguise
wholesale production. In the wonderland of shopping, we see goods that have
been transformed and transvalued by advertising and marketing. Dissociated
from their social and material contexts, objects are then associated with images
and emotions that make them more desirable. We don't see the real consequences
of our consumption. We don't see how we consume not just cloth and thread, or
plastic and metal, but people's lives. Consumer forgetfulness is the solid foundation of our consumer fantasies.[32]

Further, we don't generally ask questions. During the Clinton administration,
the U.S. Department of Labor offered a "No Sweat" card that encouraged
Americans to ask retailers about how and when their garments are made. The
card asked shoppers to ask "whether they independently monitor garment manufacturers to avoid buying at sweatshops" and "whether they support 'No Sweat'
clothing." But most of us maintain our silence: we have a "don't ask, don't tell"

The World in a Shopping Mall

policy toward our consumer goods. At the mall, therefore, we engage in what one critic calls "sweatshopping"—shopping without sweating the social consequences of our consumption.[33]

A 1990s survey by Loyola Marymount University showed that three-fourths of Americans would prefer not to shop in stores that sell sweatshop products. Yet because we remain ignorant about our consumption, most of us do. Along with manufacturers and retailers, we join in a conspiracy of silence about the sources of our shopping. When Eyal Press, for example, asked retail clerks if the clothing sold in their shop was made in sweatshops, they usually referred him to the manager, and the manager referred him to public relations people at corporate headquarters. When Press asked customers if they knew where the goods came from, he was escorted from the store. Understandably, retail clerks were more concerned with protecting their jobs than protecting foreign workers.[34]

This might not happen if shoppers focused more on the "republic" part of Banana Republic. Today's republic of the mall seems to be more about private goods than the public good, more about looking good than doing good, although, obviously, the two aren't mutually exclusive. Indeed, in the September 2001 issue of *Shopping Center World*, an article entitled "From Sweatshops to Shopping Malls" asks, "Will retailers bend to increasing pressure to eliminate global labor abuse?" The article notes that "shopping centers are the ideal place [for protesters] to get the message across to consumers and retailers." It notes that such pressure, combined with other efforts like shareholder activism, can make a difference at every level. When consumers put their money where their values are—at retail stores, in shopping centers, and in socially responsible investing—companies begin to pay attention.[35]

Anthropologist Renato Rosaldo suggests that Americans and other First World people sometimes engage in what he calls "imperialist nostalgia," a wishful memory of the good old days when there was a place for everything and everybody stayed in their place. Both the exoticism in malls and the "outsourcism" of the mall's products constitute just such an imperialist system. In it, we can purchase symbols of class privilege without ever thinking about the substance of it.[36]

THIRTEEN

Shopping Center World

Just as we trade in images, and the natural and human resources of other cultures, so too other cultures trade in American images and American resources. As early as the 1860s, ads for shipping lines, emigration societies, and land developers used images of wide-open spaces, the rugged West, Indians, and the frontier to suggest both the political freedom and economic independence available in America. In the twentieth century, images of Uncle Sam, the Statue of Liberty, the American flag, and blue jeans also provided a visual shorthand for ideas associated with America. More recently, commercial icons as diverse as Ronald McDonald and the Marlboro Man have joined movie and TV and music and sports stars as international symbols of our society. Paradoxically, these images of America help other people to express their own identity and desires.[1]

These days, images of America are ubiquitous, because

the world watches American movies and television. A writer in the *Shopping Center Development Handbook* notes that China "has 250 million TV sets, many of them receiving satellite feeds from Hong Kong and Japan. These consumers are the MTV generation, eastern style." Ian Watt reports that "increasing rates of television ownership and strong advertising campaigns have made South African consumers very brand conscious." Throughout the world, says *American Demographics*, "TV is creating a common culture of consumption. More than ever, people around the world know about and want the same types of branded goods and services. Rather than a global village, mass exposure to TV is creating a global mall."[2]

Shopping Center World

People in other countries trade these images of America in shopping centers that are themselves images of America. Malls are an American invention, but they're no longer strictly American. These days, the United States almost always has a negative balance of trade, but its most important export isn't goods and services—it's culture, including American retail culture. Indeed, one of the most important products of a trading culture is its patterns of trading, as Judith Dobrzynski suggests in a *New York Times Magazine* essay on retailing called "The American Way." Even in an era of intense economic competition, she says, American retailing "is the most sophisticated, the most dynamic, the most brutally competitive in the world—which is why visitors from around the world are streaming in to learn its secrets. Like the 18th-century British aristocrats who traveled to Italy to study its art, history and manners, they embark on a grand tour"—of shopping centers.[3]

At an academic conference on the Mall of America held in Minneapolis in 1997, one speaker mentioned that the megamall attracts more visitors annually than all the national parks and national monuments combined. A Frenchman speaking later expressed some confusion: "I thought the Mall of America *was* a national monument." Americans average twenty-three square feet per person in shopping malls, which is 75 percent of all our retail space. The world average for all retail space (not just shopping malls) is four square feet per person, and American shopping centers comprise 29 percent of that total. If shopping isn't the heart of American culture, it's at least a vital organ.[4]

It's a Mall World, After All

Although many foreign executives and managers visit American malls on their own, custom tours are now available. The International Council of Shopping Centers began to sponsor such tours in 1995, and the National Retail Federation followed the next year. A 2000 ICSC "educational study tour" invited mall owners and managers, leasing agents and retailers, architects and designers to "join your colleagues from around the world for a study tour of some of the leading entertainment-oriented shopping centers in the U.S." As visitors learn from America's malls, the American style slowly becomes the new International Style in commercial architecture.[5]

As its name suggests, the ICSC is increasingly international. Starting in 1998, the ICSC began to call its convention a World Congress. At the spring 2000 meeting in Las Vegas, more than five hundred representatives from thirty-nine countries outside North America attended sessions and browsed the Trade Expo and Leasing Mall. *New York Times* columnist Thomas Friedman addressed a breakfast session on "Understanding Globalization" and signed copies of his book, *The Lexus and the Olive Tree.* Panelists from London, Hong Kong, and Rio de Janiero anchored a panel on "New Lands and Opportunities." The ICSC web site features a 104-page report on "Shopping Centers: A World of Opportunity," and the ICSC's Worldwide Commission also compiled a CD-ROM containing eighteen reports on international retail development.[6]

Driven in part by global advertising expenditures that are increasing a third faster than world economic activity and three times faster than world population, shopping centers proliferate throughout the world, often in business and tourist destinations. These centers serve the local population but also world travelers. And like American shopping centers, they also market the world. In his book *Global Soul,* Pico Iyer describes one Hong Kong mall that invited people to "Go around the world in one day" by visiting its six hundred shops. Another Hong Kong center sold itself as "a world of delights under one roof." Featuring "the great department stores of Britain, Hong Kong, and Japan," it also housed four cinemas, twenty places to eat, and ninety-seven boutiques, including Gucci, Guess, Valentino, Vuitton, Boss, Hugo Boss, and the Armani Exchange.[7]

Some of these foreign malls feature American retail firms. The saturation and intense competition of domestic markets, the aging of the baby boomers, minimal population growth, and slow increases in consumer spending have caused

American retailers to look overseas for growth. In 1998, for example, Toys "R" Us opened fifteen new stores in the United States but thirty-five overseas. At the beginning of the new millennium, almost all of America's top one hundred retailers have a presence overseas. And American manufacturers are asking, as IBM did in one of its ads, "How do we sell more stuff to more people in more places?"[8]

Stores that cater to the world's young people have particular advantages. In *The Kids Market: Myths and Realities,* consultant James McNeal notes that American kids are a magnificent market, but "there is ten times as much market potential among children in the rest of the developed and developing world." McNeal contends that "the U.S. model of consumption, in general, has become the guiding model for consumers the world over, suggesting great opportunity for many existing U.S. products and brands." Observing that the number of kids aged four to fourteen outside the United States is fourteen times greater than the number of American kids, he advises marketers that "the kids market doesn't end at U.S. borders."[9]

A writer in *American Demographics* notes that "in a world united by satellite technology, teenagers the world over share many of the same consumer attitudes because they watch many of the same TV shows and commercials. Global teens already have some strong brand preferences, but there's still plenty of room to develop global brands by paying attention to youth." MTV, for example, channels messages into 288 million homes in more than eighty-eight countries. And "the good news for marketers is that teens who watch commercial TV also tend to consume more. For example, teens who watch MTV music videos are much more likely than other teens to wear the teen `uniform' of jeans, running shoes and denim jacket."[10]

In *The $100 Billion Allowance: Assessing the Global Teen Market,* Elissa Moses reports on the New World Teen Study of thirty-four thousand teenagers in forty-four countries. She contends that the American Dream "has become synonymous with the Chinese Dream, the Brazilian Dream, even the French Dream. The universal dream [for teenagers] is to lead a good life with a rewarding job, have satisfying family relationships, enjoy rich experiences, manifest freedom and self-expression, and possess lots of consumer goods." Despite cultural differences, teenagers essentially constitute a global youth culture unified by "unabashed consumption," "passion for technology," "perpetual entertainment," and seven other "unifiers." "From Manhattan to Madras and Milan to Melbourne," she says, "teens

It's a Mall World, After All

who speak different languages (although many speak English) all speak the same language of global brand consumption."[11]

In Europe, malls have been sited both in historic landscapes and on the outskirts of cities. An ICSC report estimates that 43 percent of the European population visits a shopping center each week. "The French," an American journalist reports, "are adopting many of the things I did not miss about the U.S. . . . and racing full speed into partial Americanization. Shopping centers are constructed practically overnight in warehouses that feel like monuments to the aluminum siding industry." The ICSC sponsors an annual convention in Europe and has affiliates in Germany, Austria, Hungary, Belgium, Holland, Italy, Spain, Portugal, and the Scandinavian countries.[12]

Harun Farocki's 2001 documentary film *The Creators of Shopping Worlds* (*Die Shopfer der Einkauswelten*) shows German planners working on a shopping center with a *Miami Vice* theme for the city of Munster. As they work on this "true American design," they speak mainly in German, but some words—"anchor tenant," "food court," "marketing," and "real life"—are spoken in English because it's the international language of shopping centers. And the basic idea of malls as an investment project designed to channel traffic into retail stores needs no translation at all.

In Central and Eastern Europe, shopping centers are very popular. In Budapest, citizens were stricken by "retail hysteria" when the 500,000-square-foot Polus Center opened in 1996. A shop clerk explained the attraction: "Finally we have something Western in this boring country. I can't say why I like this mall so much. It's just nice to have something new."[13]

In Asia, an emerging middle class has money to spend, and they expect to spend it like Americans do. In some Asian countries, the savings rate has been as much as 38 percent, so there's a market for malls. In Japan, per capita income exceeds American averages, and retail expenditures are 30 percent higher, but the country is, by American standards, woefully "under-stored," with only four square feet of retail space per person. The Japanese youth market is also powerful, accounting already for the success of retailers like the Body Shop, Tower Records, AMC Theaters, and Starbucks. And shopping centers are making inroads: the ICSC gave a 2001 Maxi award to Gotemba Premium Outlets for a publicity campaign that successfully convinced Japanese consumers that they should shop at an out-of-town outlet center.[14]

In his book *Fantasy City: Pleasure and Profit in the Postmodern Metropolis*, John Hannigan states that "Asian consumers are embracing western retail formats, specialty boutiques, entertainment concepts . . . and even discount retailing. Shopping malls, for example, have sprouted up everywhere, both in city centers and in the new suburbs. From 1993 to 1996, more than a dozen malls were built in Jakarta, Indonesia with an average size of 1 million square feet. Bangkok is now home to two of the largest shopping malls in the world; one of them, the 5 million square foot Seacon Square, hosts as many as 200,000 shoppers every week." Singapore has staked its growth on the development of shopping. As Tran Vinh says in *The Harvard Design School Guide to Shopping*, "Singapore sees itself as a shopping center: Singapore has more retail space per person than any of its neighboring cities in Southeast Asia"—and almost as much as the United States. In its Central Area, for example, a two-mile stretch of Orchard Boulevard has been developed with over fifty huge, mixed-use shopping centers, largely tenanted with shopping chains and franchises. Because 50 percent of branded shopping sales came from tourists, the Singapore Tourist Promotion Board has introduced a plan called "Tourism Unlimited" to theme its various shopping districts and promote shopping as a tourist attraction as well as an indigenous activity.[15]

In Asia, although suburban malls are beginning to show up, shopping centers and megamalls tend to be part of mixed-use projects located in central cities and accessed primarily by public transportation. With a strong emphasis on food and entertainment, these projects become destinations for families, who often shop and play together. An analysis of "Retailing in Thailand" reports that "going shopping has developed into a form of relaxation for Thai people during their free time, and shopping malls and department stores can be very crowded on weekends." They're especially crowded after payday, although the development of credit is spreading Thai spending throughout the months.[16]

Even in China, a second "cultural revolution" is occurring, this time due to the invasion of consumer culture. Especially in the cities, Chinese people encounter Western advertising and material culture, and they like it. Companies like Amway, Mary Kay, and Tupperware are enlisting Chinese representatives and selling both consumer goods and the idea of consumer spending. Anthropologist James Watson contends that "the Chinese want the American lifestyle, a modern lifestyle, the way they think Americans live." "For the

Chinese," says a Saatchi & Saatchi executive in China, "it's the lifestyle they aspire to, the spirit of America." That life-style includes shopping centers, so projects like the Grand Gateway in Shanghai have blossomed. Designed by the Jerde Group International, the Grand Gateway is a 1.1-million-square-foot mall attracting about 3 million visitors a month.[17]

In Latin America, the story is similar. The 1990s were "the mall decade" and "shopping" is one of the most commonly used English words. "When in Rio de Janiero," advises William Ecenbarger, "do as the *cariocas* do. It's a rainy day, and everyone's going to the Barras Shopping Center, which is surrounded by a lake of shimmering cars. Inside, the Muzak is colonizing my ears with Broadway show tunes. Except that people are speaking Portugese, this could be Sawgrass Mills." If the United States is "over-stored," Latin America is under-malled (about 2.5 square feet per person). Bogota, however, now boasts the Unicentro Mall, with 360 stores, and the city is also graced by other malls: the Metropolis, Granahorrar, Andino, Hacienda Santa Barbara, Centro 93, and Plaza de las Americas. In Quito, there are eight malls, one of which has 400 stores. In the Mall San Pedro, Costa Rican citizens can discover Victoria's Secret amid 259 other establishments. After decades of following an economic strategy of "import substitution," using high tariffs to protect locally produced goods, Latin American countries have embraced "free trade," including the importation of name-brand Western products. Latin American malls allow the middle classes to shop like the consumer classes of the developed world.[18]

The malling of the world is not a cookie-cutter operation. Shopping centers are always adapted to local conditions. In Riyadh, Saudi Arabia, for example, Altoon and Porter designed the new Kingdom Mall with the third floor exclusively for women. With a business center, spa, and theme restaurant—in addition to the top floor of each of the department stores—the mall creates a space where women can hang out in jeans and t-shirts, instead of the coverings required in other public places. In some countries, shopping centers are anchored by supermarkets and hypermarkets, like the first generation of American shopping centers. In countries without a lot of cars, shopping centers flourish more in city centers than in suburban districts, and near train and transit hubs. In countries such as France, the legal environment is relatively hostile to shopping centers, and in other countries, laws requiring majority local ownership stifle the plans of foreign retailers and developers. In most countries, therefore, shopping center development is an indigenous process, inspired by, but not dictated by, American models.[19]

In all of these places, as in the United States, shopping centers are a force for change. In *Shopping Centers: A World of Opportunity*, Jorge Agustin Justo reports that "Argentina's shopping centers owe their success to consumers' embrace of the new shopping format and their rapid change in shopping habits." In Brazil, "large shopping malls have had negative impacts on the surrounding urban infrastructure, especially in terms of traffic. They usually raise real estate values for commercial and retail uses at the expense of the surrounding residential neighborhoods." Fernando Zobel de Ayala notes that "over the last five years, retailing in the Philippines has increasingly shifted to shopping malls. The Philippine tourism office estimates that 60 percent of all shopping occurs in malls, and shopping centers' market share continues to grow." A group of Spanish correspondents notes that during the 1980s and 1990s "the shopping center clearly caught on, and it triggered a major change in the habits of the Spanish consumer." In Hong Kong, Jolyon Culbertson reports that "the one-stop shopping experience has become an integral part of the local lifestyle. The mall culture is here to stay."[20]

Malls of Americanization?

Malls bring aspects of American consumer culture to the world, just as the media broadcast American entertainment culture in movies and TV. William Ecenbarger contends that "the world has become a Mickey Mouse operation. For all its industrial problems, the U.S.A. reigns supreme as an exporter of music, film, television, sports, food and hundreds of consumer products ranging from Levi's to Pampers to Barbie dolls. America, winner of the Cold War, is now the Great Communicator, world role model and global disc jockey."[21]

In some places, shopping centers are seen as malls of *America*, as agents of unwelcome Americanization. Local critics don't worry about the architecture of shopping centers so much as the culture of shopping centers, the culture of consumption. In Korea, for example, consumer culture causes worry about the erosion of Confucianism, with its emphasis on restraining the self for the greater good. In Malaysia, shopping culture creates anxiety about the extension of credit

Brand-new flag (Image courtesy of www.adbusters.org)

to different ethnic groups, and in Indonesia, conspicuous consumption aggravates agitation over politically sensitive income inequalities.[22]

In Singapore, where household spending increased 76 percent between 1988 and 1993, and where "window-shopping" ranks as the number one leisure activity outside the home, critics worry about the "excesses" of consumer culture, compared to past consumption patterns. They also worry that young people's symbolic attachment to American brand names will undermine their own distinctive traditions. Young people are attracted to America as "the land of the free," and American products are often promoted as symbols of freedom. Kids are less culture-bound than adults, and more open to new ideas, including American malls and consumer goods, so many modern retailers target the international children's market. But to an older generation, American individualism, and the moral laxity of our cultural liberalism, threaten the collective cultural values that bind people together.[23]

When Americans shop at an American mall, we buy into a set of values and assumptions that seem natural to us but may be utterly foreign to other people. In an essay on "Marketing, the Ethics of Consumption, and Less-Developed Countries," George Brenkert suggests six axioms of an American "ethics of consumption." The first is "the pursuit of happiness" ethic, which suggests that people are consumers and "products are for individual satisfaction." We assume that "more satisfaction is better than less satisfaction; [and that] present or immediate satisfaction is superior to delayed or future satisfaction." The second is the "identity" axiom. We assume that "a person's identity tends to be bound up with the products he or she owns and uses," and that "consumerism enhances self-esteem." Third is the "free choice" axiom. We believe that individuals have a right to free choices at the mall. This axiom entails corollaries, including a free market and limited government intervention. The fourth assumption, the "success axiom," emphasizes material success as a primary goal for individuals in a consumer society. Its corollary, the "good life corollary," assumes that the good life is defined in large part by one's possessions. Brenkert's fifth ethic, the "exchange axiom," assumes that "products are acquired for the exchange of money." The "price corollary" assumes that "their price captures their interchangeability." And the "ignorance corollary" suggests that "consumers need have little knowledge of how or where the objects they consume are produced." Brenkert's last axiom, which I would call the "resource axiom," suggests that "the world is a collection of resources whose primary value lies in their use for consumption purposes according to the preceding precepts."[24]

This consumption ethic is embodied in American malls, and implied in malls of everywhere else. If a society already shares this ethic, then a mall isn't out of place. But in societies with a different ethic, this American "cosmallogy" is an intrusion, however pleasurable. The attractions of commercial culture can undermine not just patterns of exchange but also traditional cultures that have existed for centuries. People who have been contented with "the good life" of local cultures find that increased contact with commercialism makes them ashamed of their own culture and eager to pursue the new fantasies of advertising and television. The "demonstration effect" of America's consumer culture often encourages poor people to spend their income on conspicuous consumption instead of saving it for economic development. Even Third World consumers come to aspire to a "standard package" of consumer goods.[25]

Still, it's not the case that malls make other countries American. Each culture adapts shopping centers to their own needs. Nevertheless, malls have common cultural consequences. An Indonesian shopping center isn't a mall of

It's a Mall World, After All

America, but it's not just a mall of Indonesia either. A shopping center's impacts, and the local culture's resistance and adaptations, are part of a larger conversation about what it means to be American and what it means to be oneself.[26]

Controversies over Americanization and cultural imperialism continue. To some extent, as Richard Pells suggests in *Not Like Us: How Europeans Have Loved, Hated, and Transformed American Culture Since World War II*, "the debate over Americanization [is] an argument over the meaning and consequences of modernity." Americanisms, like rock music and blue jeans and shopping centers, are employed by some members of a society, often the young or the working classes, against their own traditions. Even the English language, or its American version, can be interpreted as an Americanism. By the 1990s, 70 percent of young people (age eighteen to twenty-four) in Western Europe spoke English, and 83 percent of teenagers were studying English in school. But only 40 percent of people over twenty-five and a mere 20 percent of people over fifty-five spoke the English of American media and advertising. The spread of English as a second language, therefore, assists the spread of American media and commercialism as a first language. American movies and TV have a great advantage over other countries' products, because the language facilitates their market penetration—and vice versa. Up to 90 percent of the films shown in Europe are American made.[27]

Several European countries have passed laws to restrict the growth of hypermarkets and shopping centers. This resistance, says Chuihua Judy Chung, "is an attempt to preserve the European identity. . . . Europeans define themselves by their cities, and an unanticipated alteration of this spatial and material order amounts to an abrupt physical assault on the European character." The legislation maintains traditional limitations on shop hours (including Sunday closing), but includes newer restrictions, including environmental (and social) impact statements, tightened permit processes, limitations on the size of shopping developments, or preferences for urban development. Except for the Scandinavian countries, which have successfully channeled retail development primarily into their urban centers, the results have been mixed.[28]

We should be cautious, of course, in thinking about Americanization. For one thing, it's hard to say precisely what the term means. Critics often assume that American media and institutions send a single message, but one of the most important messages of modern American media is that variety sells. Second, it's fairly clear that consumerism isn't peculiarly American. In fact, as Leslie Sklair suggests, "the global-capitalist system works through the culture-ideology of consumption, rather than through a glorification of the American way of life." Third, it's difficult to say if even Americans are fully Americanized, since the United States in the new millennium is still a nation of immigrants and a multi-cultural, cosmopolitan country. Fourth, the debates on Americanization tend to highlight the negative aspects of American influence; they seldom invoke more positive cultural patterns, such as democracy, religious membership, or partici-pation in volunteer organizations. Fifth, it's important to remember that other cultures often adapt Americanization to their own needs. In "American Empire and Cultural Imperialism: A View from the Receiving End," Dutch scholar Rob Kroes argues that "in this allegedly `American Century,' then, Americanization should be seen as the story of an American cultural language traveling and of other people acquiring that language. What they actually said with it is a dif-ferent story altogether."[29]

"Americanization" gets even more complicated when the second largest oper-ator of malls in America isn't American but Australian. With acquisitions in 2001 and 2002, Westfield America, a division of Westfield Holdings, took second place to the Simon Property Group. Westfield also owns and operates shopping centers in Australia, New Zealand, and Europe, and has experienced double-digit growth in profits over the last ten years. Chairman Frank Lowy contends that "there are no other shopping-centre companies in the world that are global." And according to the *Economist*, Westfield is "fast becoming the mall equivalent of, say, McDonald's or Marriott." If malls are Americanizing the world, they seem to be doing so with a peculiar accent.[30]

The International Council of Shopping Centers publishes a magazine called *Shopping Center World*. Increasingly, the title looks prophetic. As tourists and busi-ness travelers, we Americans spend our dollars in foreign shopping centers that make us feel at home. As experts in retail practices, we serve as examples and consultants to the rest of the world. Even more fundamentally, however, our daily consumption practices have become an inspiration for the world. As Richard Wagnleitner says, "Whatever the social reality of millions in the United States might be, America first and foremost signifies wealth, power, youth, and success.

It is not only the center of twentieth-century capitalist culture of consumption but, at the same time, itself its most important product." Americans teach the world what to wish for: "The pursuit of success is the common philosophy, the transformation of success into consumption is the common practice. . . . I consume, therefore I am: Credit Card instead of Descartes."[31]

So—it's a mall world after all. At the mall, we market the world, using images of the world as a counterpoint to our everyday lives. We employ images and fantasies of the exotic to sell products that are assembled in the sweatshop republics of the new millennium. We use the fantasies of one world to conceal the realities of another world. And as shopping centers become more central in all the nations of the world, we impose our commercial "cosmallogy" on the other people of the planet—not just Planet Reebok or Planet Hollywood, but planet Earth.

From one perspective, the malling of the world is a story of American imperialism—imaginative, economic, and cultural. We imaginatively colonize the rainforests and the Serengeti to sell merchandise from bandana republics. We economically colonize sweatshop republics to provide an objective correlative for our dreams. We culturally colonize the world by broadcasting commercial images of the good life which are bound up in the world of goods. From another perspective, it's the story of freedom—free trade, free time, and, most of all, free choices that people worldwide make in embracing elements of a mall world.

Is a mall world a good thing or a bad thing? The answer, of course, is yes, it is! When we go to the mall, we literally buy into ideas and institutions that translate and transform our world. As consumers, as citizens, and—in a *small* world, as neighbors—people need to sort out the real goodness in the goods of the mall and determine, both individually *and* collectively, how in the world we can really live the good life.

FOURTEEN

Shopping for a Better World

As we have seen in this book, shopping centers are us. They reflect and affect our lives and our values. They help us to learn the common sense of our culture, and they do a tremendous amount of cultural work in American society. The shopping centers of today were shaped by the "us" of yesterday, people "just looking" for their American dreams. Right now, we're inventing the shopping centers of the future. So what do we want them to be?

American malls developed during the twentieth century. Each mall was planned, but the larger history of malls was unplanned, the result of small decisions made by developers, designers, institutional investors, manufacturers, managers, retailers, salespeople, and customers. Each of these actors made rational decisions to participate in the malling of America. Over time, most of us have been satisfied with the immediate results. In general, malls have succeeded at doing what they're designed to do. They provide a convenient place for finding a variety of consumer goods. They provide semipublic spaces for strolling or "hanging out." They're often beautiful, exhibiting a wide variety of commercial art. They reinforce American values of individualism and choice. Malls get people to buy stuff, and they generate a substantial repeat business. They provide jobs for workers, taxes for governments, and profits for managers, owners, and investors. In the process, at some level, they help us deal with important issues like identity and community and progress, race and gender and sexuality. Malls are an American success story.[1]

The historical improvements in shopping centers have all come within a paradigm of increased profits and progress. The profit motive is a remarkable stimulus, and there's a lot of good that comes from it. Mall developer James Rouse claimed that "profit is the thing that hauls dreams into focus." And historian Neil Harris reminds us that "the best of these buying machines reminds us, once again, that the commercial spirit has nurtured much of our most interesting American design."[2]

Many of us know that shopping centers have their costs. Although America's malls have accomplished most of their immediate goals, they've also had unintended consequences. Sometimes their success has social costs. Many of us regret the loss of independent local retailers and the homogenization of retailing. We regret the replacement of vital public spaces by pseudo-public spaces like shopping centers. Some Americans regret the connection between the malling of America and the sprawling of America. Many of us worry about the materialism of our kids and our culture. Sometimes malls succeed in helping us deal with the symptoms of social problems, like our lack of time, but they fail to help us cure the social problems themselves.[3]

Unfortunately, the imaginative design of American malls hides the larger designs of a consumer culture. "The problem," David Orr suggests, "is that we do not often see the true ugliness of the consumer economy. . . . The distance between shopping malls and the mines, wells, corporate farms, factories, toxic dumps, and landfills, sometimes half a world away, dampens our perceptions that something is fundamentally wrong." Sometimes the success of shopping centers comes at the expense of the environment. Shopping centers are, in fact, the showplace of an environmental catastrophe. Malls—or, more broadly, the consumer culture that they represent—play a large part in the depletion of natural resources, the decline of animal habitats, the poisoning of air and water and soil, and the entropy of the biosphere. Inside the mall, it's easy to forget the earth. But shopping and consumption are major causes of environmental degradation, as our purchases set in motion processes of extraction and extinction that we don't intend. The era of oblivious shopping is coming to an end. If the whole world consumed like Americans do, we would need two more planets to support us. If we don't reform our shopping, wc will, in fact, "shop 'til we drop."[4]

Because many Americans are concerned about the changes involved in the malling of America, we try to imagine other possibilities for meeting our human needs—material, social, and spiritual. In this society, malls do many good things for us. But they're not all good, and they could be better. In a better society, they might be better yet. So improving malls might be one small part of improving society, and vice versa.

In many ways, shopping centers of today are better than shopping centers of the 1950s and 1960s, because individuals in the industry have experimented with ideas and institutions to improve customer satisfaction. Shopping center professionals have responded to the changing needs and values of Americans, and they are likely to respond similarly in the future. So we need to be clear about what might increase our customer satisfaction—and, more important, our human satisfaction. In a world of supply and demand, we can demand different dreams. As individuals, as groups, and as citizens, we can shape shopping for a new century.

Shopping happens in the present, but it's connected to the past and the future. History happens in malls. When we go shopping, we *embody* a history of economic and social (and political) relations that have evolved in American history. When we go to the mall, we also *make* history, because our choices have far-reaching effects, making the future, shaping the institutional and social choices of people who will follow us. Shopping today, we affect the lives of our children and grandchildren.

Toward a Politics of Consumption

Today's malls are the end product of a certain kind of American utopianism. As early as Edward Bellamy's best-selling 1888 utopian novel, *Looking Backward*, Americans have imagined the good life as one of order, leisure, and abundance. In Bellamy's story, protagonist Julian West falls asleep in the year 1887. When he awakens in the year 2001, he finds that Americans have embraced a socialist society that provides for all its people. Influenced by the country's first department stores, Bellamy envisioned a country in which people earned equal incomes payable in advance on what was basically a credit card. With these cards, they shopped in central stores located throughout the country. Julian West describes his first experience of such a shopping center in Boston:

> There was nothing in the exterior aspect of the edifice to suggest a store to a representative of the nineteenth century. There was no display of goods in the great windows, or any device to advertise wares, or attract custom. Nor was there any sort of sign or legend on the front of the building to indicate the character of the business carried on there; but instead, above the portal, standing out from the front of the building, a majestic life-size group of statuary, the central figure of which was a female ideal of Plenty, with her cornucopia. . . . It was the first interior of a twentieth-century public building that I had ever beheld, and the spectacle naturally impressed me deeply. I was in a vast hall full of light, received not alone from the windows on all sides, but from the dome, the point of which was a hundred feet above. Beneath it, in the centre of the hall, a magnificent fountain played, cooling the atmosphere to a delicious freshness with its spray. The walls and ceiling were frescoed in mellow tints, calculated to soften without absorbing the light which flooded the interior. Around the fountain was a space occupied with chairs and sofas, on which many persons were seated conversing. Legends on the walls all about the hall indicated to what classes of commodities the counters below were devoted.[5]

Shopping centers still contain such utopian promises of peace and plenty, stuff, and sociability. Malls embody the values and ideals of what we might call "commercial utopianism"—freedom, abundance, leisure, happiness, individualism, and community. Our shops and stores display the bounty that American enterprise has made possible. They celebrate our freedom to choose things that express our individuality as well as our commitment and conformity to certain communities. They give us a place to cultivate our leisure and to pursue our happiness.

Yet even though malls appeal to our utopian sensibilities, they almost always ask us to settle for less. By its very nature, commercial utopianism always leaves something to be desired. After all, desire is the source of the repeat business that keeps the mall humming. Even though malls suggest that they satisfy our desires, and in a piecemeal fashion they do, they would go out of business if they ever succeeded.

Contemporary commercial utopianism embodies many of our values (see table 2), but it can't satisfy other utopian desires. Commercial utopianism allows us to realize some of our values, but it marginalizes others. It's big on freedom, but small on responsibility. It's great on choice, but not on democracy. It's good for some people, but not for nature. It emphasizes opportunity, but not equality. It evokes passion, but not much compassion. The mall is a good place for "just looking," but not if you're looking for justice. It's a fine place for materialism, but not so fine for spirituality. Malls sell "the good life," not the good society.

Still, commercial utopianism gives us a good place to start thinking about a good society. Right now, shopping centers offer utopias for the affluent, which is no utopia at all. But a deeper utopianism could make the promises of contemporary commercial utopianism more inclusive and extensive. A deeper American dream would celebrate freedom—but for all people and all time. In the future, commercial utopianism could offer abundance, or at least sufficiency, for all people and all time. It could encourage good leisure and genuine happiness—for all people and for all time. And it could encourage not just community, but solidarity, with all people for all time.

Extending the values of commercial utopianism to all people for all time would involve changes in our values, our politics, and our commercial practices. Assuring sufficiency for all people forever would change the reasons and the ways we produce and consume goods. Assuring a sufficiency for all garmentworkers, for example, would drastically alter the character of the mall, the structure of workplaces in the Third World, and the nature of shopping. Striving for sufficiency for all time would result in reductions in consumption, because our current culture of consumption simply isn't sustainable. Accepting freedom as a value available not just to people with money but to all people would make consumer culture more democratic. And working for good leisure would require a new politics of work, because nothing makes good leisure better than the satisfactions of good work.

Peter Maurin, the cofounder of the Catholic Worker movement, once said that institutions should be designed to make it easier for people to be good.

If we took a similar perspective toward malls, and tried to imagine what malls might do for human fulfillment and happiness, we might arrive at a list something like this:

The mall of tomorrow empowers people.

The mall of tomorrow values different people, and difference itself.

The mall of tomorrow promotes good work.

The mall of tomorrow provides good leisure.

The mall of tomorrow promotes responsible consumption, conspicuous frugality, and a genuinely conservative (or conserving) outlook.

The mall of tomorrow sells new stuff, but also secondhand goods and goods made locally by hand.

The mall of tomorrow nurtures the full humanity of children.

The mall of tomorrow connects generations instead of segmenting them into niche markets.

The mall of tomorrow is home to millions of Americans because it's located within walking distance of new urban (and suburban) villages.

The mall of tomorrow promotes learning, not consumer forgetfulness.

The mall of tomorrow is a tool for conviviality, where committees, communities, and coffee klatches all come to meet.

The mall of tomorrow is artful architecture and a gallery of commercial and critical art.

The mall of tomorrow nurtures not just self-love and romantic love, but compassion, which is love for people we don't see and aren't yet alive.

The mall of tomorrow liberates the oppressed.

The mall of tomorrow heals the earth with regenerative design.

The mall of tomorrow contains sacred space, a place to encounter the mystery of the universe and to live with it.

Because this mall of tomorrow reflects tomorrow's American values, it necessarily reflects and affects the family of tomorrow, the school of tomorrow, the media of tomorrow, and the workplace of tomorrow. It's not possible to have a brand new mall in an old country. It will require a New World. But fortunately, the New World is an old American tradition.

Shopping for a Better World

The mall of tomorrow seems a long way off, but people are already building the foundations for this new social structure. Americans are reevaluating the values of commercial utopianism. Some people are remaking their own lives to remake their society. Some of us are challenging the institutions that structure our commercial life. Others are proposing political innovations that would foster institutions that would make it easier to be good.

Rethinking Shopping

At the mall, people are looking for the good life. But we don't seem to find it because we keep going back. Our recurrent, ritual attendance at the mall can be seen as both a sign of the mall's success and a sign of its failure. It can't sell us what we really need for fulfillment as human beings, even though our culture keeps telling us that happiness is connected to consumption.

But polls show that consumption doesn't, in general, make us happy. It's true that people with some money are generally happier than people with no money. In a provocative essay called "If We Are So Rich, Why Aren't We Happy?" Mihaly Csikszmentmihalyi points out that

> material advantages do not readily translate into social and emotional benefits. In fact, to the extent that most of one's psychic energy becomes invested in material goals, it is typical for sensitivity to other rewards to atrophy. Friendship, art, literature, natural beauty, religion, and philosophy become less and less interesting. . . . As income and therefore the value of one's time increases, it becomes less and less "rational" to spend it on anything else besides making money—or on spending it conspicuously. The opportunity costs of playing with one's child, reading poetry, or attending a family reunion become too high, and so one stops doing such irrational things.[6]

After a certain point, money and materialism don't offer much satisfaction because we don't always appreciate our possessions for their intrinsic value. Instead, since we are social beings, we notice what our neighbors have and what we don't yet have. "Like a street drug," says Gregg Easterbrook, "materialism requires more and more to produce the same brief high." In 1957, about a third of Americans told the

It's a Mall World, After All

National Opinion Research Center that they were "very happy." And about a third of us are still very happy, even though, on average, we consume more than twice as much stuff. Deep down, we know that you can't buy happiness, although sometimes you can buy a pretty good imitation of it. It's wisdom to know the difference.[7]

Polls also show that we have serious reservations about our consumer culture. A 1995 report shows that we "believe that materialism, greed, and selfishness increasingly dominate American life, crowding out a more meaningful set of values centered on family, responsibility, and community." Eighty-six percent of us think that "today's youth are too focused on consuming and buying things," but we're not easy on ourselves either: 82 percent of respondents agree that "most of us buy and consume far more than we need." In short, we believe that we are increasingly "a society at odds with our values."[8]

There's some evidence, too, that ordinary Americans have begun to experience "shopping fatigue," feeling "overstuffed and underwhelmed" with shopping. Retail analyst Wendy Leibmann, who publishes a biennial survey called "How America Shops," notes that even before 11 September 2001, Americans were visiting fewer stores on their shopping trips. "This is a sure sign that shoppers are no longer searching for something more," she says. "Either they have it already, or they don't need it or don't want it." The "overstuffed consumer" may not have given up on materialism, but he or she seems to have cut back significantly.[9]

Liebmann also found that customers are bored with shopping, giving retailers an average grade of D+ for their shopping experience. As a retail analyst, of course, Liebmann's job depends on reversing these "dangerous" trends toward underconsumption, so she suggests that retailers pay more attention to creating unique environments and experiences to draw customers back to the stores. "Retailers," she says, "have to create a total experience that's competitive with any number of experiences I can spend my time and money on." Instead of embracing America's shift away from shopping, the shopping center industry will try to combat it. But there are other possibilities: our discontent could lead to both better shopping and better living.[10]

Rethinking Our Lives

Responding to concerns about consumer culture, some individuals are taking action. Individuals have played an essential part in the malling of America, and

Shopping for a Better World

they will play a crucial role in reinventing the mall. Both the mall's pleasures and its problems have developed from what economist Thomas Schelling calls "the tyranny of small decisions," the accretion of individual choices that makes for social change. The movie *You've Got Mail*, about an independent bookstore owner who loses her customers to a large bookstore chain, illustrates many of these processes. We like the small, intimate shops with personable proprietors, but we also like the benefits of the larger chains, including variety, predictability, and (sometimes) lower pricing. We appreciate the images and values offered in the chains' national advertising. There's a gap between a Gap t-shirt and the generic one we buy at a local boutique, and it's a gap that's often filled with images and associations from TV and magazine ads. We shop at chains like Gap because, in some ways, a Gap t-shirt *means* more than a local product. We like the little shop on the corner, but we appreciate the way that shopping centers have cornered the market on so many interesting shops. Without intending to drive our local retailers out of business, then, we patronize our shopping centers. The result is, of course, "You've got mall."[11]

The result, too, is that many of us are unsatisfied with the way our lives reflect our values. As Peter Marin suggests, many Americans aren't sure that they live in right relation to the world. "For many of us these days, at the heart of our relation to the world around us, [there is] an ethical tension or a sense of moral ambiguity. In the first place, we are aware of the nature of the world, the kinds of suffering and injustice at work in it; and, in the second place, we more or less dimly sense the ways in which our own roles and station amount, at best, to a kind of unintentional complicity with much that we abhor."[12]

"Thus," concludes Marin, "we are often at odds not only with the world but also with ourselves, for few of us choose to live in relation to the world, or have the *chance* to live in relation to the world, in ways which reflect precisely how we feel about it. Whether this is enough, in itself, to make us guilty of anything is a question perhaps only a god might answer; but such questions of guilt and responsibility nonetheless nag at us beneath the surface of consciousness." Sometimes these questions even nag at us at the mall. Robert Bellah suggests, for example, that "we know how deeply interdependent we are. All we have to do is look at the labels on our clothes. . . . But by and large, that [interdependence] has no moral meaning." We haven't yet adjusted our actions to our deepest values.[13]

But the "tyranny of small decisions" is also the opportunity of small decisions. As individuals, for example, we could be what Wendell Berry calls "responsible consumers." For Berry, this means meeting our needs—not our every desire. It means paying attention to the quality of what we consume and the health of the systems, both social and natural, that provide for us. To be a responsible consumer, then, is always to be more than a consumer. It's to be a parent, a partner, a neighbor, a world and local citizen, concerned with how our practices of consumption affect our children, our loved ones, our neighbors, our countrymen, the countryside, and the world, both human and natural. It's to extend the circle of love and care that we express in consumption from the shopping center to the world. It's to develop an extended ethics of shopping, paying attention to the moral ecology of consumption.[14]

We already make ethical decisions at the shopping center. We think about good and bad taste, but also about good and evil. "Within a largely secular society," Daniel Miller contends, "almost all of us still see ourselves as living lives directed to goals and values which remain in some sense higher than the mere dictates of instrumentality. Daily decisions are constantly weighed in terms of moral questions about good and bad action indicated in traits such as sensitivity as against style, or generosity as against jealousy." A lot of our shopping reflects not selfishness but love for the people around us. Even though most of us don't understand the world as a gift economy, we're deeply involved in gift economies in our own homes.[15]

Even so, ethics is not a standard part of the public discourse in American malls. Ethical reflection would slow things down and work against the profits of impulse purchases. Standard mall ethics assume a free individual in a free market, and very few communal responsibilities. They assume both moral relativism (I can't criticize your free choices, to each his own, and so forth) and economic and political libertarianism (it's OK if it sells).

Ethics is a way of telling stories about the goodness of the good life. Shopping centers have always been in this storytelling business. And the products of the mall are amply interwoven with stories, often about the personal benefits of buying this product. We already pay for stories with our products; but we could demand more and better stories for our money. We could look for environmental stories, for social stories, for political stories in our products. We could

Shopping for a Better World

buy a product precisely because we want to tell a story about a sustainable society with it. We could buy a product because we want to be a part of a story of social justice. We could buy a product because we like its story of political responsibility. And, in fact, at times, we already do.

We already shop for better stories. Many of us buy "green" products precisely because they allow us to tell a hopeful story about the future. Some mall retailers have begun to tell better stories to their customers. The Body Shop, for example, sells skin and hair care products, but it also sells a story about a new way of doing business. Aveda Corporation has also committed itself to providing organic-based hair products and cosmetics for women and men who want to make a difference without stopping shopping. In 1989, Aveda signed the CERES Principles, an extensive set of environmental guidelines developed by Corporations for Environmentally Responsible Economics. Both Body Shop and Aveda have profited from their commitment to environmentally and socially responsible production. They tell stories that appeal to responsible consumers.[16]

In apparel, both Patagonia and EcoSports have shifted production to organically grown cotton as a way of combating the toxic effects, for both people and the environment, of chemically dependent agricultural production. Critics say that we can't afford to grow organic cotton. These retailers, however, argue that we can't afford not to grow it, because production laced with pesticides and herbicides is inimical to the earth.[17]

Sometimes, too, we shop at certain shopping centers because they tell a story we need to hear. Sometimes, shopping centers affirm our deeper values with "cause marketing." Linking their name with a charity or a noncontroversial cause, the shopping center provides space for fund-raising activities. The Mall of America, for example, sponsors a Thanksgiving Walk for Hunger and a Walk for the Cure (for the Juvenile Diabetes Foundation). The ICSC gives awards every year for community service. Malls engage in such philanthropic activity all the time. Indeed, when the ICSC tried to calculate the amount of community service and support in American malls, they found the task literally impossible. If we support shopping centers for supporting these events and philanthropies, we can help them to extend their commitments to causes broader than shopping.[18]

It's a Mall World, After All

All of these acts of responsible consumption make a difference, but they generally don't envision a different consumption system. Some people, though, have tried to imagine a different system, one based on "post-materialist values." In shopping for a better world, they try to shop for better cultural (and commercial) values. Some of those values may be "new and improved," but most of them will probably be tried and true—the pre-materialist values that preceded the great American shopping spree of the twentieth century. David Orr asks, for example, "What virtues in our lives would produce actions that were harmonious in a larger commonwealth of plants and people? And what sort of communities must we create in order to encourage the harmonious action that we expect from individuals?" He suggests that we could learn something from the Amish and other so-called backward peoples, who have shaped cultures that preserve the virtues of humility, simplicity, moderation, prudence, frugality, hard work, neighborliness, and family stability. And he insists that, although individuals practice them, these virtues are not just individual values but also social values, and societies must nourish them to keep them.[19]

Almost all human faith traditions speak to the issue of materialism. In reviewing the teachings of the founders of the world's great religions, Arnold Toynbee found that "they all said with one voice that if we made material wealth our paramount aim, this would lead to disaster." In the United States, most of us are nominally Christians. But at America's malls, we seem to forget that the Christian gospel promises an abundance of life, not a life of abundance.[20]

Sometimes the affirmation of our pre-materialist values may suggest possibilities for post-materialist values. The Copenhagen Institute for Future Studies states that "the major growth in consumption in the future will be of a nonmaterial nature." What does this mean? People already buy some stuff not so much for the stuff itself but for the immaterial meanings expressed by the stuff. If such *meanings* make our lives rich, then it's possible to consume more meanings without consuming more stuff, maybe even by consuming less stuff. And if we can fulfill our experiential needs without buying stuff at all, it might be possible to pursue more happiness with fewer environmental consequences. As Mihaly Csikszentmihalyi says, "We need a new way of thinking about consuming, one that maximizes the quality of experience while minimizing the amount of entropy produced as a result."[21] Some post-materialist values that might contribute to such a satisfying and sustainable future might be:

1. Voluntary simplicity, elegant and conspicuous frugality. Ads repeatedly suggest that more is better. Sometimes they even suggest that you need more stuff to simplify your life. But sometimes less is more, and we can simplify by buying less and enjoying it more. Voluntary simplicity isn't a program of voluntary poverty, nor is it a movement of people determined to take the fun out of life. Instead, it's a way of dealing with the time poverty of American life by spending time instead of spending money. "Less stuff, more fun," says a slogan for the Center for a New American Dream.

2. A preference for painstaking and pleasurable production over quick consumption. Currently, a lot of consumption consoles us for the work we do. "Thank God it's Friday," we say, as we prepare for a weekend of leisure and consumption. But there's probably more pleasure (and more productivity) in good work than in commodified leisure, so it makes sense to work for better work, work that produces not only goods and services but also good human beings in service to each other.

3. A celebration of the body, both as a beautiful organic form and as a productive tool in the work of creation. A lot of consumer culture depends on the devaluation of the body and the commodification of cures. Ads tell most of us that we're not good enough the way we are, and that we need soaps, shampoos, cosmetics, chemical preparations, Botox, plastic surgery, diets, and clothes to hide our essential ugliness. Such ads also treat the body as a sight instead of as an active organism. So post-materialist values might sing the body eclectic, the different ways of being embodied and moving beautifully and productively.

4. A delight in self-expression, in word and deed, in music and dance, in painting and poetry, in arts and crafts and cooking, in relationships and child-rearing. Consumer culture tells us now that we need to buy mass-produced goods to express ourselves. But we can also express ourselves in the arts and crafts of daily life, and with far less environmental impact. By taking pleasure in our own manufacturing (the word literally means "to make by hand"), we could develop the aesthetic imagination that's often stimulated but not fulfilled in our malls. And by expressing ourselves in the communities we manufacture from good conversations, we could develop our social imagination and social capital too.

5. A somebodiness that comes from participation in the beloved community, from the activity of communities of memory and hope. All of us want to be somebody, and ads often promise that purchases will help us to become somebody. The consumer culture of malls seldom suggests, as Martin Luther King did, that somebodiness comes from activism in the name of the community. Such a concept of somebodiness suggests that we become somebody not by standing out from the group, but by standing in solidarity with it, and such participation is inevitably political.

6. Whole-systems thinking (and acting). Malls invite us to look at one thing at a time, one shop at a time. They generally conceal the systematic nature of shopping. Within a framework of post-materialist values, however, people could value the complexity and completeness of whole-systems thinking and acting. We would understand that isolated acts aren't, in fact, isolated, and we would pay more attention to the wider consequences of our actions. Instead of seeing the mall simply as a place to go, we might see it as a network of ideas and institutions with global reach.

7. Groundedness—some genuine relationships with nature. American materialism developed as Americans themselves moved from agricultural land to cities and suburbs. We love nature, but the nature we love is often scenic, romantic, and remote. And so our relationships to nature are also distant and mediated. Americans need to get back to nature, and the nature we need to get back to is both the nature of wilderness and the nature of our own back yards, our own daily lives.

8. Sacred ground. In American culture, Bill McKibben contends, "people are everything. Most cultures, historically, have put something else, God or nature or some combination, at the center. But we've put God and nature at the periphery. A consumer society doesn't need them to function, and it can't tolerate the limits they might impose; there's only need for people." Although most of us have a sense of the sacred, it's an underdeveloped resource in contemporary culture. We can't continue to put a price on priceless things. Something has to be sacred.[22]

9. Materialism. Materialism is "the belief that physical well-being and worldly possessions constitute the greatest good and highest value in life." Few Americans admit to such a stark belief in materialism, but we act as if it were our consuming passion. A new and improved materialism, an ecological materialism, might

Shopping for a Better World

promote a reverence for materials and for the stuff of creation. This new materialism might revive pre-materialist ideals of thrift, frugality, and sufficiency, and it might encourage us to design products for repair and re-use, and to consume materials fully before discarding them.[23]

10. A new kind of worldliness—the sort of virtue that keeps us conscious of the world even while we're focused on our localities. In the twentieth century, Americans have become increasingly worldly—more concerned with the pleasures of the flesh than with the pleasures of the heart and soul, more concerned with the here and now than with elsewhere or with the hereafter. This worldliness is on display at America's malls. But the interconnections of the modern world, including our shopping centers, also invite us to another kind of worldliness, a care and concern not just for the self but for the people of the world, a sense of stewardship not just for our own resources but for the resources of the planet.

Americans already embrace many of these values, and we won't ever agree on all of them. But if we hope to move beyond modern materialism, we'll need to begin a sustained conversation about the values we really value.

Living Values

Rethinking our values is one thing, enacting them is another. People try to incarnate these new/old values in all sorts of ways, but these days, downshifting is one of the most popular and most potent. Downshifting is a way of telling stories about the good life, a way of enacting post-materialist values in the present. For many Americans, the main story of their lives is "work and spend." For others, it's "shop 'til you drop." Downshifting is a way of responding to the time poverty of American life caused by the standard cycle of work and spend. About 10 percent of the population, downshifters tend to believe that you're rich if you have a lot of money but you're really wealthy if you have a lot of time. So downshifting works for people who want more personal time, less stress, and more balance in their lives. If you spend less, downshifters argue, you can work less. And if you work less, you have time for more fulfillment, from family and friends, from community involvement, from genuine leisure instead of rushed recreation. Downshifting can take many forms: flextime arrangements at work, voluntary demotions, and phased early retirement. And it mainly works for people who have control over their work, who aren't trapped in a job to make ends meet. Whatever the form, it's an affirmation that something more important than money makes the world go round (see table 5).[24]

In their book *Your Money or Your Life*, Joe Dominguez and Vicki Robin argue that money *is* life, because we exchange the time of our lives to make money. They invite Americans to calculate their spending not just in dollars but in the currency of time. Is it worth a month of work to fly to Paris for a long weekend, or a year in the office to buy a luxury car? Would we rather have a gourmet meal in a trendy restaurant or the time it took to pay for it? Dominguez and Robin also ask us to think about our real wage rate, which involves calculating the real costs and real returns of our work lives. The real costs of work are often more than we expect, including time on the job but also time spent commuting, buying work clothes, reading journals at home, buying takeout food because we don't have time to cook, and paying for counseling due to work-related stress. The real returns from work are also usually less than we assume, because we calculate our salary before taxes, and forget that the more we work for the company, the more we also work for Uncle Sam.[25]

Organizing for Change

While some people consume responsibly and others downshift to more sustainable life-styles, other people have voiced their concerns about malls and materialism in organizations and movements. Two organizations with particular relevance for shopping centers are the Media Foundation of Canada and the Center for a New American Dream. The Media Foundation publishes *Adbusters*, a "journal of the mental environment" to explore the ways that commercial images and ideas get inside our heads and our institutions. Both in the magazine and on its web site, articles and photo essays show how marketing and merchandising try to capture our consciousness, and how we might resist. The Media Foundation is also a catalyst for culture jamming, which is activism devoted to jamming the marketing messages that permeate our mental environment. In addition to the essays, *Adbusters* publishes advertising satires that sometimes expose the invisible complexities that ads often cover up. One parody satirizes the religion of con-

Table 5

Upscale Living versus Downshifting

Upscale	Downshifting
More stuff	Less stuff
Richer	Poorer
More work	More leisure
Less time (time bind, time poverty)	More time
Convenience	Convening
Quality time	Time
Conspicuous consumption	Conspicuous frugality
Consumption communities	Communities
Fast food, prepared food	Food, preparing food
Outsourcing household tasks	Houseworkers
Wired	Weird
Social status	Social questioning
Gadgets, inventions	Inventiveness
McMansions	Homes
Stuff to fill the house	Time to enjoy the house
Luxury goods	Goods
Making money	Making do
Financial capital	Social capital
Stress	Different stresses

sumption. Another skewers the Tommy Hilfiger "Declaration of Independence" ads with a flock of sheep photographed in front of an American flag and the tag line "Follow the Flock." A Nike parody links the company's fashion footwear to the poor people who manufacture the shoes with text reading "You're running because you want that raise, to be all you can be. But it's not easy when you work sixty hours a week making sneakers in an Indonesian factory and your friends disappear when they ask for a raise. So think globally before you think it's so cool to wear Nike." *Adbusters'* parodies help contemporary consumers recontextualize the decontextualized images they receive in ads.[26]

Recently, too, the Media Foundation has sponsored an annual Buy Nothing Day as a counterpoint to the compulsive shopping activity of a consumer culture. Observed on the day after Thanksgiving, Buy Nothing Day transforms this high holy day of shoppers into a holiday from consumption. Across the world, activists engage in a kind of street theater, dramatizing the deeper dilemmas of consumption. In Vancouver, Mr. Materialism, dressed entirely in gold, thanks shoppers for spending with such vigor. In Boston, carolers sing "Uh oh, we're in the red, dear" to the tune of "Rudolph the Red Nosed Reindeer" and pass out "gift exemption certificates." At the Mall of America in 1998, protesters from the Ruckus Society unfurled a six-hundred-square-foot banner showing a cartoon of Earth falling through a shopping bag with the pointed question, "Shop Til We Drop?" Buy Nothing Day is, in fact, a counterpoint to every other day in America, which is Buy Something Day.[27]

In a consumer society, buying nothing is very hard work. In Seattle, activists distribute a checklist of questions to help shoppers think twice about things they plan to buy. It's a different kind of shopping list, one that makes us more mindful of the complexities of consumption. Here are some questions a person might responsibly ask before making a purchase:

What good is this thing?

Do I need it?

Could I borrow one?

What's the environmental impact of this purchase?

Is it made of recycled materials and is it recyclable?

What does this purchase teach people around me?

Is this purchase a good way to support the values I believe in?

How could I explain this purchase to my God?

How does this purchase affect the quality of the future?

Does this purchase support institutions and practices that will help my kids raise their kids well?

Who lives well as a result of this purchase?

Who lives poorly?

The Center for a New American Dream is a second important organization advocating cultural changes in consumption. With five thousand members in more than thirty countries, the center works as a catalyst for changes in the culture of con-

"I need a belief system that serves my needs right away."

Dean Sachs has a mortgage, a family and an extremely demanding job. What he doesn't need is a religion that complicates his life with unreasonable ethical demands.

Spiritual providers in the past have required a huge amount of commitment — single-deity clauses, compulsory goodness, and a litany of mystifying mumbo-jumbo. It's no wonder people are switching to Mammon.

Mammon isn't the biggest player in the spiritual race. But our ability to deliver on our promises is unique. And our moral flexibility *unmatchable*.

MAMMON   *Because you deserve to enjoy life – guilt free.*

The religion of consumption
(Image courtesy of www.adbusters.org)

sumption. Its main public presence is a web site at www.newdream.org, but it also publishes a newsletter called *Enough!*—a quarterly report on consumption, quality of life, and the environment, as well as several e-mail publications. One such publication, *Step by Step*, helps people become active advocates for a new American Dream. Another, called *Turn the Tide*, asks people to take action in their homes and workplaces and report back to the center. When you log on the web site to record your action—say, "Replace one beef meal each week"—you learn the environmental impact of that decision. Finally, a monthly publication called *In Balance* reports stories of success. At the end of 2001, the center listed its accomplishments for the year: 25 million web hits, production of a film called *More Fun, Less Stuff:*

The Rewards and Challenges of a New American Dream, contracts for two books on *What Kids Want that Money Can't Buy* and *As If the Future Mattered: Visions of a New American Dream*, work with religious congregations in exploring the hidden costs of consumption, help for government purchasing agents interested in buying environmentally preferable products, pressure on Staples (the office supply store) to increase their stock of recycled paper, and collaboration with the World Wildlife Fund to develop a youth education program.[28]

In general, the center's programs are meant to raise awareness and involve people in responsible consumption. They ask people to reflect on their deepest values and to consider whether they practice what they believe. While the Media Foundation encourages protest and political action, the Center for a New American Dream is primarily involved in consciousness-raising and incremental action. Both organizations invite people to imagine new American dreams and to try to realize those dreams in their own lives.

But individual reforms, even coordinated actions by individuals, only go so far because shopping centers are a "social trap," and social traps, according to David Orr, "draw their victims into certain patterns of behavior with promises of immediate rewards and then confront them with consequences the victims would rather avoid." A social trap is a situation in which "individually rational behavior in the near term traps victims into long-term destructive outcomes." Arms races, traffic jams, population explosions, and overconsumption are examples of this irrationality of rationality. As British anthropologist Daniel Miller clearly shows in *A Theory of Shopping*, we shop for good reasons, and malls provide a good place for that shopping. But the overall result is not always good, because shopping has larger consequences than the ones we usually see. We may understand our shopping within a cosmology of love, but it also functions within a cosmallogy of expansive capitalism. We have good intentions, but we also cause unintended consequences.[29]

Social traps require social solutions. Although individuals can have a remarkable impact by consuming responsibly and by downshifting, they still won't get to the root of the problem, which is systemic. In shopping for a better world, and for better shopping centers, individuals will need to act in social and political movements to bring about cultural changes.

Conservatives often justify the market by saying that consumer choices drive it. They note the high failure rate for retailers and the ways in which the con-spiracy of customer satisfaction makes individual consumers powerful. When consumers vote with their purchases, they cast a ballot for what they want. This is, as we have seen, true. But the myth of the sovereign consumer is also false, because we only get the choices that appear on the shelves. We don't get a choice between malls of today and malls of tomorrow; we just get a choice between one product and another. And we make our choices in the face of established and powerful institutions, like advertising and public relations, organized to influ-ence those choices. So if consumers choose to remember that they are also cit-izens, if consumers respond to these institutional pressures with their own insti-tutional pressures, it only evens up the balance of power. And if consumers choose to exercise their political sovereignty to enhance their consumer sover-eignty, then politics can be an appropriate way to shop for the good life—and for better shopping centers.[30]

Malls of today already fulfill some of the goals of utopian malls of tomorrow, but there's still a long way to go. To get from here to there, Americans will need to use their social power and their political power to make changes. Any move-ment to reform malls is inevitably involved with modifying incentive structures throughout the American economy. And a lot of these incentives need the force of law, because right now the law offers incentives to bad neighbors, to the entre-preneurs who are willing to cut corners. American trade policy, for example, makes it easy for apparel makers to shift production to the Third World. When Levi's finally closed most of its American plants in 2002, one analyst commented that "they made a valiant effort to be a good corporate citizen, but they had to do this. It was just getting too expensive for them to do business here." The utopian "mall of tomorrow" depends on an economic market where people aren't penalized for good behavior. The labor legislation of the Progressive era did just this: child labor laws, minimum wage, maximum hours, and worker safety regu-lations assured good working conditions for workers but also a fair competitive market for employers. So a new politics of consumption could also help us to create institutions that make it easier for corporations to be good.[31]

Responsible consumption as a society doesn't mean eating less red meat and recycling. It means living so we replenish the earth. It means a regenerative society. Right now, the United States is the most powerful nation on Earth, but we don't yet have the power to live *sustainably* in a society that satisfies the soul. If we keep moving in the direction we're going now, we'll end up using our power to fight wars to make the world safe for consumption. A better choice is to invent a politics to make our consumption safe for the world. What follows are a few possibilities.

First, we should put our money where our values are, both individually and collectively. We've already discussed the ethics of individual spending, and it's important. But individual spending becomes collective spending when people engage in organized boycotts and "buycotts." Sometimes consumers organize politically to boycott, refusing to buy things because we don't like the narrative that goes with it. A boycott is a way of buying what you want without buying anything. If you want justice, and Adidas or Nike aren't selling it, then a boycott is a way of building justice by not buying the shoes. It's an old American tradition, as old as the American Revolution, and it can be effective.

A "buycott," on the other hand, asks people to reward manufacturers and merchants who are doing things right. If you have a choice between a retailer that destroys local communities and one that invests in the local community, patronize the one that invests in your values—and publicize your choices. If you believe in organic production, buy your shirts at a shop that makes products, and the world, the way you want it. If a shopping center near you sponsors events that you approve of, let them know, and let them know that such choices influence your shopping choices.

Second, we should tell the truth about products and pricing. One prerequisite for responsible consumption is truthful pricing. Right now, the price of a pair of jeans doesn't tell the whole story. It tells us how cheaply a manufacturer can produce the pants for us. But it doesn't tell us about the full cost: its economic value, social and environmental costs, ethical and spiritual implications, and opportunity costs. The price tells us how much money we must exchange for the product, but it doesn't tell us how much life, both human and natural, has already been exchanged to get the pants to the mall. We need to remember that the lowest price isn't always the best price. In fact, the lowest price can often indicate the highest long-term cost. Even in the information age, we don't know enough to make our best choices as consumers.[32]

A policy of full-cost accounting would make it possible for consumers to know what they're really getting for their money. Right now, the government

Shopping for a Better World

requires manufacturers to list the country where a product was made, but why not require information on environmental impacts, working conditions, the social impact on communities, and eventual waste? As Mihaly Csikszentmihalyi suggests, "If the true entropic costs of a sport utility vehicle were kept in mind . . . even the most attractive vehicle of that sort would seem indecently coarse."[33]

Full-cost accounting isn't a wild or radical idea. It's basically truth in packaging, and it's absolutely essential for markets to work well. If people know what they're buying, and buying into, we can make rational choices. But if we don't know, we can't make markets work for the human good. In a section on "Doing Well by Doing Good" in his book *The Dream Society,* Rolf Jensen predicts that consumers will increasingly demand social and environmental responsibility from manufacturers and retailers. Already, 66 percent of Americans say that they would switch brands if a company were connected to a cause they supported. Among affluent Americans, the major target market for malls, the proportion is even higher, with 82 percent saying that a company's connection to a cause could cause them to switch brands. In the age of "the political consumer," Jensen suggests, "the traditional, for-profit-only company is on its way to becoming a thing of the past."[34]

Third, we should use the power of taxation to encourage behavior that's socially and environmentally beneficial. In recent years, the Republican Party and its "depublican" agenda have convinced Americans that taxes are un-American, so the only good tax legislation is a tax cut. This is bullshit. A carbon tax, for example, could raise money for environmental programs at the same time it discouraged the burning of fossil fuels that cause global warming. Consumption taxes, based perhaps on the amount of entropy a product causes, could tax consumption before consumption overtaxes the earth. A progressive sales tax could make people pay for the status items that keep consumption increasing apace. "The principle would be," as Juliet Schor suggests, "that the high-end, status versions of certain commodities would pay a high tax, the midrange versions would pay a midrange tax, and low-end versions would be exempt." Luxury taxes could tell consumers that Americans in general—we, the people—think that enough is enough. We already do some of this, and the sky isn't falling. Property taxes, for example, require people to pay more for the social and environmental costs of larger houses. Finally, a tax on advertising might reverse the escalation of desire. As it stands, American taxpayers subsidize their own seduction, because advertising is fully deductible from corporate profits.[35]

Fourth, we should prove that "enough is enough" by providing "enough for everybody." Usually the slogan "enough is enough" invites affluent Americans to consider the problems of overconsumption—social, environmental, and spiritual. But as Daniel Miller points out in "The Poverty of Morality," overconsumption is not a problem for most people on the planet. "We live in a time when most human suffering is the direct result of the lack of goods. What most of humanity desperately needs is more consumption." A comprehensive politics of consumption thus invites us to think not just about the distribution of goods in the shops of the mall but also the distribution of goods in the world. And seemingly unrelated topics like development policy and foreign aid need to be considered in thinking about the prospects of a new world of shopping and consumption.[36]

In *How Much Is Enough?* Alan Durning shows the extraordinary inequalities of consumption, both in the United States and the world. He divides the world into three classes: a consumer class, a middle-income class, and a class of poor people. The 1.1 billion consumers who make more than seventy-five hundred dollars a year live mainly in Europe and North America (but also in Australia, Japan, Hong Kong, and many major cities of the Third World), take in 64 percent of the world's income, and spend it on the delights of consumer society. The middling class, people whose income ranges from seven hundred to seventy-five hundred dollars, live mainly in the Latin America, the Middle East, China, and East Asia. These 3.3 billion people earn about a third of world income and spend it on a life of moderation—a diet based on grains and water, simple shelters, and rudimentary stocks of consumer goods. The poorest class, a class as large as the consumers, live in privation, mainly in rural Africa, India, and South Asia. Twenty percent of humanity, they earn just 2 percent of world income.[37]

In his book *Global Soul*, Pico Iyer points out that "one of the most troubling features of the globalism we celebrate is that the so-called linking of the planet has, in fact, intensified the distance between people: the richest 258 people in the world, by UN calculations, have a financial worth as great as the 2.3 billion others, and even in the United States, the prosperous home of egalitarianism, the most wired man in the land (Bill Gates) has a net worth larger than that of

40 percent of the country's households, or perhaps 100 million of his compatriots combined (according to Robert Reich)."[38]

In the United States, people in the top fifth of incomes make almost as much as the other four-fifths of Americans combined. Households in the upper quintile average $141,621 a year, while households in the bottom fifth average just $10,188 annually. Even though the United States is the world's preeminent consumer society, 31.1 million Americans (11.3 percent of us) live in poverty. This basic inequality of American society affects consumption patterns, because people can't shop with an income of only $10,000 a year. Generating more income for poor people could be good for business at malls of America. In malls themselves, a first small step toward enoughness might be to support unionization of retail workers. Henry Ford made money when he decided that his workers should be able to buy his cars, and retailers might also generate more business by paying mall workers a living wage.[39]

Fifth, we should pay for good design. The whole fashion system of the mall operates on assumptions about good design and designers, and it's reinforced daily in American media. But it would be possible to get better design by offering incentives for *ecological* design.

In his brilliant book *Earth in Mind*, David Orr suggests that the purpose of American education should be the development of "designing minds." But Orr wants people to pay attention to more than mere style and designer labels. "The problem," he says, "is not how to produce ecologically benign products for the consumer economy, but how to make decent communities in which people grow to be responsible citizens and whole people who do not confuse what they have with who they are." Arguing for *ecological* design, Orr suggests that good design fits with the design of nature. Its logic is the "biologic" of natural systems, emphasizing harmony and pattern so that the design of shopping centers would be understood not just as the design of buildings, but as the design of communities, both human and natural. Good design involves synergies of the human and natural worlds, so that both people and places are improved. Good design doesn't just produce stuff to satisfy our desires; indeed, it might involve "the improvement of desire." So far, even the best shopping center architects haven't done much with such comprehensive ecological design.[40]

Good design, in our malls or in the products sold inside, has five characteristics: it's beautiful, meaningful, efficient, humanistic, and regenerative. We already know that good design should be beautiful: we pay designers to give us creative and elegant places and products. We also know that good designs are deeply meaningful, conveying ideas in material form. Good design is a sign and a symbol, helping us feel the possibilities of the world. Nike's swoosh, for example, combines suggestions of speed and style with classical allusions. Good design is efficient, getting the job done. The most stylish pair of one-legged pants won't work for most of the population, no matter how lovely the lines or lustrous the fabric. Good design is also humanistic: it improves people by improving their lives, and it makes it easier to be good. A character in the movie *Gandhi* says that "there is no beauty in the finest cloth if it makes hunger and unhappiness." In the same way, good design is beautiful not just because it looks good, but because it does good. Good design encompasses both good products, and good processes of production. Finally, good design is regenerative. It improves nature by making human life beneficial to the biosphere. These five characteristics are the design challenge of the twenty-first century, our common vocation as we contemplate shopping for a better world.

Sixth, we should pay for the public/private synergies that can make malls more vital as community centers. According to Jeff Gunning, "People are citizens, workers, and consumers simultaneously. Consequently, they demand more complex and satisfying environments to satisfy them." Malls already have extensive community connections, but they could easily become a more vibrant part of their local communities. And the shopping center industry is already moving in that direction. "The ideal shopping center," notes the 1999 edition of the *Shopping Center Development Handbook,* "will become a center of community life, with such public facilities as a library, community center, and government service offices located within the complex. The era when shopping centers included only retail tenants and were separated from the community by vast parking lots is rapidly drawing to a close."[41]

"Rather than revile malls," say researchers at Rutgers University's Walt Whitman Center, "we propose to change them" by designing democratic functions into malls—functions like "voting, community meetings, constituent contact with elected officials, leafleting, soapbox speeches, charity drives, membership recruitment for grassroots groups, information booths on government services—from cultural and recreational activities to education and worship." The researchers contend that mixed use is essential to civic synergies. "Imagine a mall that included community theater, a childcare center, a public health station, a 'Hyde Park' corner for political debate and pamphleteering, a community art gallery, an interior court with music performances, a public library/community center with access to the Internet, a kid's playground, and a storefront 'city hall' where local representatives could face their public. And imagine an architecture that integrated and interspersed these kinds of civil society facilities with shops and stores and offered surrounding communities full and easy access by public as well as private transportation."[42]

Such a strategy would mark a return to the vision of shopping center pioneers like Victor Gruen and James Rouse. In *Shopping Towns USA*, Gruen argued that good planning benefited society and that "the shopping center which can do more than fulfill practical shopping needs, the one that will afford the opportunity for cultural, social, civic and recreational activities will reap the greatest benefits." He always thought that a center for society was more important than a center for shopping.[43]

Is this practical? Yes and no. It's not practical if we assume that the world will always be the way it is. But it is practical, and necessary, if we want our children and grandchildren to live a truly good life. David Orr contends that we're quickly approaching a time when altruism and necessity will coincide, when the impractical idealists will be the practical realists. In fact, one of the primary virtues of today's impractical idealists is to show the impracticality of the so-called real world. In the real world of nineteen major industrial nations, for example, Americans are first in greenhouse gas emissions and first in contributing to acid rain; first in air pollutants per capita; first in forest depletion; first in paper consumption per capita; first in garbage per capita; first in hazardous waste per capita; first in gasoline consumption per capita, first in oil imports, and first in oil spills affecting our shores; first in TVs per capita; first in cars per capita, and first in use of cars instead of public transportation. Is that practical?[44]

In the real world of industrial nations, the United States is number one in infant mortality, number one in percentage of low birth-weight babies, number one in children and old people in poverty, number one in inequalities of wealth,

Back to the future: new American dreams
(Photo courtesy of Southdale Center; reprinted by permission)

number one in big homes and in homelessness, number one in credit cards and in private consumption, and number one in executive salaries and inequalities of pay. We're number one in time devoted to TV, and last in books published per capita. Is this practical?[45]

Not all of these impracticalities are related to shopping centers, but few of them are unrelated to our culture of consumption. Too often in America, the insistence on practicality is a call to conform to the world the way it is, whether or not it is the way it ought to be. When practicality is an efficient means to an inhuman end, however, then the practical is practically immoral. The practical world often accomplishes so much because it encompasses so little. These days, to "be practical" is to set aside whole dimensions of the human person—aesthetic, spiritual, ethical, and sometimes even political. The purely practical is often a game of "Let's Pretend" that asks us to act as if human beings weren't really fully human. Accepting our conformity and our compliance, this practicality rejects the rest of us. At their best, America's impractical dreamers remind us of our full humanity. By keeping our minds apart from the world's presumed practicality, they free us to wonder how, practically, we might become as good as we could be.

In Daniel Quinn's novel *Ishmael*, a character says, "You can't just stop being in a story, you have to have another story to be in." Malls are an essential part of our current imaginative reality; if we want to inhabit a different American dream, we need to be as imaginative as mall designers and developers have been. We need to imagine another story to be in. And we need to start imagining it now.[46]

Some people will say this is just a dream, and I agree. But as Rolf Jensen says in *The Dream Society*, "Dreams create realities—through hard work." At the shopping center, we're already walking around in a field of dreams. We drive dreams to and from the mall, and we buy dreams packaged in different forms. We already live in a dream society, but right now, we live in yesterday's dreams. If we work at it, tomorrow's shopping centers will embody a better dream. It is a dream—an American Dream—and it's what Americans do.[47]

Notes

Introduction: Shopping for American Culture

1. International Council of Shopping Centers (ICSC), "Scope USA," at the ICSC web site, www.icsc.org; John Fetto, "Mall Rats," *American Demographics* 24 (March 2002): 10; Judith Ann Coady, "The Concrete Dream: A Sociological Look at the Shopping Mall" (Ph.D. diss., Boston University, 1987), 720; Ira G. Zepp Jr., *The New Religious Image of Urban America: The Shopping Mall as Ceremonial Center*, 2d ed. (Niwot: University Press of Colorado, 1997), 10.

2. As my colleague Eric Nelson says, malls "are the last place anyone would go to think seriously. There is nothing, however, that demands more serious thought." Eric Nelson, *Mall of America: Reflections of a Virtual Community* (Lakeville, Minn.: Galde Press, 1998), 152.

3. Zepp, *New Religious Image*, 10.

4. John C. Ryan and Alan Durning, *Stuff: The Secret Lives of Everyday Things* (Seattle: Northwest Environment Watch, 1997), 4–5.

5. Barry J. Babin, William R. Darden, and Mitch Griffin, "Work and/or Fun: Measuring Hedonic and Utilitarian Shopping Value," *Journal of Consumer Research* 20 (March 1994): 646–47.

6. Mark Gottdiener, "Recapturing the Center: A Semiotic Analysis of Shopping Malls," in *The City and the Sign: An Introduction to Urban Semiotics*, ed. Mark Gottdiener and Alexandros Ph. Lagopoulos (New York: Columbia University Press, 1986), 291.

7. Paul Lauter, *From Walden Pond to Jurassic Park: Activism, Culture, and American Studies* (Durham N.C.: Duke University Press, 2001), 11.

8. Leon G. Schiffman and Leslie Lazar Kanuk, *Consumer Behavior,* 5th ed. (Englewood Cliffs, N.J.: Prentice Hall, 1994), 437.

9. Jon Goss, "Once-upon-a-Time in the Commodity World: An Unofficial Guide to Mall of America," *Annals of the Association of American Geographers* 89 (March 1999): 47.

10. Mary Douglas and Baron Isherwood, *The World of Goods* (New York: Basic Books, 1979), 57.

11. Elizabeth Chin, *Purchasing Power: Black Kids and American Consumer Culture* (Minneapolis: University of Minnesota Press, 2001), 12–13.

12. Goss, "Once-upon-a-Time," 49.

13. David Orr, *Ecological Literacy: Education and the Transition to a Postmodern World* (Albany: State University of New York Press, 1992), 5.

14. Gene Wise, "Some Elementary Axioms for an American Culture Studies," *Prospects* 4 (1979): 529–33.

1. Inventing Malls

1. Richard Longstreth, "The Diffusion of the Community Shopping Center Concept During the Interwar Decades," *Journal of the Society of Architectural Historians* 56 (September 1997): 268–73. See also Longstreth's *City Center to Regional Mall: Architecture, the Automobile, and Retailing in Los Angeles, 1920–1950* (Cambridge: MIT Press, 1997).

2. William Leach, *Land of Desire: Merchants, Power, and the Rise of a New American Culture* (New York: Vintage, 1993), 8–9; Susan Porter Benson, *Counter Cultures: Saleswomen, Managers, and Customers in American Department Stores, 1890–1910* (Urbana: University of Illinois Press, 1986).

3. Johann Friedrich Geist, *Arcades: The History of a Building Type* (Cambridge: MIT Press, 1983), 12.

4. ICSC, "A Brief History of Shopping Centers" (June 2000), at www.icsc.org/srch/about/impactofshoppingcenters/briefhistory.html; Carole Rifkind, *A Field Guide to Contemporary American Architecture* (New York: Dutton, 1998), 317.

5. Longstreth, "Diffusion of the Community Shopping Center," 268–73.

6. Howard Gillette Jr., "Evolution of the Planned Shopping Center in Suburb and City," *APA Journal* (Autumn 1985): 449; Michael Beyard, W. Paul O'Mara, et al., *Shopping Center Development Handbook,* 3d ed. (Washington, D.C.: Urban Land Institute, 1999), 3. Despite the influence of Country Club Plaza, some historians consider Highland Park Village in Dallas to be the first planned shopping center because its sales spaces were not bisected by public roads; in fact, it was the first center to turn its back on traffic.

7. Lizabeth Cohen, "From Town Center to Shopping Center," *American Historical Review* 101 (October 1996): 1051–52.

8. ICSC, "Brief History of Shopping Centers"; "New City," *New Yorker* 32 (March 17, 1956): 33; Sze Tsung Leong with Srdjan Jovanovich Weiss, "Air Conditioning," in *The Harvard Design School Guide to Shopping,* ed. Chuihua Judy Chung and Sze Tsung Leong (Cologne: Taschen, 2001), 93–127.

9. "A Break-Through for Two-Level Shopping Centers," *Architectural Forum* 105 (1956): 114–26.

10. William Severini Kowinski, *The Malling of America: An Inside Look at the Great Consumer Paradise* (New York: William Morrow, 1985), 117–22; Gillette, "Evolution of the Planned Shopping Center," 451–54; "New City," 33.

11. Victor Gruen and Larry Smith, *Shopping Towns USA: The Planning of Shopping Centers* (New York: Reinhold, 1960), 24; Sze Tsung Leong, "Gruen Urbanism," in *The Harvard Design School Guide to Shopping*, ed. Chuihua Judy Chung and Sze Tsung Leong (Cologne: Taschen, 2001), 381, 384.

12. Cohen, "From Town Center to Shopping Center," 1056; Gillette, "Evolution of the Planned Shopping Center," 454.

13. Kent A. Robertson, "Downtown Redevelopment Strategies in the United States: An End-of-the-Century Assessment," *APA Journal* (Autumn 1995): 429–37. On the impact of malls on smaller cities, see Cohen, "From Town Center to Shopping Center," 1061–68. On the meanings of Main Street, see Richard V. Francaviglia, *Main Street Revisited: Time, Space, and Image Building in Small-Town America* (Iowa City: University of Iowa Press, 1996), 164–92. Starting in the 1970s, as a direct response to shopping centers, the National Trust for Historic Preservation also began a Main Street program, trying to help Main Street merchants create niche markets that might preserve diminishing downtowns. By the late 1990s, the National Trust had worked with more than fourteen hundred cities. "Antisprawl Pioneer Moe Speaks Out," *Shopping Centers Today* (May 1999), at www.icsc.org/srch/sct/current/sct9905/46.htm.

14. Cohen, "From Town Center to Shopping Center," 1064–67; Gillette, "Evolution of the Planned Shopping Center," 450, 454–56; John McMorrough, "Suburban Model," in *The Harvard Design School Guide to Shopping*, ed. Chuihua Judy Chung and Sze Tsung Leong (Cologne: Taschen, 2001), 721–27.

15. Both of these urban developments benefited from federal "seed money" subsidies first offered in the Carter administration through the National Urban Policy Administration. They are also eligible for Federal Economic Development Administration grants. Coady, "Concrete Dream," 710–11.

16. Rifkind, *Field Guide*, 331; David Bosworth, "Endangered Species: The Mall as Political Habitat," *Salmagundi* (Spring–Summer 1998): 232–33.

17. Gillette, "Evolution of the Planned Shopping Center," 457–58; Boyd Gibbons, *Wye Island* (Washington, D.C.: Resources for the Future, 1987), 16–18. When Rouse designed the new town of Columbia, Maryland, in the 1960s, he also played up the power of the mall. Like Country Club Plaza and Southdale, he envisioned the Columbia Mall as the civic center of the design.

18. Bosworth, "Endangered Species," 232–34.

19. ICSC, "Brief History of Shopping Centers."

20. Ibid.

21. On West Edmonton, see Margaret Crawford, "The World in a Shopping Mall," in *Variations on a Theme Park: The New American City and the End of Public Space*, ed. Michael Sorkin (New York: Hill and Wang, 1992), 3–30. On Mall of America, see Nelson, *Mall of America*, and Goss, "Once-upon-a-Time," 45–75.

22. Beyard et al., *Shopping Center Development Handbook*, 33.

23. Victor Gruen, "The Sad Story of Shopping Centres," *Town and Country Planning* 46 (1978): 351–52.

2. Designing Malls

1. Kenneth Clark, *Civilisation: A Personal View* (New York: Harper and Row, 1970), 330, quoted in Coady, "Concrete Dream," 525.
2. Louis G. Redstone, *New Dimensions in Shopping Centers and Stores* (New York: McGraw-Hill, 1973), 4. On market research, see, for example, *Market Research for Shopping Centers*, ed. Ruben A. Roca (New York: International Council of Shopping Centers, 1980).
3. Charles Kober in Robert Davis Rathbun, *Shopping Centers and Malls: Book 2* (New York: Retail Reporting Corporation, 1988), 88.
4. Richard Keller Simon, "The Formal Garden in the Age of Consumer Culture," in *Mapping American Culture*, ed. Wayne Franklin and Michael Steiner (Iowa City: University of Iowa Press, 1995), 233.
5. Ruben A. Roca, "Introduction," in *Market Research for Shopping Centers*, ed. Ruben A. Roca (New York: International Council of Shopping Centers, 1980), 2–3. See also William J. McCollum's "Basic Research Procedures" in the same volume and the chapter on "Project Feasibility" in Beyard et al., *Shopping Center Development Handbook*, 37–93.
6. Roca, "Introduction," 4, 51. See McCollum, "Basic Research Procedures."
7. Janet Moore, "Mall Hopes Renovation Will Attract Shoppers, Retailers," *Star Tribune*, 19 November 2000, p. D1.
8. Rancho Cucamonga ad in *Shopping Center World*, December 2000, 15. See also add for Chandler, Arizona, in *Shopping Center World*, September 2000, 31.
9. See ad for Festival Bay in *Shopping Center World*, February 2001, 7, and for Santana Row in *Shopping Center World*, September 2000, C21.
10. Ann Satterthwaite, *Going Shopping: Consumer Choices and Community Consequences* (New Haven: Yale University Press, 2001), 319.
11. Warren I. Susman, "Personality and the Making of Twentieth Century Culture," in Warren I. Susman, *Culture as History: The Transformation of American Society in the Twentieth Century* (New York: Pantheon, 1984), 271–85.
12. "You Are Where You Live," Claritas, Inc., at http://cluster2.claritas.com/YAWYL/ziplookup.wjsp. For a good introduction to psychographics, see Hiromi Hosoya and Markus Schaefer, "Psychogramming," in *The Harvard Design School Guide to Shopping*, ed. Chuihua Judy Chung and Sze Tsung Leong (Cologne: Taschen, 2001), 559–75. For a good discussion of the implications of such marketing, see Joseph Turow, *Breaking Up America: Advertisers and the New Media World* (Chicago: University of Chicago Press, 1997).
13. James Atlas, "Beyond Demographics: How Madison Avenue Knows Who You Are and What You Want," *Atlantic Monthly* (October 1984): 51, 55.
14. SRI Consulting Business Intelligence, "The Proven Segmentation System," at http://future.sri.com/VALS/vals2desc.html.
15. "The VALS Segment," at www.sric-bi.com/VALS/types.shtml. To determine your own VALS type, take the survey available on line at www.sric-bi.com/VALS/presurvey.shtml.
16. Schiffman and Kanuk, *Consumer Behavior*, 84.
17. Ibid.
18. Crawford, "World in a Shopping Mall," 9.

19. Karen L. Gentleman, "The 1997 Mall Customer Shopping Patterns Report," in *Consumer Retail Spending: ICSC Research Reports* (New York: International Council of Shopping Centers, 1998), 17; Fetto, "Mall Rats," 10. For an example of a shopper intercept survey, see Kim A. Fraser, *Marketing Small Shopping Centers* (New York: International Council of Shopping Centers, 1991), 145–48.

20. Gentleman, "1997 Mall Customer Shopping Patterns Report," 17; Karla M. Kirtland, "The 1996 Mall Customer Shopping Patterns Report," in *Consumer Retail Spending: ICSC Research Reports* (New York: International Council of Shopping Centers, 1998), 22.

21. Stafford Cliff, *50 Trade Secrets of Great Design: Retail Spaces* (Gloucester, Mass.: Rockport Publishers, 1999), 9.

22. Beyard et al., *Shopping Center Development Handbook*, 59–68.

23. Tae-Wook Cha, "Ecology," in *The Harvard Design School Guide to Shopping*, ed. Chuihua Judy Chung and Sze Tsung Leong (Cologne: Taschen, 2001), 321; Alan A. Alexander and Richard F. Muhlebach, *Shopping Center Management* (Chicago: Institute of Real Estate Management, 1992), 178.

24. Redstone, *New Dimensions*, 6–9.

25. Charles Kober in Rathbun, *Shopping Centers and Malls: Book 2*, 89.

26. Redstone, *New Dimensions*, 8–9.

27. Gottdiener, "Recapturing the Center," 296; Margaret King, "Disneyland and Walt Disney World: Traditional Values in Futuristic Form," *Journal of Popular Culture* 15 (Summer 1981): 121.

28. Redstone, *New Dimensions*, 51.

29. Ibid.; Roy Higgs, "Renovation: Facelift or Major Surgery?" in Rathbun, *Shopping Centers and Malls: Book 2*, 132.

30. Beyard et al., *Shopping Center Development Handbook*, 121.

31. Tran Vinh, "Coopetition," in *Harvard Design School Guide to Shopping*, ed. Chuihua Judy Chung and Sze Tsung Leong (Cologne: Taschen, 2001), 205–15; Simon Property Group, "2000 Annual Report," http://media.corporateir.net/media_files/NYS/SPG/reports/Simon%2000AR.pdf; Beyard et al., *Shopping Center Development Handbook*, 196.

32. Gottdiener, "Recapturing the Center," 296–99; Rifkind, *Field Guide*, 315; Coady, "Concrete Dream," 496; Beyard et al., *Shopping Center Development Handbook*, 8, 71–74.

33. Rifkind, *Field Guide*, 315; Robert F. Lusch, Patrick Dunne, and Randall Gebhardt, *Retail Marketing*, 2d ed. (Cincinnati: South-Western Publishing, 1993), 94.

34. Coady, "Concrete Dream," 715.

35. Beyard et al., *Shopping Center Development Handbook*, 53; Michael D. Beyard, *Dollars and Cents of Shopping Centers: 2000* (Washington, D.C.: Urban Land Institute, 2000), 346; "The Gap and the Limited's Prominence in Enclosed Malls," *Finard Retail Research* (July 1997), at www.finard.com/Finard%20Research/gap.htm.

36. Christopher D. Boring, "Using Market Research to Find the Right Tenant Mix," in *ICSC Guide to Operating Shopping Centers the Smart Way* (New York: ICSC, 1993), 35–36; Beyard et al., *Shopping Center Development Handbook*, 168–70.

37. Lawrence J. Israel, *Store Planning/Design: History, Theory, Process* (New York: John Wiley, 1994), 81, 121–22; Srdjan Jovanovich Weiss and Sze Tsung Leong, "Escalator," in *The Harvard Design School Guide to Shopping*, ed. Chuihua Judy Chung and Sze Tsung Leong (Cologne: Taschen, 2001), 346.

295

38. Israel, *Store Planning/Design*, 121; Redstone, *New Dimensions*, 69. Escalators are a part of the upbeat quality of American life, literally uplifting people, helping them move up in the world. Even though escalators go up and down, we never call them "descalators." Americans almost universally agree that, physically, what goes up must come down, but we're not convinced it's a *social* principle. This is what we might call the escalator clause of the American social contract. And so we ride on, ever upward, on the infinite escalator of commercial progress.

39. Gottdiener, "Recapturing the Center," 296–99; Beyard et al., *Shopping Center Development Handbook*, 130; Goss, "Once-upon-a-Time," 47; Tim McGill at a conference on "Learning from the Mall of America," Minneapolis, 20–23 November 1997.

40. Charles Kober in Rathbun, *Shopping Centers and Malls: Book 2*, 88. See also Beyard et al., *Shopping Center Development Handbook*, 141–63.

41. Daniel Herman, "The Next Big Thing," in *The Harvard Design School Guide to Shopping*, ed. Chuihua Judy Chung and Sze Tsung Leong (Cologne: Taschen, 2001), 528.

42. Stuart Ewen, *Captains of Consciousness: Advertising and the Social Roots of the Consumer Culture* (New York: McGraw-Hill, 1976).

43. Herbert J. Gans, *Popular Culture and High Culture: An Analysis and Evaluation* (New York: Basic Books, 1974); John Fiske, *Reading the Popular* (Winchester, Mass.: Unwin Hyman, 1989); Michael Schudson, *Advertising: The Uneasy Persuasion: Its Dubious Impact on American Society* (New York: Basic Books, 1984); Michael Schudson, "Delectable Materialism: Were the Critics of Consumer Culture Wrong All Along?" *American Prospect* (Spring 1991): 26–35.

3. The Nature of Malls

1. The ideas in this essay have been inspired primarily by Jennifer Price's brilliant "Looking for Nature at the Mall." Although her essay focuses on the now-defunct Nature Store (purchased by the Discovery Channel), it has taught me not just *what* to think about the nature of the mall, but *how* to think about it. The essay first appeared in the groundbreaking *Uncommon Ground: Toward Reinventing Nature*, ed. William Cronon (New York: W. W. Norton, 1995) and now resides in Price's own *Flight Maps: Adventures with Nature in Modern America* (New York: Basic Books, 1999).

2. Beyard et al., *Shopping Center Development Handbook*, 120, 158.

3. Simon, "Formal Garden," 231–32.

4. Ibid., 234–36.

5. J. Madeleine Nash, "The Gilded Age Grandeur," 46–47, quoted in Coady, "Concrete Dream," 551.

6. Mall of America postcard, in possession of the author.

7. Louise Wyman, "Replascape," in *The Harvard Design School Guide to Shopping*, ed. Chuihua Judy Chung and Sze Tsung Leong (Cologne: Taschen, 2001), 622.

8. Simon, "Formal Garden," 244.

9. Beyard et al., *Shopping Center Development Handbook*, 121.

10. See the web site of the Plants for Clean Air Council at www.plants4cleanair.org.

11. Kevin Kenyon, "Innovations Slash Cost of Renovations," *Shopping Centers Today* (6 December 1998), at www.icsc.org/srch/sct/current/sct9812/06.htm.

12. Ibid.

13. NatureMaker web site, www.naturemaker.com.

14. Wyman, "Replascape," 619–31.

15. NatureMaker web site, www.naturemaker.com.

16. Ibid.

17. American Wilderness Experience, *Go Wild in the Mall!* brochure, 1997; B. J. Bergman, "The Great Indoors," *Sierra Magazine* (March/April 1998), at www.sierraclub.org/sierra/199803/indoors.asp.

18. American Wilderness Experience, *Go Wild in the Mall!*

19. Ibid.

20. Ibid.

21. Michael Sorkin, "See You in Disneyland," in *Variations on a Theme Park: The New American City and the End of Public Space* (New York: Hill and Wang, 1992), 210; Simon, "Formal Garden," 241.

22. John Dube, "Science Items a Natural for 'Wonders,'" *Shopping Centers Today*, at www.icsc.org/srch/sct/current/sc9807/13.htm. It's interesting to note how we seem to see nature education as part of the life cycle, as a necessity for kids, but not necessarily for adults.

23. Price, "Looking for Nature at the Mall," 188–89.

24. Ibid., 188–91, 195. "In the nature stores," observes Jon Goss, "consumers purchase not only commodified nature, but an educational and spiritual experience, and a natural way of being. . . . A piece of nature comes with the peace of mind that nature is somehow not exploited." Goss, "Once-upon-a-Time," 61.

25. Goss, "Once-upon-a-Time," 61.

26. Rolf Jensen, *The Dream Society* (New York: McGraw-Hill, 1999), 59; Joan Raymond, "Happy Trails: America's Affinity for the Great Outdoors," *American Demographics*, August 2000, 52–58.

27. Martin M. Pegler, *Lifestyle Stores* (Glen Cove, N.Y.: PBC International, 1996), 77.

28. William Cronon, "The Trouble with Wilderness; or, Getting Back to the Wrong Nature," in *Uncommon Ground: Toward Reinventing Nature*, ed. William Cronon (New York: W. W. Norton, 1995), 89–91.

29. Dube, "Science Items a Natural for 'Wonders.'"

30. Price, "Looking for Nature at the Mall," 199.

31. Ryan and Durning, *Stuff*, 20–24.

32. Ibid., 23–25.

33. Nelson, *Mall of America*, 206, 228.

34. Tom Dwyer and Heidi Shay, "The Changing Nature of Retail Seasons," in *Consumer Retail Shopping: ICSC Research Reports* (New York: ICSC, 1998), 39; Martin Pegler, *Visual Merchandising and Display*, 3d ed. (New York: Fairchild Publications, 1995), 180.

35. Dwyer and Shay, "Changing Nature of Retail Seasons," 39.

36. Leong and Weiss, "Air Conditioning," 93–127.

37. Richard White, *The Organic Machine* (New York: Hill and Wang, 1995).

38. Renato Rosaldo, "Imperialist Nostalgia," *Representations* 26 (Spring 1989): 108; Goss, "Once-upon-a-Time," 60.

4. Retail Designs

1. Paco Underhill, *Why We Buy: The Science of Selling* (New York: Simon and Schuster, 1999), 31; Gottdeiner, "Recapturing the Center," 300; Vilma Barr and Charles Broudy, *Designing to Sell: A Complete Guide to Retail Store Planning and Design*, 2d ed. (New York: McGraw-Hill, 1990), 9, 12.

2. J. Paul Peter and Jerry C. Olson, *Consumer Behavior and Marketing* (Boston: McGraw-Hill, 1999), 256.

3. Barr and Broudy, *Designing to Sell*, 11; Kenneth H. Mills and Judith E. Paul, *Applied Visual Merchandising*, 2d ed. (Englewood Cliffs, N.J.: Prentice Hall, 1988), 4; Dik Glass, "Foreword," in Vilma Barr and Katherine Field, *Stores: Retail Display and Design* (Glen Cove, N.Y.: PBC International, 1997), 8.

4. Barr and Broudy, *Designing to Sell*, 8.

5. Lusch, Dunne, and Gebhardt, *Retail Marketing*, 406; Vilma Barr and Katherine Field, *Stores: Retail Display and Design* (Glen Cove, N.Y.: PBC International, 1997), 10, 38.

6. Barr and Broudy, *Designing to Sell*, 106. During the 1960s, pop art used commercial art both to critique American consumer culture and narrow definitions of art that would exclude commercial artists.

7. Mills and Paul, *Applied Visual Merchandising*, 1.

8. Ibid., 57.

9. Mary Portas, *Windows: The Art of Retail Display* (New York: Thames and Hudson, 1999), 8–9, 36; Barr and Broudy, *Designing to Sell*, 42.

10. Lusch, Dunne, and Gebhardt, *Retail Marketing*, 408–9; Underhill, *Why We Buy*, 84; Barr and Broudy, *Designing to Sell*, 42.

11. Portas, *Windows*, 52–53.

12. Steven Lagerfeld, "What Main Street Can Learn from the Mall," *Atlantic Monthly* (November 1995): 110–20.

13. Barr and Broudy, *Designing to Sell*, 38.

14. Underhill, *Why We Buy*, 47–49; Weishar, "Using Visual Merchandising to Increase Sales," in *Increasing Retailer Productivity: A Guide for Shopping Center Professionals* (New York: International Council of Shopping Centers, 1988), 33–34.

15. Weishar, "Using Visual Merchandising to Increase Sales," 34.

16. Barr and Broudy, *Designing to Sell*, 104.

17. Ibid., 91.

18. Weishar, "Using Visual Merchandising to Increase Sales," 36; Underhill, *Why We Buy*, 82–84.

19. Russell Redman, "Small Centers Can Utilize Entertainment," *Shopping Centers Today*, December 1995, reprinted in *Entertainment in Shopping Centers: A Compendium of ICSC Information Resources* (New York: International Council of Shopping Centers, 1996), 144.

20. Underhill, *Why We Buy*, 80; Weishar, "Using Visual Merchandising to Increase Sales," 34; Barr and Broudy, *Designing to Sell*, 17.

21. Underhill, *Why We Buy*, 17–18.

22. Ibid., 77.

23. Barr and Broudy, *Designing to Sell*, 97–99.

24. Ibid., 43, 89; Linda Cahan, "Designing Winning Looks for Terrific Temporary Stores," in *The ICSC to Operating Shopping Centers the Smart Way* (New York: International Council of Shopping Centers, 1993), 175.

25. Weishar, "Using Visual Merchandising to Increase Sales," 34; Mills and Paul, *Applied Visual Merchandising*, 33.

26. Mills and Paul, *Applied Visual Merchandising*, 6–7, 12, 25.

27. Pegler, *Visual Merchandising and Display*, 225. See also RoxAnna Sway, "New Mania for Mannequins," *Display and Design Ideas* (1 August 2001), at www.ddimagazine.com /displayanddesignideas/search/search_display.jsp?vnu_content_id=1272486.

28. Pegler, *Visual Merchandising and Display*, 225.

29. Julie Clark, "A Torrid Affair," *Design and Display Ideas* (1 July 2001), at www.ddimagazine.com/displayanddesignideas/search/search_display.jsp?vnu_content_id=94 7680; Pegler, *Visual Merchandising and Display*, 84.

30. Joan Jacobs Brumberg, *The Body Project: An Intimate History of American Girls* (New York: Random House, 1997).

31. Mark Crispin Miller, *Boxed In: The Culture of TV* (Evanston, Ill.: Northwestern University Press, 1988).

32. Underhill, *Why We Buy*, 158–59.

33. Portas, *Windows*, 142.

34. Weishar, "Using Visual Merchandising to Increase Sales," 41: Barr and Broudy, *Designing to Sell*, 66–67, 72–74; Mills and Paul, *Applied Visual Merchandising*, 95.

35. Portas, *Windows*, 143.

36. Barr and Broudy, *Designing to Sell*, 57; Weishar, "Using Visual Merchandising to Increase Sales," 32–34; Cahan, "Designing Winning Looks," 175.

37. Barr and Broudy, *Designing to Sell*, 58–59.

38. David Bodamer, "From Classical to Rock, Music Sets Mood for Malls," *Shopping Centers Today* (October 2001), at www.icsc.org/srch/sct/current/page66.html.

39. Michael Fickes, "The Sound of Retail," *Shopping Center World* (30 October 1999), at http://shoppingcenterworld.com/ar/retail_sound_retail_index.htm. AEI's web page (www.aeimusic.com) contends that "the right music . . . at the right time . . . in the right place . . . will move the right people." AEI, the web site says, "is the music and video partner of choice for today's most powerful brands. We create memorable experiences with music and video to increase sales opportunities and promote return visits."

40. Fickes, "Sound of Retail."

41. *Stay Free!* magazine (issue 15), at www.biblio.org/stayfree/15/foreground.htm.

42. Weishar, "Using Visual Merchandising to Increase Sales," 34.

43. Underhill, *Why We Buy*, 64.

44. Ibid., 162.

45. Mills and Paul, *Applied Visual Merchandising*, 65.

46. Underhill, *Why We Buy*, 26.

47. Barr and Broudy, *Designing to Sell*, 22.

48. Barr and Field, *Stores*, 11.

49. Barr and Broudy, *Designing to Sell*, 11, 12.

5. Home Shopping

1. Barbara Kingsolver, *Small Wonder* (New York: HarperCollins, 2002), 134.

2. Einstein, quoted in *Star Tribune*, 19 July 2001, p. E1.

3. James U. McNeal, *The Kids Market: Myths and Realities* (Paramount Market Publishing, 1999), 11.

4. Raj Mehta and Russell W. Belk, "Artifacts, Identity, and Transition: Favorite Possessions of Indians and Indian Immigrants to the United States," *Journal of Consumer Research* 17 (March 1991): 408. American consumption depends on the American family home. Because so many of us live in detached, single-family homes, each household needs one of every-thing. And this is a long tradition. At the beginning of the twentieth century, for example, manufacturers who wanted to increase the market for their goods combined with trade unionists who wanted a "family wage" for men to increase incomes and improve housing to guarantee urban social order and corporate social control. As one corporate leader said, "Get them [the workingmen] to invest their savings in homes and own them. It ties them down so they have a stake in our prosperity." Or as a housing expert said in praise of long-term mortgages, "Good homes make contented workers." Loren Baritz claims that "the fact of home ownership made propertied workers susceptible to middle-class preoccupations. They hungered for order and regularity, for the security of an ethnically homogenous neighborhood. . . . [Homes] made them politically conservative and placed them at the service of the middle class, so long as it did not change the rules that these propertied workers assumed were necessary to safeguard their property—their security and pride." Baritz, *The Good Life: The Meaning of Success for the American Middle Class* (New York: Alfred A. Knopf, 1989), 75.

5. Constantine Von Hoffman, "Branding Baby's Brain," *Sierra* (November 2000): 56–59, 95. Von Hoffman suggests that many times the nursery is "themed," using characters available in commercial culture.

6. Daniel Miller, *A Theory of Shopping* (Ithaca, N.Y.: Cornell University Press, 1998).

7. Hoffman, "Branding Baby's Brain," 58; McNeal, *Kids Market*, 76.

8. James U. McNeal, *Kids as Customers: A Handbook for Marketing to Children* (New York: Lexington Books, 1992), 35; McNeal, *Kids Market*, 67–74; "Teach Wisdom with $20 a Week," *Business Week*, 25 September 2000, 192.

9. McNeal, *Kids Market*, 67, 71–74. Thanks to St. Olaf student Annie Sateren for this insight on allowance and extrinsic rewards.

10. Russell W. Belk, "Materialism and the Making of the Modern Christmas," in *Unwrapping Christmas*, ed. Daniel Miller (Oxford: Clarendon Press, 1993), 85. For more on gift giving and Christmas, see chapter eight.

11. Linda Barbanel, *From Piggy Bank to Credit Card: Teach Your Child the Financial Facts of Life* (New York: Crown, 1994); Deborah Roedder John, "Consumer Socialization of Children: A Retrospective Look at Twenty-Five Years of Research," *Journal of Consumer Research* 26 (December 1999): 183–213.

12. David W. Orr, *The Nature of Design: Ecology, Culture and Human Intention* (New York: Oxford, 2002), 201.

13. McNeal, *Kids Market*, 14–16; Dan Cook, "Lunchbox Hegemony? Kids and the Marketplace, Then and Now," *Lip Magazine* (20 August 2001), at www.lipmagazine.org/articles/feat-cook_124.shtml.

14. Shelly Reese, "Kidmoney: Children as Big Business," *Arts Education Policy Review* 99 (January–February 1998): 37–41; McNeal, *Kids Market*, 19–22.

15. John, "Consumer Socialization of Children," 200–201. James McNeal estimates that kids

make around 3,000 product or service requests a year, and that parents honor about half of them. McNeal, *Kids Market*, 79–85, 90, 209.

16. Juliet Schor, *The Overspent American: Upscaling, Downshifting, and the New Consumer* (New York: Basic Books, 1998), 84–88; "Who's in Charge Here?" *Time*, 6 August 2001, 44; McNeal, *Kids Market*, 79.

17. McNeal, *Kids Market*, 39–43, 83; Ellen Seiter, *Sold Separately: Children and Parents in Consumer Culture* (New Brunswick, N.J.: Rutgers University Press, 1993), 21; Miller, *Theory of Shopping*, 42–43.

18. McNeal, *Kids Market*, 43–46.

19. McNeal, *Kids as Customers*, 47.

20. McNeal, *Kids Market*, 39–45.

21. This paragraph is an extrapolation from the discussion in John, "Consumer Socialization of Children," 183–213. On kiddie rides, see "Impulse Manufacturing," at www.impulsemfg.com/impulse1.htm.

22. Barbara A. Hogan, "Activities for Kids Lure Shoppers of All Ages," *Shopping Centers Today*, February 1996, reprinted in *Entertainment in Shopping Centers: A Compendium of ICSC Information Resources* (New York: International Council of Shopping Centers, 1996), 43–44.

23. McNeal, *Kids Market*, 15, 183.

24. Ibid., 177.

25. Ibid., 13–14, 185; Hilary Townsend, "Kids Clubs Cram Centers with Adults," *Shopping Centers Today* (11 September 1997), at www.icsc.org/sctadv/sct/97-09-11-517.html.

26. Ann Merrill, "More Fun than a Box of Cereal," *Star Tribune*, 28 December 2000, pp. D1, D4.

27. Pat Riedman, "Mall Tours Boost Mall Sales: Retailers and Marketers Are Both Winners When the Stars Come to Town," *Kidscreen* (January 1997): R1; Duncan Hood, "Marketers Buy into Added Promo Mileage from the Mall Net," *Kidscreen* (May 1999): 29.

28. Maura K. Ammenheuser, "Day-Care Dilemma," *Shopping Centers Today* (1 August 2000), at www.icsc.org/srch/sct/current/sct0800/08.html.

29. Kim Johnson, "Area Retailers Marketing to Generation Y," *Eden Prairie Sun-Current*, 8 August 2001, pp. 1A, 10A.; Mercedes M. Cardona and Alice Z. Cuneo, "Retailers Reaching Out to Capture Kids' Clout," *Advertising Age*, 9 October 2000, p. 16.

30. McNeal, *Kids Market*, 125; John, "Consumer Socialization of Children," 202–3; "Who's in Charge Here?" 44.

6. Hanging Out at the Mall

1. Reese, "Kidmoney," 37–41; Channel One ad in *Advertising Age*, 11 May 1998, reproduced in *Adbusters* (Autumn 1998): 14.

2. See also Peter Zollo, *Wise Up to Teens: Insights into Marketing and Advertising to Teenagers*, 2d ed. (Ithaca, N.Y.: New Strategist Publications, 1999) and Gene Del Vecchio, *Creating Ever-Cool: A Marketer's Guide to a Kid's Heart* (Gretna, La.: Pelican Publishing, 1997).

3. When TRU asked teenagers in 1997 what makes a person your age cool, the responses included good looking (49 percent), funny (49 percent), outgoing personality (45 percent), lots of friends (38 percent), popular with opposite sex (34 percent), smart (28 percent), good athlete (26 percent), how they dress (25 percent), independent (20 percent), big partygoer (17 percent), owns cool stuff (13 percent), rebellious (8 percent). Zollo, *Wise Up to Teens*, 200–204.

4. "Teens Spend $172 Billion in 2001," Press Release of Teenage Research Unlimited at www.teen-research.com/PRview.cfm?edit_id=116; Cindy Rodriguez, "Teens Become an Even Bigger Market Target," *Star Tribune*, 7 March 2002, p. E12; "Trends in Retail Trade," OSU Extension Facts, WF-565 (n.d.) Oklahoma State University, 3.

5. The most influential article on coolhunting is Malcolm Gladwell, "The Coolhunt," *New Yorker*, 17 March 1997. But see also Shelly Reese, "The Quality of Cool," *American Demographics*, July 1997, and especially the PBS documentary "Merchants of Cool."

6. "Socializing vs. Spending: The Ratio at the New Teen Spaces," www.look-look.com/look-look/html/Test_Drive_Socializing.html.

7. See the descriptions of the firm on the company's web site, at www.look-look.com/look-look/html/Test_Drive_Press.html.

8. Teenage Research Unlimited, at www.teenresearch.com; Zollo, *Wise Up to Teens*, 170–80.

9. Teenage Research Unlimited, at www.teenresearch.com; Zollo, *Wise Up to Teens*, 25, 36.

10. Zollo, *Wise Up to Teens*, 135–47; Elizabeth Canning Blackwell, "What Do Teens Really Want," *North Shore Magazine*, at www.teenresearch.com/Prview.cfm?edit_id=60.

11. "Teens Serious in Quest for Fun," press release (18 October 2000), at www.teenresearch.com/Prview.cfm?edit_id=74; Zollo, *Wise Up to Teens*, 195–96. "High-tech is such a (huge) part of our lives" was a strong second choice, appearing on 41 percent of ballots. Other choices paralleled adult attitudes, noting the speed of modern life, and the stress of having too many things to do. All of these, of course, are marketable attitudes.

12. Zollo, *Wise Up to Teens*, 215–17.

13. John, "Consumer Socialization of Children," 210.

14. Ibid., 183–213.

15. Zollo, *Wise Up to Teens*, 145–47, 190, 211–13.

16. Mark Ritson and Richard Elliott, "The Social Uses of Advertising: An Ethnographic Study of Adolescent Advertising Audiences," *Journal of Consumer Research* 26 (December 1999): 260–77; Zollo, *Wise Up to Teens*, 31, 282–83. Thanks to Laura Henderson for some of the insights contained in this paragraph.

17. Zollo, *Wise Up to Teens*, 49, 206–7. "If your target is 12-to-15-year-olds," advises Zollo, "consider using 17-year-old actors. You'll grab the youngest teens because they aspire to be as old as the actor."

18. Selina Guber and Jon Berry, *Marketing to and Through Kids* (New York: McGraw-Hill, 1993), 121.

19. Susan M. Valentine, "Consumer or Loiterer?" *Chain Store Age with Shopping Center Age* (November 1990): 108.

20. Some malls are officially "safe places," affiliated with Project Safe Place to provide refuge and counseling to kids who are experiencing family turmoil or abusive situations. "Better Safe than Uninvolved," *Chain Store Age* (May 2000): 132.

21. Guber and Berry, *Marketing to and Through Kids*, 122; Satterthwaite, *Going Shopping*, 112–13.

22. Zollo, *Wise Up to Teens*, 50–52. Many thanks to Elise Braaten for her insights on the importance of this mall culture.

23. Ibid., 72–79, 108–9, 134. Market researchers also read this magazines: Teenage Research Unlimited provides a clipping service (with commentaries) called *teen.bits* for their clients.

24. Zollo, *Wise Up to Teens*, 53–55, 108–9.

25. "Racking 'em Up: Teen Stats Provide a Glimpse into the Lives, Stomachs and Pocket Books of American Teens," *Kidscreen* (July 1999), at www.kidscreen.com/articles/ks25983.asp; Scott Carlson, "Teen Survey Reshapes Analyst's Outlook for Apparel Chains," *Knight-Ridder/Tribune Business News*, 21 April 2001.

26. McNeal, *Kids Market*, 127; Anna Kuchment and Malcolm Beith, "How Old?" *Newsweek International*, 2 October 2000, 6.

27. Rachel Carlton, "A World of Her Own," *Design and Display Ideas* (24 November 2001), at www.ddimagazine.com/displayanddesignideas/search/search_display.jsp?vnu_content_id=1097103.

28. Zollo, *Wise Up to Teens*, 234.

29. "Racking 'em Up"; Zollo, *Wise Up to Teens*, 80–84, 130.

30. ICSC, "2001 Maxi International Awards Winners," www.icsc.org/srch/education/awards/maxi2001/maxi_p13.html and www.icsc.org/srch/education/awards/maxi2001/maxi_p21.html.

31. Ibid.

32. Ibid., 15.

33. Zollo, *Wise Up to Teens*, 186–97.

7. Christmas Shopping

1. Robert D. Holsworth and J. Harry Wray, *American Politics and Everyday Life*, 2d ed. (New York: Macmillan, 1987), 31.

2. ICSC, "Consumers to Spend an Average of $817 on Holiday Purchases," at www.icsc.org/Consumer02.pdf. For a lively and smart introduction to Christmas, see Karal Ann Marling, *Merry Christmas! Celebrating America's Greatest Holiday* (Cambridge: Harvard University Press, 2000).

3. ICSC, "ICSC Holiday Fun Facts 2002," at www.icsc.org/FunFacts02.pdf.

4. Belk, "Materialism and the Making of the Modern Christmas," 76.

5. Ibid., 77; Michael Barton, "The Victorian Jeremiad: Critics of Accumulation and Display," in *Consuming Visions: Accumulation and Display of Goods in America, 1880–1920*, ed. Simon J. Bronner (New York: Norton, 1989), 70–71; Jeffrey L. Sheler, "In Search of Christmas," *U.S. News and World Report*, 23 December 1996, 60–62. As Elizabeth Pleck points out, "The effect of a child-oriented holiday, with gift-giving as its central feature, was to make class distinctions visible, if not painful." Despite the season's sentiment, and despite the charities that try to provide gifts to poor kids, Christmas is often a bitter time for poor people. Elizabeth Pleck, *Celebrating the Family: Ethnicity, Consumer Culture, and Family Rituals* (Cambridge: Harvard University Press, 2000), 57.

6. Martin M. Pegler, *Christmas Displays and Promotions* (New York: Visual Reference Publications, 1993), 7.

7. Melanie Conty, "Holiday Themes Unite World's Centers," at www.icsc.org/sctadv/sct/97–11–30-56.html.

8. ICSC, "Holiday Fun Facts 2002."

9. Pegler notes that "for children it is all wonder—all beauty; it is dreams come true—fantasy turned into tangible reality and magic that you can actually see. For the adults—it is a look back to the carefree or careless times when they were young and believed in magic—in

make-believe and 'happily-ever-after endings.'" Pegler, *Christmas Displays and Promotions,* 139.

10. Pegler, *Christmas Displays and Promotions,* 111. On social capital, see Robert Putnam, *Bowling Alone: The Collapse and Revival of American Community* (New York: Simon and Schuster, 2000).

11. Pegler, *Christmas Displays and Promotions,* 167, 198.

12. Ibid., 62.

13. www.aeimusic.com/pagetemplate/qtxg3b.asp?pageid=816.

14. Conty, "Holiday Themes Unite World's Centers."

15. "Shoppers' Solid Start Gives Hope to U.S. Retailers," *Star Tribune,* 26 November 2001, p. A11.

16. Sandra Eckstein, "Toy Firms Bank on Harry Potter Holiday Magic," at www.startribune.com/stories/384/846120.html; Anne D'Innocenzio, "Scarce Commodities," *Star Tribune,* 30 November 2001, pp. D1–3; Sheryl Harris, "Toys Come, Go, But Classics Are Forever," *Star Tribune,* 3 December 2001, p. E4.

17. See, for example, Daniel J. Vargas, "Not Your Average Toys, These Are for Kids of the Very Rich," *Star Tribune,* 7 December 2001, p. E27.

18. Belk, "Materialism and the Making of the Modern Christmas," 78.

19. Leigh Eric Schmidt, *Consumer Rites: The Buying and Selling of American Holidays* (Princeton: Princeton University Press, 1995), 134–48; Belk, "Materialism and the Making of the Modern Christmas," 83.

20. Rachel Beck, "Agencies Supply Santa for Season," *Augusta Chronicle,* at www.augustachronicle.com/stories/121398/bus_124–1620.shtml; ICSC, "ICSC Holiday Fun Facts 2001," at www.icsc.org/holiday_fun_facts01.pdf.

21. Beck, "Agencies Supply Santa for Season."

22. Earnest Winston, "A Tough Job, but Santas Do It," *Cincinnati Enquirer* (24 December 1999), at www.enquirer.com/editions/1999/12/24/loc_a_tough_job_but.html.

23. Ibid.

24. Cherry Hill Photo, at www.cherryhillphoto.com.

25. ICSC, "ICSC Holiday Fun Facts 2001."

26. Belk, "Materialism and the Making of the Modern Christmas," 82–83, 91.

27. Children's Defense Fund, *The State of America's Children Yearbook* (Boston: Beacon Press, 1999), xi. For a description of a poor people's Christmas, see Chin, *Purchasing Power,* 81–87.

28. Theodore Caplow, "Rule Enforcement Without Visible Means: Christmas Gift Giving in Middletown," *American Journal of Sociology* 89 (May 1984): 1306–7.

29. Belk, "Materialism and the Making of the Modern Christmas," 89–90.

30. Ibid., 90–91.

31. Caplow, "Rule Enforcement Without Visible Means," 1307, 1319–22.

32. Ibid., 1313–15.

33. Ibid., 1315.

34. Ibid., 1315–16.

35. Ibid., 1312–13.

36. Belk, "Materialism and the Making of the Modern Christmas," 93–94.

37. Belk, "Materialism and You," *Journal of Research for Consumers* (May 2001), at www.jrconsumers.com.

38. James Carrier, "The Rituals of Christmas Giving," in *Unwrapping Christmas,* ed. Daniel Miller (Oxford: Clarendon Press, 1993), 55–74.

39. Ibid., 59, 62–64.

40. Ibid., 63–64.

41. Ibid., 63.

42. Jim Jones, "Balancing Gift-Giving with the Spiritual Celebration," at www.reporternews.com/1999/religion/jones.html.

43. Alternatives for Simple Living, at www.simpleliving.org/index.shtml.

44. S.C.R.O.O.G.E., at www.geocities.com/EnchantedForest/Palace/4079.

45. Bill McKibben, *Hundred Dollar Holiday: The Search for a Joyful Christmas* (New York: Simon and Schuster, 1998).

46. ICSC, "ICSC Holiday Fun Facts 2001."

47. Leigh Eric Schmidt, "Christianity in the Marketplace: Christmas and the Consumer Culture," at www.crosscurrents.org/schmidt.htm.

48. I am indebted to George Wertin for many of these insights about the cultural complexities of Christmas.

49. Sheler, "In Search of Christmas," 64.

50. Richard Morin, "The Favorite Time of the Year," *Washington Post*, 22 December 1997; Jones, "Balancing Gift-Giving with the Spiritual Celebration," at www.reporternews.com/1999/religion/jones.html.

51. Morin, "The Favorite Time of the Year," *Washington Post*, 22 December 1997; Sheler, "In Search of Christmas," 62.

8. Just Looking

1. Susan Fournier and Michael Guiry, "'An Emerald Green Jaguar, A House on Nantucket, and an African Safari': Wish Lists and Consumption Dreams in Materialist Society," *Advances in Consumer Research* 20 (1993): 352–58.

2. Crawford, "World in a Shopping Mall," 3–30.

3. Phyllis Rose, "Shopping and Other Spiritual Adventures in America Today," in *Common Culture: Reading and Writing About American Popular Culture*, ed. Michael F. Petracca and Madeleine Sorapure (Englewood Cliffs, N.J.: Prentice Hall, 1995), 621–24.

4. Alan Dundes, "Seeing Is Believing," in *The Nacirema: Readings on American Culture*, ed. James Spradley and Michael A. Rynkiewich (Boston: Little, Brown, 1975), 14–19.

5. Babin, Darden, and Griffin, "Work and/or Fun," 646; see also Hilary Radner, *Shopping Around: Feminine Culture and the Pursuit of Pleasure* (London: Routledge, 1995).

6. Randall Jarrell, "A Sad Heart at the Supermarket," in *A Sad Heart at the Supermarket: Essays and Fables for Our Time* (New York: Atheneum, 1962), 64–89.

7. See Grant McCracken, "Diderot Unities and the Diderot Effect," in *Culture and Consumption: New Approaches to the Symbolic Character of Consumer Goods and Activities* (Bloomington: Indiana University Press, 1988), 118–29.

8. Alan Warde, "Consumption, Identity Formation and Uncertainty," *Sociology* 28 (4): 878.

9. Pegler, *Visual Merchandising and Display*, 133.

10. John Berger, *Ways of Seeing* (New York: Penguin, 1977).

11. Charles Horton Cooley, *Human Nature and the Social Order* (New York: Scribner's, 1902), 179–85.

12. Jerry Jacobs, *The Search for Acceptance: Consumerism, Sexuality and Self Among American Women* (Bristol, Ind.:

Wyndham Hall Press, 1988), 23–24. A popular t-shirt pronounced this philosophy: "It is not who you are, but what you wear. Besides, who really cares who you are anyway?" See also Lauren Langman, "Neon Cages: Shopping for Subjectivity," in *Lifestyle Shopping: The Subject of Consumption* (New York: Routledge, 1992), 40–82.

13. Satterthwaite, *Going Shopping*, 124.

14. Mills and Paul, *Applied Visual Merchandising*, 147.

15. Barnes & Noble press release (26 October 2000), at www.barnesandnoble.com/ir/press/archive/2000/102600.asp.

16. Kirtland, "1996 Mall Customer Shopping Patterns Report," 20; Yankelovich Partners, "Trends in Communication: Know Your Customers," (21 June 2001), at www.drpt.state.va.us/resource/downloads/SMC_Yankelovich.pdf.

17. Herbert Gans, "The Uses of Poverty: The Poor Pay All," *Social Policy* (July–August 1971): 20–24.

18. Yankelovich Partners, "Trends in Communication"; Schor, *Overspent American*, 11–14.

19. "Yearning for Balance: Views of Americans on Consumption, Materialism, and the Environment," prepared for the Merck Family Fund by the Harwood Group (July 1995), 1–5; Schor, *Overspent American*, 11–19.

20. Heidi Shea and Michael Baker, "African-American Consumers," in *Consumer Retail Spending: ICSC Research Reports* (New York: International Council of Shopping Centers, 1998), 52–53.

21. Ibid., 54–56.

22. Ibid., 56–57.

23. Ted Ownby, *American Dreams in Mississippi: Consumers, Poverty and Culture, 1830–1998* (Chapel Hill: University of North Carolina Press, 1999), 149–58.

24. "Children's Place Settles Race-Bias Claim," *Star Tribune*, 22 December 2000, p. A14.

25. Kenneth Meeks, *Driving While Black: Highways, Shopping Malls, Taxi Cabs, Sidewalks: How to Fight Back If You Are a Victim of Racial Profiling* (New York: Broadway Books, 2000), 76–111. Meeks also shows the rationalizations for this practice.

26. Brad Knickerbocker, "New Face of Racism in America," *Christian Science Monitor* (14 January 2000), at www.csmonitor.com/durable/2000/01/14/p1s1.htm.

27. Timothy Henderson, "Perception that Some Merchants Practice Racial Profiling Generates Debate," *Stores* (June 2001), at www.stores.org/archives/jun01edit.html.

28. Ownby, *American Dreams in Mississippi*, 61–81; Chin, *Purchasing Power*, 34–43.

29. Alex Kotlowitz, "False Connections," in *Consuming Desires: Consumption, Culture, and the Pursuit of Happiness*, ed. Roger Rosenblatt (Washington, D.C.: Island Press, 1999), 67–68.

30. Kotlowitz, "False Connections," 70–71.

31. Chin, *Purchasing Power*, 143–73. See also Susan Willis, "I Want the Black One: Is There a Place for Afro-American Culture in Commodity Culture?" in *A Primer for Daily Life* (New York: Routledge, 1991), 108–32.

32. Gary Cross, *An All-Consuming Century: Why Commercialism Won in Modern America* (New York: Columbia University Press, 2000).

33. Mihaly Csikszentmihalyi, "The Costs and Benefits of Consuming," *Journal of Consumer Research* (September 2000): 270.

34. Jane Janedis, "Understanding the Process of Fashion," in *ICSC Guide to Operating Shopping Centers the Smart Way* (New York: ICSC, 1993), 179.

306

35. Leach, *Land of Desire*, 268.

36. Myra Stark, "The State of the U.S. Consumer 2000," at www.saatchikevin.com/workingit/myra_stark_report.html. Juliet Schor and others contend that Americans are working more. But Geoffrey Godbey and John Robinson argue that we have more leisure than ever. They agree that Americans feel harried, and suggest that the time bind comes not so much from a lack of leisure time, but from a lack of lengthy leisure. We have lots of free time, but it comes in short bursts, and so we spend it watching TV, which doesn't accomplish much for our sense of busy-ness. See Juliet Schor, *The Overworked American* (New York: Basic Books, 1992) and John Robinson and Geoffrey Godbey, *Time for Life: The Surprising Ways Americans Use Their Time* (University Park: Pennsylvania State University Press, 1997).

37. Yankelovich Partners, "Trends in Communication." According to the National Opinion Research Center, Americans in 1982 felt more unrushed than rushed—25 percent to 20 percent. By 1996, more Americans were feeling the rush, with only 18 percent feeling unrushed, and 30 percent feeling constantly rushed. John Head, "Life's a Rush, as Americans Feel the Time Crunch," *Star Tribune*, 9 July 2001, pp. E1, E7.

38. Fetto, "Mall Rats," 10; *The Harvard Design School Guide to Shopping*, ed. Chuihua Judy Chung and Sze Tsung Leong (Cologne: Taschen, 2001), 74–75.

39. David Lewis and Darren Bridger, *The Soul of the New Consumer: Authenticity—What We Buy and Why in the New Economy* (London: Nicholas Brealey, 2000), 8; Annetta Miller, "The Millennial Mind-Set," *American Demographics*, January 1999, 62–63.

40. Beyard et al., *Shopping Center Development Handbook*, 18–19.

41. Wendy Leibman, "How America Shops: The Consumer Paradox," *Vital Speeches of the Day* 64 (15 July 1998): 596–98; Stark, "State of the U.S. Consumer 2000."

42. "Mall Bawl: A Promo in Every Shop," *Promo* (1 August 2001): 57.

43. Miller, *Theory of Shopping*, 15–72. Miller contends that many women especially see the purpose of life "in its relation to something that transcends it. Shopping, so far from being, as it is inevitably portrayed, the essence of ungodliness, becomes as a ritual the vestigial search for a relationship with God." Miller, *Theory of Shopping*, 150.

44. Ibid., 102–3.

45. Portas, *Windows*, 101.

9. Shopping for the Fun of It

1. Debra Hazel, "That's Entertainment," *Shopping Centers Today* (June 2000), at www.icsc.org/srch/sct/current/sct0600/05.html.

2. Karal Ann Marling, *As Seen on TV: The Visual Culture of Everyday Life in the 1950s* (Cambridge: Harvard University Press, 1994, 116; Alan Bryman, "The Disneyization of Society," *Sociological Review* (1999): 33–36.

3. "The Architecture of Reassurance," Museum of Building, Washington, D.C., 11 June 2001.

4. See especially George Ritzer, *Enchanting a Disenchanted World: Revolutionizing the Means of Consumption* (Thousand Oaks, Calif.: Pine Forge Press, 1999).

5. Chuihua Judy Chung, "Disney Space," in *The Harvard Design School Guide to Shopping*, ed. Chuihua Judy Chung and Sze Tsung Leong (Cologne: Taschen, 2001), 292.

6. "Chronology" compiled by Andrew Landsbury in *Designing Disney's Theme Parks: The Architecture of Reassurance*, ed. Karal Ann Marling (Montreal: Canadian Centre for Architecture, 1997), 219–22.

7. Bryman, "Disneyization of Society," 31–32.

8. Beth Dunlop, *Building a Dream: The Art of Disney Architecture* (New York: Harry N. Abrams, 1996), 23. Vincent Scully reminds critics of "theming" that all architecture is themed. Even college campuses are themed "to create secret gardens of mythic character, weaving a special transcendent spell, suggesting the ritual of magic." Scully, "Disney: Theme and Reality," in Dunlop, *Building a Dream*, 7–8.

9. Marling, *As Seen on TV*, 92–93; Dunlop, *Building a Dream*, 13; Chung, "Disney Space," 276–77.

10. Marling, *As Seen on TV*, 93; Huxtable, quoted in Martin M. Pegler, *Streetscapes: Façade, Entrances, Storefronts* (Washington, D.C.: Urban Land Institute, 1998), 16; Chung, "Disney Space," 288.

11. King, "Disneyland and Walt Disney World," 125; Marling, *As Seen on TV*, 96.

12. Karal Ann Marling, *Designing Disney's Theme Parks: The Architecture of Reassurance* (Montreal: Canadian Centre for Architecture, 1997). "'When you wish upon a star your dream comes true' makes a lovely fiction for a while," according to Vincent Scully, "but it is, after all, pure bullshit in the long run." Scully, "Disney: Theme and Reality," in Dunlop, *Building a Dream*, 8.

13. King, "Disneyland and Walt Disney World," 130–31; Bryman, "Disneyization of Society," 31.

14. Sorkin, "See You in Disneyland," 208.

15. Alan Bryman calls this "the dedifferentiation of consumption," the process by which forms of consumption associated with different institutions produce synergies. Bryman, "Disneyization of Society," 33.

16. Kevin Kenyon, "In New Twist, Entertainment Pursues Retail," *Shopping Centers Today* (1 May 1998), at www.icsc.org/srch/sct/current/sct9805/14.html; Chung, "Disney Space," 292; "The Architecture of Reassurance," Museum of Building, Washington, D.C., 11 June 2001. For a look at Disney retailing, see Lissa Poirot, "The Magic of Disney," *Display and Design Ideas* (March 2000), at www.ddimagazine.com/mar00stor4.cfm.

17. Paul Jacob, "Really Artificial, Genuinely Surreal," *Shopping Center World* (July 1999), at www.scwonline.com/publs/scw/99jul/scw9907e20.html.

18. "Shopping in Las Vegas," at www.ussx.com/feature_shopping.asp.

19. Richard N. Vellotta, "Forum Shoppes Unfazed by Rivals," *Las Vegas Sun* (19 July 2000), at www.lasvegassun.com/sunbin/stories/text/2000/jul/19/510524807.html.

20. Lisa Snedker, "Desert Passage to Specialize in 'Shoppertainment,'" *Las Vegas Sun* (13 August 2000), at www.lasvegassun.com/sunbin/stories/text/2000/aug/13/510616944.html.

21. Hubble Smith, "Mall Hopes for Some Retail Magic," *Las Vegas Review-Journal* (14 August 2000), at www.lvrj.com/lvrj_home/2000/Aug-14-Mon-2000/business/14113953.html.

22. "Many Are Spending Vacations at Malls: Shopping Centers Are Common Tourist Stops," *Baltimore Sun* (3 August 1998), in Beyard et al., *Shopping Center Development Handbook*, 10; "The Mall's Next Mission: Trap Those Tourists," *Shopping Center World*, July 2001, 6; "Taubman Centers and TIA Release First Ever Survey on U.S. Shopping and Travel Experience," at www.taubman.com/pressrel/releases/01/4_26_01.htm.

23. Dan Fost, "That's Entertainment," *Marketing Tools* (June 1998), at www.demographics.com/publications/mt/98_mt/9806_mt/mt980618.htm.

24. Nelson, *Mall of America*, 63.

25. Francaviglia, *Main Street Revisited*, 164–92; Mark Gottdiener, *The Theming of America: Dreams, Visions, and Commercial Spaces* (Boulder, Colo.: Westview Press, 1997), 86.

26. Dunlop, *Building a Dream*, 18, 23; Francaviglia, *Main Street Revisited*, 167–80.

27. Chung, "Disney Space," 277.

28. Susan Doubilet, "Entertainment Retail: Reinventing the Mall," *Architectural Record*, October 1999, 152; Redstone, *New Dimensions*, 236; Heidi Gralla, "Simon Says Entertainment Is Essential," *Shopping Centers Today*, January 1995, reprinted in *Entertainment in Shopping Centers: A Compendium of ICSC Information Resources* (New York: International Council of Shopping Centers, 1996), 135; Jacob, "Really Artificial."

29. ICSC, "Educational Study Tour of U.S. Entertainment-Oriented Shopping Centers," at www.icsc.org/srch/mt/deses/2000HSL.html.

30. Albert Warson, "Experts: Canadian Centers Need Novelty, 'Main Street' Retail to Capture Youth Sales," *Shopping Centers Today* (14 June 1999), at www.icsc.org/srch/sct/current/sct9906/14.htm.

31. Paul Goldberger, "The Store Strikes Back," *New York Times Magazine*, 6 April 1997, 45; Martin M. Pegler, *Retail Entertainment* (New York: Visual Reference Publications, 1998), 11–13.

32. Goldberger, "Store Strikes Back," 45–46.

33. Ginia Bellafante, "That's Retail-tainment," *Time*, 7 December 1998, 64; Annetta Miller, "The Millennial Mind-Set," *American Demographics*, January 1999, 62–63.

34. Ronald Mendoza, "Themed Retail Design," at www.where-its-at.com/articles/spotlightarticles/spotlight4.html.

35. Anna Robaton, "Conference Preps Mall Executives on Entertainment," *Shopping Centers Today*, May 1995, reprinted in *Entertainment in Shopping Centers: A Compendium of ICSC Information Resources* (New York: International Council of Shopping Centers, 1996), 62.

36. Kevin Kenyon, "Entertainment's Not Fun for Everyone," *Shopping Centers Today* (7 April 1998), at www.icsc.org/srch/sct/current/sct9804/07.htm.

37. Doubilet, "Entertainment Retail," 152; Hogan, "Activities for Kids Lure Shoppers of All Ages," 44. See also "Carousels Add a Promotional Spin" and "Carousels Add Appeal to Malls" in the same publication.

38. Barbara A. Hogan, "Turnkey Events Offer High Traffic at Low Cost," *Shopping Centers Today*, February 1996, reprinted in *Entertainment in Shopping Centers: A Compendium of ICSC Information Resources* (New York: International Council of Shopping Centers, 1996), 151–54.

39. John Fetto, "Let's Go to the Movies," *American Demographics*, March 2000; Shannon Dortch, "Going to the Movies," *American Demographics*, December 1996.

40. Jon Springer, "Multiplexes Alter Movie Theater Picture," *Shopping Centers Today* (16 July 1998), at www.icsc.org/srch/sct/current/sct9807/16.htm; Peter and Olson, *Consumer Behavior*, 265.

41. Springer, "Multiplexes Alter Movie Theater Picture"; Barbara A. Hogan, "Mega-Cinemas Gain Star Status at Malls," *Shopping Centers Today*, February 1996, reprinted in *Entertainment in Shopping Centers: A Compendium of ICSC Information Resources* (New York: International Council of Shopping Centers, 1996), 118.

42. Kenyon, "Entertainment's Not Fun for Everyone"; Dortch, "Going to the Movies," 47, 22–23; Beyard et al., *Shopping Center Development Handbook*, 98–99.

43. Peter and Olson, *Consumer Behavior*, 265.

44. Kenyon, "Entertainment's Not Fun for Everyone"; Dortch, "Going to the Movies," 4–7, 22–23.

45. Allyson H. Sicard, "Leasing: Retail and Entertainment: A Family Affair," *Shopping Center World* (August 1997), at www.scwonline.com/pubs/scw/97aug/ scw9708h.html.

46. Barbara A. Hogan, "Themed Restaurants Take a Bite Out of the Retail Pie," *Shopping Centers Today,* October 1995, reprinted in *Entertainment in Shopping Centers: A Compendium of ICSC Information Resources* (New York: International Council of Shopping Centers, 1996), 149.

47. John G. Edwards, "That's Entertainment," *Las Vegas Review-Journal,* 16 February 1998.

48. Barbara A. Hogan, "Defining Entertainment: Retailers and Owners Are Serious About Having Fun," *Shopping Centers Today,* February 1996, reprinted in *Entertainment in Shopping Centers: A Compendium of ICSC Information Resources* (New York: International Council of Shopping Centers, 1996), 81.

49. "'Shoppertainment'—Every Day a Holiday," at www.nareit.com/portfoliomag/ july2000/feat_mega_side.shtml.

50. Clifford A. Pearson, "Metreon, San Francisco, California," *Architectural Record,* October 1999, 154–59; Colleen Cason, "Technology Reinvents the Store," at www.insidevc.com/special/projects/stories/stuff03a.shtml.

51. Ed Leibowitz, "Crowd Pleaser," *Los Angeles Magazine,* February 2002, 48–55.

52. Ibid., 48–55; Michael Cannell, "John Jerde: Neon Urbanist," *Architecture,* August 2000, 113.

53. "Urban Legend," *Trojan Family Magazine* (Summer 2001), at www.usc.edu/dept/pubrel/trojan_family/summer01/Jerde/Jerde.html; "The Jerde Partnership International: Philosophy," at www.jerde.com/philosophy.html; Leibowitz, "Crowd Pleaser," 48.

54. "The Jerde Partnership International: Philosophy," at www.jerde.com/ philosophy.html; Jim Davis, "Power and Light Designer Seeks Community," *Kansas City Business Journal,* 29 August 1997, 3–4.

55. "The Jerde Partnership International"; Leibowitz, "Crowd Pleaser," 48; Cannell, "John Jerde," 113; *The Jerde Partnership International: Visceral Reality* (l'Arca Edizione, 1998), 10.

56. Leibowitz, "Crowd Pleaser," 48–55.

57. Daniel Herman, "Jerde Transfer," in *The Harvard Design School Guide to Shopping,* ed. Chuihua Judy Chung and Sze Tsung Leong (Cologne: Taschen, 2001), 403–5.

58. Herman, "Jerde Transfer," 403–5; Daniel Herman, "Separated at Birth," in *The Harvard Design School Guide to Shopping,* ed. Chuihua Judy Chung and Sze Tsung Leong (Cologne: Taschen, 2001), 711.

59. "The Entertainment Economy," *Business Week,* 14 March 1994, 58–64.

60. Martha Wolfenstein, "The Emergence of Fun Morality," *Journal of Social Issues* 7 (1951): 22–24; Simon, "Formal Garden," 246.

61. Richard Butsch, "Introduction: Leisure and Hegemony," in *For Fun and Profit: The Transformation of Leisure into Consumption* (Philadelphia: Temple University Press, 1990), 3–27.

62. Witold Rybczynski, *Waiting for the Weekend* (New York: Penguin, 1991), 225; Mary Jo Deegan, "The Americanization of Ritual Culture: The 'Core Codes' in American Culture and the Seductive Pleasure of American 'Fun,'" in *The American Ritual Tapestry: Social Rules and Cultural Meanings* (Westport, Conn.: Greenwood, 1998), 77.

63. Rybczynski, *Waiting for the Weekend*, 218–19.

64. Bernice Kanner, "Hungry, or Just Bored?" *American Demographics*, January 1999, 15; Tom Kuntz, "Word for Word: Boredom," at www.utexas.edu/courses/ hilde/Phl_304/boredom.html.

65. Patricia Meyer Spacks, *Boredom: The Literary History of a State of Mind* (Chicago: University of Chicago Press, 1995), 9–30.

66. Neil Postman, *Amusing Ourselves to Death: Public Discourse in the Age of Show Business* (New York: Viking, 1985), 87; Warson, "Experts."

67. Ritzer, *Enchanting a Disenchanted World*, 174.

68. Mary Catherine Bateson, *Peripheral Visions: Learning Along the Way* (New York: HarperCollins, 1994), 56.

69. Sorkin, "See You in Disneyland," 223.

70. Ibid., 206.

10. Making a Purchase

1. Pamela Muston, "Training: The Route to Increased Sales," in *Increasing Retailer Productivity: A Guide for Shopping Center Professionals* (New York: International Council of Shopping Centers, 1988), 73–79.

2. Deborah Caulfield Rybak, "30% in State Earn Less Than $10 An Hour, Report Says," *Star Tribune*, 2 February 2002, pp. D1, D10.

3. Barry Bluestone, Patricia Hanna, Sarah Kuhn, and Laura Moore, *The Retail Revolution: Market Transformation, Investment, and Labor in the Modern Department Store* (Boston: Auburn House, 1981), 80; Rifkind, *Field Guide*, 315.

4. Bluestone et al., *Retail Revolution*, 83.

5. Ibid., 83–86, 91.

6. Ibid., 112–15.

7. Ibid., 110–11; Eyal Press, "Sweatshopping," in *No Sweat: Fashion, Free Trade and the Rights of Workers*, ed. Andrew Ross (New York: Verso, 1997), 224.

8. Bluestone et al., *Retail Revolution*, 116, 146–47.

9. Misty Milioto, "Bad Customer Service Drives Shoppers Away from Stores," *Shopping Center World* (3 April 2001), at www.shoppingcenterworld.com/ar/retail_bad_customer_service/ index.htm; Judith Sains, "What Makes a Successful Salesperson," in *ICSC Guide to Operating Shopping Centers the Smart Way* (New York: ICSC, 1993), 173.

10. Rebecca L. Morgan, *Calming Upset Customers: Staying Effective During Unpleasant Situations* (Los Altos, Calif.: Crisp Publications, 1989), 6, 40, 45.

11. Arlie Russell Hochschild, *The Managed Heart: Commercialization of Human Feeling* (Berkeley and Los Angeles: University of California Press, 1983), 7–9, 147–53; Lusch, Dunne, and Gebhardt, *Retail Marketing*, 533.

12. Michael Moffatt, *Coming of Age in New Jersey: College and American Culture* (New Brunswick, N.J.: Rutgers University Press, 1989), 43–44.

13. Putnam, *Bowling Alone*.

14. Underhill, *Why We Buy*, 36. For an example of how a company measures service quality, see the information on SERVQUAL at www.arl.org/stats/newmeas/libqualplus.html.

15. Michelle Lowe and Louise Crewe, "Shop Work: Image, Customer Care, and the

Restructuring of Retail Employment," in *Retailing, Consumption and Capital: Towards the New Retail Geography* (London: Longman, 1996), 204.

16. Hiromi Hosoya and Markus Schaefer, "Bit Structures," in *The Harvard Design School Guide to Shopping*, ed. Chuihua Judy Chung and Sze Tsung Leong (Cologne: Taschen, 2001), 158.

17. Bluestone et al., *Retail Revolution*, 114.

18. David Orr, "Prices and the Life Exchanged: Costs of the U.S. Food System," in David Orr, *Earth in Mind: On Education, Environment, and the Human Prospect* (Washington, D.C.: Island Press, 1994), 172.

19. William Cronon, *Nature's Metropolis: Chicago and the Great West* (New York: W. W. Norton, 1991), 256.

20. Orr, *Ecological Literacy*, 5–6, 64–67, 160–61. See also Richard North, *The Real Cost* (London: Chatto and Windus, 1986). On the real costs of cars, for example, see Alan Durning, *The Car and the City* (Seattle: Northwest Environment Watch, 1996), 48–62.

21. Leah Hager Cohen suggests that in reifying money, we almost deify it, and both elements are essential. Money cannot be pure abstraction; we must think of it as real. And it cannot be purely rational; we must treat it as sacred. Cohen, *Glass, Paper, Beans: Revelations on the Nature and Value of Ordinary Things* (New York: Doubleday, 1997), 233.

22. Ibid., 225–27.

23. Mihaly Csikszentmihalyi, "The Costs and Benefits of Consuming," *Journal of Consumer Research* (September 2000): 270.

24. David Evans and Richard Schmalensee, *Paying with Plastic: The Digital Revolution in Buying and Borrowing* (Cambridge: MIT Press, 1999), 7.

25. Ibid.

26. Nancy Shepherdson, "Credit Card America," *American Heritage* 42 (1991): 125–32.

27. Evans and Schmalensee, *Paying with Plastic*, 3, 31.

28. Ibid., 1–3.

29. Robert D. Manning, *Credit Card Nation: The Consequences of America's Addiction to Credit* (New York: Basic Books, 2000), 6; Evans and Schmalensee, *Paying with Plastic*, xi.

30. Laura Pappano, *The Connection Gap: Why Americans Feel So Alone* (New Brunswick, N.J.: Rutgers University Press, 2001), 37.

31. Henry David Thoreau, *Walden* (New York: Harper and Row, 1965), 23.

32. ABC News, "You've Got Mail" (15 March 2001), at www.abcnews.go.com/sections/business/DailyNews/creditcards_010315.html.

33. "Trends in Retail Trade," OSU Extension Facts, WF-565 (n.d.) Oklahoma State University, 2; Anne D'Innocenzio, "What Will Massive Debt Mean for Young Consumers?" *Star Tribune*, 9 March 2002, pp. D1–D2; Manning, *Credit Card Nation*, 5, 9.

34. Evans and Schmalensee, *Paying with Plastic*, 8, 33.

35. Ibid., 5–6.

36. Ibid., 5, 33; Schor, *Overspent American*, 72; Manning, *Credit Card Nation*, 13.

37. Manning, *Credit Card Nation*, 5, 27.

38. Dee DePass and Donna Halvorsen, "Who Is to Blame for the Rise in Personal Bankruptcy?" *Star Tribune*, 24 January 1997, p. A19.

39. "Historical Retail Evolution," at www.pwcglobal.com/extweb/newcojou.nsf/
e056f88ddbc206c7852565d3005ae4f7/1a9de849c09b41b0852566260074f735/
$FILE/Outl_.PDF.

40. DePass and Halvorsen, "Who Is to Blame for the Rise in Personal Bankruptcy?" p. A19;
Manning, *Credit Card Nation*, 5.

41. Jennifer Lach, "In the (Credit) Cards," *American Demographics*, April 1999, 43; "E-Business Intelligence," at
www.businessobjects.com/company/ebi/mastercard.htm; Lewis and Bridger, *Soul of the New Consumer*, 13.

11. The Politics of No Politics

1. Ironically, there's even a virtual Town Square at www.townsquareshops.com/index.htm.

2. Cohen, "From Town Center to Shopping Center," 1080–81.

3. Kowinski, *Malling of America*, 354–59.

4. Ibid., 1068.

5. Satterthwaite, *Going Shopping*, 114–17.

6. Cohen, "From Town Center to Shopping Center," 1068–69; Michael Fickes, "Freedom of
Speech in the Mall," *Shopping Center World*, 1 September 2000, 150–53. See also ICSC,
"Scorecard of Pruneyard Litigation," at www.icsc.org/law/prune.pdf.

7. Kowinski, *Malling of America*, 355.

8. Coady, "Concrete Dream," 618.

9. Ibid., 568–69.

10. ICSC, "Scope USA."

11. Beyard et al, *Shopping Center Development Handbook*, 66.

12. Ken Jones and Jim Simmons, *The Retail Environment* (New York: Routledge, 1990), 1.

13. Edmund Mander, "Antisprawl Raises PR Issues for Industry," *Shopping Centers Today* (May
1999), at www.icsc.org/srch/sct/current/sct9905/48.htm.

14. ICSC, "ICSC PAC," at www.icsc.org/government/pac.html, and ICSC, "Government," at
www.icsc.org/government.

15. ICSC, "Government Relations Issues," at www.icsc.org/cgi/dispgri.

16. ICSC Fast Action Center, at www.capitolconnect.com/icsc.

17. ICSC, "ICSC PAC."

18. "Government Affairs," at www.imra.org/govaff-fed_agenda.asp.

19. Gentleman, "1997 Mall Customer Shopping Patterns Report," 17.

20. Lizabeth Cohen, *A Consumer's Republic: The Politics of Mass Consumption in Postwar America* (New
York: Knopf, 2003).

21. Jane Pavitt, "In Goods We Trust?" in *Brand.new*, ed. Jane Pavitt (Princeton: Princeton
University Press, 2000), 32. For an excellent discussion of the Kitchen Debate, see
Karal Ann Marling, "Nixon in Moscow," in her *As Seen on TV*, 243–83.

22. Lizabeth Cohen, "Citizens and Consumers in the United States in the Century of Mass
Consumption," in *The Politics of Consumption: Material Culture and Citizenship in Europe and America*
(Oxford: Berg, 2001), 204–5.

23. Ibid., 213–20.

24. Richard Flacks, "Making Life, Not History," in *Making History: The American Left and the American
Mind* (New York: Columbia University Press, 1988), 32–37, 51–57.

25. Godfrey Hodgson, *America in Our Time* (Garden City, N.Y.: Doubleday, 1976), 51.

26. Edward Purcell, *The Crisis of Democratic Theory: Scientific Naturalism and the Problem of Value* (Lexington: University of Kentucky Press, 1973); David and Cecile Shapiro, "Abstract Expressionism: The Politics of Apolitical Painting" in *Prospects* 3 (1977): 175–214.

27. "Cheers to 100 Years . . . 20th Century Timeline," *Shopping Center World* (1 December 1999), at www.industryclick.com/magazinearticle.asp?releaseid=4532&magazinearticleid=52314&siteid=23&magazineid=109.

28. Ownby, *American Dreams in Mississippi*, 149–58.

29. Ibid.

30. Lipsitz, "Who'll Stop the Rain? Youth Culture, Rock 'n' Roll, and Social Crises," in *The Sixties: From Memory to History*, ed. David Farber (Chapel Hill: University of North Carolina Press, 1994), 224. For a brilliant analysis of this story, see especially Thomas Frank, *The Conquest of Cool* (Chicago: University of Chicago Press, 1997).

31. Alan Wolfe, "Undialectical Materialism," *New Republic*, 23 October 2000, 29. According to Dan Cook, this ideology of liberty applies even to children: "The children's market works because it lives off of deeply-held beliefs about self-expression and freedom of choice—originally applied to the political sphere, and now almost inseparable from the culture of consumption." Cook, "Lunchbox Hegemony?"

32. Gary Cross, *An All-Consuming Century: Why Commercialism Won in Modern America* (New York: Columbia University Press, 2000), 193–213.

33. Wolfe, "Undialectical Materialism," 30–31.

34. Holsworth and Wray, *American Politics and Everyday Life*, 40.

35. Ibid., 43.

36. Ibid., 213–14.

12. The World in a Shopping Mall

1. The title of this chapter comes from Margaret Crawford, whose essay is a brilliant exploration of West Edmonton Mall. Crawford, "World in a Shopping Mall," 3–30.

2. Goss, "Once-upon-a-Time," 52–55.

3. Daniel Boorstin, *The Image: A Guide to Pseudo-Events in America* (New York: Harper, 1961), 77–117.

4. Rosaldo, "Imperialist Nostalgia," 108. "In this ideologically constructed world of ongoing progressive change, putatively static savage societies become a stable reference point for defining (the felicitous progress of) civilized identity."

5. Goss, "Once-upon-a-Time," 63; Ritzer, *Enchanting a Disenchanted World*, 66; Mark A. Schneider, *Culture and Enchantment* (Chicago: University of Chicago Press, 1993): ix.

6. Michael Sorkin notes that in the nineteenth century, "winter gardens became hugely popular places of amusement and assembly. Those tropical landscapes in Berlin or Brussels helped . . . to invent the idea of simulated travel, initiating the great touristic dialectic of appearance and reality." Sorkin, "See You in Disneyland," 210.

7. Stephen M. Fjellman, *Vinyl Leaves: Walt Disney World and America* (Boulder, Colo.: Westview Press, 1992), 221–27.

8. For an excellent discussion of the origins and attraction of the Rainforest Café, see Nelson, *Mall of America*, 219–27.

9. Timothy Luke, *Ecocritique: Contesting the Politics of Nature, Economy, and Culture* (Minneapolis: University of Minnesota Press, 1997), 128–29.

10. Leach, *Land of Desire*, 104–11.

11. Bill McKibben, *The Age of Missing Information* (New York: Random House, 1992), 95–97.

12. Marilyn Halter, *Shopping for Identity: The Marketing of Ethnicity* (New York: Schocken Books, 2000), 17; Goss, "Once-upon-a-Time," 70.

13. According to a VP of Westcor Partners, people don't want just another mall. They want to be "in an experience. We're trying to make people feel like they're on vacation." Debra Hazel, "Inside/Out: New Hybrid Malls Offer Best of Both Worlds," at www.icsc.org/srch/sct/current/sct0500/01.html.

14. "From Jungle to Drawing Room," *Economist*, 14 March 1987, 65.

15. Clive Gammon, "Banana Republic's Survival Chic Is Winning Bunches of Trendy Buyers," *Sports Illustrated* (19 August 1985): 88; Roy H. Campbell, "Banana Republic Stores Undergo a Fashion Makeover," *Knight-Ridder/Tribune News Service*, 10 December 1998.

16. Debra Hazel, "Bearing Fruit," *Shopping Centers Today* (1 May 1999), at www.icsc.org/sct/9905/33.htm.

17. Ibid.

18. The Zieglers meant no harm by the name. They called the business Banana Republic "because our merchandise came from countries where one regime had deposed another and declared all the old uniforms surplus . . . and [it was] part of a whimsy of creating an imaginary republic where I was Minister of Propaganda and Finance and Patricia was minister of culture." Paul Smith, "Visiting the Banana Republic," in *Universal Abandon? The Politics of Postmodernism*, ed. Andrew Ross (Minneapolis: University of Minnesota Press, 1988), 129–31.

19. Smith, "Visiting the Banana Republic," 142–45.

20. Naomi Klein, *No Logo: Taking Aim at the Brand Bullies* (New York: Picador, 1999), 195–228.

21. Alexander Goldsmith, "Seeds of Exploitation: Free Trade Zones in the Global Economy," in *The Case Against the Global Economy: And for a Turn toward the Local*, ed. Jerry Mander and Edward Goldsmith (San Francisco: Sierra Club Books, 1996), 267–72; Pamela Varley, ed., *The Sweatshop Quandary: Corporate Responsibility on the Global Frontier* (Washington, D.C.: Investor Responsibility Research Center, 1998), 83–85; Klein, *No Logo* 205.

22. Varley, *Sweatshop Quandary*, 85.

23. Ibid., 86; Robert J. S. Ross and Charles Kernaghan, "Countdown in Managua," *Nation* (August 2000), at www.usleap.org/Nation8-00reChentex.html.

24. Cynthia Enloe, *Bananas, Beaches and Bases: Making Feminist Sense of International Politics* (Berkeley and Los Angeles: University of California Press, 1989), 151–76.

25. Rosaldo, "Imperialist Nostalgia," 112. For a description of life in the export processing zones, see Klein, *No Logo*, 195–228.

26. Smith, "Visiting the Banana Republic," 133–34.

27. Ibid., 134–35; Michael Liedtke, "Levi Cutoffs," *Star Tribune*, 9 April 2002, pp. D1–D2.

28. On the Kathie Lee Gifford affair, see Klein, *No Logo*, 327–29.

29. "Business Ethics: Sweatshop Wars," *Economist*, 27 February 1999, 62.

30. Ellen Braunstein, "From Sweatshops to Shopping Malls," *Shopping Center World*, September 2001, 42–45; Leslie Kaufman and David Gonzalez, "Labor Standards Clash with Global Reality," *New York Times* (24 April 2001), at www.nytimes.com/2001/04/24 (accessed May 3, 2001); "Getting

Organised with Western Help," *Economist*, 1 December 2001, 57–58. Critics see the Fair Labor
Association as a cover-up, and have organized the Worker Rights Consortium instead.

31. Leslie Kaufman and David Gonzalez, "Labor Standards Clash with Global Reality," n.p. If
Gap were to replicate the efforts at the Charter factory in each of its four thousand subcon-
tractors, it would cost about 4.5 percent of its $877 million annual profit.

32. Bosworth, "Endangered Species," 237.

33. Department of Labor, "Shopping Clues for Consumers," at
www.dol.gov/opa/nosweat/card.htm; Press, "Sweatshopping," 221–26.

34. Press, "Sweatshopping," 221–26.

35. Braunstein, "From Sweatshops to Shopping Malls," 42–45.

36. Rosaldo, "Imperialist Nostalgia," 107–21.

13. Shopping Center World

1. Rob Kroes, "American Empire and Cultural Imperialism: A View from the Receiving End,"
Diplomatic History 23 (Summer 199): 467–71.

2. Kenneth Munkacy, "Operations and Management: East Meets West," in Beyard et al.,
Shopping Center Development Handbook, 214; Chip Walker, "Can TV Save the Planet?" *American
Demographics*, May 1996, 42.

3. Judith Dobrzynski, "The *American* Way," *New York Times Magazine*, 6 April 1997, 79–80.

4. *The Harvard Design School Guide to Shopping*, ed. Chuihua Judy Chung and Sze Tsung Leong
(Cologne: Taschen, 2001), 51–52.

5. ICSC, "Educational Study Tour."

6. "ICSC Spring Convention Kicks Off in Las Vegas," *Shopping Centers Today* (22 May 2000), at
www.icsc.org.

7. Benjamin R. Barber, *Jihad vs. McWorld: How Globalism and Tribalism Are Reshaping the World* (New
York: Ballantine, 1995), 62; Pico Iyer, *Global Soul: Jet Lag, Shopping Malls, and the Search for
Home* (New York: Alfred A. Knopf, 2000), 85, 88; Ron Gluckman, "The Americanization of
China," at www.gluckman.com/Americanization.html.

8. "Trends in Retail Trade," *OSU Extension Facts*, WF-565 (n.d.) Oklahoma State University, 3;
Orr, *Nature of Design*, 171.

9. McNeal, *Kids Market*, 247.

10. Walker, "Can TV Save the Planet?" 42–47.

11. Elissa Moses, *The $100 Billion Allowance: Assessing the Global Teen Market* (New York: John Wiley,
2000), 2, 9, 37.

12. Karen Fawcett, "Living and Working in France," *Bonjour Paris* (January 1999), at
www.bparis.com/newsletter1464/newsletter_show.htm?doc_id=7211&attrib_id=1834; ICSC,
"Shopping Centers: A World of Opportunity" (2000), at
www.icsc.org/international/index.pdf.

13. Chuihua Judy Chung with Juan Palop-Casado, "Resistance," in *The Harvard Design School Guide
to Shopping*, ed. Chuihua Judy Chung and Sze Tsung Leong (Cologne: Taschen, 2001),
650–51.

14. Munkacy, "Operations and Management," 217.

15. John Hannigan, *Fantasy City: Pleasure and Profit in the Postmodern Metropolis* (London: Routledge,
1998), 178–79; Vinh, "Coopetition," 205–15.

16. Munkacy, "Operations and Management," 214; Antony Feeny, Theera Vongpatanasin, and Arphaporn Soonsatham, "Retailing in Thailand," *International Journal of Retail and Distribution Management* (August 1996): 38–44.

17. Ron Gluckman, "The Americanization of China," at www.gluckman.com/ Americanization.html.

18. William Ecenbarger, "There's No Escaping US," *Fort Lauderdale Sun-Sentinel,* 4 July 1993, pp. 6–9; Forrest D. Colburn, "The Malling of Latin America," *Dissent* (Winter 1996): 51–52; "U.S. Retailers Making Forays Abroad Take a Local Approach," *Shopping Centers Today* (1 June 1999), at www.icsc.org/srch/sct/current/sct9907/ 06.htm. See also Ignacio Galceran and Jon Berry, "A New World of Consumers," *American Demographics,* March 1995, 26–33.

19. Steve Lewis, "Designed with Islam in Mind," *Shopping Center World,* November 2001, 56; ICSC, "Shopping Centers."

20. ICSC, "Shopping Centers."

21. Ecenbarger, "There's No Escaping US," 6–9.

22. Laura C. Nelson, *Measured Excess: Status, Gender, and Consumer Nationalism in South Korea* (New York: Columbia University Press, 2000), 144; Beng-Huat Chua, "World Cities, Globalisation, and the Spread of Consumerism: A View from Singapore," *Urban Studies* 35 (1998): 982.

23. Chua, "World Cities, Globalisation, and the Spread of Consumerism: A View from Singapore," 981, 986–89, 997; Bishan Singh, "Development and the Youth Culture [in Malaysia]," *Sun* (27 August 1993), at http://iisd.iisd.ca/pcdf/1993/ YOUTH.htm; McNeal, *Kids Market,* 18. See also Rob Kroes, *If You've Seen One, You've Seen the Mall: Europeans and American Mass Culture* (Urbana: University of Illinois Press, 1996).

24. George G. Brenkert, "Marketing, the Ethics of Consumption, and Less-Developed Countries," in *The Business of Consumption: Environmental Ethics and the Global Economy,* ed. Laura Westra and Patricia H. Werhane (Boulder, Colo.: Rowman and Littlefield, 1998), 91–112.

25. Kevin Gallagher, "Globalization and Consumer Culture," in *The Consumer Society,* ed. Neva R. Goodwin, Frank Ackerman, and David Kron (Washington, D.C.: Island Press, 1997), 302–4. See, too, Helena Norberg-Hodge, *Ancient Futures: Learning from Ladakh* (San Francisco: Sierra Club, 1991).

26. Satterthwaite, *Going Shopping,* 276–93.

27. Richard Pells, *Not Like Us: How Europeans Have Loved, Hated, and Transformed American Culture Since World War II* (New York: Basic, 1997), 202; Rob Kroes, "Introduction: America and Europe— A Clash of Imagined Communities," in *European Readings of American Popular Culture,* ed. John Dean and Jean-Paul Gabilliet (Westport, Conn.: Greenwood, 1996), xxvi.

28. Chuihua Judy Chung with Juan Palop-Casado, "Resistance," in *The Harvard Design School Guide to Shopping,* ed. Chuihua Judy Chung and Sze Tsung Leong (Cologne: Taschen, 2001), 632–59; Satterthwaite, *Going Shopping,* 277–93.

29. Leslie Sklair, "The Culture-Ideology of Consumerism in the Third World," in *The Consumer Society,* ed. Neva R. Goodwin, Frank Ackerman, and David Kron (Washington, D.C.: Island Press, 1997), 322; Kroes, "American Empire and Cultural Imperialism," 477. Pells, *Not Like Us,* 279–83.

30. "Mall Content," *Economist,* 1 June 2002, 64.

Notes to Pages 254–260

31. Reinhold Wagnleitner, "The Empire of the Fun, or Talkin' Soviet Blues: The Sound of Freedom and U.S. Cultural Hegemony in Europe," *Diplomatic History* 23 (Summer 1999): 521–22. "To the world," Benjamin Barber suggests, "America offers an incoherent and contradictory but seductive style that is less 'democratic' than physical culture: youthful, rich urban, austere cowboy, Hollywood glamorous, Garden of Eden unbounded, good willed to a fault, socially aware, politically correct, mall pervaded, and, ironically, often dominated by images of black ghetto life—black, however, as in hip and cool rather than in crime-ridden and squalid, 'baaaad' but not bad." Barber, *Jihad vs. McWorld*, 61.

14. Shopping for a Better World

1. Beyard et al., *Shopping Center Development Handbook*, 3.
2. Michael Demarest, "He Digs Cities," *Time*, 24 August 1981, 46; Neil Harris, "Spaced Out at the Shopping Center," in *Cultural Excursions: Marketing Appetites and Cultural Tastes in Modern America* (Chicago: University of Chicago Press, 1990), 288.
3. "Yearning for Balance: Views of Americans on Consumption, Materialism, and the Environment," prepared for the Merck Family Fund by the Harwood Group, July 1995, 1–5.
4. Orr, *Nature of Design*, 179. For more on the environmental costs of consumption, see Alan Durning, *How Much Is Enough? Consumer Society and the Future of the Earth* (New York: Norton, 1992); Ryan and Durning, *Stuff*; and Csikszentmihalyi, "Costs and Benefits of Consuming," 267–72.
5. Edward Bellamy, *Looking Backward* (Ticknor, 1887), at www.eserver.org/fiction/bellamy/contents.html.
6. Mihaly Csikszentmihalyi, "If We Are So Rich, Why Aren't We Happy?" *American Psychologist* 54 (October 1999): 823. See also Tim Kasser, *The High Price of Materialism* (Cambridge: MIT Press, 2002).
7. Csikszentmihalyi, "If We Are So Rich, Why Aren't We Happy?" 821–27; Csikszentmihalyi, "Costs and Benefits of Consuming," 268–69; Gregg Easterbrook, "I'm OK, You're OK: Psychology Discovers Happiness," *New Republic* (5 March 2001), at www.thenewrepublic.com/030501/easterbrook030501_print.html.
8. "Yearning for Balance," 1–5.
9. Keith H. Hammonds, "Retail's Challenge: The Overstuffed Consumer," *Fast Company* (December 2001), at www.fastcompany.com/build/build_feature/liebmann.html.
10. Hammonds, "Retail's Challenge," n.p.
11. Barry Schwartz, *The Costs of Living: How Market Freedom Erodes the Best Things in Life* (New York: W. W. Norton, 1994), 172–73.
12. Peter Marin, "Body Politic," *Harper's* (December 1985): 15–17.
13. Ibid.; Robert Bellah, "Habits of the Heart: Implications for Religion," at http://hirr.hartsem.edu/Bellah/lectures_5.htm.
14. Wendell Berry, *The Unsettling of America: Culture and Agriculture* (San Francisco: Sierra Club, 1977), 24–26.
15. Miller, *Theory of Shopping*, 19.
16. Tae-Wook Cha, "Ecologically Correct," in *The Harvard Design School Guide to Shopping*, ed. Chuihua Judy Chung and Sze Tsung Leong (Cologne: Taschen, 2001), 308. See also Anita Roddick, *Body and Soul: Profits with Principles—The Amazing Success Story of Anita Roddick and the Body Shop* (New York: Crown, 1991), and Anita Roddick, *Take It Personally: How to Make Conscious Choices to Change the World* (New York: HarperCollins, 2001).

17. Cha, "Ecologically Correct," 309.

18. "Mall Bawl: A Promo in Every Shop," 57.

19. Orr, *Ecological Literacy*, 173.

20. Durning, *How Much Is Enough?* 143–45; Stuart Walker, "The Inflatable Plastic Moose-Head," *Environments* (1994): 87–88.

21. Csikszentmihalyi, "Costs and Benefits of Consuming," 270–71.

22. McKibben, *Age of Missing Information*, 226.

23. For a primer on designing products for sustainability, see William McDonough and Michael Braungart, *Cradle to Cradle: Remaking the Way We Make Things* (New York: North Point Press, 2002).

24. Schor, *Overspent American*, 114.

25. Joe Dominguez and Vicki Robin, *Your Money or Your Life: Transforming Your Relationship with Money and Achieving Financial Independence* (New York: Penguin Books, 1992); Schor, *Overspent American*, 135.

26. The spoof ads are on line at www.adbusters.org/spoofads. In addition to the magazine, see Adbusters' Culture Jammers Toolbox www.adbusters.org/Toolbox/index.html. See also Mark Dery, *Culture Jamming: Hacking, Slashing and Sniping in the Empire of Signs* (Westfield, N.J.: Open Magazine Pamphlet Series, n.d.), also available at www2.sva.readings/Culture-Jamming.html.

27. See www.adbusters.org/campaign/bnd.

28. See www.newdream.org, and Brian Howard, "The Center for a New American Works for a Less Materialistic Society," *E! The Environmental Magazine* (8 March 2002), at www.enn.com/news/enn-stories/2002/03/03082002/s_46492.asp.

29. Orr, *Ecological Literacy*, 5.

30. Juliet Schor, "The New Politics of Consumption," in *Do Americans Shop Too Much?* ed. Joshua Cohen and Joel Rogers (Boston: Beacon Press, 2000), 3–33.

31. Liedtke, "Levi Cutoffs," p. D2.

32. David Orr, *Earth in Mind* (Washington, D.C.: Island Press, 1994), 172–73.

33. Jack Gibbons, "The Price Is Right?" in *Do Americans Shop Too Much?* ed. Joshua Cohen and Joel Rogers (Boston: Beacon Press, 2000), 49–52; Csikszentmihalyi, "Costs and Benefits of Consuming," 271.

34. Jensen, *Dream Society*, 43–44, 110.

35. Schor, *Overspent American*, 164.

36. Daniel Miller, "The Poverty of Morality," *Journal of Consumer Culture* (November 2001): 227.

37. Durning, *How Much Is Enough?*

38. Iyer, *Global Soul*, 25–26.

39. Durning, *How Much Is Enough?* 28; U.S. Census Bureau, *Money Income in the United States: 2000*, at www.census.gov/prod/2001pubs/p60-213.pdf.

40. Orr, *Earth in Mind*, 104–11; Orr, *Nature of Design*, 27–28.

41. Jeff Gunning et. al., "Retail's New Hook," *Urban Land* (July 1998), in Beyard et al., *Shopping Center Development Handbook*, 67, 156.

42. Benjamin Barber, Kevin Mattson, and Michael Moody, "Creating Mall-Town Square: What Can Be Done to Recreate Public Space in America's Suburbs?" (Walt Whitman Center, Rutgers University, 1997), at wwc.rutgers.edu.mallspace.htm.

43. Gruen and Smith, *Shopping Towns USA*, 23, 267. For a wealth of suggestions on the synergies of shopping and community, see Satterthwaite, *Going Shopping*. Some malls already provide

such creative combinations, and they've been particularly attractive in retrofitting older malls. The Crossroads Mall in Bellevue, Washington, has been renewed by its integration with the community. And at Mashpee Commons in Cape Cod, developers "literally built the mall into a new community which also follows the principles of higher density and mixed use." Barber et al., "Creating Mall-Town Square"; Debra Carlton Harrell, "Mall Has Been Cornerstone of Diverse Community's Renaissance," *Seattle Post-Intelligencer* (11 January 1997), at www.seattlepi.nwsource.com/neighbors/crossroads.

44. Andrew L. Shapiro, *We're Number One! Where America Stands—and Falls—in the New World Order* (New York: Vintage, 1992).

45. Ibid.

46. Daniel Quinn, *Ishmael* (New York: Bantam Books, 1992), 214.

47. Jensen, *Dream Society*, 24.

Index

325

market multiculturalism, 154
market research: 15–20, 23, 54, 99, 102, 211, 231, 241; area research, 16; consumer research, 16, 17; psychographic research, 18
Marling, Karal Ann, 165, 169–70
Massachusetts Commission against Discrimination, 152
MasterCard (credit card), 206
materialism, 21, 31, 99, 124, 127–28, 130–33, 224, 228, 263, 266, 268–69, 273, 275–79
Mattel, 244
Maurin, Peter, 266
Maxim, 99, 104
McKibben, Bill, 129–30, 239, 275
McNeal, James, 81, 83–84, 88, 252
Media Foundation of Canada, 277–78, 281
middle class, xxi, 22, 42–43, 79, 101, 112, 149, 152, 246
Miller, Daniel, 160, 161, 271, 281, 285
minimum wage, 193, 223, 224, 243, 244, 282
mirrors, 56, 67, 102, 142, 143
Moffatt, Michael, 197
morality. *See* ethics
movies, 5, 40, 86, 89, 94, 98, 103–6, 108, 113, 118, 156, 165, 167, 170, 179–81, 189, 234, 236, 249–50, 256, 259, 270
movie theaters, 151, 177, 180–81
MTV, 60, 96, 98, 106, 250, 252
multinational corporations, 243–46
multiplexes, 180–81
Muzak, 10, 67–68, 115, 129, 255

Nast, Thomas, 112
National Association of Homebuilders, 221
National Labor Committee, 246
National Mall Network, 89
National Retail Federation, 223, 251
National Trust for Historic Preservation, 174
Naturally Untamed, 41–42
natural resources, 51, 242, 263
Natural Wonders, 42, 45
nature, 33–52; as adventure, 43–45; as art, 39; as

garden, 35–38; as resource, 45–51; as season, 46–49; as souvenir, 42–43
NatureMaker, 39–40, 42
Navy Pier (Chicago), 182
neophilia, 157
niche marketing, 20
Nichols, J.C., 3, 6, 7, 173
Nickelodeon Store, 170
Neiman-Marcus, 118
Nike, 97, 99–100, 176, 244, 246, 278, 283, 287
NikeTown, 56, 176
Nordstrom, 196
Northgate (Seattle), 7
Northland Center (Detroit), 8–9
nostalgia, 19, 115, 168, 176
novelty, xvi, 51, 105, 115, 132, 139, 155–57, 163–64, 174, 188–89

Old Navy, 28, 97, 103, 105, 196
Ontario Mills, 13, 39–40
opportunity costs, 130, 202, 268, 283
Orr, David, 83, 201, 263, 273, 281, 286, 288
outfitters, 33, 44–45
outlet centers, 13, 26, 162, 253
outsourcing, 242–44
overdevelopment, 246

parking, 4–6, 8–10, 13, 23–24, 34, 47, 51, 76, 147, 151, 177, 180, 198, 287
Patagonia, 247, 272
pedestrianism, 10, 216
peer pressure, 83, 99, 103–4, 109, 117; among teenagers, 99, 103–4, 109
peer socialization, 92
Pegler, Martin, 44, 47, 63, 112–15
people's capitalism, 225
people-watching, xx, 144–46, 216
perfect gift, the, 117, 123–24, 127
Planet Hollywood, 181, 261
Politics, 215–32; local, 218–20; of free speech, 216–18; of consumption, 223–32, 240, 264–68, 281–90; of taxes, 220–23; state, 220–21

326

328

This book was published by Smithsonian Books, Washington D.C. The book printer was Maple-Vail Book Manufacturing Group in York, Pa. The jacket printer was The Lehigh Press, Inc., in Pennsauken, N.J.

The book was set in Quark 4.04. The body typeface used in this book is set in 10.5 x x15.5 Weiss. The display face is set in 54 point Futura condensed Light all caps.